# Cultural Diversity
# in the United States

# Cultural Diversity in the United States

Edited by
**LARRY L. NAYLOR**

**BERGIN & GARVEY**
Westport, Connecticut • London

**Library of Congress Cataloging-in-Publication Data**

Cultural diversity in the United States / edited by Larry L. Naylor.
    p.  cm.
  Includes bibliographical references (p.  ) and index.
  ISBN 0–89789–478–2 (cloth: alk. paper).—ISBN 0–89789–479–0
(pbk. : alk. paper)
   1. Pluralism (Social sciences)—United States.  2. Minorities—
United States.  3. United States—Ethnic relations.  4. United
States—Race relations.  5. Ethnicity—United States.  I. Naylor,
Larry L.
E184.A1C845  1997
305.8′00973—dc20      96–26936

British Library Cataloguing in Publication Data is available.

Library of Congress Catalog Card Number: 96–26936

ISBN: 0–89789–478–2 hc   0–89789–479–0 pb

First published in 1997

Bergin & Garvey, 88 Post Road West, Westport, CT 06881
An imprint of Greenwood Publishing Group Inc.

Printed in the United States of America

The paper used in this book complies with the
Permanent Paper Standard issued by the National
Information Standards Organization (Z39.48–1984).

10 9 8 7 6 5 4 3 2 1

# Contents

# Preface

This collection of readings addresses culture and cultural diversity, topics that generate some of the most significant social issues in the world today, and issues that promise to carry well into the next century. Out of the general lack of understanding of culture and its role in people's lives, when most Americans think of cultural diversity, images of broad-based "racial" groups (black and brown, maybe yellow), or various "ethnic" groups (Hispanic Americans, Asian Americans, Native Americans, etc.), immediately come to mind, and this is the diversity of the United States. For many of them, a "race" is a natural grouping of people based on some shared physical characterisitics, more often than not, color. "Ethnic" groups come into existence by virtue of people sharing as little as a common language or perhaps having the same regional origins. But, "racial" and "ethnic" groupings such as these are nothing more than gross, arbitrary, and artificial categorizations of people with little or no meaningful basis in reality, and certainly no relationship to culture. The tendency of Americans to rely on such overgeneralized categorizations tends to obscure more than it clarifies. While such groupings (categorizations) are well established and commonly used when addressing the topic of diversity, they by no means convey the actual number of cultural groups that come together and make up what is commonly known as the "American Culture." The real diversity of America is represented in the many different groupings established on the basis of shared culture, on "ethnicity," and a whole host of "special interests" that have come with the complex and fragmented modern nation-state.

The idea for this volume was born out of a need for a basic introduction for students only beginning their sojourn into the diversity of cultural groupings that make up the whole of the culture of the United States (American Culture). Up to now, to undertake a broad study of diversity, one would have to go to a large number of different resource materials to gain even the most basic exposure to the diversity of America, and most of this would focus on only specific "ethnic" or "racial" groupings. This volume brings the most basic information on culture and cultural diversity together in one place. It not only provides discussion of the basic vocabulary, concepts, and understandings associated with the topics, through presentations on representative groupings, but it also is designed to help the reader begin developing an increased awareness, understanding, and appreciation of the diverse cultures that altogether contribute to the multiculturalism of American Culture and Americans.

The term American is the common designation for citizens of the United States, and *America* is a well-established and utilized synonym for the United States. Usage of both terms goes far back in U.S. history. The world has come to know the citizens of the United States as *Americans,* and although others would also stake some claim to that identification, throughout this volume it is used strictly with reference to those holding citizenship in the United States. It is recognized that many people of South America, Central America, and the Caribbean Islands also use the term *American* to identify themselves and are sensitive to its use strictly with citizens of the United States. This tendency is particularly important to immigrants into the United States from many South American countries. This particular tendency would appear to have come from the geographical designations used in the New World (North *America*, Central *America*, and South *America*). On the other hand, people of Canada do not refer to themselves as *Americans.* They refer to themselves by virtue of their country of origin, *Canadians.* The same can be said for people of South America, Central America, and the Caribbean. It is well known that people from both of these areas first will identify themselves with reference to their country of origin as do the Canadians. The people of Mexico prefer to identify themselves as Mexicans, just as the people of Columbia identify themselves as Colombians. The people of Peru identify themselves as Peruvians. The same can be said for each and all people throughout South and Central America as well as the Caribbean. It is rare that a person from any of these areas first will identify themselves as American. It is in this same sense that all of the contributors of this volume opted for the use of America and American. Had that not been done, we would be left with no particular referent identifier for the people of the United States. Something like United Statesians has not made it into popular usage and probably never will. The world has come to know *Americans* and *America.* The people of the United States refer to themselves as *Americans,* and their country is known to them as both the United States (U.S.) and *America.*

The volume is designed around culture and cultural groupings. Cultural groups are relatively permanent assemblages of people who have rights and obligations (expectations) to one another, collectively recognize a reason to exist as a group, and with which members identify and take pride in doing so. Culture is the learned way of belief, behavior, and products of these that is shared within human groupings, serves to distinguish them from each other, and provides a sense of identity. Culture lies at the heart of almost everything humans think and do. A cultural group exists whenever a human grouping learns a particular set of beliefs and behaviors that distinguishes it from other groups. The United States is an identifiable nation-state culture group, for all of its members do share a core set of ideal beliefs, adhere to a set of prerequisite behaviors, and share the social/cultural systems that organize the culture's activities. At the same time, there are groupings in the United States that have their own set of beliefs and practices that designates them as cultural groups and distinguishes them within the larger nation-state context. Each of these represents a part of the whole that is the United States. Each is a constituent part of what is American Culture.

Despite the promise of America, many immigrants and other cultural groups have found it difficult to achieve the "American Dream," to experience equality or equal opportunities. Some of the actual experiences of immigrants have been due to customs and traditions they brought with them into the United States, traditions they continue to maintain in some fashion. Experiences of other cultural groups have been the result of history and/or their own historical efforts to cope with the sociocultural environment in which they have found themselves. Both kinds of groups have experienced prejudice and discrimination, both of which come with stereotyping and over-generalization. This seems to suggest that Americans need to develop some appreciation of the consequences of stereotyping, ethnocentrism, bias, prejudice, and discrimination if the country is going to successfully address problems of diversity. They need to become more aware of the origins of their own beliefs and practices, the basis of their own positions on significant issues and questions with which the United States is attempting to resolve. With awareness, one acquires the skills to become more critical in evaluating the relevant issues and aspects of cultural diversity. Cultural groupings are vital in maintaining stability and purpose for many individuals and groups of people, but promises and aspirations unfulfilled have led to much group competition, conflict and fragmentation. While "ethnic" cultures seemingly always have been recognized by Americans, other cultural groupings, such as those that are self-generated, imposed by others, or tied to social and economic conditions, occupational specialization, religion, and any number of other special interests, have not.

Some chapters in this volume focus on the terminology and allied concepts that are important to the diversity topic (e.g., multiculturalism, ethnicity, race, racism, discrimination, minorities and prejudice), some of which seemed to have lost their meaning in the current discussions of the topic. Other chapters focus on group categories commonly recognized by Americans (e.g., African American, Asian American, Hispanic American, Native American) and those which are not (e.g., Christians, gender, sex, deaf, etc.). Because of the continued use of such generalized categories and the usual stereotyping which accompanies that practice, attention is devoted to the problems of generalizing people into such categories and specific cultural groups subsumed within them. In addressing specific cultural groups subsumed within such categorizations, a special effort is made to relay just what makes specific cultural groups different, the histories that created them, and their complex interactions and relationships with other cultural groups of the larger nation-state context. Chapters on specific cultural groups will attempt to convey, insofar as possible, just what distinguishes one particular group from another. Given the complexity and actual cultural diversity of the United States, it is not possible in a single volume such as this to treat every identifiable cultural group in the United States. It will be important to remember, that this volume represents only a beginning to increased awareness and understanding. Space dictates some selection. The examples chosen from each category for explicit treatment are based on their particular significance to specific social problems created out of the diversity of the United States. Each specific culture discussion attempts to convey to the reader, who may not be a member of the specific group under discussion, just what they need to know to begin to develop a better understanding of that group and what distinguishes them from others. In their limited numbers, these discussions can represent only a beginning for those attempting to develop greater understanding and awareness. Altogether, they can provide only some basics that can serve as a foundation for more in-depth study at a later time.

The volume is organized into five sections, each with its own introduction. Part I is introductory, designed to introduce the reader to the basic concepts of culture and cultural groupings, as well as some allied ideas and terminology relevant to the cultural diversity topic. Part II primarily is concerned with the problems of race and racism, race and culture, and the idea of a minority. Part III introduces ethnicity, exposing the reader to selected representations of the full-range of America's ethnic cultures, usually subsumed within highly generalized categories that already are well established in the minds of most Americans. Part IV examines religious, business and professional, gender and sex, and other special interest groups that also contribute to the cultural diversity and multiculturalism of the United States. Part V takes into account the actual diversity and complexity of the problem as it comes together in the urban environment, in the workplace, and as it contributes to the many social issues that continue to confront the society and its people. It provides some practical considerations to help people begin to develop better skills in working and living with others in the context of diversity.

Although not all inclusive, this collection of readings presents a substantial body of information relevant to culture and cultural diversity in the United States. It is not presented as a comprehensive statement on these very important topics, rather it is presented as a basic introduction. In providing discussions of the basic vocabulary, diversity categories, and examples of specific cultural groups within these, the reader should be in a better position to critically evaluate the many issues and aspects of cultural diversity that now confront every American, and hopefully become part of the solution as opposed to part of the problem. Questions of critical importance surrounding cultural diversity will be with us for many years to come. All Americans need to develop a greater awareness and understanding of the cultural diversity that makes up America and themselves. All Americans need to become more sensitive to the cultural groups with which they live, work, play, and constantly interact. It is the belief of all of the contributors of this collection that with a better understanding of culture and diversity, the promises of the American culture ultimately may be fulfilled. At the least, this particular volume represents a start in that direction.

Larry L. Naylor

# PART I

## Culture and the American Context of Diversity

To begin the process of building an increased awareness, understanding, and appreciation of all the actual diversity that has come to characterize American (U.S.) culture, the chapters of Part I are focused on the core concepts of diversity: culture, the culture grouping, and the allied concepts of prejudice, discrimination, and political minorities. Chapter 1 is concerned with culture, that uniquely human characteristic which underlies the entire human experience, its groupings, and diversity. Both the ideas of culture and cultural groupings are fundamental to any attempt to deal with the topic of cultural diversity or multiculturalism. The many definitions of culture that have been proposed are discussed in this chapter, as are other difficulties and problems that have come to be associated with the concept. Throughout this volume, culture is defined as the learned way (or ways) of belief, behavior, and the products of these (both physically and socially) that is shared (at least to some degree) within human groups and serves to distinguish that culture group from another learning different beliefs and behaviors. Culture lies at the very heart of cultural diversity questions, discussions, and any solutions to be proposed to deal with its problems. Also key in the discussions of diversity is the cultural group, a relatively permanent assemblage of people who have rights and obligations (expectations) to one another, collectively recognize a reason or purpose in existing as a group, and with which members identify and take pride in doing so. After all, it is in groups of people that ideas and behaviors of culture are actualized and then utilized to determine actions. No effort to obtain a better understanding of cultural diversity is possible without first gaining some control over the culture concept and what this means to individuals and groups of people.

In addressing cultural diversity, other ideas and terms immediately come to mind—prejudice, racism, discrimination, and minority—all of which have evolved with the topic. In a large measure, these concepts reflect the problems that have accompanied increased diversity as both a consequence and a cause of a great many of the social problems Americans are experiencing. In Chapter 2, Norma Williams discusses the concepts of minority groups, prejudice, and discrimination in the historical context and as discrimination that has been experienced by African Americans, Hispanic Americans, and others. From this discussion comes a better understanding of the use of stereotyping and overgeneralizing culturally learned ideas onto groups of people and then discriminating against them based on that practice. The author critiques the assimilationist orientation and perspective (top-down model) and advances a multicultural model that promises a better response to the growing diversity of the United States. No discussion of cultural diversity would be complete without some better understanding and awareness of the basis and consequences of prejudice, discrimination, and stereotyping.

In a highly revealing and informative essay, Laura Zimmer-Tamakoshi provides us with a personal look at the culture normally associated with white (Anglo-Saxon) Protestant Americans (WASP) and their perceptions, ideas, and behaviors with regard to others. In her discussion of growing up as a WASP, the author discusses the roots of the beliefs that have come to characterize this group of Americans, the standards of behavior expected of people who would fall into this group, the vocabulary that has come to be associated with it, and how members of the group find out "who they are" and "what they stand for." With the emergence of a new conservatism in America, increasingly larger ethnic populations, and the rise of ulta-right militancy, the author suggests that although things are changing, the continuing danger comes from those who want it only one way—their way.

Together, the authors of this section provide the foundation for the discussions to follow that will address the actual ethnic and special interest cultural groupings that are present in the United States and serve to characterize American culture as a diverse or multicultural one. The question is not whether the United States has something that can be called the American culture, but a recognition that there is an American (U.S.) Culture based on shared beliefs, prerequisite behaviors, and organizational systems. The task is to identify those things in more specific terms, as the foundation for finding some common ground among the diversity of groups that are also there. In the building of an increased awareness and understanding of diversity, one has to understand the context of it and as culture applies to human groups. Culture underlies all the discussions of cultural groupings that make up the diversity. The topics and concepts discussed throughout this part naturally are associated with diversity or are germane to its understanding.

# 1

# Culture and Cultural Groupings

## Larry L. Naylor

Culture is that unique characteristic that separates the human from the rest of the world of living things. It is the primary means of human adaptation, the basis for the majority of human thought and behavior. Culture distinguishes humans in the animal kingdom, and it helps to define them. Humans create, learn, and use culture to respond to the problems of their natural and sociocultural environments, to control them, and even to change them. With culture, humans produce the socio-cultural environment, with a physical component of its own that overlays much of the natural environment. Humans use their cultures to respond to both kinds of environments with which they must be concerned. Culture makes all humans basically the same, yet it also makes them different as each human group creates and develops its own version of culture designed to respond to their own particular needs and wants, and because of the choices they make. Culture is created by people in response to the specific conditions, problems, or limitations that they face in the natural environment, and the sociocultural ones that they create. At the very least, culture represents a set of problem-solving solutions. On another level, culture is also an analytical creation *of* people *for* other people, used to help them make sense out of other people and groups that somehow believe and behave differently than themselves. Lastly, it serves as a guide to living for both the individual and the group, helping them to move through the days of their lives with some assurance and security that comes with knowing what to expect from others, what to believe, and what is the correct thing to do.

Multiculturalism or cultural diversity presents some of the most critical issues and problems facing modern nation-states, and culture rests at the core of such difficulties and discussions. The current upsurge in interest in culture and cultural diversity does not mean that people have not been interested or concerned with the ideas of culture and diversity in the past. Rather, it means that the significance of these things in the lives of people has changed considerably. No longer can such things be taken for granted or simply ignored. The role that culture plays in the lives of individuals and groups is substantial, impacting nearly every aspect of the human experience. Government agencies and leaders, educators and scholars, businessmen and corporate officers, and even the individual American, all must now face culture and cultural differences in ways they rarely thought about just a few years ago. The constantly growing interdependence of nations and peoples of the modern world, the development of a global economic system, and the rise of transnational business and international corporations, have brought all people of different cultures into face-to-face interactions on a scale unequaled in history. The growing migrations of people, the improvement and spread of technology, the fragmentations and complexity of the modern nation-state, and increasingly violent conflicts tied to ethnic groups all have brought the topics of culture and diversity into the daily lives of people just about everywhere in the world. All of these things have significantly highlighted the need for increased awareness, understanding, and sensitivity to cultural differences, for cultural difference is something found in every nation-state, in the context of international relations, in the workplace and in the daily lives of all peoples.

It is fairly safe to say that up to the 1990s, many Americans simply took culture and cultural diversity for granted. The United States (U.S.) was built by diverse groups of people coming to America from throughout the world in a search for new beginnings, new opportunities, and new lives. Because of that history, the culture of the United States has been viewed as the "melting pot" of nations, or likened to a "garden salad" or a "tapestry" made up of many unique threads that combine to make up something nominally known as American Culture. Americans have always taken pride in their diversity, in their own individual heritages, and in certain ideas that they have assumed were uniquely American. Their "heritage" was something they used to refer to their individual ancestry and linkage to the "old country," wherever that might have been. Tradition has been something linked to their "Fourth of July," "Labor Day," or having a day off from work to celebrate the birthdays of historical figures or major events in the history of the nation somehow related to cherished rights and freedoms of Americans. Although all of these things might have been vaguely equated with culture, it clearly was something more easily applied to "other" people. When called upon, assumed, or used by Americans, culture has been used to characterize those "other" people, or to identify the differences between the American way of life (culture) and that of other groups of people "somewhere out there" in the world. Some Americans might have seen culture as something only studied by anthropologists, associated with people in the remotest parts of the world whose way of life was vastly different from their more "civilized" world.

While culture has been one of the primary concerns of anthropologists, perhaps even the cornerstone of the discipline, many other disciplines and scholars also have been concerned with it, or aspects of it. Educators have explored the cultural basis of education and the school curriculum. Historians have been concerned with explaining or documenting the history of it, while sociologists have emphasized society and its social conditions. Various groups throughout the history of the United States have recognized their own cultural uniqueness within the larger nation-state context and argued for acceptance of that uniqueness. Major business corporations have had to consider differences in cultures as they expanded their markets abroad and/or attempted to reach potential consumers—consumers who obviously were not part of the mainstream "American Culture" as they commonly understood it. Seemingly, most Americans have always recognized differences among "races" or groups they created by categorizing people together on the basis of physical characteristics. They are quite used to speaking of minority groups and cultures, and they are certainly familiar with such related concepts as stereotyping, prejudice, discrimination, and racism.

Although these observations about culture and cultural diversity evidence a concern by Americans with culture and cultural diversity over the years, recent events at home and abroad have changed the degree of importance attached to such things. Violent conflicts among culture groups are increasing. Social problems, which have defied resolution through the years, now promise even more conflict and upheaval, threatening the stability and comfort of local communities and the nation at large. In the United States, the much laudable "union" is showing a decided lack of unity, and a new sense of urgency now accompanies the topics of culture and diversity. Where culture was assumed to be something characterizing other people, Americans must now recognize that it applies to themselves as well, and this somehow means more than simply "American." While Americans are becoming more conscious of their culture or cultures, conflicts and seemingly unresolvable social issues appear to being getting worse. This has forced them to think about such things as they never have before. But just what "it" (culture) is, seems to be less and less clear every day. The actual diversity of the U.S. culture (known throughout the world as the American Culture) has become a central concern of every group and every individual in America. Political correctness, cultural sensitivity, and a whole host of seemingly intractable social issues and problems touch everyone. The laissez-faire, and almost "cavalier," attitude of most Americans to the idea of culture has been altered almost overnight. Across the nation, in its classrooms, its universities, in nearly every government and business circle, in the everyday life of every American, at home, work, or their leisure activities, culture and cultural diversity are making their presence felt. While culture and cultural diversity clearly are becoming a major focus of the twenty-first century, just what these things mean is not all that clear. People find culture difficult to understand, and they experience great difficulties in applying it to their lives. Some even question whether it has any meaning at all. Obviously, there are problems associated with both concepts, beginning with the definition of culture itself.

## DEFINITION AND DIFFICULTIES

While the idea of culture and its importance are becoming well recognized by everyone, what culture actually means is not so clear, especially for those who now find that they must take it into account in every aspect of their daily lives. Up to now, culture has been pretty much an unconscious thing for the people who have learned it and simply go through life according to it. When pressed to speak of it, most Americans simply see it in terms of customs or traditions, a way of life, or the heritage of a people. Others see it as an assemblage of observable behavior (the practices) of people, while others see it as a set of rules that generate behavior. For still others, culture is a combination of beliefs, behaviors, and the physical and social products these produce. Apparently, how culture is viewed depends on one's interests or purpose. This means that culture can be used for a number of different things all at the same time. Because the concept is defined in so many different ways, it can obviously mean different things to different people. It has been used with reference to the entire human group, and it has been applied to very specific groups of people. A number of different definitions of culture have been proposed for the concept by anthropologists and other scholars over the years, generated out of the desire and need to clarify this thing that seemed so pervasive in the human experience. They were developed to provide for its intellectual understanding, and to help us to understand why people do what they do, and/or make some reasonable sense out of something that so often seems to defy logic. While the resulting cultural constructs and multiple definitions have certainly contributed to a better intellectual understanding of this human characteristic on one level, on another they have produced considerable confusion. Many people find themselves in a quandary as they try to determine just what the anthropologists or other scholars are talking about. It is a creation, an analytical concept spoken of symbolically in abstract and idealistic terms, yet it is real for people who live by it and according to its precepts. It provides the basis for most human thought and action. It is something every human must learn and practice. It lies at the very heart of almost everything that humans think and do. Yet, for most people, it is rarely thought of on the conscious level. Given all of these things, it should come as no surprise to anyone that there are some problems with this thing called culture.

## Definition

As originally conceived by Edward Burnett Tylor in 1871, culture was "that complex whole which includes knowledge, belief, art, law, morals, custom, and any other capabilities and habits acquired by man as a member of society" (Haviland 1994:304). Since that time, however, definitions have proliferated substantially as anthropologists and other scholars have tried to intellectually understand this human characteristic (Kroeber & Kluckhohn 1952; Harris 1968; Freilich 1972; Gamst & Norbeck 1976; Barrett 1984). Out of these efforts have come topical, historical, normative, behavioral, functional, mental, structural, and symbolic definitions of the concept. Topical definitions, such as that of Tylor, usually attempt to "laundry list" culture, providing lists of all those things that together make up what culture is, and they usually include social structure and organization, political, and religious, economic systems or patterns, and so on. Historical conceptualizations of culture emphasize it as a social heritage or tradition, something passed on from generation to generation. Behavioral constructs stress culture as consisting of learned behavior and shared way of life. Normative definitions portray culture as ideals, values, or rules for living, while functional characterizations see it as the way people solve environmental problems. Mental constructs see culture as a complex of ideas that distinguish humans from other animals, and structural definitions focus on patterned ideas, symbols, or behaviors. There are symbolic presentations of culture that see it as coming from arbitrarily assigned meanings that are shared among members of a society, and it even has been viewed as a superorganic process that overrides the individual, with a life and power of its own (White 1959). It is safe to say that all of these constructs have been generated to further our understanding of the concept rather than to confuse it. But with all of these possible constructs to chose from, it is not surprising that confusion abounds or that so many people have so much difficulty with the concept. If the variety of constructs tell us anything at all, it is that culture may well include, or be, all of these things.

Traditionally, anthropologists have used culture to describe groups of people inhabiting certain geographical areas who share beliefs, behaviors, customs, or a total way of life. In their usage of culture, anthropologists try to provide some measure of understanding of the particular way of life of a group, to describe them for others who might gain from that understanding. In addition to trying to understand culture through comparisons of different groups throughout the world, they try to help people make sense out of what they hear or see others doing. Of course, anthropologists are also trying to understand why humans do what they do, and how and where culture originated and developed into what they see in the contemporary world. In the process, anthropologists refined the ethnography or cultural description, but ethnographies have never been more than representations or abstractions that allow them to talk about and understand differences and similarities that exist as one group was compared to another. Their focus largely has been on difference, and their representations have been based on the norms, or what the majority of the members of the group believe and/or do. As they concentrated on traditional small-scale or "primitive" groups, this seemed to work quite well. In working with such groups, culture did appear as something that was shared among all members of a group. With less population and complexity, it did seem that everyone in the small-scale type of society did share the same beliefs and behaviors.

As anthropologists moved into the study of the more complex societies that evolved with civilization, they found that virtually every nation-state and individual is multicultural. Because of the complexity born out of the rise of specialization and fragmentation, and the arbitrary nature of them, nation-states are naturally going to be composed of many distinct cultural groups, while individuals themselves will assume membership in many different cultural groupings at the same time and across their lifetimes. The more traditional and linear models of culture that produced representative ethnographies based on norms have become less and less useful. While few would dispute the idea that culture in its earliest form focused on human adaptation to the natural environment, with the development of civilization, cultures became more complex and humans found that they had to adapt to the sociocultural environments they created with their cultures. They still had to be concerned with the problems posed by the natural environment, but increased attention had to be paid to the sociocultural environment, for culture began to impact them more, even changing the natural environment. With the advent of larger populations, specialization, and the development of the territorially based state, with its complexity and fragmentations, the sociocultural environment began to place heavy demands on human groups. In these contexts, all of the members of the culture group do not necessarily share the same beliefs and behaviors. The incorporation of many already well-defined cultural groups—through conquest, coercion, and migrations—into these artificially created cultures occasioned part of the very diversity that now characterizes them. The fragmentation of nation-state populations that comes with increasing complexity and larger social groupings further differentiate the nation-sate group. In today's world, some cultural groups even defy national boundaries, in essence having become international or transnational cultures. Of course, the widespread tendency for everybody to take culture for granted and assume that they already understand what it is, has not made overcoming the difficulties any easier. In emphasizing the role of culture in the understanding of humans and their development, and because of the focus of the anthropologist historically on the small-scale groups that tend to exist outside the mainstream of the so-called "civilized" world, culture has been reduced to an intellectual or esoteric conceptualization, an abstraction that only minimally applies in the "real world." There are other difficulties associated with the concept of culture as well.

All definitions of culture start with an idea about reality—grounded on a conviction of what is real. The answer to this question comes largely from philosophy. Philosophers provide us with a number of different premises as to what reality is. Depending on which premise is used, the perspective taken to it will be determined. On the one hand, reality is equated with matter, existing in what you can see, touch, feel, or taste. This dictates a largely behavioral approach to culture. On the other hand, reality is seen as existing in the mind, as a set of rules about the world. This dictates an ideational or mentalistic approach to culture. With different premises, the differences between the two positions cannot be resolved—neither mind nor matter can be reduced to the other. But it can be argued that both matter and mind have parts to play in defining culture, each speaking to a different aspect of it, but both aspects complimentary to one another. This is more reasonable and in keeping with how most anthropologists perceive the human experience and culture, as a totality or whole (the *holistic perspective*). Those who see culture as a set of rules or a mental construct acknowledge that such things do generate behavior. Behavioralists acknowledge that behaviors are based on ideas. The tendency to emphasize one or the other may be a product of attempts to break the phenomenon down into its smallest parts for intellectual understanding, but in the process the whole thing can become skewed or overly simplified. Others who try to make sense out of it merely end up very confused.

Despite differences in how culture is conceptualized, anthropologists do agree on some things. Culture is more than just beliefs or just behaviors, just mind or matter. Anthropologists agree that culture is something that is learned, shared, integrated, and always changing. Most anthropologists view culture as a uniquely human characteristic that must be taught and learned. Individuals are not born with culture; they have to learn it. Although the biological basis or capacity for culture is obvious, it is not something inherited along with one's physical characteristics. On the contrary, each generation of humans has to learn it all over again or it will not survive. Cultural transmission and acquisition represent the means by which cultures are reproduced. Many Americans sincerely believe that being born in the United States is all that is necessary to be an American. Being born in America does give a person the rights of U.S. citizenship, but to become members of American culture they must learn the beliefs and behaviors which make and identify them as members of the American Culture. In the United States, the primary means of accomplishing this comes with the formal educational system, but it proceeds through more informal means as well. The fact that culture is learned points to the fact that it is also something shared within groups of people. While there are serious unanswered questions remaining about how much must be shared and practiced, there is no question that it is shared. It is also related to the environment in which the group attempts to live and survive. But no culture today is the same as it has always been, for as circumstances of the natural environments and sociocultural environments have changed, humans have had to change aspects of their culture or not survive. Cultures continually change simply because environments are continually changing.

Culture is the learned way or ways of belief, behavior, and the products of these shared by members (at least to some degree) within human groupings, which serve to distinguish the individual and the group from other individuals and groups. The question is not whether culture can be defined, or whether we even need agreement among the scholars who dissect and examine its parts. The real question is how to operationalize that definition, and this comes with its application and assignment to human groupings. Culture is a collective and integrated whole consisting of learned ideas, behaviors, and products, all shared and all related to the needs of human groups. Because of this, it represents an integrated system. Ideas are generated out of people's concerns and needs, and these are translated through behaviors into products (either physical artifacts or social systems). All three of these aspects of culture are complimentary and dependent on each other. Together, they produce the whole of culture. Even as culture can be broken down in relation to the basic concerns of people living together in large groups, the systematic and integrated nature of it remains. Culture has never been a haphazard grouping of things that somehow accumulated over time. The ideas, behaviors, and products of culture are associated with satisfying one or another of the concerns, needs, or desires of people. What is done in one area will be related to what may have to be done in another area. It can even necessitate what *must* be done in specific areas of the culture. All of these represent the whole of culture and ultimately determine the way of life of the group's members. Most people's ideas and practices exist in combinations, as complexes or patterns of related behaviors, ideas, and products. These patterns serve purposes, and most are woven together in relation to the basic interests and needs of social living. Some apply to everyone in the group, and some represent alternatives that allow for choices acceptable within the group. Still others apply to only certain categories of people within the group. While these can be seen as the bits and pieces of culture, some of them are clearly more important than others.

What is important as one moves from cultural group to cultural group can vary quite substantially, but some things are important to all groups. They determine how the group will live, and whether the group and its culture will, or can, survive. These sometimes are referred to as the core systems of culture, or those things necessary for the survival of any group and its culture. They reflect the basic needs of individual human beings and groups of them. They must be provided for simply because people live together in groups, sometimes very large groups. For example, for any culture to survive, the people who share it must survive. Food and shelter are basic concerns of all people. Food may be the most important of all basic human needs, for if people do not have enough food to survive, they die and the rest of their concerns become moot points. Food and shelter are both tied to the natural resources available to the people that can be used to satisfy these needs. It is not surprising that food and shelter then lie at the heart of what we call the economic pattern or system found in all societies and cultures. Economic systems focus on who has access to available natural resources, their transformation into those things people require to meet their needs, and ways of getting those things to the people who need them. Customs that determine who has access to natural resources, how they will be transformed into the products people require, and how the finished products will be distributed to those who want or need them, together represent a core area common for all cultural groups, referred to as the economic system in the United States.

Because people attempt to live together in groups, the need for social order is essential. This creates a prime concern for social order, structured social relations, and customs for establishing and maintaining behavior deemed desirable by the group. There must be structured social relations whereby individuals know what to expect from others and what is expected of them—the social claims and obligations of people. A society's social structure stipulates the relationships among members of the group, even the means by which these are established. It can include marriage and family patterns, social stratifications, and a great many other things that focus on the rights and responsibilities of individuals to other members of their group. In the complex and fragmented nation-state, the problems of social order transcend the ability of the social structure to take care of it, hence the evolution of political or legal systems. Whether the society is a traditional and small-scale one or a complex one, it must make provisions for maintaining order among its people. It must have some means of establishing the norms of acceptable behavior and ways of dealing with disorder or violations of behavior expectations as they arise. All groups have ways of doing this, some highly formalized and some very informal. All cultures set the minimum standards of behavior for the group and provide the means for their enforcement. How individual members of the group acquire this knowledge of what is expected of them and what they can expect from others (their social relations), and how they acquire the other basic understandings of the group, represent another area of core concern for all cultural groups.

The cultural transmission and acquisition process refers to how groups teach and individuals learn their cultures. Some cultural transmission and acquisition process must exist if a culture is to survive. The central role of language in the process can be assumed without prolonged discussion, for without language, culture as it exists would be simply impossible. Within this systematic code, all the rules, behaviors, and products of the culture are symbolically encoded. Not only is language where the culture is encoded, but it is also the means by which people acquire their culture and part of what they acquire. In the process of acquiring culture, people also obtain their world view that also represents a core aspect of all cultures, albeit a little more abstract and less tangible than some of the others. This world view provides people with both attitudes and perceptions of the world in which they live. It encompasses attitudes about what the world is all about. It helps people make sense out of their world. It provides the means by which they will perceive it, as it defines their place and role in that world. It serves as the basis for many of their beliefs, and it provides for answers as to what is, why it is, what it should be, and what the individual's relationship to that might be. Such views or attitudes can be organized around religion, political ideology, economic ideology, social structure, or they can come from a combination of these.

## Cultural Forms

Saying that humans have culture is not enough. Saying that culture is *a* learned way of believing and behaving is not enough either, for people learn many cultures in their lifetime. Culture also comes in a variety of forms, and the differences between these need to be understood as well. Ask anyone to tell you about their culture, explain some idea, belief, or action, and they will tell you. All people are taught the standards of the group, the expectations, rules, ideas, and values that must be learned to become part of the group. This represents the *ideal culture*, but there is also the *real culture* that can be quite different, and there are *culture constructs* that attempt to bridge these two for specific purposes. These different forms of culture must be understood if one expects to understand the role of culture in the lives of humans and their responses given certain circumstances.

*Ideal culture* is taught to aspiring members of culture groups by those who already know and are already members of the group. It is provided and transmitted as the required knowledge, beliefs, and behavioral expectations of the group. To become a member of a group, to be identified and accepted into full membership, requires that an individual acquire the knowledge, ideas or expected behavior patterns. One is also expected to adhere to the group's rules, ideas, and behaviors. For example, Americans learn about the value placed on the individual, freedom, democracy, equality, equal opportunity, and to be responsible and law-abiding. All Americans know what their culture is *supposed to be* like for they are taught such things at home, in school, in church, and in the training or orientation programs where they work. This ideal culture is the product of the cultural group members deciding what needs to be taught and learned by new members of the group. This "statement of culture," which outlines the required beliefs and expected behaviors, is presented to each new recruit in its most idealized form as the beliefs and behaviors to which the group subscribes. It represents what the group believes itself to be all about, how they think of themselves, or how they wish others to see them. It is designed to bend the individual to the group, create solidarity or unit, and to establish some consistency and regularity in what is taught and learned. On the other hand, it is actually rare that real thoughts and actions live up to the ideals presented for the group. Ranges of behavior are acceptable in all societies, and these are learned right along with the ideal ones. Individuals learn how far they may deviate from the expected norms and still be accepted by the group. Because of the nature of their arbitrary origins, the cultures of most nation-states are the result of compromise. This is certainly true in the case of the United States, where the national culture resulted from a group effort. While American culture was the result of a group compromise effort, the individual American is left to "play it out" or "live up to it." It simply may be impossible for any individual to live up to the ideals established by a group.

In actual practice, the United States is a stratified society, socially structured into classes and other groupings that have unequal access to economic resources, status positions, prestige, etc. Inequality is structured into the society. The socio-economic class system of the U.S. revolves around stored wealth, the bulk of which increasingly is monopolized by fewer and fewer members of the society. Thus, it would appear that American society is not really the land of equality or even equal opportunity. Various cultural groups in the United States (e.g. African-Americans, Mexican-Americans, women, etc.) certainly understand inequality and the lack of equal opportunity in the society. Neither equal opportunity laws nor affirmative action programs have changed that reality for them. While individuality and freedom are highly valued in American society, neither is possible within any large social group. Individuality has to be sacrificed for the "common good," stability, and order in the group. Individuality represents a threat to any group and so, too, is the idea of absolute freedom. America is thought of as the "land of the free," but only up to the point where individual actions do not impinge on the rights of others. To allow individuals to impinge on the rights of other would represent a threat to the continued survival of the group. Contradictions such as these and a great many others that can be found in American culture point to the difference between the ideal and the real culture. What Americans may like to think or wish to think about themselves rarely correlates with what they actually believe and do as individuals or in groups. While on the one hand it can suggest how well individuals actually live up to the stated ideals of the group, on the other it might suggest that real culture includes learning the limits of variation the group will accept. As a general rule, most people do not go around with a list to remind themselves what their culture expects of them. They learn what the culture expects of them, even what it is supposed to be all about, they learn the limits of acceptable variation and then they simply go through the process of living on a day-to-day basis. They simply think as they have been taught and do what they know must be done insofar as what they interpret that to mean or what they might be capable of. Ideal culture is a group phenomenon, whereas real culture is played out on an individual basis, and people learn how far they can go in stretching, bending, or even violating the rules.

Sometimes there is a small difference and sometimes there is a substantial difference between our *ideal* and our *real* cultures, between that we have been taught to think and do, and what we actually think and do. Recognizing this difference between ideal and real forms of culture is an essential step in understanding culture and its influence on the lives of people, their behavior and beliefs as individuals or as groups. Regardless of the group, members must learn ideal culture, but they function in the real culture context and therefore also must learn just how far they can deviate from the ideals. There are other areas in which a substantial difference can be noted between the ideal and real cultures of American society, and the same can be said for any other culture grouping. Given the development of the modern nation-state, the difference between these forms of cultures can be extreme because of the arbitrary and artificial basis of such societies that frequently necessitates compromises as to what will be or how they wish the rest of the world to see them. The fact that most people in cultural groups recognize the difference between their stated ideals and the realities of everyday living produces yet another form of culture, the construct.

In a very real sense, all cultures are creations and thus all are *culture constructs*, produced out of the efforts of groups of humans and individuals to adapt to the problems of their environments and live within the limitations imposed by them. Another kind of culture construct also comes into being as people attempt to make some sense out of the beliefs and behaviors of others, to describe the culture of others in an attempt to understand them. While individuals and groups produce culture constructs as they attempt to live on a day-to-day basis within the constraints of their sociocultural environments, they also create culture descriptions for other people with different beliefs and behaviors. These constructs are created and then allowed to stand as descriptions for groups, and they in turn guide the interactions of the groups. For the individual, and for categories of people within the larger group, culture constructs also are generated as a means of adapting to the peculiar social circumstances in which they find themselves. The constructs allow them to confront those circumstances and perhaps deal with the apparent gaps between the group's stated ideals and their own realities. For the individuals who may not be able to adhere to the stated ideals of the culture because of their own limitations or the particular circumstances in which they might find themselves through no fault of their own, and for categories or groups within the larger society who find themselves in similar circumstances, these culture constructs help them account for, and respond to, the contradictions and paradoxes inherent in the larger culture context. In the complex nation-state, individuals and groups create their own cultural constructs in order to adapt to the reality they perceive or that in which they are expected (forced?) to function.

Individuals who find that they simply cannot live up to the ideals of the nation, those who are not permitted to do so, or those who might choose not to subscribe to all of the ideals that might have been established for them, in essence, create their own individualized constructs. Each individual puts together his/her own unique combination of beliefs and practices based on their own reality. This individual set is constructed from the different sets of beliefs and practices of groups with which they affiliate—in essence creating a personal culture. These constructs are like an individual's fingerprints—no two individuals will be exactly alike. Groups of people categorized together and sharing social circumstances also do much of the same thing. Ethnic groupings within nation-states are construct cultures that are created out of common origins or heritage and self-identified as a response to the circumstances in which they find themselves. Mexican-Americans are not groups of people that put together the Mexican culture and the American culture; rather, they create a unique culture all their own because of their common origins, shared characteristics, and common treatment in the social context of the United States. In the case of both the individual and categorized groupings of people, the culture constructs they create are designed to help them survive the socioeconomic conditions they might face or maximize their efforts at becoming full participating members of the larger group. Construct cultures are created for others for the same operational purposes of understanding and action.

Creating cultural descriptions for others helps people make sense out of the differences they see. Their generations then become the basis for interacting with them. Anthropologists have always been involved with cultural constructs as they have attempted to describe cultures using the norms of belief and behavior exhibited by a group. But anthropologists are not the only ones to create cultural descriptions that then are allowed to stand for a cultural grouping. All people do this as a way of trying to make sense out of what others think and do. When members of one cultural group see others doing something different from themselves, or hear something different from what they think, they have to make sense out of it. To do this, they will refer to their own experiences, beliefs, and practices to interpret what they see or hear. Based on their own learned ways of belief and behavior, they will interpret what they hear or see and put the differences in perspective. They will draw conclusions and make judgments about the ideas or practices of others based on what they have learned to be the most correct or best way to think and behave. The conclusions drawn then are allowed to stand as part of the description of that other culture. But the ethnocentrism introduced by culture provides that such interpretations are quite likely to be incorrect. The interactions  between members of different groups are made more difficult in that many of these generated perceptions can prove to be quite faulty. For example, Americans hold very different views on time than might be the case in other cultures. Americans, Mexican, and some Middle Eastern groups simply do not approach or value time in the same way. This will almost always insure some misunderstanding. An American's interpretation of the value and use of time in those other cultures might be that they are unmotivated, waste a lot of valuable time, or even that members of such groups are lazy. In actual practice, the importance of time to people in those cultures may not reflect any of these characterizations. However, the misconception will underlie the American's approach to members of these groups. While most people create culture descriptions based on what they think they hear or see, anthropologists do this a little more systematically, limiting the ethnocentric bias as much as might be humanly possible and thereby reducing misinterpretations and misconceptions.

## CULTURAL GROUPINGS

Humans tend to live together in collective groups and form societies wherein they share culture. Human societies represent aggregates of people who have claims and obligations to one another. Culture is the glue that holds them together. This means that culture can be attributed to all manner, kinds, and sizes of human groups regardless of origin or makeup. A cultural group is not simply an aggregate of people who come together for a passing moment; rather, it is a group with a relatively permanent existence, recognized rules for membership, and reason to exist. Their existence is evidenced in the ideas and behaviors they share, in the claims and obligations its members have to one another, and in organizational structures which insure that the group will continue over time. It may be that the group has nothing more than a general or specific goal of surviving given a particular set of circumstances of a natural or sociocultural environment. It may be that a group comes together for the pursuit of a common interest or purpose. A cultural grouping comes into being as a group of people attempting to survive in a particular environment and with a particular set of circumstances. It also can come into being as a group that may wish to carry forward a particular ideology or agenda. Members of such groupings are recruited through recognized rules and procedures, but actual membership is based on the individual learning all of those things that ultimately distinguish the group from others. Through an established and recognized structure, the group can continue irrespective of the loss of individual members. There is a clear sense (pride) of belonging to or being associated with culture groups, as members gain elements of individual identity in the process and as a consequence. By extension, the group is identified as a cultural grouping by themselves and members of other groups who perceive the differences.

When people learn all of the rules, duties, or expectations required of members of any group, they have learned its culture. A cultural grouping can be identified wherever a human group learns a set of beliefs and practices that distinguishes it from others learning different beliefs and practices. Once members have learned their culture, identifying "us" from "them" (those "others"), or the *we* versus *they*, is a natural and common practice. Once learned, culture becomes the measure of every other culture. People judge the actions of others based on what they have learned, and every member of cultural groupings must learn the "right" things, their own brand of "truth" that determines and guides the actions of its members. As members of different culture groups come into contact with each other, that contact and interaction will be one of conflict, for truths come into conflict. In the interaction of different groups, the learned truth of one group will compete with the truth of the other. Each will be equally believed, followed, and defended as the "ultimate," "best," or "most correct" truth. There are many culture groups and thus many different truths. Because humans learn their cultures as truth, they naturally tend to judge the cultures of others based on what they have learned and believe to be true or correct (Downs 1975). Anthropologists refer to this as *ethnocentrism*, and recognize it as a natural consequence of learning one's culture. All human groups and the individual members who comprise them are ethnocentric. No cultural group in the world teaches its new or aspiring members that someone else's culture is more correct than their culture. This insures that when members of different cultures come into contact, there will always be conflict between their truths. To understand the ramifications of this, and because culture can be attributed to the most generalized grouping of humans down to the most specific of groups, it is necessary to examine the kinds, types, or levels of human groupings to which the culture label can be applied. Culture is used with reference to the entire human species group, and it is used to characterize specific groupings.

### General Culture Group

On the most generalized level, culture can be used to characterize the entire human group as their adaptation to environment(s). In this sense, all humans have culture, for all humans rely on culture to respond and adapt to their environments. On this level, culture pinpoints that rather unique ability of humans to adapt to different environments, change them to suit their purposes and even control them to a degree no other animal has been able to achieve. When culture is used with reference to all humans on the species level, it simply represents this unique characteristic that separates the human from all of the other animals with whom they share the planet. Because all humans share and exercise this ability, all humans are essentially the same in that they will use it to provide for all of their basic and derived needs. Such basic needs as food, shelter, human association, and whatever warmth that seems to be required as part of that are common to all humans regardless of where they might be found. People in any part of the world are just as concerned about sufficient food, shelter from the elements, and the security and warmth that comes with human association as is the individual in the United States. Humans everywhere laugh when they are happy and cry when they are sad or hurt. In the satisfaction of basic needs, every human is the same as every other human, regardless of how they meet such needs. It is only in the specific beliefs and behaviors they select in attempting to satisfy or meet similar needs that humans and groups appear different from one another; it is because humans elect different means for satisfying their needs from all of the alternatives that might be available that the concept of culture becomes a bit more complicated, for this means that culture can be attributed to all manners of specific human groupings.

### Specific Culture Groups

While all humans use culture to adapt to the environment, they tend to develop local varieties, brands, or manifestations of this universal human characteristic because they live in different kinds of places and under different conditions. Representing local adaptations, cultures can be seen for what they really are—sets of problem-solving solutions. On this level, it is a common practice to distinguish cultures according to some highly generalized geographical type of environment, e.g., desert, arctic, tropical, etc. But it is also used to refer to specific groupings created according to size and complexity, e.g., small-scale traditional cultures or complex cultures. It is also used to identify people who share common origins or characteristics that exist within the complex states, e.g., ethnic cultures and those based on some special interest. This is a function of the fact that while human groups adapt to natural environments, they also must adapt to the sociocultural environments they created with their cultures. As environments differ, one would expect that individual groups inhabiting them will be different. Even groups within particular environments can differ simply because choices are made from among all of the alternatives available to them. As particular groups of humans adjust to the specific circumstances of the particular environments in which they find themselves, they create their own cultures that are specific to them, distinguishing them from other groups of humans.

Each type of natural environment has its own distinct conditions, problems, and/or limit of possibilities. But physical environments do not determine culture(s); they only limit or provide the possibilities. They limit the choices available, but choices still must be made, and thus cultures within the very same type of environment can be dramatically different. If this were not so, one would expect that all groups inhabiting a particular type of environment would have the same culture, and this is simply not the case. In the choices made to meet needs, not all of which will be the same, groups can take on very different appearances from one another. In choosing from among all of the alternatives available, humans create their own particular or specific cultures, obviously reflective of that environment and the choices that they have made. Cultural characteristics of any group are a function, at least in part, of the particular natural environment in which it is trying to survive. But humans also must adapt to more than just the limit of possibilities provided by any natural environment.

In adapting to varied natural environments, and in the making of choices from available alternatives to satisfy their needs, human groups create the sociocultural environments to which they also have to adapt. There are natural environments in the natural order of things, and there are sociocultural environments created by humans to deal with them. This sociocultural environment even produces its own physical component to augment that of the naturally occurring environment.This environment then poses its own limit of possibilities and provides for more choices to be made from still more alternatives that are available. In the case of the sociocultural environment, it quickly becomes obvious that there were many more alternatives from which to chose, and thus much more diversity appears among groups. As humans grouped together in larger and larger numbers, and as the territorially based states developed, this environment became even more complex as specialization and fragmentation became the norm. In every area of concern, people simply had all manners of choices to make. Specific cultural groupings began to appear along very different lines than those associated with just the natural environments. New kinds of cultural groupings appeared as a consequence of specialization, fragmentation, and stratification based on economic, political, religious, race, and/or special interests. New groups also appeared out of the movement of groups with distinct cultures from one nation-state to another.

Among the many kinds of cultures created out of the sociocultural environment was the nation-state culture, normally associated with territorially based states (e.g., the United States, Germany, Russia, etc.). Unfortunately, the advent of this type of culture obscures more than it clarifies, for such cultures are largely arbitrary and artificial creations. Because of this, they will nearly always be multicultural. They are arbitrary in the sense that they incorporated many already established and quite distinct cultural groups into the artificially created nation-state through some form of coercion. They are artificial in the sense that a set of beliefs and practices was consciously decided upon by some members of the group for all of its members to learn and practice. In the case of the United States, the culture came about as the result of compromise and the adoption of beliefs and behaviors that ideally would stand for the United States. Using the concept of culture with nation-states is a major source of difficulty and confusion. Nation-states are political units with varying levels of sociopolitical integration. It presupposes that all people given membership in the group will share the same set of cultural beliefs and behaviors. Whether this is or is not actually the case, people tend to believe and subscribe to it because it is what they will be taught. According to some current thinking, a nation is a community of people that sees itself as one people based on common traditions, ancestry, institutions, ideology, language, and perhaps religion (Clay 1990:28). This perception rarely coincides with the actual cultural diversity present in all nation-states. Few, if any, nation-states exhibit the homogeneity implied in such a definition. In point of fact, the more complex the society, the less likely its members will, or can, share, all of the same beliefs and behaviors.

Nation-states are societies with clearly defined territorial borders separating them from others. They are almost always characterized or associated by a state level of sociopolitical integration in which some specific group or authority exercises a monopolistic control over the use of force to insure that its members comply with the rules of the society. It has been used synonymously with culture as well, for centralized governments have been concerned with creating a national culture—a set of beliefs and practices that is supposed to apply to everyone within its borders. There is no nation-state in existence where a single set of cultural beliefs and practices is shared by all of its citizens. While nation-states may achieve some success in getting their people to share some things, that does not mean that they will share all of it to the exclusion of other sets of beliefs and practices. The tendency is for most people to perceive the nation-state as a culture based on the assumption that all of the people included in the grouping must learn and share national values (at least ideally), follow the same prerequisite behavior required of all its citizens, and function within the same organizational structures. Nation-states become cultural groupings by virtue of such things, but this does not mean that no cultural differences will be present within them. Significant differences among various groups that together make up such nation-states do exist. For the sake of unity and conformity within the state, any recognized differences almost always are portrayed as secondary to the beliefs and practices advocated by the state for all of its citizens. But, creating nation-state culture by fiat, legislating or mandating a "national culture," or simply insisting that all members of the nation-state share the same thoughts, values, beliefs, and behaviors does not necessarily mean that all of its citizens will actually do it. Groups incorporated into the state come with their own set of beliefs and practices already learned, practiced, and believed as truth. They normally elect to continue some aspects of their older cultural pattern insofar as they may be allowed to. This means that the cultural beliefs and practices they brought with them will be continued to some degree, despite any superficial acceptance of a nation-state culture. Current events have dramatically demonstrated that traditional beliefs, while subdued in the context of nation-states, are not forgotten. They apparently wait for the right opportunity to be fully expressed once again. Because of this, and the steadfastness with which all cultural groups hold on to their valued beliefs and practices, most nation-states are actually made up of *constituent cultures.*

Along with the assignment of culture to the nation-state grouping comes the use of culture for groups incorporated into any one of them; these groups together make up the modern nation-state. The most popular tendency has been to refer to such cultural groupings as *subcultures*, suggesting that they are simply microcultures within the macroculture, somehow less viable than that of the state—actually subservient to it. The term would be acceptable if it recognized the legitimacy, viability, and even primacy of such cultures, but this is not the case. The term has also come to mean that such groups have been absorbed or assimilated into the culture of the state, when in fact this is rarely the case. Examples of this are easy to find. Native-American groups have a distinct heritage and way of life. They continue many of their traditional ways, while at the same time, they have adopted many of the ways, beliefs, and practices peculiar to the culture of the United States, simply because they had to do so to survive in that context. In the process, they created a new culture, neither traditional nor American. They constructed a culture pattern quite unique to them, and this can be said for all ethnically based American groups, each of which has a different heritage and history within the American context. This accounts for why the hyphen is used throughout this volume with such ethnic groups as Mexican-American, Japanese-American, etc. *Constituent culture* would seem to be a more appropriate way to identify or refer to groups of this type. While they help to constitute the national culture and play a role in the definition of that group, each is identifiable as a distinct culture group in its own right, and its members believe just as strongly in it as might be the case with any other culture. Constituent cultures can be used to identify the different ways of belief and behavior that distinguish all manners of cultural groupings that make up the modern complex state, for in addition to ethnic groups all manners of special interest culture groups also can be viewed as constituent groups of the modern state.

Most people in the United States readily associate the idea of cultural difference with ethnicity and race. For them, ethnic difference is based on racial difference, language, common origins, or other shared characteristics. Many people resist the idea of distinct cultures for ethnic groups within the nation-state, arguing that such groupings are still part of the national culture. Others suggest that it is a combination of cultural patterns that originated out of migrations of well-defined cultural groups from one place to another, while still others argue that it is contextual, created out of a social need or circumstance favoring a combination of older traditions with new ones, in essence creating something quite unique. This group argues that ethnicity is primarily for the purpose of group self-identification. Still other researchers argue that ethnicity has lost all of its meaning, or that it is nothing more than another label for culture. However we approach it, ethnic groups are part of the modern complex society, and they contribute to the reality and definition of that society. Generally, these kinds of constituent groups appear to subscribe to many of the same ideas and behavior required of all people within the boundaries of the nation-state. Sharing some ideas and practices allows them to coexist within the nation-state, but this is not the same as saying that they will share all of the same beliefs and behaviors established for, or expected in, the state. They tend to adhere to many of the same behavioral expectations of the larger national group of which they have been made a part—the prerequisite behavior for everyone living within the nation's borders. But it does not mean that they will adhere to all such expectations. They may not because they chose not to adhere to all of them, or they may not have been allowed to share in certain aspects of the nation-state culture. While such groups share in some of the beliefs and behaviors of the larger grouping, it is apparent that they maintain their own distinct patterns of belief and behavior that distinguish them from other equally identifiable groups. They are distinct cultural groupings, even though they may contribute to the definition or characterization of the nation-state culture. The term *constituent* means to form, compose, or make up something. Every nation-state is actually composed of people with distinct ethnic cultures that have been brought together. But other kinds of culture groups produced by the social context also help to constitute the complex modern society, and these are tied to all manners of special interests. Both kinds of groupings are viable cultural groupings, and both represent constituent groups that make up the diversity of modern complex societies.

Cultural groupings arise in complex societies based on all kinds of special interests. These groups represent viable cultural groupings (constituent cultures) that contribute to the makeup of the modern nation-state. These are a function and product of the specialization and fragmentation that characterizes such complex societies. On this level of human grouping, the culture concept is perhaps the most difficult to deal with, for members of such groups are drawn from others groups within the society to form new cultural groups for very specific purposes. They can be created by drawing their members from throughout the world, in essence transcending physical geography, national boundaries, and/or nationality. Spradley and McCurdy (1972) refer to these kinds of cultural groupings as *cultural scenes*, denoting their legitimacy as culture groups. The cultural scene is where one finds information and behavior being shared by a select group, perhaps even as few as two. Cultural groupings of this type are related to social situations, emphasizing their relationship to the complex sociocultural environment. In essence, these types of groupings arise in response to the actual conditions of the social environment and are created to cope with those conditions. Along with ethnic groups, they also reflect the limited sharing of culture that is actually possible among people in an age of fragmentation, complexity, and specialization.

As constituent groups of the complex societies, special interst groups contribute to the cultural diversity or multiculturalism that has come to characterize modern states. They are created for a variety of purposes and nearly all are tied to the specialization and fragmentation of complex states. Some are created along regional geographic lines (e.g., Southerners, Yankees, Texans, New Yorkers, Californians, etc.) or according to where the members might live (e.g., urban, rural, small towns, farms, metroplexes, etc.). Some are created on the basis of sex and gender (e.g., male, female, homosexual, heterosexual), while still others can be based on age (infant, teenager, young adult, mature adult, retired, etc.) and occupation (business, professional, academic, white collar, blue collar, etc.). Such cultural groupings will be found in religions (Moslem, Christian, Catholic, Baptist, etc.), in politics (democratic, socialistic, communistic, republican, democrat, etc.), and a whole host of other special interests (environmentalism, conservationism, pop culture, specific physical disabilities, and leisure activities). Even within these categorical groupings, further breakdowns are possible. The business culture can be broken down into distinct types (restaurant, industrial, shipping, service, etc.), and from these even more specific groupings are possible. For example, in the restaurant business there are the cooks, hostesses, waitresses, waiters, the management, and the customers. Distinguishable cultures can be identified for transportation and communication, and to distinguish one company from another and how they do business—IBM from Texas Instruments, McDonald's from Burger King and Wendy's. The culture of Harvard University can be distinguished from that of the East State University or the City Community College. Virtually any special interest group can be viewed as a cultural group at this level, and the possibilities are almost endless, depending on how specific one wishes to get. The only criteria that must be met to be identified as a cultural grouping is whether a group does learn specific beliefs and behaviors that distinguish it from other groups.

Members of constituent cultures such as these simply follow many of their own distinct beliefs and behaviors, while at the same time subscribing to many of the same ideas and rules of prerequisite behavior as do all of those who have been incorporated, willingly or unwillingly, into a particular nation-state. Some groups are made necessary out of the complexity of the state or the conditions within which some groups are forced to exist. The way such cultures interact with each other usually is addressed in terms of dominant or submissive status, traditional and assimilated, minority and majority, or who has held the political/economic power over whom. The very fact that nation-states are made up of so many constituent cultural groupings accounts for the cultural diversity that will characterize them, and the problems that accompany that diversity. All nation-states are multicultural, they all exhibit these kinds of cultural diversity. The multicultural nature of modern society is reflected in the multiculturalism of its individual members.

## CULTURE DIVERSITY / MULTICULTURALISM

Multiculturalism is a term that frequently is used synonymously with cultural diversity. It generally is used whenever a multitude of cultures can be identified in the context of any human society. The world is multicultural, for it contains many cultures. The United States is multicultural, for it too contains many distinct cultures. Often overlooked is the fact that most individuals in the complex society are, out of necessity, multicultural as well.

As people learn many cultures in their lifetime, they will identify with a number of them simultaneously at any given point in time. An individual can be an American, a Mexican-American, a female, an anthropologist, a Southern Baptist, an environmentalist, a republican, and working at Harvard all at the same time. A worker carries into the workplace all of the cultural beliefs and behaviors obtained from all of their cultural group memberships. The workplace itself simply represents another cultural context. An individual's other cultural beliefs and practices are not left at the door as they enter another culture for work. This frequently can produce great conflicts for the individual who must choose which culture set (beliefs or behaviors) to follow in particular circumstances. The different cultures with which they are affiliated may actually be in direct contradiction or conflict with one another, e.g., their political, national, and/or religious cultures. The demands of their occupational culture can easily conflict with religious, political, or social cultures. In such cases, individuals are forced to chose which culture set will influence their decisions and/or guide their actions. Most people separate aspects of their lives into distinct categories of activity and then use the culture set most appropriate in each. But it may very well be that one of the cultures becomes the dominant or the primary cultural force in an individual's life, thus becoming the sole determinant of the choices made in all circumstances, even to the exclusion of all other cultural groups with which they may affiliate. Some people are more influenced by politics and political groups, others by economics and economic groups. Still others are influenced more by their religious beliefs and particular religious group than anything else. Normally, when individuals are perceived as oriented and focused to the beliefs and practices of a single group, they are judged to be shortsighted, narrow in view, and perhaps even fanatical in their steadfastness. Sometimes the choice of culture set to operate from will be determined entirely by the circumstances or context of the moment. Most humans are not simply influenced or motivated by a culture; rather, most are motivated by cultures, anyone of which can exert the greater influence on their actions at any given moment in time or given any particular set of circumstances. Unfortunately, the multicultural nature of the individual is not well studied or understood.

## CONCLUSION

Every society, regardless of size, has a distinct culture all its own. What they have is an integrated, adaptive, and always changing complex of learned ideas, behaviors and products suited to the particular environments in which they find themselves. Culture is created in response to problems posed in environments. It is a set of problem-solving solutions learned as truth. They will judge all others based on it. What they learn is actually different forms of that culture, and each will play a role in the culture change process. Any one form of it can guide, determine, and impact the people's response to particular situations and actions. Humans group with others for all kinds of reasons. They group together in response to problems or interests that arise in the natural or sociocultural environments created out of their actions in responding to the natural environment. But not everyone chooses the same solution to the same problem. When all of the needs are satisfied, we end up with a system of solutions to problems that together we call culture. All of these solutions are related to one another and form a coherent whole. The system is an integrated one that then is passed down from generation to generation as *the* way of thinking, believing, and doing. It has been created by them, and it becomes their reality. Culture becomes life's blueprint for thinking, acting, and believing. It becomes the road map that gets them from one day to the next. Putting together all the learned ways that individuals accumulate over the course of a lifetime, culture in one form or another, or altogether, provides them with all that they need to know, the prescriptions for what they will think and do. It represents truth, their truth as they have learned it. They operate as if it is the only truth or, at the very least, the more correct one.

In the final analysis, given that culture can be applied on all of these different levels of human groupings, it is not surprising that the concept is a difficult one for many people to understand and apply. While it can make sense to scholars who study it specifically, for others it is simply not so meaningful. While culture is something that can be credited to all kinds of human groups, more important is the realization that culture is something that characterizes any relatively permanent human group that learns specific beliefs and behaviors that then serve to distinguish it as a group from other groups that have learned different things. Viewed in this manner, a culture group becomes any distinguishable group of people who learn their own ways of thinking and behaving, and then pass these on from generation to generation or to each new member. All nation-states are culturally diverse or multicultural. It is precisely from this diversity that many intractable social issues and problems must be confronted by people nearly everywhere in the world.

## REFERENCES

Barrett, R. A. 1984. *Culture and Conduct*, 2nd edition. Belmont, CA: Wadsworth.

Clay, J. W. 1990. What's a nation? *Mother Jones* 15(7):28.

Downs, J. F. 1975. *Cultures in Crisis*, 2nd edition. Beverly Hills: Glencoe Press.

Freilich, M. (ed). 1972. *The Meaning of Culture*. Lexington, MA: Xerox College.

Gamst, F. C. & Norbeck, E. 1976. *Ideas of Culture: Sources and Uses*. New York: Holt, Rinehart & Winston.

Harris, M. 1968. *The Rise of Anthropological Theory*. New York: Thomas Y. Crowell Company.

Haviland, W. A. 1994. *Anthropology*, 7th edition. Fort Worth: Harcourt Brace College Publishers.

Kroeber, A. & Kluckhohn, C. 1952. *Culture: A Critical Review of Concepts and Definitions*. Papers of the Peabody Museum of American Archaeology and Ethnology, Vol. 1. Cambridge: Harvard University Press.

Naylor, L. L. 1996. *Culture and Change: An Introduction*. Westport, CT: Bergin & Garvey.

Spradley, J. P. & McCurdy, D. 1972. *The Cultural Experience*. Prospect Heights, IL: Waveland Press.

White, L. 1959. *The Evolution of Culture*. New York: McGraw-Hill.

# 2

# Multiculturalism: Issues for the Twenty-First Century

## Norma Williams

Race and ethnic relations are a topic of intense discussion and debate not only within the United States, but also on the world scene. As race and ethnic issues increase in significance, scholars and the broader citizenry are debating the issue of just what kind of a society the United States should become. In somewhat simplified terms, we find, on the one side, a number of scholars who continue to advocate the ideals of the assimilationist perspective, while another group of scholars reason that we should think in terms of some type of multicultural order if the United States is to begin to resolve the problems and issues associated with the tensions that result from racial and ethnic diversity in the nation (and in the world). If participation in the democratic process is to be meaningful for all groups in the United States, then we must confront racial, ethnic, and special interest diversity in a constructive manner.

In this chapter we discuss the limitations of the assimilationist orientation in light of the empirical data that have come to light in recent decades. The problems of the assimilationist model are especially acute as it emphasizes a top-down approach to the resolution of various racial and ethnic issues, and fails to take into account the perspective of minorities within the society as a whole. After examining some of the limitations of the assimilationist perspective, we will advance a multicultural frame of reference. Although we offer no simple solution to the difficulties that lie ahead, it seems quite reasonable to assume that if persons of different racial and ethnic minorities are to live, work, and play together in a democratic social order, they must come to understand and respect one another. Equal concern and respect for members of different racial and ethnic groups become one basis for overcoming what Gunnar Myrdal (1944) discussed, about a half-century ago, in *An American Dilemma*. This will be possible only when Americans develop a greater awareness, sensitivity, and understanding of others who are different from theselves. Before considering the main issues, certain concepts need to be clarified, and the historical context is provided for the discussion.

## SOME BASIC CONCEPTS

What is the meaning of race and ethnicity? Some scholars persist in seeking to interpret racial and ethnic differences in terms of biological characteristics. This form of "scientific racism," which has surfaced on various occasions for well over a century, while always popular, has always had some fundamental weaknesses. Biologists and physical anthropologists have long known that, in terms of genetics, the notion of a pure race is a social fiction. No human group has a monoplogy on any specific physical trait. They have shown that race is an artificial and arbitrary context. And efforts to tie human social or cultural actions or capabilities to the collective or specific physical characteristics or biological makeup of any particular group are doomed to failure.

It is not that outward physical characteristics are unimportant while scholars continue to determine the significance of physical differences that exists between groups of humans, it is what people learn about these differences that becomes important. They become significant because of the way they are defined by the cultural beliefs and values of different groups. Skin color and other physical characteristics often are used as a basis for prejudice and discrimination. Still, prejudice and discrimination typically involve more than physical appearance. Prejudice and discrimination are associated not only with physical but with linguistic and cultural differences as well. The idea of discrimination is emphasized rather than prejudice because the former reflects actual practices while the latter refers to attitudes. Discrimination is overt behavior or actions. It may involve either direct or indirect discrimination. One of the difficulties in coping with various forms of discrimination in modern society is that the process of exclusion from social and cultural activities is typically indirect (not direct in nature). (For further reading on this topic see Gonzales (1990). Various forms of discrimination often are based on an overgeneralized use of stereotypes that have been learned. Stereotypes involve negative exaggerations or distortions of individuals or groups in terms of their racial and ethnic characteristics. Such concepts as these are fundamental to any analysis of racial and ethnic diversity in U.S. society.

Race and ethnic relations cannot be separated (in real-life situations) from issues of social class and gender. Still, this discussion will focus specifically on race and ethnicity, while keeping in mind that race and ethnic relations have class as well as gender dimensions. Within each minority group there are typically class divisions, and these exist within the majority or dominant group as well. But race and ethnicity have an independence apart from social class. For example, middle-class black Americans or middle-class Mexican-Americans are not the same as middle-class whites (Anglo-Americans). So, too, gender divisions cut across class, racial, and ethnic lines. Poor African-American and poor Mexican-American women are discriminated against on the basis of their gender, but their interests and cultural values are typically very different from privileged Anglo-American women. In a more complete treatment of race and ethnic diversity, the issues of social class and gender would be given more consideration than is possible in this context. (For further reading on this topic see Andersen & Collins (1992).

## BACKGROUND CONSIDERATIONS

The history of race and ethnic relations in the United States is a complex one, yet it should be recognized that current racial and ethnic patterns are to a considerable degree the product of a long historical process. While a complete history would take far more time and space than allocated here, we can highlight some of the trends and patterns, and in addition, some of the major changes in racial and ethnic diversity that have occurred in the United States in recent decades can be discussed. A good starting point for this discussion is the "American Dream."

The founding fathers (and they were men) spoke of the "unalienable rights" of human beings. While they wrote and spoke in terms of this ideal, the reality was quite different. In actual practice, blacks or African-Americans and American Indians (Native Americans) were not viewed as human beings and thus possessed no unalienable rights. Slavery was an extreme form of discrimination. It was accepted by the founding fathers as legitimate for the South, but blacks also suffered exclusion in the North and the West, albeit in a less severe form. The issue of slavery was one factor that resulted in the Civil War. Yet freeing the slaves did not resolve the problem of exclusion of the blacks from fully participating in U.S. society with rights equal to those of everybody else. The backlash following the Civil War led to the creation of Jim Crow laws and the separate but equal doctrine. These laws were to remain in effect until they were struck down by the U.S. Supreme Court in *Brown v. Board of Education of Topeka* (1954).

Other racial and ethnic minorities also have experienced discrimination. What happened to various American Indians, the Asian American, and the Mexican-Americans cannot be ignored. All of these social categories and groups have suffered from discrimination and exclusion at the hands of dominate organizations in U.S. society, largely controlled by Anglo Americans (or Anglos). In the case of the so many American Indians, many historians have already well documented the destruction of large sectors of their population. In recent decades, all Americans have learned about the role of conquest in bringing about the subordination of Mexican- Americans. The Asian American category has suffered distinct forms of exclusion. For example, just after the outbreak of World War II, the Japanese-Americans were forcibly evacuated from the West Coast to internment camps (or what some call "concentration camps") because they were seen as potentially subversive. Similar exclusions were experienced by the Chinese brought in to help build America's railroad system, and most recently the Vietnamese who came to the United States following the Vietnam conflict. (For further reading on this topic see Williams and Coleman (1992).

Exclusionary practices are as much a part of the American heritage as are the ideals on which U.S. society was founded. The severe tensions between the ideal and real still await resolution. The particular situation in the United States is greatly complicated by the changing nature of majority and minority relations in recent decades. The growing complexity of racial and ethnic relations in U.S. society must be understood if one wants to understand the importance of cultural diversity in contemporary U.S. society.

### Increases in Racial and Ethnic Diversity

Fundamental changes in the United States are on the horizon because of significant increases in the nonwhite populations of the society. Harrison and Bennett speak of the increase in racial and ethnic diversity during the past few decades. They observe that the white population dropped from nearly 84 percent in 1970 to 80 percent in 1980 and to just a little over 75 percent in 1980. They go on to state:

The trends are even more visible in many large urban areas and a few states: 6 of the nation's largest 10 cities, and 14 cities were over one-half million persons were "majority minority" in the 1990 census; New Mexico, with a minority population of 49.6 percent, nearly joined the District of Columbia (73 percent) and Hawaii (69 percent) as a "majority minority" state in 1990, and California (43 percent) is expected to do so by the year 2000 (1995:141).

If present trends continue, the United States will approximate a "majority minority" population in the year 2050, well within the expected life span of many readers. These demographic patterns point to the fact that racial and ethnic diversity is increasing, not decreasing, and these indicate the need for all Americans to rethink the manner in which different groups come to interact with one another.

## THE ASSIMILATIONIST PERSPECTIVE

The assimilation perspective calls on racial and ethnic minorities to become like those who control and dominate the major institutions of society, and it is this majority sector (defined in terms of power) that defines the cultural values and beliefs that are to be emulated. It is clear that in throughout the twentieth century the assimilationist orientation has dominated discourse regarding race and ethnic relations not only in the society at large, but also within the social sciences (McKee 1993). Instead of surveying the limitations of the assimilationist orientation (cf. Williams et al. 1995), we shall concentrate on selected issues, particularly the built-in asymmetry between the top-down versus bottom-up orientation toward social life in general and majority/minority relations in particular. Persons in positions of privilege typically do not recognize that their views are necessarily shared by persons below, especially by racial and ethnic minorities (cf. Williams & Sjoberg 1993). Our reasoning can be clarified by first examining interpersonal relations.

Rollins (1985), in a highly informative field study, found that black women who served as domestics for whites understood their employers better than their employers understood them. The less privileged adapted to their plight as domestics by becoming keenly aware of the expectations of their employers. Because of their social power, the employers could disregard many of the views of their employees.

As one moves from the interpersonal level to the societal one, the patterns regarding the top-down and bottom-up orientations are not as easy to grasp. Nonetheless, the manner in which the dominant group (the Anglos) comes to define racial and ethnic minorities differs considerably from the manner in which the racial and ethnic minorities (the less privileged) define the dominant Anglo sector of the society.

### The Perspective from Above

The dominant Anglo sector of society has responded to racial and ethnic minorities in a variety of ways. Today this has come to mean that many forms of discrimination are more indirect than they were a half-century ago. Overt legal forms of discrimination are far less prevalent than they were in the past. However, we are also learning that the civil rights movement and the civil rights legislation of the 1960s did not lead to the equality that many persons assumed would be the product of these efforts.

The patterns associated with education are instructive. In the *Brown vs. Board of Education of Topeka* in 1954, the U.S. Supreme Court found that discrimination in public schools on the basis of race was unconstitutional. The separate but equal doctrine was in theory overturned. Yet the negative reactions to the Brown decision in many parts of the United States, especially in the South, were very strong. What has occurred since that decision points to the subtle ways in which the Brown decision has, in part, been undermined. First, the U.S. Supreme Court ruled in the Rodriguez case (1972) that education is not a fundamental right guaranteed by the U.S. Constitution. Therefore, if education is not a fundamental right guaranteed by the U.S. Constitution, and if states are expected to provide a minimal education, the conclusion must be that that is all the poor (including racial and ethnic minorities) can expect. A second retreat from the Brown decision was that involved in *Milliken vs. Bradley*. In this decision, the U.S. Supreme Court found that independent suburbs could not be included in legal efforts to desegregate the school system in the city of Detroit.

The question then arises: What have these decisions meant? In effect, they have meant that the most privileged sector of Anglo society has been able to isolate itself from racial and ethnic issues with respect to the desegregation of schools. They have been able to bypass desegregation issues in a legal manner. If one has sufficient wealth and is able to live in a suburb of one's own choosing, then one can avoid sending one's children to schools that are integrated. This does not mean that poor whites are exempt, however. But it does mean that the privileged sector of Anglo society has legally avoided the tensions posed by efforts to desegregate schools. These rulings also have provided indirect support for the "white flight" from the central cities in which so many of the poor racial and ethnic minorities live. In light of these patterns, sociologists such as Massey and Denton (1993) have come to speak of American apartheid.

The kinds of data outlined above indicate that the existing legal structure permits an indirect form of discrimination with respect to the education of the poor in general and racial and ethnic minorities in particular. While desegregation efforts have permitted the rise of a segment of African-Americans and Mexican-Americans into the middle class, the decisions by the U.S. Supreme Court after the case of

Brown have not made it possible for most persons, especially racial and ethnic minorities, to attain equality of opportunity. In a society in which education is the route to success, restricted educational opportunities mean that most members of racial and ethnic minorities cannot hope to succeed. (For further reading on this topic see San Miguel (1987).) This situation is complicated by the persistence of "science racism." The recent popularity of the book on *The Bell Curve* (Herrnstein & Murray 1994) points to the fact that the most privileged sector of the Anglo community can justify their academic success on biological grounds. In turn, the racial and ethnic minorities are stereotyped as biologically inferior. The cultural beliefs justify the very privileged Anglo sectors' lack of commitment to providing equal educational opportunities for racial and ethnic minorities.

## A View from Below

If discrimination (or exclusion) is viewed from below, the definition of the situation with respect to majority versus minority relations comes into sharper focus than when viewed from above. This is most clearly seen in the criminal justice system, for it is in this realm that tensions and conflicts are especially severe. Theoretically, the criminal justice system is used to maintain law and order within the society. From the perspective of the Anglos in positions of privilege, this system typically is viewed as treating persons in a rather fair manner. However, the same cannot be said if we take the perspective of members of racial and ethnic minorities, especially African-Americans and Mexican-Americans.

The trial of O.J. Simpson has highlighted the differences in the manner in which blacks view the criminal justice system in contrast to the way in which whites define this system. Social surveys conducted on the attitudes toward this system indicate that whites believe it is far fairer than do blacks. Moreover, when it was discovered that a detective in the Los Angeles Police Department (who testified for the prosecution at the O.J. Simpson trial) had slurred blacks on a tape, many blacks took the position that they knew this all along (Cohen 1995). Actually, the riots in Los Angeles a few years earlier indicated that the questions about the criminal justice system were not only held by blacks, but also by disadvantaged Mexican-Americans. These riots clearly pointed out that minorities had serious questions about actions of local police. The doubts expressed within the black and Hispanic communities about the fairness of the criminal justice system were heightened by the growth of the prison–industrial complex. Prisons are expanding at an enormous rate, often at the expense of higher education. Hispanics and especially black or African-American males are going to prison at a much higher rate than whites (for further reading on this topic see Duster (1995).) Many members of the Anglo sector of society assume that this pattern exists because racial and ethnic minorities have broken the law. However, fieldwork by sociologists such as Chambliss (1994) indicates that many black males are arrested in violation of their constitutional rights. The rising number of racial and ethnic minorities housed in the prison system has resulted, to a considerable degree, from a system with a built-in pattern of discrimination within U.S. society. The criminal justice system is not the only realm in which discrimination against racial and ethnic minorities can be found. Slowly but surely social scientists are pulling data together which indicate that racial and ethnic discrimination occurs in many social realms (e.g., Feagin & Vera 1995).

## MULTICULTURALISM

A columnist for the *New York Times*, Thomas Friedman (1995) has suggested that "Diversity without a spirit of community leads to tribalism. Community without a spirit of diversity leads to alienation of all minorities." This discussion will build on and modify some of the social science principles that are implicit in Friedman's statement. In some respects we are able to come to terms with multiculturalism by emphasizing what it is not (cf. Marable 1995). Multiculturalism is not a return to the separate but equal doctrine that existed in the United States prior to the Brown decision in 1954. The proponents of multiculturalism are not calling for racial and ethnic minorities to live apart on separate islands in the society. At the same time, multiculturalism needs to move beyond the assimilationist perspective which has been built on a conformity to the beliefs and values of the Anglo dominant sector of the society. Because a true multicultural society has yet to be created in the United States, we can point to the extremes of what is not, but we cannot fully describe just what it is (or will be). However, we can delineate some of the social conditions that will make it possible for a multicultural social order to exist.

First, if a multicultural order is to become a reality, groups need to have overlapping interests or beliefs. By giving everyone a stake in the society, especially in terms of attaining political and economic power, then the overlapping interests will help glue a multicultural order together. Second, instead of speaking of common values, it is advantageous to speak of a commitment to the principle of human rights. If people are to work and live together, they must share a commitment to the principle that all persons deserve to be respected as human beings.

Third, if a multicultural order is to be created and sustained, then we need some organizational structures that will make it possible for persons of different racial and ethnic backgrounds to interact with one another. The public school system remains the single most important organizational basis for achieving this goal. Unfortunately, many of the persons who most sharply attack multiculturalism also are seeking to find ways to escape from a public school system. But it is through public schools that persons from diverse cultural backgrounds are most likely to interact with one another and to lose their fear of diversity.

Fourth, it is important to rethink the meaning of "taking the role of the other." We need to think in terms of taking the role of multiple others. Only by taking into account the orientations of, for example, blacks, Hispanics, Asians and American Indians will we be able to interact with one another in a meaningful manner. And, as noted earlier, in addition, the race and ethnic differences also will have to consider social class and gender dimensions. Although these conditions are not the only ones that could be discussed, they do represent an important starting point for the creation of a multicultural order in which diverse racial and ethnic groups can work and live together. Tensions will arise but these can be managed through the democratic process.

## CONCLUSIONS

This brief chapter has had two objectives. One has been to examine the limitations of the assimilationist model. We focused our attention on the problems associated with a top-down versus bottom-up orientation. An examination of this assimilationist perspective demonstrates that it tends to emphasize the views of the privileged sector of society, and it fails to take into account the orientations of racial and ethnic minorities. The failure to take account of their definition of the situation is highlighted by a consideration of the criminal justice system.

The multicultural model appears to be a more reasonable and promising alternative to the assimilationist perspective. This orientation reflects an effort to come to terms with the growing racial and ethnic diversity in the United States. This diversity must be emphasized because it is increasing, not decreasing. A multicultural orientation emphasizes not only the perspective of the dominant sector of society, but also the views of the rising number of persons who are members of racial and ethnic minority groups, especially black Americans, Hispanics, Asians, and American Indians. In the end it is difficult not to agree with the assessment of the sociologist Troy Duster (1993), who contends that a multicultural orientation will enhance, not undercut, the functioning of U.S. society.

## REFERENCES

Andersen, M. L. & Collins, P. H. 1992. *Race, Class, and Gender*. Belmont, CA: Wadsworth.

Chambliss, W. J. 1994. Policing the ghetto underclass: The politics of law and law enforcement. *Social Problems* 24:177–194.

Cohen, R. 1995. Surprise? Fuhrman tape doesn't shock blacks. *Dallas Morning News* (August 18), p. 25A.

Duster, R. 1993. The diversity of California at Berkeley: An emerging reformulation of 'competetence' in an increasinging multicultural world. In *Beyond a Dream Defrerred: Multicultural Education and The Politics of Excellence*. B. W. Thompson & S. Tyagi (eds). Minneapolis: University of Minnesota Press, pp. 231–255.

———1995. The new crisis of legitimacy in control, prisons, and legal structures. *The American Sociologist* 26:20–28.

Feagin, J. R. & Vera, H. 1995. *White Racism*. New York: Routledge.

Friedman, T. L. 1995. Me fellow immigrants. *The New York Times* (September 10), p. E17.

Gonzales Jr., J. L. 1990. *Racial and Ethnic Groups in America*. Dubuque: Kendall / Hunt.

Harrison, R. J. & Bennett, C. E. 1995. Racial and ethnic diversity. In *State of the Union America in the 1990s. Volume Two: Social Trends*. R. Farley (ed). New York: Russell Sage, pp. 141–210.

Herrnstein, R. J. & Murray, C. 1994. *The Bell Curve*. New York: Free Press.

Marable, M. 1995. Black studies, multiculturalism, and the future of American education. *Items* (June–September) 49:49–56. New York: Social Science Research Council

Massey, D. S. & Denton, N. A. 1993. *American Apartheid*. Cambridge: Harvard University Press.

McKee, J. B. 1993. *Sociology and the Race Problem: The Failure of a Perspective*. Urbana: University of Illinois Press.

Myrdal, G. 1944. *An American Dilemma*. New York: McGraw-Hill.

Rollins, J. 1985. *Between Women*. Philadelphia: Temple University Press.

San Miguel, Jr., G. 1987. *"Let all of Them Take Heed": Mexican Aemricans and the Campaign for Educational Equality in Texas, 1910–1981*. Austin: University of Texas Press.

Williams, J. E. & Coleman, A. M. 1992. *Lest We Forget: The Japanese and American's Wartime Mistake*. East Rockaway, NY: Cummings & Hathaway.

Williams, N., Himmel K. F., Sjoberg, A., & Torrez, D. J. 1995. The assimilation model, family life, and race and ethnicity in the United States. *Journal of Family Issues* (May):380–405.

Williams, N. & Sjoberg, A. 1993. Ethnicity and gender: The view from above versus the view from below. In *A Critique of Contemporary American Sociology*. T. R. Vaughan, G. Sjoberg, & L. T. Reynolds (eds). Dix Hills, NY: General Hall, pp. 160–202.

# 3

# We Call Ourselves "Americans"

Laura Zimmer-Tamakoshi

## INTRODUCTION

This chapter examines some of the varieties of ethnic experience among white Anglo-Saxon Protestants in the United States. Just as Micaela di Leonardo (1984) found Italian-Americans to be divided by historical circumstances, place of origin in Italy, class, and gender, so too, are there significant differences in the experiences and ethnic identities of white Anglo-Saxon Protestants (WASP). Focusing more on the majority of white Anglo-Saxon Protestants than on the elite WASPs of Boston or Philadelphia, a historical perspective will be used to help illustrate some of the differences and changes in mainstream white Americans' ethnic experiences and self-perceptions. A discussion of white Americans' anxieties and the recent proliferation of cults and anti-government militias, radical religious fundamentalism and eco-warriors, physical fitness and virtual reality devotees, and yuppy commuters and escapees from America's cities and ethnic war zones also will be provided. Much of this discussion is based on personal experience and from the point of view of the people themselves. This goes well beyond the usual WASP stereotypes in illuminating the lives and value systems of white Anglo-Saxon Protestants and, since there has been much mixing among them (Alba 1990:47), white European Americans more generally.

## WASPS BY ANY OTHER NAME?

The first time I was called a "WASP" to my face was at the University of Pennsylvania, in an undergraduate class on American Ethnicity. At the time, I was a thirty-two-year-old, part-time "nontraditional" student in anthropology. Non-traditional referred to my being a mother and housewife, while commuting to Philadelphia two or three times a week from the suburbs. Hurt by my accuser's evident hostility, I was further stunned by the realization that I was indeed the closest thing to a WASP in the class of twenty-five or so students. My defense that I am an American mongrel (part English, Scots Irish, German, and Cherokee) and that I came from a less privileged background than any of the other students was swept aside. I was a member of an "oppressive ethnic group" and as such was on the giving (versus the receiving) end of WASP snubs and prejudices. Because of my "privileged ethnicity" I was seen as more likely to succeed and to enter the ranks of America's elite society.

Over the years I have pondered my classmates' assessment of my ethnicity and future life chances. Certainly WASP was not my chosen identity, nor was it a fair reflection of my experiential reality. To lump together millions of white, Anglo-Saxonish type peoples is to ignore distinctive varieties of white ethnic experience in this country. One need think only of the Shakers or Mormons to realize the distortions involved in assuming a homogeneity among white Anglo-Saxon Protestants (Kephart 1982). Moreover, it is as wrong to assume that all WASPs occupy the same level in society as it would be to assume that the men hanging out on Talley's Corner in Liebow's classic (1967) are representative of all black men in this country, or that the youthful gang members from the Italian slum described in Whyte's *Streetcorner Society* (1955) are typical of all Italian-Americans. Recently, there has been a chipping away of such monolithic categories as "WASP" and "white power structure," more among the academic community, however, than among the general populace. In a book of essays on the multicultural experience in America (Aguero 1993) several apparently white, Anglo-Saxon Protestant contributors deny having—as women, formerly working class white males, and gay men—any part in the "white power structure" in this country. While "power structure" implies an elite aspect to the term WASP, the essays suggest that most white middle-class males are also "in the soup" as it were.

Interestingly, while many Americans are struggling with their identities, elite WASPs who are part of America's real power elite have no such crisis to deal with. While they may or may not like the term, they are a self-conscious and proud elite, well bred, well educated, well connected, and capable of protecting their economic and social privileges against persons of the "wrong" class, religion, ethnicity, or race (Mills 1956:64). For example, while America's elite occasionally welcome "new money" into their families through the marriage of a son or a daughter, money is only one requirement for acceptance. The other requirement is that the newcomer be white, Anglo-Saxon Protestant. In *The Proper Bostonians*, Cleveland Amory (1947:12-13), himself a proper Bostonian, noted that out of a city of some 2,350,000 people in the mid-1940s, only 8,000 were listed in the Boston Social Register. Out of these 8,000, there was only one Jewish man and less than a dozen Catholic families. Excluded were some one million Irish Bostonians, as well as hundreds of thousands Bostonians of Italian, Jewish, Polish, German, and other backgrounds, including several hundred thousand persons whose backgrounds were Anglo-Saxon and Protestant. No blacks or Asians were included in the Register.

A member of the Philadelphia elite, Digby Baltzell (1964), criticized this ethnic and racial exclusiveness and class snobbery as detrimental, keeping out many clever and bright people from America's leadership class. Elizabeth Ameisen, a "main line WASP" and anthropology student, took a different approach to the subject of WASP racism, arguing that it perpetuates WASP position and privilege by making clear the boundaries of this particular social group. Ameisen recounts how she and a group of friends were once refused admittance to the Premier Club, to which her family belonged, because one of the girls had a "Jewish-sounding name" (1990:54). Ameisen gives plentiful examples from her interviews with main-line WASPs of open and ingrained racism. This racism came in the form of jokes and other behaviors. Asking her younger informants if they ever would consider marrying a black person or person of the Jewish faith, one young girl said she was dating a Jewish boy but that her father would likely disinherit her if she married him. Another said, "I could never marry anybody black, my father would kill me" (1990:73). In a recent case where the son of a respected Philadelphia family did marry a black woman, "They have been virtually ignored by his family and Philadelphia society in general" (1990:73).

By contrast, my identity and that of many other white Americans is based less on "good breeding" and wealth than on a sense of being a fundamental part of America's history. Most people, including white Anglo-Saxon Protestants, simply call themselves "Americans." In the case of my own family, although our ancestors helped wrestle this land from its original heirs, they have been here for centuries, in many cases before the American Revolution. Our English or German heritage is no longer salient to our self-identities, and no stories are passed down in my family about "life in the old country." Rather, it is clear that my ancestors came here to make a better life for themselves. The stories that have come down to me, the product of a Pennsylvanian and a Floridian, are part of an American history text. I have, for example, forbearers who fought on both sides of the American Revolution and Civil War, who farmed and homesteaded in Pennsylvania, in the mountains of North Carolina and Florida Keys. Daniel Boone was a relative who pushed forward the American frontier into Kentucky and Missouri. Two of my ancestors, Frankie and Johnny Silvers, had a folksong written about them. Frankie was the first woman to be hanged in North Carolina for killing Johnny, and then chopping up his body and burning it in the wood stove in their log cabin.

While elite WASPs left the old country for many of the same reasons as non-elite WASPS (e.g., religious freedom, economic opportunity, and adventure), they generally came to this land already wealthy, in charge of the new religions and settlements, and conscious of themselves as America's power elite. Elite WASPs did not start from scratch like other settlers, and they felt no affinity with the "American Rabble." In his account of the Boston Brahmins and Philadelphia Gentlemen, Baltzell (1979:248) demonstrates how many of the founding families of Puritan Boston (e.g., Adamses and Cabots) and Quaker Philadelphia (e.g., Biddles) have enjoyed an unbroken tradition to the present of upper-class affiliations and leadership in church, state, and business. These privileges were maintained in part through private education. Baltzell points out that of the 207 institutions of higher learning in America founded before the Civil War (Harvard was founded in 1636), all but 27 were founded by religious groups, most of which were "heirs of rational and hierarchical Calvinism" stirring the "passions of the successful to use their privileges to take the lead in many areas of American Life" (1979:38-39). C. Wright Mills noted how many of the nation's command posts were occupied by the elite in 1942. He points out that, "of the thirty-two ambassadors and the top ministers of 1942, almost half were graduates of private preparatory schools frequented by children of the Metropolitan 400; and of the top one hundred and eighteen officers in the Foreign Service, fifty-one were Harvard, Princeton, or Yale" (Mills 1956:207). While many of our nation's presidents and congressmen have come from elite WASP families, just as significantly, the majority of their advisors and White House staff have come from the same backgrounds, including attendance at Ivy League colleges (Mills 1956:234).

While the power WASPs snub the *nouveau riche*, money *is* an important element of their power, and, unlike most Americans, they started out with it and have continued making a lot of it. While my own ancestors were working small farms, wealthy Americans were cooking up schemes that resulted in land speculation and higher land taxes (e.g., Flagler's Railroad to Key West, Florida). The resulting higher taxes drove most of my grandparents' generation off their farms and into towns and cities where they worked as nurses aides, clerks, or in unskilled jobs for meager wages. During the Great Depression of the 1930s, they and their children suffered considerable hardships. Being too proud to accept charity, they deepened their work ethic and desire never to be poor again. Later, with the help of working wives, night classes, and, in some cases, the G.I. Bill, some of my uncles became small-town insurance agents, realtors, and bankers. In contrast, most elite families made it through the Depression with few difficulties, being connected to one another and economically well advised against total ruin. Mills argued that middle-class competitiveness and mistrust is lacking among America's power elite (1956:66). He points out that the chief executives of America's financial institutions, many well-known lawyers and politicians, and the very rich are not distinct and segregated groups (1956:119). Rather, they are friends, relatives, partners, and members of the same clubs, churches, and schools. They are "insiders" who share information and tips with one another. Their pride is in their class and extended families, not the individual or nuclear family that is the obsession of most Americans. While the middle class grew rapidly following World War II, and came to include members of many different ethnic and racial groups, the upper class remained content to keep their wealth and power within their white, largely Anglo-Saxon Protestant ranks. One need only look at the back of today's stock reports to see that the top executives and board members are almost to a man white and upper class. Multicultural and egalitarian gender images are more hype than corporate reality.

For my generation of "baby-boomers," being female, white, and middle class looms larger in my self- or ascribed identity than my WASP ancestry. For my kind of "American," America stands for freedom, high aspirations, and the possibility of success, unless you are a woman and then there are limitations on your choices, aspirations, and the degree of success you are likely to achieve. Many middle-class and working-class women of all ethnic and racial groups have been fighting to improve their working and living conditions and to achieve parity with men. Not so among women of the upper class. According to Elizabeth Ameisen, WASP women are satisfied to take second place to their husbands, busying themselves with their families, friends, homes, charities, and clubs. In the mid-1980s, when a few younger women wanted to challenge the Premier Club's all-male member policy, some women were shocked and agreed with the harsh words of one matron that, "We don't need a woman on the Board of Governors. Women are putting themselves in places they don't belong today. The men have the last say. It's a men's club and it should stay that way" (Ameisen 1990:53). Lest we think elite women are more passive than other women, it should be remembered that many are educated at places like Bryn Mawr and Vassar, where they are taught to reject organized feminism as "unnecessary" and "unseemly," but where they also are encouraged to become self-confident and competent women. In a chapter on "The Boston Woman," Amory describes the "female of the Proper Bostonian species" as possessing an incredible vitality and determination to fill their lives with activity. During World War II, one First Family woman, "in the neighborhood of seventy," spent her Mondays and Fridays running ward errands for four hours a day in the Massachusetts General Hospital, her Tuesdays traveling all over town for Boston's Family Welfare Society, and her Thursdays at the Red Cross" (1947:95–97). Amory goes on to recount that she liked to keep her Wednesdays and Saturdays open for gardening and other compulsory pursuits of Proper Boston women: lectures, concerts, indignation meetings, etc. Further, while such women deferred to the men in the family, they did not do so, however, to men of lower classes (1947:110).

In much of the world, the term "American" has become a negative or dirty word as Americans and members of other core countries are blamed (justifiably or unjustifiably) for the destruction of the environment and exploitation of indigenous peoples. White Americans especially are blamed for destroying the planet with their heavy consumption patterns. There are various degrees, however, of guilt and differences in white Americans' powers and ethics. Moreover, it would be fairer to say that all Americans out-consume the rest of the world. To be sure, the major decision-makers and owners of the multinational companies live far from the consequences of their actions, and it is the middle and lower classes who must face the consequences of the misjudgments and the misdeeds of the higher-ups. An example of the intertwining and direction of consequences from elite policy-making is the case of "red-lining." In the 1950s and 1960s, America became a nation of suburbs with white ethnics fleeing the discomforts of city life. Poor rural blacks left the South to seek work in the northern cities and took their places. Watching the trends, big-city bankers and realtors bought up urban neighborhoods. Rather than make low-cost home improvement loans and mortgages available to the new arrivals, they circled large residential areas in red ink on their maps as "undesirable" for such loans and better slated for future business development.

They then rented the rundown properties at exorbitant cost to the millions of blacks seeking a "better life" in northern cities (Polenberg 1980). Old neighborhoods were turned into soul-destroying places and the center of the race riots of the 1960s and 1970s. Predictably, the persons hurt were not the elite whites, but lower-class blacks and whites.

## THE THINGS WE DO (OR DON'T DO)

According to Polenberg (1980), during World War II there was a sense of equality among the different ethnic, racial, and religious groups in America. This sense was captured in cartoonist Ernie Pyle's soldiers portrayed as individualistic, democratic, optimistic, and united with their comrades. This same image was fostered by the nation's leaders with such notions as "the battlefield does produce a brotherhood" and "America is the international country" (Polenberg 1980:46–54). That the "new brotherhood" was temporary and more ideology than anything became apparent soon after the war ended. In the expanding suburbs of "four thousand identical houses," and as the nation and civil rights movement began the push for racial integration, suburban dwellers were choosing to live in segregated neighborhoods where they would have minimal or no interactions with persons of different race, ethnicity, and class (Polenberg 1980:127–137).

The small-town neighborhood I grew up in, however, *was* integrated and provided me with an opportunity to observe ethnic differences and prejudices close up. On my block there were Irish and Italian Catholics living alongside white Protestants, Jews, and an old Black woman who took in boarders, (including Puerto Rican labor migrants). Closer to the center of town and the Catholic Church, there was more segregation with a block of blacks, a block of Irish, and a block of Italians, each with its own small family-run corner grocery store. Closer to the country club were the "rich folk," genuine WASPs with large estates and homes. My mother was friendly with all the neighbors, learning the art of making "real Italian" spaghetti sauce, being best friends with the kids of the only Chinese family in town, joining the Episcopal Church, and participating in an acting group with some of the equally less conservative "rich people" from the north end of town. There were, however, pressures to conform to particular standards of behavior, to not get "too close" to the neighbors. My uncles (on my mother's side) were the primary "culture police" in this regard, teasing my sister and I as we grew up about our use of makeup and instructing us that we were never to marry Catholics, Jews, Negroes, or "Spicks." They forgot to warn us against marrying a "Japanese" man, for, at the time, there were no Japanese anywhere near where we lived and the possibility that any one in the family would know much less marry one of the "perpetrators of Pearl Harbor" was unthinkable.

The process of making "others" seem more peculiar than mysterious, and less desirable, and of teaching us "who we are" and "what we stand for" took place in many ways. We learned the reasoning behind our uncles' prejudices by listening in on their conversations during family visits, in school, at the movies, on television, and in the books we read. We made our own limited observations of the differences between the things we were being taught and what we did in church and the religious practices and beliefs of our neighbors. As a child I was morbidly fascinated by one uncle's assertion that because Catholics believe a child is less sinful than its mother, Catholic doctors will sacrifice a mother's life in favor of her newborn child if it is a question of one or the other. This uncle truly feared for my life when I had a Catholic doctor in attendance for the births of my three children. Another stereotype was that Catholic women are little more than baby-makers. "Proof" of this was the young woman I baby-sat for who bore her husband one child a year (several were stillborn) until after seven pregnancies she looked like a bedraggled woman in her forties instead of her late twenties. Catholics and blacks alike were accused of "living for the moment" and deserving of their poverty due to their lack of thrift and family planning. The fact that most of our Irish and Italian neighbors were more prosperous than we were at the time, and had only two or three children, was conveniently overlooked!

While we played with the neighborhood kids on weekends and in the summer, the rest of the time we went to separate schools and belonged to separate clubs and organizations. Even scout troops were segregated, a process begun in the mid-1930s when the Catholic Church accepted scouting as part of the church's program for its young people on the condition that the troops it sponsored would be primarily for Catholic boys and girls (Gordon 1964:223). When I was a girl scout in the 1950s, scouting groups were sponsored by Protestant and Catholic Churches and Jewish Synagogues as well as by the YMCA and other sectarian groups. Our parents also led segregated lives belonging to different churches (there were both white and black Episcopal Churches in our small town) and clubs, like the Italian Social Club and the Star Social Club where only Italians or blacks went to dance on weekends. Because of this social and religious segregation, we had only vague notions of what the neighbors said and did in their schools and organizations. Today, with two of my children married to Catholics, the nuns seem less bizarre to me. Back in the 1950s and 1960s, however, in their black habits and extreme sanctimony, they were more than a little scary.

What we learned, on the other hand, was that we are not bizarre. Rather, we were the central characters in the school books we and every other kid in America read—the Dicks and Janes versus the Silvios and Eileens. We learned that America was a strong and powerful country, largely—it was asserted—because of people like our parents, who worked hard, saved their money, bought second-hand cars rather than buy on credit, invested in their children's education, went to church on Sunday, stayed home on the weekends to teach "junior" how to play ball and "sis" how to sew rather than hang out in "pubs" and "saloons," were patriotic, supporting no foreign prince or Pope, and practiced simple (e.g., Protestant) Christian virtues. The biases and assumptions about other races and religions in this self-portrait are blatantly obvious! Back then, however, the "all-American" image of white Anglo-Saxon Protestants was everywhere: on the cover of *Life* magazine and the *Saturday*

*Evening Post* (e.g., Norman Rockwell paintings), on television, and at the movies. Our favorite pulp fiction provided WASP models for adolescent success. For girls there was Nancy Drew (Montague 1976), for boys the Hardy brothers (Wasylyshyn 1982). As a teenager I read every Nancy Drew mystery ever written, and from her I learned that a girl could be and do anything she wants as long, that is, as she knows when and for whom to take a back seat. Nancy had the best of both worlds (the male and the female) by being a successful sleuth *and* demure girlfriend, the latter made possible by her Ivy Leaguer boyfriend Ned conveniently being away and engrossed in his studies most of the time, and her widowed father treating her like the son he never had (Montague 1976:114).

Mixed messages were common in our upbringing, with both boys and girls encouraged to attend college but, in the case of girls, more as a back-up policy for what to do if your husband died or lost his (presumably more important) job. The women in my family worked in addition to being primary caretakers of their children, but, like Nancy Drew, they "knew their place". At Thanksgiving the women did the shopping, preparing, cooking, setting the table, and cleaning up after. The men's sole Thanksgiving duties were to carve the turkey and to watch football—the quintessential American sport. (It amuses me now to realize that women, who used all kinds of knives in their food preparation, were not allowed to touch the "men's carving knife" or that they were seen as incapable of carving a turkey!)

One thing that was taught less at school or Girl Scouts but was ingrained in us at home was the fear of what "they" thought. Along with learning table manners and "proper" morals (do unto others as you would have them do onto you), we learned to fear public censure ("What will people think?!"). In addition to learning who we should or should not marry then, we also learned never to show weakness in public ("They'll never let you live it down."), never to seek psychiatric care ("They'll think you're crazy."), never to get arrested ("They'll think we're a family of criminals."), and never, ever, to carry tales outside of the family ("They don't need to know."). The sum of these prescriptions and proscriptions is a tremendous insecurity *and* work ethic that often places family pride and business often taking priority over family life and pleasure.

## CAMELOT AND ITS AFTERMATH

In the 1960s and 1970s, however, my generation chucked our inhibitions and the contradictions that had ruled our lives. John F. Kennedy proved to non-Catholics that a Catholic could uphold the principle of the Separation of Church and State. He and his wife and family were attractive and sophisticated models for a younger generation hungry for a less constrained life-style. And, tapping into the social forces emerging against white privilege (especially upper-class privilege) and poor working conditions, Kennedy ended up receiving more votes from Protestants than from the Catholics and the Jews combined (Polenberg 1980:169). For Catholics,

Kennedy's election as president of the United States produced a greater sense of identification with "America" (Polenberg 1980:172).

Ecumenism was the order of the day, and young people everywhere gave themselves up to the romantic, idealistic "Age of Aquarius." As their hard-headed elders shook their heads in shock and dismay, young Protestants, Jews, and Catholics worked together against racial injustice and in Lyndon Johnson's "War on Poverty". Assimilation and the coming together of the American people as one nation, united in purpose *and* marriage, seemed ever more possible and desirable. Intermarriage between white ethnics (but especially white Protestants and Irish Catholics) took place in unprecedented numbers. And in a rainbow of friendships and relationships white Protestant youth discovered the lies and half-truths of their parents' teachings. Blacks, Catholics, and Jews were *not* simply more superstitious or self-indulgent than we were, they were just as committed to life in America, and they were as bright, friendly, sensitive, hard-working, and young.

In actuality, however, I and most young Americans of all backgrounds were not immersed in the 1960s and 1970s "youth culture." As a very young mother and housewife, I taught Sunday School and Girl Scouts, bowled with and attended meetings of the Junior New Century Club (a middle- to upper-middle-class social club for women in the 20–40 age bracket), and when I wasn't taking the kids to the park or pre-kindergarten I read a lot of romantic mysteries (the grown-up versions of Nancy Drew). Even when I returned to school and was exposed to college activists, I did not march on Washington or Selma. I did not smoke dope or go to Woodstock. And only rarely did I dress like a hippie or wear flowers in my hair. I did, however, participate in some of the liberation of mind and spirit. I went back to college after reading Betty Friedan's *The Feminine Mystique* (which was mystifying to many of my Junior Club associates who advised me to "have another baby" instead!). And while some of the men then in charge of American colleges and universities radicalized me with their put-downs of married women returning to school, I gained support from other students *and* my mother and aunts—older and more experienced than the Junior Club women—who assured me that they, too, would do what I was doing if they had been born in my generation.

Like many in my generation, I socialized my children far differently than I had been. There were no lectures from either me or their father on whom they should or should not marry. And although they heard racist remarks from time to time from their German grandfather and other relatives, they did not take effect. The environment my children grew up in was very different from the one I was nurtured in. This was reflected in the liberal attitudes portrayed on television (e.g., the biracial and sexually egalitarian "Mod Squad") and at the movies (e.g., the interracial and icon-busting Jesus Christ Superstar and other, sexually liberal and explicit movies). Above all, there was less worry about what "they would think" and more emphasis on personal and individual development. Some children, like my own, attended alternative schooling, and there was more concern about developing children's self-esteem. Dr. Spock was the expert on child-rearing, and there was little of the old "children should be seen and not heard" pedagogy.

Trouble was on its way, however, and hopes for a more just world were about to be shattered, or at least severely tempered. Those of us who lived through them will never forget the television images of the assassinations of JFK, Martin Luther King, Robert Kennedy, and so many others. In elementary school, we had been taught to look down on Latin American countries with their dictators and weekly political assassinations. Now *we* felt shame. We also shall never forget the shock and horror of Vietnam, race riots, and the burning down of America's cities. We Northerners, who had felt superior to "dumb prejudiced Southerners," were now humbled that so much ugliness and hate had been smoldering in our own society. It was even more shocking when a small group of radicals from Philadelphia came to our hometown to stir up the local "Negroes" and a few office and store windows had bricks thrown through them. Suddenly, we (meaning we supposedly "upstanding white people") did not feel safe and in charge of America anymore, much less the universe.

It was a harsh but overdue comeuppance. It was obvious that America's "melting pot" was not working and that the structural assimilation of blacks and other oppressed minorities had not taken place (Gordon 1964:114). On a more positive note, at least from the perspective of everyone but die-hard WASPs and white supremacists, after the riots there followed a flowering of ethnic consciousness, a realization on the part of many ethnics that they could pull together and bring about their own economic improvement and pride (Gordon 1964:244–247). While some of us looked on with more than a touch of envy and a sense that we were no longer at the center of American history, blacks and other ethnics openly touted their rediscovered (or newly created) cultural heritage and values, moved into the political mainstream, and snubbed and mocked us as often as they could (or so some of us felt).

## LATE CAPITALISM AND RADICAL AMERICANS

Snubs and nasty shocks were not the worst of it for the majority of white Americans, however. Not only were Americans getting older, but the 1980s and early 1990s ushered in a period of late capitalism and devastating economic uncertainty that struck the middle class almost as hard as the lower classes of American society. As Baby Boomers and Flower Children turned middle-aged and their parents enjoyed their "Golden Years" and the support of social security and Medicare, the Vietnam war, more liberal immigration laws, and changes in industry were loosing floods of "exotic" new immigrants (Haitians, Vietnamese, Thai, etc.) into the country, and mainstream Americans felt as if their jobs and homes were being plucked right from under them. My Florida relatives are now mostly out of Miami. But they were there during the time of the first boatloads of Cubans fleeing Castro's oppression, the Haitian inundations, and all of the other legal and illegal immigrations that have turned Miami, once a sleepy lower-middle- and middleclass area with a fringe of tourism, into what has been variously called by white

Americans "Little Havana," a "third-world country," and "Hell." More humiliating and almost as bothersome as the drugs and crime (which are bad) and the loss of jobs to hungry, hustling immigrants, has been the Cubans' success at turning Miami into a Hispanic economic and social success story. For people who were born in Miami and whose parents settled the area, people who went through the Depression and World War II to preserve the "American Way," and now face an unknown and financially insecure future, seeing Spanish street signs and advertisements and hearing Spanish take over as the primary language in their hometown is a bitter pill. The same restructuring of the American economic and social scene is taking place all over, with Mexicans and Thai workers moving to the Heartland to work in the meat-processing plants that have moved there from Chicago and other Midwestern cities, and Koreans and other Asians moving into and revitalizing crumbling neighborhoods in Philadelphia and other Rustbelt cities (Lamphere et al. 1994).

Sensibly, local leadership, following national guidelines and policies, coped with the major influx of immigrants and the social pressures they brought to bear on American cities with affirmative action, bilingual education, "political-correctness" education, an ethos of multiculturalism, and other liberal policies. While this has not always worked out well, there are large numbers of new immigrants who are successfully adapting into the American way of life in both economic and social terms. Displaced blacks and whites, on the other hand, feel (and in some cases justifiably so) extremely threatened. In such a climate, a large segment of the white European population, from lower to middle class, feels let down by their leaders and especially big business. While some may say that they deserve a taste of injustice, human nature is such that the newly down-and-out will not agree and will try to find someone else to blame. With television announcers reminding us daily of yet a newer form of "victimization," the dastardliness of our leaders, crooked doctors, lawyers, and welfare recipients, and all sorts of other depredations on the average American citizen, it is no wonder (whether justifiable or not) that many white Americans are beginning to see themselves as victims, too.

Accordingly, more and more white Americans are participating in and joining the ranks of radical fringe and majority fundamentalists groups, seeking a return to more "natural" or older ways of life (from the flaccid New Age fascination with the various Native American life-styles in places like Boulder, Colorado, to even more dangerous flirtations with pioneer and survivalist ethics that mark some of the new anti-government militia groups) and seeing demons and destroyers in every corner of society (the New Agers fearing the fundamentalists, the fundamentalists the New Agers and liberal government). In many American families, it is no longer possible to hold a conversation with the born-again Christians in the family who have added to their demons pro-choice advocates, women's libbers, homosexuals, affirmative action, the National Wildlife Federation, testing on animals, and a host of liberal causes. New Republican member of the House of Representatives, Helen Chenoweth from Idaho, speaks for millions of disgruntled Americans when she equates many right-wing movements (anti-environmentalists, the religious right, advocates of states' rights, citizens militias, gun owners, and "country sovereignty" anarchists) with "real Americans" fight for our freedoms and our liberties, and our way of life. We're fighting for our culture" (Blumenthal 1995:27). It does not need to be said that most of the people in those right-wing groups are white European Americans (although not all by a long shot). Similar sentiments are echoed by Montana Militiamen Bob Fletcher and John Trochmann. Their targeted conspiracy is the New World Order, an alleged mega-conspiracy that is seeking to destroy the United States (meaning "real Americans" like themselves). Just how paranoid such people are is their belief that a map on the back of a 1993 Kix cereal box, showing the country divided into eleven regions, is a "representation of the New World Order plan for dividing the United States into regional departments after the invaders emerge to take over the country, which is scheduled to happen any day now" (Kelly 1995:61). Kelly drolly adds, "Why the conspirators have chosen to publicize their intentions on the back of a cereal box is not clear."

## CONCLUSION: THE POLITICS OF ETHNICITY AND CLASS

With the emergence of militancy among white European Americans and their increased sense of themselves as an oppressed group, one might assume that white Anglo-Saxon Protestants and other white European Americans are becoming America's new underclass and that WASPs are no longer in control of America. It is true that there are many poor white Americans (there always has been more white Americans living below the "poverty line" than any other category of Americans). It is also true that Caroline Kennedy married a Jew and that former president George Bush has grandchildren who are half-Hispanic. None of which necessarily means, as Christopher (1989) has argued, that WASP defenses have been irrevocably breached by increased intermarriage with outsiders or that a majority of white Americans still cannot achieve the American Dream. What is most interesting and useful to understand about the changes going on in white society is not ethnic mixing and lost privilege so much as a perceived and possibly real moral break between upper- and lower-class whites. Upper-class persons of all ethnic backgrounds are reaping the rewards of a more "multicultural" society (especially cheap labor of many of the new immigrants) and promoting liberal ideologies of pluralistic harmony and national economic growth. At the same time, lower-class persons and all those who are not part of cyberspace (as the students at the University of Pennsylvania are, according to Meyer (1995)) and cannot afford BMWs or to live in very expensive, postmodern communities where street names like Hunters Run and Hummingbird Lane evoke the very world they have destroyed (MacCannell 1992) and for who ethnicity is a survival strategy and not a trivial "what kind of ethnic shall we do tonight?" are very angry that their lives, their beliefs, and their aspirations are being mocked, ignored, and no longer are part of the American Agenda. No longer, that is, until the Republicans focused on the negative feelings running through large portions of white society and have tried to channel it into a new agenda or "contract," as Newt Gingrich likes to call it. Neither Gingrich, however, who believes America can be a better place if all the "victims" and "poor ethnics" stop "whining" (1995:26) nor Adler, who worries about whether or not our country can survive all the diversity (1995:16) have it right about the direction some white ethnics want this country to take. For many, if the ones I know are any indication, what they are engaged in is more of a religious war than an ethnic or class battle. America is not just a land of freedoms to them. It *is* a religion. One they died for in World War II. One they are willing to share with most other immigrants (as long as they continue to act "American"). One that contradictorily they see as based on diversity and freedom of choice versus special privilege and the watering down of cherished morals.

## REFERENCES

Adler, J. 1995. Sweet Land of Liberties: If everyone has his own niche, what do we have in common anymore? *Newsweek* (July 10), pp. 18–23.

Aguero, K. (ed). 1993. *Daily Fare: Essays From the Multicultural Experience*. Athens: University of Georgia Press.

Alba, R. D. 1990. *Ethnic Identity: The Transformation of White America*. New Haven: Yale University Press.

Ameisen, E. R. 1990. Exclusively in an Ethnic Elite: Racial Prejudice as Boundary Maintenance. In Encounters *with American Ethnic Realities*. P. Kilbride, J. Goodale, & E. Ameisen (eds), in collaboration with C. G. Friedman. Tuscaloosa: University of Alabama Press, pp. 25–76.

Amory, C. 1947. *The Proper Bostonians*. New York: E. P. Dutton & Company.

Arens, W. & Montague, S. P. (eds). 1976. *The American Dimension: Cultural Myths and Social Realities*. Port Washington, NY: Alfred Publishing Co.

Baltzell, E. D. 1964. *The Protestant Establishment: Aristocracy and Caste in America*. New Haven: Yale University Press.

———1979. *Puritan Boston and Quaker Philadelphia: Two Protestant Ethics and the Spirit of Class Authority and Leadership*. New York: Free Press.

Blumenthal, S. 1995. The political scene: Her own private Idaho. *The New Yorker*, (July 10), pp. 27–33.

Christopher, R. C. 1989. *Crashing the Gates: The De-WASPing of America's Power Elite*. New York: Simon & Schuster.

di Leonardo, M. 1984. *The Varieties of Ethnic Experience: Kinship, Class and Gender Among California Italian-Americans*. Ithaca: Cornell University Press.

Gingrich, N. 1995. *Renewing* America: In his new book, Newt says stop whining. *Newsweek,* (July 10), pp. 26–27.

Gordon, M. M. 1964. *Assimilation in American Life:The Role of Race, Religion, and National Origins*. New York: Oxford University Press.

Kelly, M. 1995. A reporter at large: The road to paranoia. *The New Yorker,* (June 19), pp. 60–75.

Kephart, W. M. 1982. *Extraordinary Groups: The Sociology of Unconventional Life-Styles,* 2nd edition. New York: St. Martin's Press.

Kottak, C. P. (ed). 1982. *Researching American Culture*. Ann Arbor: University of Michigan Press.

Lamphere, L., Stepick, A. & Grenier, G. (eds). 1994. *Newcomers in the Workplace: Immigrants and the Restructuring of the U.S. Economy.* Philadelphia: Temple University Press.

Liebow, E. 1967. *Talley's Corner: A Study of Negro Streetcorner Men.* Boston: Little, Brown & Company.

MacCannell, D. 1992. *Empty Meeting Grounds: The Tourist Papers.* London: Routledge.

Meyers, M. A. 1995. Cyber U: Whither the modern university in this age of technological quakes? *The Pennsylvania Gazette: Alumni Magazine of the University of Pennsylvania,* (May), pp. 30–35, 41.

Mills, C. W. 1956. *The Power Elite.* New York: Oxford University Press.

Montague, S. P. 1976. How Nancy gets her man: An investigation of success models in American adolescent pulp literature. In *The American Dimension.* S. P. Montague & W. Arens (eds). Sherman Oaks, CA: Alfred Publishing Co., pp.99–116.

Polenberg, R. 1980. *One Nation Divisible: Class, Race, and Ethnicity in the United States Since 1938.* New York: Penguin Books.

Wasylyshyn, J. 1982. A neo-Freudian analysis of the *Hardy Boys Mystery Series.* In *Researching American Culture.* C. Kottak (ed). Ann Arbor: University of Michigan Press, pp.111–115.

Whyte, W. F. 1955. *Street Corner Society: The Social Structure of an Italian Slum,* 2nd edition. Chicago: University of Chicago Press.

# PART II

## Race, Ethnicity, and Culture

A great many Americans see such things as the *race, ethnicity,* and *culture* as basically all the same. In fact, most Americans tend to think: "racial groups" are the same thing as "ethnic groups;" that ethnic groups are easily identifiable on the basis of racial classifications; and that both "race" and "ethnic group" are the same thing as a cultural group. From this practice has come the tendency to use the terms interchangeably, despite the fact that the practice repeatedly has been shown to be based on many false premises and assumptions, and generalizations and stereotypes that have led to many of the social problems associated with cultural diversity. Although some of the misunderstandings and negative consequences of *race* already have been discussed in Part I, it is imperative that special attention be directed at these things because of the significance and importance placed on them by most Americans. The tendency for people to categorize others on the basis of *race*, or observed physical characteristics, and then attribute social or cultural significance to them—superior or inferior status—is historically well established in Western culture. The resulting cultural minority status then attributed to such categories has produced dire consequences for a great many people, some of which continue to impact many Americans. The tendency to categorize ethnic groups on the basis of a single trait (e.g., language, food, etc.) is also historically grounded, and this too has produced dire consequences for many people. Another serious consequence of this practice has been the general loss of meaning with such concepts as *ethnic* and *ethnicity*. Both the concept of *race* and the concept of *ethnicity* generally have been used with culture, but they are not always equal to it.

The idea of race extends far back in human history, at least to the point where civilizations evolved with their complexity and fragmentation favoring society being broken down into groups for a variety of purposes. Creating groups on the basis of observed physical characteristics probably seemed a simple way of doing it. Unfortunately, people now view the legacy as fact and race as something that just naturally (and really) exists. They fail to recognize how artificial and arbitrary such groupings actually are, even when used by scientists who already know them to be true. The next step to judging such artificially and arbitrarily created groups, measuring one against the other, was then probably equally simple. Attributing social or cultural skills and capabilities to groups based on physical characteristics produced *racism*. Once this reared its ugly head, it has remained with us in one form another right up to the present. All racial classifications are arbitrary and artificial. There are no "pure races," and there is no group that can be created that would not overlap all of the other groups one might establish. This applies even to the scientific use of race as breeding populations, wherein members of groups share some statistically significant combination of physical characteristics. They remain in this context, as in all contexts, artificial and arbitrary. They will always depend on who is looking at what, where they draw the lines, and for what purpose(s). That physical differences between groups of humans do exist is obvious, but no study has ever established any cultural significance (intelligence or cultural capability) to them. In culture, people learn something quite different as cultural significance is assigned to physical differences. They then generalize (stereotype) their conclusions onto anyone who may come close to the physical descriptions and groups they have arbitrarily created as a member of that (those) group(s). Once this has been done, the rationalizations and justifications for prejudice, discrimination, and racist doctrines (racial superiority based on the differences) apparently come quite easily, despite the fact they started out, and remain, largely untrue and ill-founded.

In the United States, racial groups have been created and people have learned what the differences mean. It is amazing how many groups have been created by Americans on this basis—anywhere from three to thirty or more. It is even more amazing to hear what they learn with regard to each one of them. A casual glance reveals that most Americans use color for such groupings. Black and brown are readily seen, evidenced by the fact that in some states these are the only two *races* recognized when it comes to minority rights. When pushed, Americans also will acknowledge orientals as a *race* and Indians (the American version) as a *race* (the red man) *and* a culture. With regard to the "black group," Americans tend to see any black as part of that "culture group," in part because so many blacks identify themselves as "African American," reflecting their common origins in Africa. Unfortunately, not all black people come from Africa (unless one goes back to the very beginnings of the entire human group) and there has never been an "African" culture but many culture*s*. This terminological designation is as arbitrary and artificial as the concept of race or the nation-state culture that encourages the practice of establishing racial groupings. Mike Lieber discusses race as a biological and cultural construct in Chapter 4. He discusses the basis for racial classifications through history and the legacy of race in the context of what he describes as muddled thinking and a world of "thingies." Lieber brings the reader to an acute awareness of just how complex this topic of race really is. In Chapter 5, Kimberly Martin discusses the concepts of race and racism, and the general tendency to identify *racial* groups as cultural groups based on shared ethnicity. She discusses these concepts in the context of orientations (based on certain expectations, feelings, and assumptions) people use in all of their diversity-based interactions.

When the topic of race is brought up or considered, the idea of a *minority* quickly follows. In Chapter 6, Tyson Gibbs presents a portrait of a minority group in America (U.S.). While focusing on the African-American (hyphen used when actually speaking of an identifiable cultural group), almost always the first group to be envisioned when the idea of minority arises, the author emphasizes the point that the concept of a minority is more than simply numbers; it is also tied to the denial of access to power of a group and the relationships of a group with the dominant power structure. To make the point about power and minority status, John Hartigan further emphasizes this point about minorities as he explores the question of when white Americans become a minority in Chapter 7. As the population makeup of America continues to change with the addition of more "minorities" into the general population, and as the movement of white urban dwellers out of the cities continues (leaving the *minority* in control of the cities), the circumstances described by the author for Detroit will not remain that uncommon. It is also true that, in the 1990s, there has been a growing tendency for many "whites" to see themselves as a disadvantaged group in some respects; a strange position (at least from their point of view) for those who used to be in control, and this has produced a growing conservatism—if not down right militancy—on the part of a growing number of "white Americans."

In addition to creating groups on the basis of physical characteristics (races or racial categorization), other groups in America are established on the basis of shared cultural characteristics, sometimes a single trait and sometimes a group of traits. Ethnic groups generally are seen as groups within larger societies who can be identified on the basis of language or some distinctive tradition(s) (food, custom, dress, mode of life, etc.). In Chapter 8, Frank Salamone focuses on the topics of ethnic and ethnicity, and attempts to put some meaning back into them. Given the vast number and variety of such recognized groups in the United States, this chapter serves to introduce the reader to just what ethnic cultural groupings are all about. The author suggests that the basis for ethnic groupings lies in self-identity and social interaction. He also proposes that ethnic groups are political, economic, and social action groups; thus they are always changing. In the final analysis, the continuation of ethnic groups is tied to power, and this separates groups from other groups in the competition for scarce and desired resources.

# 4

# Murky Minds, Many Muddles: The Concept of Race

## Michael D. Lieber

Studs Terkel, one of America's few truely wise men, talks of race as an American obsession. Whatever fancy terms psychiatrists use to describe obsession, all of them in some way define it as a profound muddle, lumping together different things and ideas about things until the differences disappear into a mental hash in which there is no clarity and from which there is no escape. As an obsession, no concept comes close to race (aka subspecies) for the muddles it generates.

The way out of any muddle is clear thinking, and that begins with consistently applied logic. With that in mind, I am going to subject race as a biological and as a cultural category to three fundamental logical principles: (1) logical type, (2) the map is not the territory, and (3) a correlation is not a cause. If viewing race this way makes the last couple of centuries worth of controversy look surreal, consider the possibility that it is.

We start with the fact that no living being has ever encountered a species or a race, nor is such an encounter possible. What we see, smell, hear, and touch are specific plants and animals, or a field of plants or a bunch of animals. We see that a chimp looks different from a baboon, and both of them look different from an orangutan, but we do not see three different species—only three different animals. Species is a concept, not a thing. Believing that we have seen three species requires a typically mammalian mental trick called "generalization." Species is a kind of generalization that we call "classification," the invention of classes or categories that group together things that we perceive as similar.

Species is a class (or category) that groups together a set of living things that share a common set of attributes (or properties). This _set of properties_ defines the class. Take a simple example: the English word, fruit, the reproductive organ of a seed plant. Fruit, like any class, has members—any objects that share the properties defining the class. These include apples, peaches, strawberries, plums, oranges, etc. Fruit has a feature that is common to categories. Its members are also categories. Fruit is a class whose members are classes. Each member class also has members, such as Rome apples, Granny apples, red and yellow delicious apples, etc. Species, like fruit, is a class formed from a set of properties shared by a set of organisms. It is not organisms but their shared properties, *abstracted from the organisms*, that constitute the class. Species, like fruit, is a mental, not a physical, phenomenon.

A species is also a member of a larger class, the genus, and the genus is a member of a yet larger class, and so on up to phylum and kingdom. Human beings are grouped into the genus *Homo*, whose properties are upright posture, bipedal locomotion, partially opposable thumbs, nongrasping feet, V-shaped dental arches, small canine teeth, a vertically placed *foramen magnum* (the hole in the bottom of the skull through which the spinal cord passes), and a brain size that varies from 700 cubic centimeters on up. The category *Homo* arguably has four members: *H. habilis, H. erectus, H. Neanderthal,* and *H. Sapiens.* Each of these four has all of the properties that define the genus plus other properties that distinguish it from the other three. *Homo erectus,* for example, has heavy ridges of bone that surround the upper eye sockets, low to no forehead, and a brain capacity that averages 1000 cubic centimeters. These properties distinguish *H. erectus* from *H. sapiens,* which has no bony brow ridges, a well-defined forehead, and a brain capacity that averages 1400 cubic centimeters. The point is this—genus, the higher level category, is defined by fewer properties, and is therefore more inclusive than the categories (species) that are its members. The member categories are defined by a larger set of properties, so they are less inclusive, having fewer members than the high level category. The genus *Homo* includes only four species as members. The primate order that includes *Homo* also includes hundreds of other species.

I have just described examples of the principle of *logical type*, Bertrand Russell's and Alfred Whitehead's contribution to the logic of classes. Obviously, a class is not the same as its members. The relationship of a class to its members is a form of the whole-to-part relationship. The difference between a whole and a part is that of one order of logical type. Fruit is a class that includes the class of apples, apples being one order of logical type lower than fruit, while granny apples are two orders of logical type lower than fruit, and so on. Species is one order of logical type lower than genus, while subspecies, race, is two orders of logical type lower than genus. Therefore, *no class can be a member of itself.* Fruit is not an apple, and an apple is not fruit, but a *kind* of fruit. Identifying a class with its members is an error of logical typing, a logical fallacy. So, if I ask you to bring me a piece of fruit, I have literally made an impossible demand. Now, if I'm feeling playful, I can scold you for bringing me an apple—not exactly what I asked for, which was fruit. "But this IS fruit," you say. "No, it is an apple," I reply. I've gotten you to collapse the category into one of its members, a logical type error. If you continue to play my game, I continue to double bind you. But if you are clever, you can beat me at my own game, saying "Yes it is true that this apple is not fruit. But it is a kind of fruit," gently pointing out my logical error. Now for the kill: "This apple is sweet, while the category, fruit is lacking the property of taste, and why would you want to try eating something that is tasteless anyway?" Gotcha.

These errors of logical typing are clearly absurd and nonsensical. Scholars and laypersons have been publishing books on race and intelligence, race and morality, race and criminality, etc., doing the same things with these relationships that I did with apple and fruit. Yet millions of people take it seriously. How is this possible?

## THE CONCEPT OF RACE AND RACIAL CLASSIFICATION

It does not take a Ph. D. to know that people living in Nairobi look different from inhabitants of Tokyo, and that both look different from residents of Dublin and Calcutta. Our species features a good deal of physical (read somatic or phenotypic) variability. The concept of race as subspecies employs principles of scientific classification to order this variability. The inevitable problem of ordering any kind of variability by classes is what properties define the classes? The procedure used to solve this problem entirely depends on two kinds of things—(1) the purpose of the classification and (2) the nature of the data obtainable by observation. But understand that purposes and data for scientific classification of races is part of a history of relationships between the people doing the classifying and the people being classified.

By the time that Darwin published his *Origin of Species*, Europeans had 400 years of experience with peoples whose physical appearances and life ways were radically different from anything they had known before the voyages of exploration of the fifteenth century. Europeans' initial responses to the "savages" encountered in the Americas, in Africa, and on the Pacific Islands—people who used stone tools, wore bizarre or no clothing, practiced all sorts of sexual perversion, and spoke unintelligible gibberish—were to deny that they were human at all. It took a papal bull in 1557 declaring savage peoples to be human to settle the question. This done, the problem for Europeans was working out their relationships to these savage peoples, a process that began with trying to understand what sorts of people savages were and how they got that way. This process underwent a number of phases—savage peoples were ignorant brutes, normal humans fallen from grace, childlike innocents, noble savages, and everything in between.

Somatic and behavioral differences were lumped together during these musings of the seventeenth through the nineteenth centuries. Which particular image a writer promulgated depended on the theology, political philosophy, or economic interest each had in mind. Political philosophers Thomas Hobbes and John Locke saw civil society originating as a social contract between individuals (in a savage state). Hobbes's savages were ignorant, self-interested brutes, while Locke's were something between innocents and noble savages. Justifying the exploitation of the potentially rich resources of Africa, Many British entrepreneurs used the images of child-like innocents and ignorant brutes needing the British to bring enlightenment and a civilized work ethic to the poor African. Slavers were less charitable. The theory of evolution, in other words, did not suddenly appear in a social vacuum.

Europeans and Americans never doubted their superiority to these backward primitive peoples. To them, the coincidence of their technological, organizational, and moral superiority with their distinctive physiognomy was hardly accidental. What Darwin's theory contributed to these assumptions was a mechanism, natural selection, whereby biological change in populations regularly occurred. Thus, racial classification of the human species was seen as scientific documentation of the outcomes of this universal principle of population change.

### Racial Classification of Somatic Traits

If theologians, philosophers, and entrepreneurs could play fast and loose with the definitions of race and the construction of racial categories, scientists could not. Scientists are constrained to give a rigorous, consistent listing of properties that define the categories they construct, and these constraints have forced them to face the problem of how and where to draw the boundaries between racial categories. Which properties and how many of them to use have always been the stumbling blocks of racial classification. Any classification is open to challenge, and in almost any field of classification there are lumpers and splitters. The lumpers choose fewer properties to form a few large and inclusive classes. Splitters demand more minute, differentiated sets of properties that result in more categories, each of which is smaller and includes fewer members. One finds both sorts in the racial classification industry. Three classes have been most durable: Caucasoid, Mongoloid, and Negroid. (Australian aborigines are often included as a fourth race.) Each class is assumed to include people descended from the same ancient ancestral population. Caucasoid assumes that the ancestral population of today's white-skinned people are all descendants of ancestors who lived in the Caucasus mountains. Mongoloid all are assumed to be descended from an ancestral population whose homeland was in Mongolia, and Australois from Australia. Only the category Negroid has no geographic reference. Each of these major categories has practical problems of who to include or exclude. Negroid is the clearest example.

If the defining properties of the Negroid race are limited to dark skin, broad (flat) nose, thick, everted lips, and woolly hair, then the category includes almost all of the sub-Saharan African populations, most of those of Madagascar, the populations of Melanesia (from New Guinea eastward to Fiji), and some populations from the interior of the Philippines, Malaysia, and Polynesia. The Philippine and Malaysian populations, traditionally hunters and gatherers, often are separated out with a semantic trick—the category "negrito," which also can include African Pygmy populations. It is never clear whether negrito refers to a sub-subspecies or to a separate race. The wide geographical separation of these populations and the internal diversities within both the major category and the subcategories makes the assumption of a common ancestral population a matter of speculation. One sees the same problems with the classification of the populations of South Asia with Caucasoid.

Making racial categories correspond more closely to the facts of geography, demography, and observable somatic variability requires adding properties to the defining set. It does not take an expert to see that the tall, slender, dark-skinned Tutsi population of Rwanda look very different from the short, lighter skinned !Kung of South Africa. Both of these populations look different from the short but dark-skinned Pygmy populations of the Ituri forest, and so on. Thus one becomes a splitter, and it is true that specifying distinctive somatic properties for distinct local populations solves the problem of lumping together Africans with Asian and Pacific Island populations, but the evolutionary problem of the possible relations between these populations does not go away. Their similarities remain to be explained.

## MEASURING RACES

Anthropologists and other students of human variability developed a set of techniques to make their observations of human somatic variability as precise and as replicable as possible, so that comparison of populations could be free of subjective, arbitrary decisions of classifiers. Called *anthropometry*, this set of techniques is designed to make precise measurements either on the living human body or on human skeletons. Using a set of known points on the body, say the skull (exemplified in Figure 1), the observer takes a set of measurements between these points using calipers (or flexible steel tape for measuring arcs) and measuring with a millimeter rule. For example, the measurement from the point labeled G to point OP in Figure 1 (side view) gives the maximum length of the skull. Taking the widest points on the lateral parts of the skull yields a measure of the maximum breadth, and so on. Once the measurements are completed, they are converted into a set of indices, ratios of measured lengths, that are used compare one skull (or long bone or hip bone) with others. An example of one of the indices is called the *horizontal cranial index,* derived by taking the maximum skull breadth, multiplying it by 100, and dividing the result by maximum head length. All of the indices derived from all of the measurements on one individual give a numerical description of that individual. The indices derived from the body measurements can be supplemented by matching skin, eye, and hair color against color charts and hair form against a standardized chart. By measuring enough individuals of both sexes and various ages in the population, indices can be averaged to give a statistical somatic description of the population.

Objective as the anthropometric procedure may seem, the problem of drawing boundaries between racial categories did not disappear; it just got more complicated. How different did the indexical means of two populations have to be before they could be considered separate racial categories? Were some indices more important markers of racial distinctiveness than others? The horizontal cranial index, for example, was considered a very important racial marker, although not definitive by itself. To what extent did one have to consider the effects of intermarriage with other populations—how stable were these indices in a variable environment over time? Questions such as these had no objective answers—decisions about the quantities that formed the boundary between racially distinct populations were necessarily arbitrary.

Figure 4.1.
Human skull, side view.

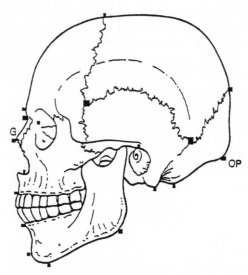

Anthropometrically derived descriptions of populations had other problems of a practical nature. First, there was nothing to prevent anyone from putting together a set of indices to describe a population that may never have existed and then using that set as criteria against which living populations could be distinguished as included within it or excluded from it. This is precisely what Nazi "scientists" did to construct the Aryan race. They took known ranges of indexical variations from known populations and selected from among the ranges to form a composite set that described their imagined ancestral Aryan population. The purpose of this statistical invention was clearly political, equating subspecies with nationality. Jews in this formulation were also a purported race, as were Slavs, and so on. The Nazis' uses of anthropometric procedures should not distract us from understanding those procedures. The Aryan race was no more and no less an invented category than the Negro, Caucasian, or Mongoloid races. All are constructed in the same ways, involving arbitrary decisions about what are important measurements, how indices are constructed, which ones are important markers for racial classification, and how differences should be selected as defining properties of the category. The biology of human races from its beginnings has been the invention of researchers trying to objectify and systematize a socially learned pattern of perceptions of human variability. How arbitrary and unreliable the choices of significant biological markers for drawing racial boundaries can be is the second problem of the use of anthropometry.

During the second decade of the twentieth century, Franz Boas, the founder of American professional anthropology, conducted a study of the Slovak population in New York City. He and his students did anthropometric measurements of three generations of Slovaks—the generation born and raised in the old country, the generation born in the old country but raised in the United States, and the generation born and raised in the United States. Because Slovaks preferred to marry others from the same village or region of Czechoslovakia, hybridization was negligible. Given this stability of genetic heritage, Boas's results were startling. Not only were the children and the grandchildren of the Slovakian born and raised generation taller and heavier than their parents and grandparents, but their head and face forms had undergone a drastic transformation from round-headed and square-faced to long-headed and long-faced. These traits had been thought to be stable and diagnostic of racial populations. Boas's research showed that it was a new environment, specifically a new diet and new patterns of physical activity that accounted for this transformation of bone form. It was clear then and even clearer now (with the development of biomechanics) that human bone is very plastic, and its shape can vary with the pattern of environmental stresses placed on it. Racial taxonomies based on anthropometric measurement of the human soma are of highly questionable scientific value.

## Genetic Classification of Races: From Measuring to Counting

If somatic traits are unreliable for classification, the emerging field of genetics provides traits that are far less responsive to environmental variability. The rapid development of genetics in this century has provided taxonomists with a growing list of stable properties for comparing human populations. Comparing genetic variation has significant advantages over comparing distances between points on human bodies. Over a series of subjects in a population, the distance between points on a bone can vary from a fraction of a millimeter to several millimeters. This means calculating an average, and a mean, and a standard deviation for that trait in the population (as well as averaging indices based on that trait). These are continuous variations. But variations of genes are not continuous. Genes on a chromosome undergo transformation through mutation, and this results in changes in some or all of the chemical components that comprise the gene. Once transformed, the new variant of the changed gene is chemically different from its untransformed parent. Each variant of the gene is called an *allele*. One either has allele A on one or both chromosomes containing that gene or one does not. Somatic traits are *measured*. Alleles are *counted*.

A genetic assay of a human population is simple in theory. Every member of the population has 23 pairs of chromosomes. In theory—and with the rapid progress of gene mapping in fact—each *locus* on a chromosome, the place on the chromosome occupied by a particular gene, is scanned to determine which allele of the gene is present there. Say that we have a population of 100 individuals. That means that for each locus on the chromosome, there are 200 total alleles to be identified and counted. Take blood type as an example. The ABO "system" is a single locus on a chromosome that can be occupied by the A, the B, or the O allele. So if Jane has the A allele on one chromosome and O on the other, then the population assay starts with one A and one O. If Jane's brother has one B allele and one O allele, the population count becomes one A, one B and two Os. Four alleles down, only 196 left to count. All of the loci on all of the chromosomes of these 100 people constitute the whole *gene pool* of the population. The genetic description of this population's gene pool consists of the percentage of occurrence of each allele out of the 200 possible loci that it could occupy. So if we find that A occurs in 49 percent of the loci while B occurs in 11 percent and O in 40 percent, we have the beginnings of a description of this gene pool. These percentages of alleles are called *gene frequencies* (or *allele frequencies*). Rapid discoveries of other alleles and ambitious gene mapping research allow a far more precise description of the stablest characteristics of a population than its somatic predecessor.

The problems of boundary drawing that beset somatically derived racial categories continue to plague classification of human races by genetic criteria. How different do the sets of allele frequencies have to be before we call them different races? Are some allelic frequencies more accurate markers of racial difference than others? If so, which ones, and what makes them better markers? All of these are questions whose answers still appear to rest on arbitrary preferences and inadequate data. There are still lumpers and splitters—those who still think of human species as comprised of four races and those who can distinguish hundreds of local races that are parts of regional races that are parts of geographic races covering whole continents or parts of continents. Race as a biological construct remains what it always was—an abstract invention of observers supposedly representing the biological variability of the human species (itself an invention of higher logical type).

### The Map and the Territory

Maps are useful representations of particular territories, but few would claim that a map *is* the territory. The philosopher, Alfred Korzybsky, contributed this important principle to the fundamental rules of clear thinking. Any map selects certain features of a territory and represents the ordering of these features, such as a road map or a hydrographic chart. Even with a road map, one can be a lumper or a splitter. U. S. road maps commonly depict the U. S. interstate highway system alone on one page against an outline of the continental United States. But turning the pages to state road maps, there are interstate roads, federal highways, state maintained highways, county roads, and township roads, each with its own distinctive line and color. If you are driving across the country with the goal of getting there fast, then the interstate map is more useful and state-by-state maps less useful. If you are wandering across the country to sightsee, then the state-by-state road maps are more useful. The purpose of the map determines which features of the territory are represented and, thus, how useful it is and in what contexts. The same is true with racial categories, which come in two varieties—somatic maps and genetic maps, illustrated in the follwing two examples.

Someone discovers a decomposed body in a field. Police take it to the coroner, who calls in a forensic anthropologist. The police have to match the body against their missing person's files, and they have to know which category of files to search. They need to know the age, sex, height, weight, and race of the deceased. Age, sex, height, and approximate weight are relatively easy to determine. Height is determined by measuring the skeleton and then correcting for shrinkage from decomposition. Weight is estimated from height and bone density. Sex and age are determined from observing the forms of several markers on the skull and pelvis. The territory is the skeleton, and the map is constructed of selected features of the bone that are observable by eye and touch. Determining race is a bit more complicated, however, requiring a different kind of map.

Genetic sampling is useless if the identity of the missing person is unknown, so the forensic anthropologist has to resort to old-timey anthropometric measurements. Here it is the 1990s, and there is the anthropologist bending over the skeleton with calipers, rulers, and a calculator to compute indices. Once the set of indices is complete, it is compared to known ranges of variation in—you guessed it—Negroid, Caucasoid, Mongoloid, and, possibly, Native-American populations. The best statistical fit with the known sets of indices is the one that the police get. The particular sets of indices the anthropologist uses for matching purposes are not the only ones available. They are merely the ones that *match the categories under which police departments file reports on missing persons.* When forensic specialists can make an unambiguous determination on a clear statistical match, they usually guess right. When a clear match with a known set of indices is impossible, the only answer the police get is "indeterminate." There are two reasons for indeterminacy. First and most obvious, when members of different populations mate, their offspring are hybrids of those two gene pools. Interbreeding usually blurs biological (if not social) distinctions. With a growing and rapidly hybridizing U.S. population, anthropologists are giving police "indeterminate" with increasing frequency. Second, the categories that police use are not totally biologically based. If a missing woman has one African-American parent or grandparent, she will be listed in the African-American files. If she has a Polish father and a mother with an Irish father and a Shoshone mother, she will be listed as white. These are social, not biological, categories.

Genetic maps of human populations are certainly possible to construct. The technology exists to map samples of any size from any population, and to compare the genetic variability of any two or more populations. This sort of mapping is now in the planning stage—the Human Genome Diversity Project. It would take a long time to complete and would be very expensive. The project, however, faces opposition from a variety of political organizations that see it as the handmaiden of large biotechnology corporations out to profit from patents on human genes.

All of these considerations of categories and their properties, anthropometry, gene frequencies, and lumping and splitting, must sound dry and very academic to newcomers to this scientific minefield. This is not where the hot controversies lie. The exciting stuff on TV is about bigotry, discrimination, race riots, criminality, I.Q., who makes better athletes, etc. Behavioral and character propensities are where the action is. Are they innate or learned, nature or environment, body or mind?

## MAPPING THE SOCIAL MINEFIELD
## WITH CORRELATIONS AND CAUSES

Applying this map–territory relation to race, let us try the relationship between race and intelligence. First, what is intelligence? Frankly, there is no consensus among scientists about what intelligence denotes. Some say that intelligence is a set of aptitudes, others that intelligence is a component of the human personality. Some say that intelligence is really a cover term for a set of diverse mental processes, such as motor intelligence, cognitive intelligence, etc., each to be measured separately. Some say that intelligence is whatever the I.Q. tests measure. There are yet other definitions. All researchers agree that whatever intelligence is, it is located in the brain somewhere. Without agreement on what this concept denotes, there is no agreement on which brain structures account for it.

One thing is clear, however: Whatever I.Q. tests measure, the distribution of test scores show a clear correlation between racial category and mean I.Q. test scores. American whites as a category consistently score higher on these tests than African Americans as a category. The numbers are not disputed. Their meaning is disputed.

One possible meaning of this consistent correlation is that white people are more intelligent than black people. But "white people" and "black people" are categories. Is intelligence—whatever it is—a property of subspecies? The attribution of more intelligent, less intelligent usually is applied to distinctions between individuals. Does it make logical sense to average (or compute statistical means of) the scores of performances of individuals and then attribute these numbers to a social category as a property of the category? This makes the same kind of logical sense as saying that fruit tastes sweet. Fruit is tasteless; so is its subcategory apple. Red or yellow delicious apples (sub-subcategories) are sweet, at least when they are mature, but Granny apples are not. Distinctive taste does not differentiate the category apple from other members of the category fruit. But it does distinguish between *members of the category*, apple. Intelligence, as it is used by scientists and laymen alike, differentiates individual people from one another. Thus, "fruit tastes sweet" and "white people are more intelligent than black people" are logically the same kind of fallacy, confusing a class with its members. Now, I doubt that the Ku Klux Klan will disband on hearing that they are all guilty of a logical typing error. Besides, they share this fallacy with a number of academics.

Logical typing fallacies aside, the correlation between I.Q. scores and racial categories remains to be explained. Let us start with correlation. A correlation between some X and some Y is a statement that Y varies whenever X varies. Statistical correlations sample a large number of instances of X and Y, and use statistical tests to determine whether or not their covariation is a coincidence. If the correlation occurs more often than we would expect from random chance, then we are reasonably certain that there is some third factor that causes Y to vary when X varies. But *a correlation is not a cause*. Take this nonaccidental correlation—when the birds fly south, the children start back to school. Only a fool would claim that either causes the other. In the same way, the correlation between I.Q. scores and racial category tells us nothing about cause other than that there is one, so we ought to look for it. The most popular cause of I.Q.–race variations is genetic differences between the racial categories. Exactly what sorts of data would be *minimally* necessary to actually demonstrate scientifically that the genes responsible for racial differences also account for differences in intelligence?

Let us assume that Caucasians and African-Americans are both biological races, i.e., populations that breed with far greater frequency within their own groups than between them. Then we can assume that these populations show greater genetic variability between them than within them. With this assumption, we then can select subjects from within each population for genetic testing. Now, here is what we would have to do to demonstrate genetic causation for variations in intelligence between the two populations.

First and most difficult would be obtaining a consensus among scientists on exactly what "intelligence" denotes. Let us say for the sake of argument that we have gotten such a consensus. The next step is to identify all of the nerve nets and their interconnections responsible for intelligence. Let us say that these research results have been obtained and we have mapped the territory in the brain controlling intelligence.

Second, we have to figure out how to organize the selection of subjects for testing from each of these two populations. Who counts as Caucasian and who as African-American? The African-American population is one of the more mixed ones genetically, including not only African but also European, Native American, Asian, and Oceanic ancestry. What will be the criteria for including and excluding individuals from the populations to be sampled genetically? Do we establish a percentage quota for non-African genes and exclude all those whose percentages are greater than the quota? How do we decide what that figure should be? How do we know which alleles are African? Or should we use a set of alleles that are markers for racial category and include only those with all or almost all of those marker alleles? Can we do this without losing any genes that affect intelligence? When we get all of these sampling criteria established, who will be left to sample? These dilemmas are typical of human populations, which are genetic mongrels, because people will breed between groups at every opportunity. This is why so many anthropologists have abandoned race as a biological category, claiming that it is a social category and nothing else. But no matter. Say that we have two test populations.

With subjects to test, we now have to show that the same genes responsible for racial traits are also responsible for intelligence. This means identifying every allele of every gene responsible for each, but this is just the beginning, and here is why. All that a gene does is to encode information about a particular protein that is produced in the cell. What that protein does is to trigger a chemical reaction in the cell, and that reaction may produce a somatic trait by itself. For example, if you have a type A blood allele, your blood type will show up somatically as type A. The same is true for the type B allele. In this case, chemical action from proteins coded for a single locus produce a somatic effect. But many other important somatic traits are the result of a chain of chemical reactions, like skin color, which results from a sequence of eight chemical reactions, each triggered by a specific protein coded for by a specific gene. These reaction chains are called *chemical pathways*.

After you have identified every allele coding for every protein and every chemical pathway from allele to racial somatic traits, then you have to do the same for every gene, protein, and chemical pathway that controls intelligence. If the chemical pathways for racial traits connect to the chemical pathways that form the nerve nets and their interconnections controlling intelligence in one individual, then you have a single, interconnected set, so you can go on to test the entire sample population. If the racial pathways do not connect with the intelligence pathways, then there is no causal relationship between race and intelligence, and you can stop right there. If there is a connection between racial and intelligence pathways, then you have to deal with the problems of population sampling and variability in both genes and physiology.

We already know that each gene comes in several varieties called alleles. Each one is capable of coding for a protein, each is capable of producing a different chemical reaction from the others. Therefore we should also expect variability in the chemical pathways and their somatic outcomes. When both populations are all sampled, then it must be shown that, (1) the form and/or functioning of the connected nerve nets in each population are different, (2) that these form–function differences are the result of differently constituted chemical pathways, and (3) that form– function differences result in differences in performance. Finally, it must be shown that the differences in alleles, proteins, pathways, nerve nets, etc., *between the two populations* are greater than the same differences *within each population*. This is what a scientific demonstration of causal connections between race and intelligence entails.

Are there any scientists offering anything like this kind of demonstration? No. Modern proponents of eugenics and social Darwinism (the victims of poverty and discrimination as evolutionarily unfit) are very good at creating the image of scientific inquiry with correlations that appear to be causes. But just as a correlation is not a cause, image is not substance. This difference is particularly important when the pseudoscience of racial difference is proposed as a rationale for public policy, such as excluding Jews from all professions in prewar Germany or proposing cuts in education funding for inner-city children in the United States.

## THE PECULIAR LEGACY OF RACE:
## A WORLD OF THINGIES

The persistence of the race concept in occidental societies has nothing to do with what we know or do not know about human biology from rigorous scientific inquiry. The race concept draws its vigor and longevity from the fact that it is a social category whose primary meanings in everyday use are socially, rather than scientifically, derived. It is not the genetic and/or physiological variability that interests people, but behavioral differences that people observe and the supposed differences in traits of character that people infer from them. Connections that occidental people make between biology and character that render character as innate come from a folk theory of heredity that is far older than modern genetics. This old theory held that conception, occurring through a single act of intercourse fusing sperm and egg, served to transmit to the offspring somatic and character traits contained in tiny corpuscles contributed by each parent. Traits like hair color, size, facial and body features were complemented by traits like sloth, biliousness, industriousness, brilliance, greed, and the like. Because people of a given category are all assumed to inherit the same corpuscles, then all of its members must *have* the same traits of character. Genetics is the modern version of this old corpuscular theory of inheritance.

In the folk theory, it is conception, not geography, that conveys inherited traits. Inherited character traits are independent of geography and are thus *portable*. The portability of inherited character explains for eugenicists why Jews, for example, are as greedy in Berlin as they are in Jerusalem. The identification of race with ethnicity (inherited nationality) was developed theoretically by Ernst Haeckle using the Darwinian evolution as an explanatory framework. His union of race and nationality was tested as a politically potent strategy in Austria during the 1890s and thereafter by several political parties vying for power on platforms of anti-semitism. Nazi party strategists developed the race–nationality–character triad contrasting the Aryan race with the Jewish race, the Slavic race, etc., in the 1930s. Hitler's Final Solution, remember, entailed eliminating an entire race, not just getting Jews out of Germany.

While eugenics (the application of controlled breeding practices to human populations) was being developed in Europe, the United States had its own eugenics movement. Eugenics offered a scientific rationale for the discriminatory practices, such as exclusion of Asians and African Americans from the industrial labor market and their economic, residential, and educational segregation in the late nineteenth and twentieth centuries. Based on knowledge gained in laboratories, farms, and businesses such as horse and dog breeding, controlled breeding was demonstrated to effectively manage the frequency of desirable and undesirable somatic traits in plants and animals. Eugenicists were convinced that these breeding methods also should work for human beings to control character traits like insanity, imbecility, and criminality and eliminate them from the population. The population to be purified, of course, was white and Christian, which needed protection from non-white (including Jewish) admixture. So influential were the ideas of eugenicists, a number of states enacted laws against interracial and first cousin marriages.

Racial pseudoscience rationalizing systematic discrimination against racial and cultural minorities was an important part of the context within which the discipline of anthropology—and particularly the theory of culture—developed in the United States. Franz Boas was an implacable foe of racial pseudoscience. He publically attacked eugenics and eugenicists, pointing out every flaw in the practitioners' logic and use of data, presenting strong evidence to contradict eugenicists' assumptions, assertions, and predictions. Boas' major contribution to these debates was the demonstration that race, language, and culture varied independently of one another. He used ethnographic data to show that any child could learn any language and any conceivable human life-style.

One of Boas' students, Alfred Kroeber, took the independence of race, language, and culture even further. He took the definition of culture as E. B. Tylor had coined it—that "complex whole" that includes art, customs, beliefs, law, and all other habits learned by people as members of society—emphasized culture as a complex and *integrated* whole, and characterized culture as *superorganic.* What Kroeber's superorganic did was  divorce culture from biology altogether. Culture represented an evolutionary leap to a new plane of human existence, an emergent phenomenon of human evolution that, once in existence, was  independent of its biological base. Culture was a phenomenon in and of itself, *sui generis,* shaping how people lived their lives and yet independent of the people it shaped.  Individuals, after all, are born and die, while culture continues on impervious to their careers. While people share culture because they learn it, this extra-somatic phenomenon lay beyond people. Race could not touch it. Kroeber's position was challenged immediately, and the debate over the nature of culture raged on until the 1950s, when Kroeber recanted his position. By that time, however, the race debates of the 1920s had left an indelible mark on the  concept of culture.

Despite unrelenting criticism of Kroeber's superorganic, the terms of that debate conceded many of Kroeber's points. That culture was not *reducible* to biology was never in question. There was little disagreement about the *facticity* of culture as a distinctly human phenomenon. It was agreed that culture could serve to shape not only how a human community saw its world, but also what a human community looked like. Marriage rules can limit the choice of mates, thereby shaping the somatic variability of a community. There was little disagreement that this thing called culture was incorporated by learning into individuals' minds but still independent of particular minds for its existence. There was no disagreement about culture as a phenomenon that constituted a determining part of a community's environment, called its *cultural environment.* Few, if any, questioned the *thingness* of culture. Not that thinkers before Kroeber did not objectify culture, but the debates over the superorganic helped crystallize that "complex whole" as a thing. This legacy of the race issue not only shaped the thinking of five generations of anthropologists, but, more importantly, it shaped how the general public now understands and uses culture.

The thing called culture is said to have properties that we ordinarily attribute to people—*moulding* thought and perception, *maintaining* its own stability, but also the ablity to *change.* One culture can *influence, change, impact,* or even *dominate* another and *spread* over space. This typically human thing comes in local variants found in specific communities. Each such community can be and is called *a culture.* Even a culture can generate local variants, called *subcultures,* that are analogous to dialects of a  language. Even the manifestations of culture in what individual people learn is objectified as people *having* a culture. Anthropologists find that this thing exists at at least two levels of awareness. Part of culture or of *a* culture is readily observable, such as rules, ideas, beliefs, and recipes for organizing people and doing things, all of which people can explicitly describe, talk about, explain, or argue about. But there is another part of culture that is not readily observable and must be inferred from the way observable action and talk are organized. The observables are called *overt* or *explicit culture*, while the inferrables are called *covert* or *implicit culture*. The legacy of race has been an even swap—the fallacy of reductionism (reducing a phenomenon of high logical type to a lower level of logical type) was traded for the fallacy of reification (also called the fallacy of misplaced concreteness).

Anthropologists are aware of the reification of culture and its implications. It may not really be a thing, but it is convenient for analytical purposes to treat it *as if* it were a thing. By acting as if culture were a thing, one can use analytical techniques that work well for things. If it is not a thing, but we act as if it were a thing, then what have we learned about it from our researches? I follow Dr. Daniel Foss, a brilliant, iconoclastic sociologist, in calling culture in this "as if" usage a *thingie*. It is a thingie in people's environment, but also a thingie that people *have*, like an arm or a car. Culture is one of several thingies used to understand human variability. Personality is another thingie, as are intelligence and aptitude. Indeed, except for genetics, nearly everything we use to explain human variability is a thingie.

Why do African-American people behave differently from white American people? Because they have different subcultures. So if African-Americans have one subculture thingie and white Americans have a different subculture thingie, then how come all African-American people don't act the same and how come all white Americans do not act the same? As members of either a category or a culture, all have the same thingies, no? The obvious answer to that one is that individual differences within each category can be explained by people having different personalities, different amounts of intelligence, and different aptitudes. Different thingies. Of course, we can be much more sophisticated than that and look at other environmental variables like social class, which is a category that people intuitively recognize but that scholars find very difficult to define. Middle-class people make more money than lower class people (except when they do not), *have* different values, and make different choices about using their time and resources. Scholars talk about middle-class culture, which I suppose is a category thingie. So does a middle class African-American family act more like people with the middle-class thingie or more like people with the African-American thingie? Or is there a difference between the white middle-class thingie and the black middle-class thingie?

Let us go back to I.Q. and race for a moment. If the scientific inquiry into genetic causes of the variability in I.Q. scores has been less than adequate, then how about environmental variability as a causal explanation? Environmental data on test-takers usually consist of information about income, neighborhood, and social class, however that is defined. Income is a reasonable indicator of the range of choices the families of test-takers have. What does it tell us? Take two families making $65,000 a year. One invests in TVs, cable, VCRs, movies, Gameboys, and Sega. The other uses the same amount of money for concert series, museum memberships and trips, theater subscriptions, and books. What does income tell us about the environments of the children of these families? If $65,000 a year equals middle class, what does middle-class environment mean? How about a cultural explanation—something like

African-American children score lower on I.Q. tests because their culture does not place a high value on test scores? Thus their culture does not foster high motivation (another thingie) to achieve on tests?

These are familiar arguments, painted in bold strokes, manipulating facts collected about thingies. But these can not be the same kinds of facts that one would collect about things that are really things, so I will follow Dr. Foss and call them factoids. In the relentless debates about race and intelligence in a dangerous world ready to use pseudoscience to justify public policy decisions, what have social scientists brought to the table? Thingies and factoids. We can do better, a lot better.

## RESOLVING THE MUDDLES: A WORLD WITHOUT THINGIES

Assuming that people from Tokyo will continue to look different from people from Nairobi, we can be reasonably certain that the concept of race will not disappear from the Western world anytime soon. The conceptual maze of muddles that characterizes race is not necessarily inherent in the Western psyche, however. Clear focus on observations that yield empirical generalizations, from which hypotheses can be inferred and tested—acting like scientists, in other words—can serve to map the differences we call racial in ways that are accurate and useful. This does not mean simplifying the complexities of biology and social life (which is what thingies do). Our conceptual tools must clarify the nature of the complexities, starting by ridding ourselves of thingies.

I do not mean to throw out concepts of culture, intelligence, society or social class, or personality any more than we should throw out the concepts of the gene or somatic variability. We just need to be clear about what these concepts denote and resist the temptation to turn them into thingies. Whatever the disagreements about what intelligence is, most researchers agree that its arena is the relationship between how the human brain processes information and how persons habitually respond to the inputs that convey the information being processed. We can observe the differences in individuals' performances of some required task (like an I.Q. test) and infer from the differences that (a) all OF the individuals are getting the same inputs carrying the same information or that (b) the task constitutes different inputs and therefore conveys different information to different individuals. If (a), then differences in performance should point us to questions about individual differences in how each processes information. If (b), then we need to look at differences in how individuals *attend to* their environments such that what is the "same" set of inputs to the observer are different sets to the performers.

To simply throw out intelligence tests is absurd. The correlation between racial categories and I.Q. scores is useful, since explaining the correlation requires us to ask important questions about biological and environmental variability. The biological data and analyses necessary to test a theory of genetic causes of differences in performance can, in theory, be had. The work will be tedious and costly. Who will pay for it depends on who is most likely to benefit from this sort of research. The kinds of research necessary to understand what environmental constraints shape human behavioral variability are also doable, but will require conceptual rigor comparable to that of genetic research. Let me use I.Q. scores and correlations one more time to illustrate the kind of research that is possible, and the conceptual clarity it requires.

## I.Q., Birth Order, and the Nature of Environments

Psychologists have done years of research on a correlation between birth order and I.Q. scores in families with two or more children. Results often show a pattern of scores where the first-born scores highest, while younger siblings' scores steadily decrease with birth order position. This pattern appears in the United States, Europe, Africa, and India. Although psychologists disagree about the significance of these correlations, the pattern remains and appears impervious to racial and cultural differences. Explaining the correlation means examining the nature of *environments.*

Take a couple who court and marry. Over time, their relationship develops with their increasingly habitual ways of dealing with and understanding each other. Then they have a child, and their relationship changes, since each now has to deal with the other, with the child, *and* with the-other-with-the-child. The child grows up with its own relationships with each parent and with both together. Then along comes another child. This child will not have the same relationship with its parents that the first one has, because each parent now has to divide attention between two children of different ages and needs. The kind of attention the second child gets will be dependent on its needs and on the kind of relationship it develops with the older sibling. The first child's relationship also will undergo change for the same reasons, while the parents' relationship also will change with this ever more complex set of relations. A third child introduces another order of complexity for everyone, since now the eldest child has two younger siblings, while the second child deals with one older and one younger sibling, and its relationship with the older one may change or develop, depending on the relationship it develops with the younger sibling. The third child, of course, contends with two older siblings, and its relations with each depends on their relationship with each other, the relations of each with the parents, and the relationship of the parents to the relationship between the older siblings, etc. Now, given the complexity of these different relationships, does it make sense to say that because the children live in the same household, *they all have the same environment?*

Taking this example a step further, is it possible that the learning environment of each child is the same? Does the child learn only about "things" or about things and about the context in which he/she learned about the things? Is it possible for any human being to learn about anything without also learning about the context of which the learning was part? Can we learn without learning how to learn? If the learning environment for each child varies with that child's set of relationships in the family, and if each child's set of relationships is different, does that not imply differences in how each child learns how to learn? Can each child's learning environment possibly be the same as that of the other children? Common sense and common experience alone are sufficient to answer no to this last question.The concept of environment viewed through the lens of relationships between people (and between people and things) as *contexts of learning* are quite different from those of income level or social class as environments.

Now go one step further. If each child's learning environment is different from the others', is it possible that each child's learning is culturally identical to its siblings'? Anthropologist Ward Goodenough says no. Each person may see, hear, and learn the same sorts of skills, rules, relationships, speech, and ceremonies as everybody else, but always in different learning environments, implying varying interpretations of what was learned. Thus, each person in a community constitutes what Goodenough calls his or her own "subculture." This would account for the fact that people can share the same general definitions of what things of their experience mean and still differ in their interpretations of the same situation or the applicability of a rule to a situation. They share a consensus about what things mean and about values, but they interpret and apply them differently. People may share the same maps but see different features of a territory such that each maps a situation differently, resulting in several different maps being used simultaneously.

Now it is time to rescue culture from the realm of thingies and make it useful to a view of environments as contexts. When E. B. Tylor first used culture in its modern sense, he used it as a way of comparing one society with others. Whatever else culture came to mean, it was always a concept used to explain the nature of differences in the way human communities organized their activities, their members, and their ideas. Culture was a kind of *explanation* before it was ever a kind of thing, so we can discard its thingness without losing its usefulness.

Culture is a *theory* that anthropologists use to explain two sorts of observations: (1) why the relationships between people who comprise a community, relationships between people and their environments, and relationships between people and supernaturals (who often are parts of the environment) appear to be so highly patterned and predictable; and (2) why the patterns of relations that organize one community can be so different from the patterns that organize other communities. Culture explains these observations by positing a causal relationship between patterns of perception that people learn and patterns of action and interaction in which they participate. Culture is, thus, a theory of human perception and of how people learn to perceive. The theory connects patterns of perception with patterns of action, thought, and interaction by stipulating that it is *meanings* of the things, persons, and relationships people encounter that organize their experiences by making sense of them. People living in communities confer meanings on the stream of experience, and those meanings differentiate experiences from one another. It is these meanings (encoded on symbols) and the relationships between meanings that people learn. To the extent that people share the same sets of symbols through learning, they share meanings of, and thus interpretations of, what they experience. Because people organize meanings in patterned ways, we can infer that part of learning symbols is learning the rules for putting meanings and symbols together. Some of these rules are taught explicitly. Other sorts of rules are learned by making inferences about repeated experiences. Rules of grammar are a good example of rules that are inferred rather than taught. People know the steps by which an active sentence is converted to a passive sentence, but they cannot explicitly state the rules. These rules are deeply unconscious assumptions or *premises* ("implicit culture"). People can share the same premises and still differ in how they interpret a specific situation, however.

Culture is a theory about how people make and use mental (or cognitive) maps and how the maps that people in one community make and share differ from those that people in other communities make and share. Because people in different communities define experience differently, cultural anthropologists are particularly sensitive to how people organize the contexts of action and interaction that we observe. But just because people may share the same general meanings and symbols that encode them does not mean that every person in the community defines a specific situation in the same way, for reasons already explained. Thus, learning about another community and its people's construction of reality does not allow us precise predictions of what people will do in specific situations. The best we can do is specify a range of possible outcomes, given what we understand about variability in people's interpretatations of situations in that community.

Now let us apply this understanding of culture to the problem of race. First, the theory would predict that this concept should be peculiar to those communities that share a corpuscular theory of human inheritance, and this seems to be true. Oceanic people, by contrast, explain ethnic differences using their own ethnobiological theories. Communities most carefully studied in Melanesia and Micronesia appear to share a theory of environmental determinism, beginning with a theory of conception as the result of repeated acts of intercourse that fuse male with female fluids. The fluids convey not only somatic traits but environmental relations, such as immunities to particular spirits gained by ingesting soil and waters they inhabit. The immunities are transformed into a biological substance and transferred through sexual fluids to the fetus. Social relations are similarly transformable. If either parent steals things during the pregnancy, this relational propensity will be transformed into biological substance and communicated to the child. Because the body is a product of relations between people and between people and places they inhabit, this sort of environmental determinism precludes a racial theory of ethnic difference. Indeed, Oceanic people's ethnic stereotypes are literally rooted in places. Racial categories are, thus, cultural artifacts of western ethnobiological theories.

Are the differences between African-Americans and "whites" cultural as well as somatic? As someone who lives in Chicago, I find it very difficult to think about the cultural category "white people" as unified in any way other than not being African-American. The difference between Mexican-Americans and Brazilian-Americans or between Irish-Americans, Polish-Americans, and Appalachian folks  is pretty hard to miss. All share American citizenship  and expectations learned through growing up here, but all are differentiated from and differentiate themselves from the others based on expectations, observations, and, of course, ethnic stereotypes. I don't see any less variation among African-Americans than among whites. Applying the concept of culture to African-American as a category demands sustained, careful, ethnographic research just to establish the range of variability among African-Americans necessary to determine what sets of meanings, cultural premises, and interaction patterns Afro-americans share in common, if any. There has been some very interesting and suggestive research along these lines, but nothing like the sheer sampling of communities that needs to be done before concluding anything.

## SO?

Race and culture are concepts invented by western people to describe and explain human biological and behavioral variability. The potential usefulness of both concepts has been vitiated by a long history of logically fallacious reasoning—collapsing properties of a category into properties of its members, confusing maps with territories, and confounding correlations with causes. The muddles that have resulted have been used to justify everything from misogyny laws to genocide using muddled biology and failed public policies using muddled notions of culture. It never had to be that way, nor does it have to be now.

Presently available technology is adequate to answer biological questions such as what percentage of the genes in the human genome are responsible for somatic differences associated with racial variety, if and how they commingle with genes influencing the formation of brain structures, etc. Whether or not this research gets done depends on whether anyone wants to know the answers badly enough to fund them. It is a lot cheaper, less time-consuming, and less rigorous to do more correlations, call them causes, and ride the talk show circuit. The best hope for getting the research done is the Human Genome Diversity Project, if it is allowed to proceed and is adequately funded.

It is not biological variability that interests the general public about race. It is behavioral variability assumed to be rooted in biology (about which we know very little in any case). The study of race as a cultural category holds great promise for an understanding of the European American societies that share this concept. For example, what do the ways that French and American people define and use the race concept tell us about the similarities and differences in French and American cultural premises, meanings of personhood, and theories of biological inheritance? The race concept, in other words, tells us a lot more about the people that use the concept than it does about the people whom the concept is used to describe. The concept of culture is, therefore, most usefully applied to the understanding of the inventors, end-users, and local distributors of the race concept.

## REFERENCES

Barkan, E. 1992. *The Retreat of Scientific Racism*. Cambridge: Cambridge University Press.

Block, N. J . & Dworkin, G. 1976. *The I.Q. Controversy: Critical Readings*. New York: Panteon Books.

Gordon, C. C. 1993. *Race, Ethnicity, and Applied Bioanthropology.* Arlington, VA: American Anthropological Association.

Gould, S. J. 1981. *The Mismeasure of Man.* New York: W. W. Norton.

Linnekin, J. & Poyer, L. 1990. *Cultural Identity and Ethnicity in Oceania.* Honolulu: University of Hawaii Press.

Shipman, P. 1994. *The Evolution of Racism.* New York: Simon & Schuster.

Terkel, S. 1992. *Race: How Blacks and Whites Think and Feel About the American Obsession.* New York: New Press.

# 5

# Diversity Orientations: Culture, Ethnicity, and Race

Kimberly P. Martin

## INTRODUCTION

Culture, ethnicity, race are three terms frequently used interchangeably in everyday conversation and which also have varying meanings depending on the interpretation of the individual using them. In this chapter, three precise and distinctive definitions for these terms will be used, not only to compare the broad range of meaning they connote, but as a vehicle for distinguishing three orientations toward diversity-based interactions. It will be shown that these three orientations represent very different assumptions about what goes on in the diversity-based interactions occurring every day in multicultural societies. These different assumptions permeate diversity-based interactions at the personal and social levels for all of us. They influence how we relate to our families, neighbors, and friends, as well as to our peers, colleagues, and co-workers. They affect how we form opinions about, meet, work and socialize with others, as well as how people in everyday life react to us. They contribute to the nature of family dynamics, community relations, and national politics. In the study of diversity as an academic pursuit, these orientations influence how teachers and students receive, process, internalize, and feel about the various issues, research, and activities that are covered in the classroom. In sum, these three diversity orientations have profound implications for how we approach personal and social interactions in a culturally, ethnically, and racially diverse social milieu, as well as how we learn and teach about diversity issues.

## CULTURE

The first definition that is central to an understanding of diversity issues is the definition of culture. Here *culture* will be defined as *the* abstract, learned, shared rules and standards for interpreting experience and organizing behavior in a society, including the behaviors and material possessions that are produced by those rules and standards (Spradley & McCurdy 1989). This definition refers to both real and ideal rules and standards for how people ought to behave, whether those standards are consciously attended to or unconsciously assumed. Our behavior and values, our material possessions, social institutions, and spiritual beliefs all reflect the underlying culture that we share with the other members of our society. Culture is the automatic pilot that guides our behavior and makes us predictable and intelligible to those around us (Goodenough 1961). It provides us with guidelines for evaluating our own behavior as well as that of others.

As long as those with whom we interact are using the same culture as we are, interactions are efficient and productive. We feel comfortable and competent. We like the feeling of belonging that comes from interacting within our own cultural milieu. We are proud when we perform according to the standards of our cultural group. Along with this pride and competency comes ethnocentrism, the belief that our culture is superior to others and that we should judge others by our superior standards. This powerful self-centeredness about the importance of our own culture negatively colors how we view and evaluate individuals and groups who are culturally different from us (Klopf 1991; Parillo 1994). Because of ethnocentrism, we may view the behavior of culturally different groups to be embarrassing, immoral, or worthy of contempt or condemnation, rather than just different.

Ethnocentrism is not the only problem we encounter when we try to interact across cultures. Being in an unfamiliar cultural setting may mean not knowing what will happen next or how to behave appropriately. It is not uncommon to become frustrated, frightened, angered, or anxious when the behavior of others does not meet our expectations. These negative emotional reactions are called *culture shock* (Oberg 1979; Klopf 1991). The anxieties and discomfort of culture shock may cause us to avoid contact with those who are culturally different from ourselves.

The definition of *culture* used here highlights one of the ways in which problems arise in everyday diversity-based interactions: the misunderstandings that occur when people are operating according to different sets of cultural rules. Sometimes this results in bewilderment when the behavior of others seems to make no sense. At other times it results in antagonism when the cultural rule sets of those involved conflict with one another and behaviors are misinterpreted as threatening or negative. Focusing on the definition of culture highlights a way of looking at diversity-based problems as misunderstandings between individuals who are using different sets of cultural rules, rather than problems based on clashes of ethnic identity or power-based struggles involving oppression.

### Cultural Orientation Assumptions

Individuals using a *cultural orientation* tend to make a certain number of assumptions about why problems occur in diversity-based interactions. The first assumption is that problems in these interactions only arise when the different sets of cultural rules and standards about how one should behave get in the way of productive communication. Individuals with this orientation believe that conflict arises for one of two reasons: (1) because people do not know enough about each other's standards and rules to interact productively with one another; and/or (2) because people make faulty ethnocentric assumptions about the superiority of their own learned cultural rules and standards. Lack of cultural knowledge creates misunderstanding, embarrassment, and anger because others are perceived as acting in ways that are rude, ignorant, foolish, or downright offensive. The assumption of ethnocentric superiority creates barriers to acquiring knowledge about other cultures, leading in many cases to the kinds of fixed, negative perceptions of others that we call *prejudice*.

Diversity-based interactions frequently result in powerful negative emotions such as anger, embarrassment, impatience, and irritation. The second assumption that cultural orientation individuals tend to make is that such negative emotions result from the seeming strangeness and inappropriateness of the behavior of those who do not share their particular cultural rules. These emotions are perceived as the consequence of misunderstanding, and not necessarily of intentional mistreatment, discrimination, or oppression.

Because of this perception, cultural orientation individuals assume that negative emotions will disappear once everyone understands that the problems are merely a misunderstanding. On the basis of this orientation, it is logical to assume that the solutions for diversity interaction problems are: (1) to be aware that different sets of rules exist for various cultural, ethnic, and racial groups; (2) to set aside the idea that your own culture is superior to all others; and then (3) to learn each other's cultural rules and standards so that those interacting with one another have the tools to correctly interpret each other's behavior. Knowing each other's rules and standards is, for the person using the cultural orientation, the key to eliminating embarrassment, discomfort, annoyance, and anger, as well as restoring clear communication in the interaction.

People who are using the cultural orientation tend to assume that cultural rules exist at an intellectual level that is easily accessible to both those who live by those rules and to outsiders, particularly when insider members of the other group are willing to explain and help with this process. The roles of insider and outsider often are defined by the cultural context in which the interaction takes place. For example, good communication and positive interaction at a Native American powwow would be made possible if Native Americans were willing to share cultural knowledge about the event with the non-Indian visitors, while at the same time the visitors were willing to learn and abide by the Native American cultural rules and standards that define the powwow. At a Native American event, the insider cultural context is Native American, and the non-Indian visitors are the outsiders who need to acquire, learn and practice new cultural knowledge in order to make the interaction work. Conversely, an interaction between European Americans and traditional Native Americans in a European American business setting would require the insider/outsider roles to be reversed; the cultural context of the interaction would be the European American, and the Native Americans would be expected to make the accommodation to the norms and rules of that culture.

Of course it is also possible for there to be some mutual adjustment of cultural rules. In the example above, this would require the European Americans to learn the rules of the powwow and do their best to follow those rules, while the Native Americans would show tolerance for European American behaviors which either intentionally or perhaps mistakenly violate the cultural norms of the pow-wow. In a European American business setting, the Native Americans might learn and follow the European American cultural rules, while the European Americans might show tolerance for the Native American behaviors that violate the cultural norms of the business setting. In these cases, both groups would have learned about each other's cultures and would accommodate each other to facilitate friendly, productive interaction.

These examples represent how individuals using cultural orientation see the task of resolving diversity-based communication problems as a process of assembling "recipes" for culturally correct interactions in different cultural contexts, and learning the recipes for future use. They assume that all of the participants in this kind of interaction should have an equal motivation and responsibility for helping to overcome the cultural misunderstandings that occur, either in making their own cultural rules accessible to others, or in learning and accommodating the cultures of others.

*Cultural orientation* individuals assume that people involved in diversity-based interactions wish to accomplish goals that are unrelated to the cultural differences between them, and that their desire to accomplish these goals is more important than any cultural, ethnic, and racial differences. For example, an American business executive who is trying to negotiate a contract with a Japanese counterpart is doing so to obtain a needed product or service. When such an interaction is viewed from a *cultural orientation*, the cultural differences between the American executive and the Japanese executive present stumbling blocks to the negotiation process but are not, themselves, directly a part of what either of the individuals is seeking in the interaction.

Individuals operating with a *cultural orientation* presume that both parties want the interaction to be mutually satisfying, and that the only thing missing is the knowledge that would allow them to communicate with one another effectively enough to get the job done. International corporations such as Arthur Anderson, Inc., and Motorola have incorporated cultural orientation training as a normal part of the job for employees who work overseas. They receive language training and use interpreters to mediate the language barriers. They train employees about ethnocentrism and culture shock. They give intensive training about the culture of the society in which the employee will work, including conventions for polite behavior, conversation styles, values, nonverbal communication, and business protocol. The goal of all of this training is to eliminate the unwanted cross-cultural complications and misunderstandings that might prevent business goals from being realized.

The cultural orientation presents a perspective that is very different from the ethnic and racially based oppression orientations. The assumptions and expectations of the cultural orientation are not only different from those of the other orientations, but frequently those differences become flash points for anger and resentment, and sometimes even prejudice and hatred. In the next section, the focus is on the definition of ethnicity and the ethnic orientation that is derived from that definition, as well as how the expectations and assumptions of the ethnic orientation are in conflict with those of the cultural orientation.

## ETHNICITY

For the purposes of this chapter, the term *ethnicity* is defined as membership in a group with which one chooses to affiliate on the basis of shared ancestry and/or cultural heritage. Boundaries are central to the idea of ethnicity. We are either insiders or outsiders because of our ethnic affiliations. We can only be insiders if there are outsiders with whom we contrast ourselves. The focus on national or geographical origins as a way of designating membership in an ethnic group works well in many cases (Parillo 1994; Farley 1995). The definition used here adds the component of choice. Increasingly, multicultural societies are made up of individuals who can trace their ancestry and origins to multiple nationalities, religions, languages, traditions, and cultures. This is particularly true of Americans. Many choose one of these heritages as the focus of their ethnic identity, while ignoring or de-emphasizing the others. Here, ethnicity becomes something the individual embraces consciously. Another reason to emphasize choice in this definition is that ethnic identification varies in strength and emphasis, depending on the individual. Some individuals will practice the religion of their ethnic group, but not retain the language. Others will adopt ethnic names, but deviate from traditional family roles or reject traditional holiday rituals. Regardless of the variations on ethnic identity that are present in American multicultural society, pride and identity based on group membership are at the center of the concept. Ethnicity is an important way to be an insider.

We mark ourselves as insiders by using distinctive communication styles and characteristic behavior patterns, that is, by acting out a shared set of cultural rules and standards. Behavioral markers such as vocabulary, gestures, clothing, and social conventions serve not only as vehicles for communicating content unambiguously within a particular cultural context, but also in several other extremely important ways.

Behavioral markers *symbolize* the distinctive heritage of the group. This heritage can reflect common experiences grounded in such factors as ancestry, nationality, language, religion, culture, or political and social experience. For individuals using an *ethnic orientation*, culturally derived behavioral markers do *not* constitute the distinctive characteristics of members of the group, they are simply the outward signs of these more substantial differences derived from shared experiences in the past. Examples of shared experiences might be the oppression of slavery or job discrimination, the pride of accomplishment in technological advancement, or the symbolism and style of the traditional music and art. Shared experiences and perspectives derived from history and heritage constitute the core of ethnic identity. Thus, for someone with this orientation, it is not the way in which people greet each other that matters, rather, the greeting is important as a symbol of underlying shared experience and perspective that allows insiders to recognize and acknowledge one another.

In addition to symbolizing the underlying commonalities of group members, behavioral markers serve as ongoing reaffirmations of group membership that are frequently a central component of personal identity for group members. Ethnic markers are used to publicly claim membership in a group whose existence and solidarity is of central importance to the individual. Pride, security, comradeship, and a sense of empowerment are all important by-products of membership in an ethnic group. This is particularly true for members of ethnic minorities, whose history includes the systematic devaluing of ethnic culture through social and political oppression. Historically, American minority groups such as Latinos and African-Americans have been effectively able to combat oppression and prejudice through group solidarity and political activism constructed around ethnic identity.

Boundaries must be maintained for an ethnic group to have meaning. In the case of ethnicity, boundaries are signaled by behavioral markers, for example, the zoot suit clothing style of Latinos in the 1940s. Insiders have the right to membership (and therefore the right to use the behavioral markers) because they share heritage together, not because they have the cultural knowledge to act like an insider. Just knowing the behavioral markers of the group does not entitle anyone to use them, unless that individual also shares the crucial core experiences that make him or her a member of the group. Outsiders who do not share the insiders' ethnic heritage, but try to participate in the group by using its behavioral markers, are seen as reducing the differences between the groups to superficialities that demean the crucial importance of the ethnic experience. In addition, for those insiders who draw self-esteem and identity from their ethnicity, de-emphasizing or ignoring the substantive historical and experiential characteristics of an ethnic group actually means denying essential parts of their personal identity.

This perspective on the behaviors that mark membership in an ethnic group is diametrically opposed to those used by individuals coming from a different cultural orientation. From the cultural orientation perspective, culture facilitates interactions among people who know the rules. From the ethnic orientation perspective, culture is symbolic of shared experience and heritage. For the former, cultural differences are to be overcome so that interactions can be productive and successful. For the latter, culture is to be guarded and protected as a symbol of membership in a select group that is not accessible to just anyone.

When the individual with a cultural orientation tries to assemble a recipe for interacting productively with members of an ethnic group, that recipe will include ethnic markers that are considered by the ethnic insider as the exclusive property of insiders. The person with an ethnic orientation is not willing to share behavioral markers with outsiders, and is not interested in teaching others how to use those markers to accomplish productive interactions within the ethnic group. Further, that ethnic insider is likely to resent and reject the well-meaning attempts of the outsider to fit in. Lack of knowledge about the importance of ethnic markers on the part of the person with the cultural orientation, combined with rejection on the part of the person with the ethnic orientation, frequently leads to further misunderstanding, avoidance, and sometimes long-standing prejudice on the part of both participants.

## Ethnic Orientation Assumptions

As in the case of the *cultural orientation*, the *ethnic orientation* presents a set of assumptions concerning what is going on in diversity interactions. One implicit assumption of this orientation is that all individuals need an ethnic affiliation of some sort in order to construct their own personal identity. For example, during discussions in college classes, individuals using an ethnic orientation frequently are patronizing toward whites or European Americans who do not claim an ethnic identity other than American. They feel that these "American" individuals are lacking a central core self-knowledge and self-identity and feel sorry for them. And it is not only the ethnic orientation individuals who see ethnic identity in this way. The white/European American individuals frequently are embarrassed by and sometimes defensive about what they perceive to be a lack of ethnic identity.

Individuals using an *ethnic orientation* further tend to assume that all ethnic identities in a multicultural society are entitled to equal respect, and that everyone in such a society should acknowledge and accommodate the ethnic characteristics that form part of the identity of others. This assumption is particularly important as a response to the devaluation and disrespect shown to ethnic minority groups in *de facto* and *de jure* discrimination and oppression throughout the history of U.S. society. Respectful acknowledgment of ethnicity by the dominant society as a whole, and by individual members of dominant society as they interact with minority individuals, is seen as a critical component for attaining and maintaining any equal status for minority individuals. Respectful acknowledgment includes recognition of the ethnic markers of others as well as refraining from using markers that are not part of one's own ethnic identity.

A third assumption is that diversity interactions represent one of the places where this kind of acknowledgment and validation of ethnic identity should occur, and that accommodation of differences is at least as important as any other goal associated with such interactions. By extension, the *ethnic orientation* assumes that many members of our multicultural society, especially members of the dominant culture, have not in the past, and do not currently, accord ethnicity its proper place in interpersonal processes, nor do they respect or accommodate the characteristics that are of central importance to many ethnic minority group members.

In fact, the history of the multicultural society in the United States is one of dominant group ethnocentrism involving devaluation of and discrimination against unassimilated groups. Dominant society and its members have not been respectful of ethnic minorities, while forcing minorities to treat white and European American ethnicities with respect. People who use an *ethnic orientation* tend to see this as a major problem in diversity interactions. For these individuals, the solution to this problem is seen as primarily the responsibility of the dominant society members (whites and European Americans), who must adjust their attitudes, behaviors, and institutions to accommodate the diverse ethnic groups that constitute the reality of American society.

People who approach diversity-based interactions with an *ethnic orientation* also frequently assume that diversity-related communication problems can be solved only if all members of the society become aware of, acknowledge, and respectfully accommodate all of the differences that mark the boundaries of ethnic groups. Ethnic orientation individuals strongly believe that no one should be asked to give up their ethnic characteristics, and hence their ethnic identity, for the convenience of others during interactions involving diversity.

A good example of a group of individuals who were using the assumptions of the ethnic orientation appeared on a recent television talk show. On this program, African-American and European American teenagers argued heatedly over the issue of "sagging." Sagging refers to wearing oversized jeans or shorts cinched in at the hips with a belt so that the waistline of the pants hits the widest part of the hip several inches below the waist, the pant's crotch falls mid-thigh to knee, and the pants are very baggy. The controversy on the show centered around the claim of the African-American teens that sagging was an African-American style of dress, and that European American teenagers had no right to sag. In this case, the European American teens were not trying to use the ethnic marker of sagging as a way of joining any ethnically defined social group of African-American teens. Instead, they simply admired the style and wanted to adopt it for themselves.

The entire hour of the talk show was devoted to a verbal battle between these two groups of teens. In essence, the African-American group was defending sagging as an ethnic symbol that could be used legitimately only by members of the African-American ethnic group. An analogy may clarify how the African-Americans felt. Imagine that England or Japan or Russia suddenly began to fly the stars and stripes as their national emblem instead of their traditional national flag. How would Americans react? Probably with outrage on the part of U.S. citizens, not because there is anything inherently American about stars or stripes or the colors (red, white, and blue), but because a particular pattern and configuration of those elements are strongly identified with the United States and its heritage. African-American youths have developed configurations and patterns of speech, dress, and movement that represent their identity in similar ways, and their reaction is not so surprising when viewed from the perspective of the ethnic orientation.

In contrast, the European American teenagers' response fits neatly into the cultural orientation outlined above. They argued that they had a right to wear their pants any way they wanted. The European American teens saw different ways of wearing clothing as options that were available to anyone who liked what they saw. They liked the style, and therefore they sagged. For them, sagging was just a stylist choice, not a statement of ethnic identity. Ethnicity was not particularly important to them, and they were not able to understand why the African-American group had such strong feelings about sagging.

The television program was intended to stimulate discussion about relations between ethnic groups, and to present an example of the kinds of conflict that arise due to ethnic boundaries. Likewise, in an academic context, the *ethnic orientation* is one of the primary orientations represented in ethnic studies courses and readings, where knowledge of the history and heritage of American ethnic groups forms the core of the curriculum.

## RACE

The third term used to delineate differences in diversity orientations is race. Anthropologists, through decades of study and research, have failed to find any *biologically* based set of characteristics that clearly establishes racial groups as scientifically accurate categories for understanding or categorizing human beings (Montague 1964, 1965). However, race continues to be a powerful concept in the *social sciences*. For the purposes of this analysis, the following social science definition of *race* is used: a social category based on arbitrary physical or cultural characteristics that is used for purposes of discrimination.

One important key to understanding this definition is in recognizing that physical characteristics only become important for classifying people into groups if the society chooses to recognize and utilize them in this way. In the United States, we have arbitrarily chosen skin color, eye form, hair texture, and certain facial features as criteria for attributing race, while ignoring other physical traits such as blood type, lactose tolerance, or ear shape. As Farley states, "Physical characteristics partially define race, but only in the context of a decision by a society to consider those physical characteristics relevant. This illustrates an important fact: Race is a socially constructed concept"(1995:5). It is also notable that, here in the United States, racial attribution based on language, religion and cultural practices becomes intertwined with that based on physical features, further emphasizing the arbitrary and social nature of racial categories. Americans also depend on different traits to recognize membership in particular racial groups. For example, eye shape is used to categorize Asian Americans apart from European Americans, but are not useful for telling African-Americans from European Americans. By the same token, skin color or tone is useful in determining whether an individual is African-American or European American, while it is frequently not useful in distinguishing Asian Americans from European Americans.

In the definition of race used here, the word discrimination is an important component. This definition focuses on the use of racial criteria to categorize people in order to discriminate either for or against them. Here the word *discriminate* is used in its most general sense, meaning to treat differently. Differential treatment becomes especially significant in the context of an imbalance of power, where one group exercises control over another. Those who have access to power benefit from positive discrimination. Membership in the power-based group (often referred to as the *majority* or *dominant* group) provides an ongoing advantage to that group, along with the accompanying pride in membership in that privileged group (Farley 1995). Conversely, the results of systematic discrimination are painful and often psychologically, economically, and politically crippling to those who do not have power and, therefore, experience negative discrimination and mistreatment. Pain, hurt, anger, and powerlessness result from the mistreatment, and are compounded both because members of oppressed groups do not have the resources and status to protect themselves from discrimination, and because they do not have appropriate channels to vent their frustration and rage. The term *minority* is used to refer to groups that have been systematically oppressed within their own societies, regardless of the numbers of individuals represented in the group (Farley 1995).

The expectation of mistreatment when interacting with members of more powerful groups is a natural consequence for minority individuals who have experienced habitual discrimination. Furthermore, children are taught by their families, friends, and peers to expect mistreatment, and to handle oppression and discrimination in the same ways that have worked for other members of their group. Suspicion, defensiveness, cynicism, and highly emotional responses that seem out of proportion to the situation at hand are commonly described in discussions of minority group oppression. These emotions are an important component of the *oppression orientation* to diversity interactions.

In this discussion, the main focus is on racial discrimination and racial oppression. Race is one of the most powerful and pervasive social concepts in American society. There are, however, other kinds of criteria that are used to categorize people into groups for the purposes of discrimination. Some examples of nonracial minority groups in the United States include women, the elderly, and homosexuals. Members of these groups also experience oppression and may operate from an oppression orientation.

### Oppression Orientation Assumptions

The basic assumption of the *oppression orientation* is that diversity-based interactions *always* result in mistreatment or oppression of the less powerfully affiliated individual or group. Oppression can be consciously perpetrated or can result from the thoughtless participation of dominant society individuals in discriminatory systems that form their normal everyday cultural milieu. People coming from an *oppression orientation* assume that diversity-based interaction problems can be resolved only if mistreatment ceases, and power is taken from the dominant group and given to the oppressed individual or group. The dominant group can yield power to the minority group, or the minority group can seize power in some way in order to avoid oppression. In either case, the *oppression orientation* individual believes it essential not only to restore power to those from whom it has been taken, but also to heal the psychological, economic, and political wounds suffered by members of the oppressed group and to provide reparation for past wrongs. Only after these things have been accomplished can relations improve between racial groups.

Because power is assumed to take a number of forms, it can be found in several partial solutions to the interaction problems as they tend to be perceived by the individual using an *oppression orientation*. Ethnic revitalization and the strength of numbers found in ethnic group affiliation provides one avenue of empowerment. Violence against the dominant society or against minority peers provides a vent for rage, and gives a temporary sense of power, even though it may not directly affect the kinds of mistreatment that are at the root of the oppression. Finally, commitment to, and action on, the part of dominant society members to the elimination of both oppressive situations and their causes is a central component to the process of shifting the power balance toward equality for oppressed groups.

The healing process itself presents a different kind of power, the psychological empowerment of individuals. The victims of oppression want the opportunity to express, in a safe context to an appropriate target audience, the hurt, anger, and frustration that accumulates from systematic oppression. Acknowledgment by dominant society members that the system in which they have prospered is responsible for great pain and suffering on the part of others is vindicating for members of oppressed groups, and also contributes to the healing process. The solutions that are considered necessary to defuse diversity-based interactions from the *oppression orientation* involve healing the wounds of those who have suffered oppression, and restoring to them their dignity, self-esteem, and personal power over their own lives.

The trial of O.J. Simpson for the murder of his wife, Nicole Brown Simpson, and her friend, Ron Goldman, provides us with an excellent example of the oppression orientation. All over the United States, in conversations with family, friends, and co-workers, in discussions on radio and television talk shows, and in newspapers and magazines, people followed this trial and voiced their thoughts and feelings about the guilt or innocence of Mr. Simpson, about the individuals involved in trying the case, and about the trial proceedings. It was not uncommon to hear observers say that the system was biased against Simpson because he was African-American. Suspicions of police racism and conspiracy, of attorney bias, and of juror prejudice based on racial considerations were commonly expressed, frequently with considerable passion.

A number of individuals voiced the opinion that even if Mr. Simpson was guilty, he should not be convicted, because so many whites have committed crimes, including murder, against African-Americans and have not been punished. In some cases, individuals expressing this opinion did not rely on evidence about police, attorney, or juror bias in the case at hand. They spoke passionately about the systemic racial bias they have experienced and observed in American society.

It is not the racially based opinions, themselves, that constitute the oppression orientation, but the fact that these individuals looked immediately and exclusively to racism to make sense of the trial. Their experience told them that because dominant and minority individuals were interacting with one another in the Simpson case, racism must be the central issue. For many minority individuals, the evidence of their lives has proven that the answer to virtually every problem lies in resolving the issue of racism. Certainly the evidence of African-American history shows that for centuries racism has been the barrier that prevented members of this group from progressing educationally, economically, personally, and socially. It should not be surprising that some African-Americans still believe that it is a waste of time to look elsewhere for explanations and solutions in diversity-based interactions.

Two major differences become apparent here between the cultural and the oppression orientations. First, the focus of the cultural orientation on cultural differences is seen by people using the oppression orientation as trivial and an attempt to evade the real issue which is power and its use and misuse. Second, the oppression orientation blames dominant society, which is seen as being primarily European American, for past injustices. From their perspective, the responsibility to share power and undo inequality rests primarily with individual European American dominant society members who have benefited from the unjust status quo. European Americans who use a cultural orientation may be accused of evading responsibility assigned them by the oppression orientation. Further, they may be accused of using the cultural orientation as a smoke screen to avoid addressing how the power structure can be made more fair, and therefore as a smoke screen for maintaining the status quo for their own benefit.

The cultural orientation does not address power or oppression, and people using this orientation tend to see themselves as nonprejudiced individuals who are trying their best to get along in a multicultural society. They are shocked when they are personally assigned responsibility for historic injustice and angry when they are accused of taking advantage of inequalities in the power structure for their own benefit.

## A DIVERSITY ORIENTATIONS MODEL

The three diversity orientations outlined above, *cultural orientation, ethnic orientation,* and the *oppression orientation*, provide complementary parts of a model for helping us to understand the complicated context in which diversity-based interactions take place. This model is based on several premises, each of which is essential to its usefulness. First, individuals approach diversity-based interactions with expectations and assumptions from one or more of the three orientations. Second, most people assume that those with whom they interact share their assumptions about what should be happening in the interaction. Third, most people are not aware that there is any orientation to diversity-based interactions other than their own. Fourth, most diversity-based interactions occur between people with orientations that are totally different from each other. And fifth, an understanding of how people operate within these orientations has the potential of making a crucial difference in the intellectual and emotional dynamics of what occurs as people reach across cultural, ethnic, and racial boundaries.

The three orientations presented here are, of course, abstract and simplified. They are not necessarily separate or mutually exclusive in the real world of people's minds and their feelings. Some individuals seem highly focused in one of these orientations, while others approach diversity-based interactions with assumptions, emotions, and expectations from some combination of the three. It is also possible for any given individual to shift orientations from one interaction to another, given variable interaction contexts or participants. It is also important to emphasize that no ranking of these orientations in order of importance or influence is implied in the model. Each orientation represents an equally valid point of view from a particular perspective, and each has an important place in our understanding of what goes on in diversity-based interactions. It is absolutely necessary to attend to all three to truly understand the dynamics of multicultural society.

Many people, however, do seem to have a primary diversity orientation that guides their interactions with others most of the time, and which is derived from their enculturation and life experience. For example, it is common for European Americans in the United States to operate from a *cultural orientation*. Such individuals take their identity from the dominant society and use that group as their frame of reference. They have not felt a compelling need for the pride and solidarity of ethnic group affiliation; rather, they take their membership in the "mainstream" social group for granted. They have not experienced systematic mistreatment because of their membership in the dominant society, and therefore they do not perceive diversity-based interactions as inherently oppressive. They frequently are surprised when others respond to their well-meaning interaction attempts with suspicion and hostility born of bitter experience, or hurt when others reject their well-meaning attempts to fit into an ethnic context where they are not welcome by using behavioral markers whose underlying symbolism they do not fully understand.

In such arenas as international business, interactions are more straightforward because, although culturally different, both participants tend to be members of their respective dominant society groups, are members of the same special interest groups, and share the *cultural orientation* to diversity-based interactions. In this case, both are implicitly focused on an interaction goal unrelated to the cultural differences between them, and both share a commitment to solving the well-meaning culture clashes (Brislin et al., 1986) that interfere with the attainment of that goal.

In contrast, minority individuals frequently approach diversity-based interactions from the *ethnic* and/or the *oppression orientation*. Those who have personally experienced systematic oppression or who have been enculturated to expect systematic oppression may operate from the *oppression orientation*. They expect to be mistreated. They feel powerless against oppression and discrimination. Anger and rage build up. They want justice, not just for the situation at hand, but for the long-term oppression experiences of their group. Their experience tells them that the solution to all problems lies in overthrowing the oppression that has plagued them and their ancestors, families, and peers.

Individuals who derive important personal identity from ethnicity are likely to operate from an *ethnic orientation*, placing a high value on ethnic markers and the underlying heritage they symbolize. They do not want to have to give up their ethnicity to succeed. They want to be free to "walk-the-walk" and "talk-the-talk" in a respectful multicultural society. Ethnicity historically has been a very important central empowerment tool for minority groups, increasing personal and social solidarity as well as political leverage against oppression. As a consequence, many minority group members operate from an orientation that combines the assumptions of both the *ethnic* and the *oppression orientations.*

All Americans find themselves in diversity-based interactions on a daily basis in their everyday lives. In today's world, we cannot escape talking and working with people of different cultural, racial, and ethnic backgrounds and different diversity orientations. Our personal, social, and economic success in a multicultural society will depend on our ability to have productive diversity-based interactions and relationships.

Successful diversity-based interactions begin with self-knowledge. It is critical for members of America's multicultural society to discover their own individual diversity orientations, to develop an understanding of how these orientations came out of their personal life experiences, and to explore how these orientations might affect their interactions with others. It is equally critical for all Americans to learn to recognize these orientations in those with whom they interact. By doing so, the chances of identifying conflicting goals and expectations before they become problematic are increased. People need to interpret the behavior of others by taking into account the different kinds of experiences and emotions that can complicate even the most straightforward diversity interaction.

## WHICH INDIVIDUAL IS MOST LIKE YOU?

One person may be repulsed and angered by the cultural traditions of another, who is, in turn, puzzled and hurt by this rejection. Which individual is most like you? Can you understand and empathize with the point of view of the other?

One person may adopt behaviors of another group in order to show respect and good will, only to be rejected and ridiculed by another who finds the behaviors presumptuous and inappropriate. Which individual is most like you? Can you understand and empathize with the point of view of the other?

One person may find relief and release by venting rage over a controversial issue, while another might find this angry behavior shocking and bewildering because s/he does not understand the full scope of the feelings engendered by experiences of discrimination. Which individual is most like you? Can you understand and empathize with the point of view of the other?

Grief and pain are overwhelming to some individuals who have experienced oppression, while these emotions seem exaggerated and overdramatized to those who have not experienced the full impact of systematic discrimination first hand. Which individual is most like you? Can you understand and empathize with the point of view of the other?

Anxiety and guilt cause denial in those who have been privileged, while denial reaffirms the existence of systematic discrimination and mistreatment to those for whom oppression has been a way of life. Which individual is most like you? Can you understand and empathize with the point of view of the other?

These three orientations to diversity can provide insight about the spectrum of expectations, feelings, and assumptions that surround daily relationships with others in a diverse society. The human multicultural experiment that faces us in the twenty-first century provides an immense challenge to humankind. The best chance for meeting this challenge comes from a better understanding of how really varied the emotional and intellectual contexts of diversity interaction can be, and how different people experience it.

## REFERENCES

Brislin, R. W., Cushner, K., Cherrie, C., & Yong, M. 1986. *Intercultural Interactions: A Practical Guide*. Beverly Hills: Sage Publications.

Farley, J. 1995. *Majority-Minority Relations*. Englewood Cliffs: Prentice Hall.

Goodenough, W. H. 1961. Comment on Cultural Evolution. *Daedalus* 90:521–528.

Klopf, D. 1991. *Intercultural Encounters: The Fundamentals of Intercultural Communication*. Englewood, CO: Morton Publishing Co.

Montague, A. 1964. *The Concept of Race*. New York: Free Press.

———1965. *The Idea of Race*. Lincoln: The University of Nebraska Press.

Oberg, K. 1979. Culture Shock and the Problems of Adjustment in New Cultural Environments. In *Toward Internationalism: Readings in Cross-Cultural Communication*. E. Smith & L. Luce (eds). Rowley, MA: Newbury House.

Parillo, V. 1994. *Strangers to These Shores*. New York: McMillan Publishing.

Spradley, J. P. & McCurdy, D. W. 1989. *Anthropology: The Cultural Perspective*. Prospect Heights, IL: Waveland Press.

# 6

# Portrait of a Minority

## Tyson Gibbs

## MINORITY POPULATIONS

From the early 1950s, through the mid-1960s, Americans considered the United States a "melting pot," a place where people from around the world mixed, and became *American*. The prevalent view during this roughly fifteen-year period was that anyone, regardless of country of origin, could prosper economically using the unwritten guiding principles of the work ethic. The work ethic principles stressed diligence to one's job honesty in business transactions and loyalty to the company that hired you. This idealized view of the American society as a melting pot was shattered by Glazer and Moynihan (1963), who studied immigrants from different countries who lived in New York City. They discovered that third-generation children (who looked like their parents, used the same language as their parents, and ate the same foods as their older relatives), voted differently, felt differently about issues of education and male/female relationships (Peoples & Bailey 1991:373). In effect, they were essentially as different from one another as their grandparents were from their ancestors. What Glazer and Moynihan discovered was that America was not a melting pot, and that the strength found in groups bonding together because of national origin, language, religious beliefs, customs, or group traditions were the ties that maintained ethnic boundaries (Peoples & Bailey 1991). Attempts to fully integrate and assimilate different cultural groupings by labeling them American, accomplished little toward breaking the protective effects that these groups found by maintaining their cultural roots. This study of the immigrant population living in New York City eventually resulted in the concept of *ethnic minority*.

### Ethnic Minority

An *ethnic minority* population is distinguished from the majority population by internal adoption, and practice, of customs, religion, dress, food habits, language, and values that promote group cohesiveness. The majority population will often distinguish *ethnic minority* group members by attributes that are easily identifiable —skin tone, dress, language, and perceived behavior. The adoption of easily identifiable attributes for *ethnic minorities* by the majority population promotes the idea of "we" and "they." *Ethnic minority* group members, in order to successfully compete for survival with the majority population, generally will take one of three options. The first is an attempt at imitating the value system, customs, language, and cultural behaviors of the majority population. Such attempts at survival can result in a measure of success by the *ethnic minority* members if their actions are accepted by the majority population. Adopting the customary behaviors of the majority population can also result in ostracism from fellow ethnic minority group members, because such actions can be viewed as traitorous. The second option for successful competition with the majority population is for the ethnic minority group member to promote their cultural heritage through ceremony, dress, food habits, language, or other distinguishable behaviors that set their group apart from the majority population. Such action from the ethnic minority group further supports the "we"and "they" concept, providing the majority population with information for purposes of acceptance, because the majority can clearly see differences, and the differences are something tolerable, or the majority can reject the ethnic minority group because the differences are more than the majority population is to accept. The last option is for the *ethnic minority* group to attempt to live in both cultures by adopting habits from their own minority group and habits from the majority population. Attempts to survive using the "foot in each camp" method generally place the ethnic group member as an outsider in both populations. African-American populations are distinguished by their participation, as ethnic minority group members, in all of the options described above. The internal struggle for survival by African-Americans using these options, in addition to their usually easy identification because of their skin tone, makes them the classic ethnic minority population. In American society, any group that bears the phenotype or outward skin tone of shades of light brown to very dark will bear the label of *African American,* and, in general, such ascription will imply negative behavioral attributes.

## Cultural Minority

The concept of a *cultural minority* is to describe population groups that have limited access to power. Cultural minority group members are distinguishable by ascription of the majority population and by self-identification. The majority population maintains power and control through promoting the differences between *cultural minority* groups, their purported goals, and the agenda of the majority population as incompatible activities. The *cultural minority* group members may seek to achieve shared power through a promotion of their population needs when such needs can be identified as resulting from the lack of attention from the majority population. All *African-Americans* have been ascribed values and goals by the majority population that are stated as incompatible with the national concept of being an American. Such ascriptions are the stuff that promotes the ethnic minority group members as one single-minded body, incapable of assimilation into the value stream of the typical American. In effect, *African-Americans* are systematically kept from power through this technique of promoting value differences between them and the majority white population.

### Racial Minority

The concept of *racial minorities* promotes the visible skin distinctions between population groups living in the United States. Such distinctions are developed, formulated, and used by the majority population to maintain distances between groups. Recent Louis Harris polls taken over the last ten years, 1985 thru 1995, continually point out that in America, both the majority white population and the minority African-American population do believe that the perceived differences between them keep the two groups apart. *Racial minorities* are distinguishable by their ascribed skin tones—yellow (Asian), black (African), brown (Hispanic), or red (Native American). Such attributes as "colors" are blurred in 1990s American society as a result of admixture of the different population groups over the last 400 plus years. Yet, many minority group members refer to themselves as black or brown to promote unity within the group. African-Americans and some Hispanic Americans have used the color label to identify themselves with their countries of origin or their perceived political unity.

### African Americans as the Classic Minority

The Merriam-Webster *Dictionary* defines classic as—"Notable, e.g., the best example." Using this definition, African-Americans are the "classic" ethnic minority group. African-Americans fit all three categories of minority population—ethnic, cultural, and racial minority. Although generations of African-Americans have lived in the United States, they cannot claim status as ethnic nationals because they never had ownership of the land. African-Americans, while occupying some mayoral, state legislative, congressional, and city council seats, are small in numbers, and many of the cities in which African-American mayors govern are plagued with low tax bases, high crime, and poor infrastructure conditions. All of these differential accesses to political and monetary power, coupled with the easy identification because of their skin tones, clearly establishes the African-American as the classic minority.

## WHO ARE THE AFRICAN-AMERICANS?

The label African-American is a compromise label that is the result of many years of struggle within a group of people living in America to develop an internal sense of identity that separates their group from other ethnic groups. African-

Americans have skin tones that range from very light to extremely dark. The label African-American encompasses much more than the simple identification of a racially based group with a common point of origin in Africa. Concealed in this label is a sense of historical identity, political ideology, group identity, and survival strategy as a minority living in a country whose majority population is of another ethnic and racial category.

Historically, African-Americans were brought into the United States mainly from the West Coast of Africa (that part of Africa with country names such as Nigeria, Sierra Leone, Liberia, Ivory Coast, Guinea, etc.). From the late 1600s until the late 1800s, African-Americans were thought of as *slaves*, because the term depicted the occupation of most of the people with dark skin tones. After the 1870s, when most people of African descent were freed as slaves,  several terms were introduced to describe this population of people. The label *Freedmen* was used because it indicated the new-found status of a people who were freed as slaves, freed before slavery had legally ended, or otherwise freed from the bonds of slavery. *Colored people* was also a very popular term for people of African descent. This term called attention to the complexion of the skin, and reenforced the concept that we (meaning white people, or people whose origins were mainly European in origin), are different from them (people of African descent). It is important to emphasize here that many African-Americans during the late to early 1900s used these labels to describe themselves.

The label *Negro* became popular during the early 1900s. This label may have gained popularity as a result of anthropological attempts at describing the four major races of humans: Negroid, Caucasoid, Australoid, and Mongoloid. Many people of African descent used this term to describe themselves, rejecting the *colored* label as more demeaning. The anthropological definition of *Negro* during this time period referred to those dark-skinned people living south of the Sahara in Africa.The term *black* became a label that resulted from the civil rights movements of the 1960s. During this time, many people of African descent decided to adopt this label to symbolize their association with dark-skinned people who live in other parts of the world. The label *black* was also intended to be a statement of the way people of African descent could unite themselves as a political group (Anderson 1990:2). But not all people readily adopted the label *black*. The label *Afro-American* was alternately used with the label *black*, while some people of African descent preferred to stick with the label *Negro*. Indeed, many other dark-skinned people, particularly older individuals, continued to call themselves *colored*.

What followed the 1960s was an internal political struggle between black intellectuals (those who were teachers and promoters of Black Studies), militant blacks (those whose politics included using any means necessary to gain parity with white America), and the general body of people of African descent (all those remaining who formed the general mass of blacks and whose income ranged from very poor to wealthy). Persons who did not wish to actively participate in the various attempts evolving to achieve civil rights through violence continue to call themselves *Negroes*, following the lead of the Reverend Martin Luther King, Jr., who used that particular label in many of his speeches. Although the civil rights issues are not as prominent in 1990s as they were in the 1960s, the split that occurred between different generations, income levels, and political ideologies over labeling continues to separate the African-American population into different communities and groupings. In the 1990s, the labels *black* and *African-American* are the most popular. This internal struggle within the black community pointed out to other Americans for the first time that not all people of African descent are of a single mind.

The importance of this discussion about labeling people of African descent who now reside in the United States is linked to the ideas of a minority group or population struggling to establish their own identity and finding their place in American society. The struggle is both internal and external since not all black people agree with, or readily adopt, the label changes. For example, the Bureau of Census (1989) indicates that there are over 29.3 million people who self-identify as black Americans. There are millions of dark-skinned people in the United States, who prefer to identify with their country of origin (e.g., Nigerians, West Indians, Jamaicans, Cubans, Ghanians, or Puerto Ricans, etc.) rather than be identified as "black Americans." With this comes the problems of overgeneralization of all black people into a black category that is then overgeneralized to the African-American. Black people who simply are lumped into this category, those who do not identify with the African-American, resent this practice, and African-Americans perceive the tendency to have serious consequences to their identity. Clearly, the external perceptions about the changes of label from *Negro, Afro-American, or black American* to *African-American* may be perceived as an exercise in folly, since everyone in America is an American. But, for many African-Americans, the rights that come with the label American have not yet fully manifested themselves. Many African-Americans continue to see that educational opportunities, community development chances, economic fortunes, good health, well-being, and status have yet to materialize for the vast majority of the black community.

## DEMOGRAPHIC PROFILE OF AFRICAN-AMERICANS

The overall trend is that African-Americans are leaving the rural areas for more metropolitan cities. The U.S. Bureau of Census (1989) indicated that over 80 percent of the African-American population now resides in what is called the "Central City." African-Americans now represent approximately 12 percent of the total population in the United States. The Bureau of Census estimates the actual number at 29.3 million people. This figure reflects a 14 percent increase in total population since the 1980 census, with about 8 percent of the African-American population being over the age of 65 years. This overall increase in the African-American population also reflects a greater percentage increase in population than that for the white population during the same time period. The overall median age for African-Americans is 27.3 years. African-American males have a median age of 25.8 years, compared to 28.8 for females (U.S. Bureau of Census 1989:1). The increase in population can be attributed to the excess births of African-Americans over deaths. Significantly, 16 percent of the total increase in population was due to immigrants from countries whose skin is dark and, because of that, are labeled as African-American.

Recall the earlier discussion of immigrants of African descent from other countries who do not classify themselves as African-Americans, but who identify with their country of origin. The Bureau of Census has not grappled with this problem of labeling all dark-skinned people now living in this country as African American, despite the fact that their language, customs, and political viewpoints may be quite different from those of African descent who were born in the United States. Furthermore, not all people of African descent born in the United States fully accept other dark-skinned people from other parts of the world. For many native-born African-Americans, the habits of Nigerians, Jamaicans, dark-skinned Cubans, Puerto Ricans, or other West Indians are as foreign to them as these customs might be to white Americans. Unfortunately, many white Americans, Japanese-Americans, Chinese-Americans, and other ethnic Americans often lump all people with dark skin into the one racial/cultural category or grouping, ignoring many of the specific cultural differences that supersede color of skin. This points out the most serious limitation of racial groupings or categorizations based on a single trait such as color. The resulting overgeneralization obscures far more than it clarifies.

Although the African-American population tends to be concentrated in the central city or metropolitan areas, well over half of the population continues to reside in the southern regions of the United States. The states with the highest concentrations of African-Americans include Virginia, North Carolina, South Carolina, Georgia, Tennessee, Mississippi, Louisiana, Florida, and Alabama. These states have experienced a 4 percent growth in their African-American populations since the 1980 Census. The Census also shows that in the northern and western portions of the United States, while 90 percent of the African-American population tends to live in metropolitan areas, in the South only 70 percent live in such communities. Linked with this rise in African-Americans living in central city is the flight of white Americans and others from these metropolitan communities. The term *White Flight* was coined during the late 1960s and early 1970s to label this move of the white Americans from the cities to the suburban areas. In many respects, in these central cities the low tax base, decaying inner core, and low levels of economic activity and urban development are the result of poor African-Americans, Hispanic Americans, and southeast Asian immigrants moving in to occupy the inner city core areas vacated by the whites. If current population trends continue, by the year 2020 more than half of the U.S. population will be able to trace their origins to Africa, Asia, Spanish-speaking regions, and the Pacific Islands (Henry 1990:28). Henry also projects that the Hispanic and Asian populations will increase an average of 20 percent, while the African-Americans will increase approximately 12 percent and the white population of America will increase less than 2 percent. The implications of this projected monumental change in the U.S. population base are staggering. The relationship of these groups, currently all minority groups, to the power structure will change considerably. For example, in the arena of politics, one can expect the formation of new alliances between these minority groups in economics. These alliances may impact "who will find work" or "who will control the nation's finances." It is certain that ethnic tensions will increase, raising the question of how this new mosaic population will be governed." In education, questions will arise as to the language of public education, the number of languages children will or should learn, and the types of history that will be taught. Currently, the current population figures and other issues already haunt many school boards around the country.

## EDUCATIONAL ISSUES

The overall percentage of African-Americans completing high school in 1988 in the South who were over 25 years of age was approximately 60 percent. This percentage for the South is slightly different than the almost 68 percent of African-Americans completing school in the North and West. The 60 percent figure for the South represents a 15 percent increase in the number of African-American adults over the age of 25 completing high school since the 1980 census of population. In the North and West, the increase of 25-year-old African-Americans completing school was 10 percent. African-Americans over 25 years of age completing college in all areas of the United States, numbered 11.3 percent of the total African-American population in 1988. The 11.3 percent figure, is an increase of 3.4 percent over the 1980 figure of 7.9 percent.

Completing high school at the minimum, and completing college as an ultimate goal, generally are considered to be key elements for personal development in the United States. These key elements are especially important for individuals seeking a way out of poverty. The above figures for 25-year-old African-Americans completing high school in the South, the North and the West illustrate a major concern in African-American communities. Low levels of education have been linked to increased teenage pregnancies, drug use and abuse, increased influence of gangs on teenagers and youth, and decreased chances for job opportunities for African-Americans under the age of 25 years. Indeed, the over 40 percent African-American males who fill the nations jails have very limited high school education. Forty percent is extremely high because the African-American population is only 12 percent of the total population in the United States.

The issue that is paramount is, "Why is there a problem of limited schooling with its negative consequences in the African-American community?" Many policy-makers, educators, civil groups, and corporations are pondering this question. John P. Newport (1989) relates the possible reasons for such dire statistics. According to Newport, the African-American population has an approximate 30 percent poverty rate. Much of the discussion about issues of low levels of education, poor job skills, increased teenage pregnancy, or youth joining gangs relates to those persons living in poverty, and must be separated from those African-Americans who are not poor. Despite the percentage being at approximately 30 percent, most other Americans tend to stereotype the "poor" or "poverty" tag to the entire African-American population. Many issues are put forth as reasons for the problems found in this population. Newport gives further cause for consideration. Some problems relate to the lack of male role models, with more than 37 out of 100 African-American men out of the eligibility category for marriage. This means that for every 100 African-American women, they are competing for 63 men. Other issues cited a focus on questions of self-esteem in children, which are difficult to improve when the role models for the children lack the necessary parenting skills to give to their children.The living environment in poor communities provides little toward increasing self-image. On the political front, many African-Americans cite the lack of interest in the African-American poor by those African-Americans not living in poverty. These scholars believe that such negligence by the more affluent African-Americans is paramount in keeping poor communities poor, because the affluent have skills, information, and knowledge about survival that could alter the futures of many poor African-Americans. Aside from these issues mentioned by Newport there is the overall sense that the poor communities are losing ground annually. Whites have almost 30 percent more in median income than African-Americans at all levels. And, African-American males aged 25–44 suffer from a 30 percent unemployment rate, compared to approximately 15 percent for white males.

## FAMILY INFORMATION

An examination of the African-American family is also enlightening. The percentage differences for families living as married couples declined only slightly between 1980 and 1988. The Census data indicates that only 53 percent of the African-Americans lived as married couples during this period. The number of single heads of households rose from 40 to 43 percent during this eight-year period between 1980 and 1988, while the number of male headed households rose from 4 to 6 percent (U.S. Bureau of Census 1989:7–9). The South had the largest percentage of married couples at 56 percent. The North and West had 49 percent married African-American couples. There were more female headed households in the North and West, 45 percent. In the South in 1988, African-American female headed households numbered 41 percent. In many respects, such data as these fuel the current arguments that almost half of the African-Americans living in the United States live in single parent households headed mainly by females. These arguments taken to the ultimate conclusion re-enforce the idea that the African-American family structure is crumbling at the central core, if the central core is defined as the nuclear family, consisting of father, mother, and siblings. On the other side of this argument, African-American Dorothy Height suggests, "social analysts...refuse to acknowledge the impact of racial discrimination on education and employment. They (social analysts) define a family as a social/economic/political unit with a man as its head. For black people, this definition has never applied. Throughout history, many black women have had to accomplish (economic survival)...without male partners"(1989:137). For many African-American scholars, the emphasis by non-black scholars on the affects of discrimination in the aftermath of slavery undermines the survival of African-Americans in spite of discrimination.

A second critique of the structure of the more typical African-American family suggests that African-Americans are no longer under the shackles of slavery, and therefore should not be excused for continuing to circumvent the boundaries of marriage and the traditional family structure. In case of point, Daniel Moynihan (1965) wrote of the disintegration of the African-American family and suggested corrective social actions. However, modern African-American scholars tend to take the view of Leanor B. Johnson: "While the black matriarchy and its role in socializing children and marriage stability receive(s) enormous attention...there exists a conspicuous absence of studies on dual job/career families, sibling relationships, dating and courtship, and housing and social policies" (1990:101). The usual tendency is to classify African-American families as varied in their manifestation, instead of lacking or showing deficits.

## SIGNIFICANT ECONOMIC ISSUES FOR AFRICAN-AMERICANS

The African-American household median income for the period from 1980–1989 was about 55 percent of the white household median income of approximately $32, 270 dollars. The overall median income showed no particular trend during this period. The purchasing power did increase a modest 1.1 percent. Income in African-American female headed households was between 50 and 60 percent of African-American male headed households. This trend reflects the national trend of women earning much less than their male counterparts. Approximately 30 percent of all African-American households live below the poverty level. What is not in these data are the high rates of unemployment experienced by African-American males. In many large urban centers, the unemployment rate for the African-American male between ages 18 and 50, ranges between 15 and 40 percent. In effect, the continued poverty in the African-American communities creates what many social analysts are calling "A Permanent Underclass."

There are many other aspects and issues of the economic status of African-American families to be considered. Julianne Malveaux (1990:135) discusses some of these, some of which have already been discussed in this chapter: a higher than white family divorce rate, a much higher number of female headed households, a greater percentage of the population deferring marriage, and a substantial decline in jobs in the manufacturing sector of the U.S. economy. These changes in society often affect the African-American much more than other ethnic groups. With the exception of the Native American population as one of the older and currently the largest minority group in the United States, African-Americans have not shown continued and sustained progress in all sectors of the economy. However, the fact that 70 percent of the African-American population lives above the poverty level is an important fact that often is missed when discussing African-American economic progress.

The issues of economic progress are the same issues that cross the questions about family structure and stability; the problems of education and opportunities opened up by educational progress; and the issues of ethnic identity for a minority population, living in a country where the majority is another group. These issues are questions of access to all sectors of society, the ability to reach the higher levels of the work force (less than 2 percent of the corporate executive officers of major corporations are African-American), and the problem of defining goals that are compatible with the majority population concept of the work ethic. Many African-Americans have received the label of "Uncle-Tom," "Sell-Out," or "Handkerchief Head" when they express work ethics and life goals similar to the majority white population. In recent times, such persons as Supreme Court Justice Clarence Thomas and economist Thomas Sowell, both successful in their fields, have received these labels. For many African-Americans, the question of economic survival often means walking a fine line between what is considered appropriate behavior for an African-American and what it really takes to achieve any economic goal in American society. Personal politics, often in the form of attempting to stay within the boundaries of what is right as an African-American, can either propel an individual forward because of the strength found in group conformity or such attempts to "do the right thing" can keep the person searching for an identity and acceptance, and from fully achieving their career goals.

## OTHER ETHNIC ISSUES

The problems facing African-Americans in the United States are not unlike those being experienced by other minorities: living in a population where the majority is of another race; equality in job opportunities and the handling of applications for jobs; lack of loans for housing; and limited opportunities in education. Quite often, the term "racism" has been used to capture what many African-Americans believe is the essence of African-American problems with the other ethnic groups in the United States. The term has been used for so many problem areas that it has become a cliché that further separates the majority white population from the African-American population. Many whites view the term racism as a word that stands for, "I can't make it using the work ethic system, so I will scream racism as an excuse for my failures." Indeed, a prominent African-American, Andrew Young, once ambassador to the United Nations for the United States, echoed these sentiments in a speech given at the West Virginia Cultural Center in Charleston, West Virginia. Ambassador Young described racism as "stubbing a toe...while it is somewhat painful and annoying...there are greater problems such as gender and poverty." Responding to Ambassador Young's comments, Dr. Betty Cleckly quotes Derrick Bells' statement in the May 6, 1991 issue of *Newsweek:* "In a society that is becoming increasingly multicolored, there is no escaping the ancient conflicts, the race relations among all the races—Asians and Hispanics, as well as African-American and white—have never been easy in the United States. But the conflict between blacks and whites remains particularly thorny because of America's history of slavery and discrimination."

The concept of racism is one that carries sentiments of the history of African-Americans in the United States. This history is one that has slavery, widespread racially targeted discrimination against African-Americans specifically, and massive attempts to keep African-Americans out of mainstream America. With the passage of the 1964 Civil Rights Act, many of the overt forms of the past few hundred years of discrimination were challenged. Subsequent legislation outlawed and provided legal remedies for changing most individual and corporate discriminatory behavior against the African-American group. Many African-Americans took advantage of the "opening-up" of American society and made great achievements as a result of these new laws. The African-American middle class grew at an unprecedented rate, to a degree never before witnessed in the United States. In the 1990s, the question remaining in the minds of many white Americans is: "Why are African-Americans still calling for an end to racism, given these monumental achievements in the African-American community?"

The fact is, not all segments of the African-American community are crying racism in a loud voice. Many are fulfilling their version of the American Dream of "a reasonably good job, children, and a house outside of central city." Recall the earlier statement that many affluent African-Americans do little to assist those living in poverty, in a particularly overt way. Not all African-Americans believe that there is anything wrong with the way of conducting personal economic growth and development via the work ethic touted by the majority white population. In fact, the African-American middle class, although not at the same economic level as the mostly white middle class, has adopted the values of "working hard, a conservative approach in financial matters, education as a major key to improving one's station in life, and achievement as something earned, not given."

## CONCLUSION

The African-American population in the United States is a heterogeneous grouping of persons whose skin tone ranges from light brown to dark complexions. This grouping of individuals is heterogenous because it encompasses all peoples from around the world whose skin tones fit within the color range of brown to black. The persons within this grouping speak many different languages, have a wide variety of customs and habits, believe in a multiple array of religions, and are easily distinguishable by their skin tones. Skin tone (color) is the classic method for identifying a racial minority. This African-American population has limited access to political and economic power in America, relegating them to the status of a cultural minority. The wide distinctions between the poor and the middle-class African-Americans also were pointed out in this chapter. Yet, the limits to power affect not only the poor group, but also the middle class equally as much. The self-identification of African-Americans as an ethnic minority group and the ascription of African-Americans as an ethnic minority group by the majority population further solidifies the African-American as the classic minority population group. As was pointed out earlier, such ascription comes from the linkage of skin tone and extends to expected language, behavior characteristics, and expected customary activities.

The African-American population is not one group with a single mind. There is a range of political, economic, and social ideologies that run the gamut of the American belief system and routine cultural activities. What generally appears in the media, particularly on television and in the movies, is the portrayal of African-Americans living below the poverty level. Many African-Americans have grown up for generations without the benefit of knowing poverty and it sequelae. As was indicated earlier, only 70 percent of the African-American population lives above poverty. What most Americans know about African-Americans comes from images of the actions of the poor.

## REFERENCES

Anderson, T. 1990. Black studies: Overview and theoretical perspectives. In *Black Studies*. T. Anderson (ed). Pullman, WA: State University Press, pp. 1–10.

Glazer, N. & Moynihan, D. 1963. *Beyond the Melting Pot*. Cambridge: Harvard University Press.

Height, D. 1989. Self-Help—A black tradition. *Nations Magazine* (July 24/31), pp. 136–138.

Henry, W. 1990. Beyond the melting pot. *Time Magazine* (April 9), pp. 28–31.

Johnson, L. B. 1990. Perspective on black family empirical research—1978. In *Black Families*, 2nd edition. H. Pipes McAdoo (ed). Newbury Park, CA: Sage Publications, pp. 91–106.

Malveaux, J. 1990. The economic statuses of black families. In *Black Families*. 2nd edition. H. Pipes McAdoo (ed). Newbury Park, CA: Sage Publications, pp. 133–147.

Moynihan, D. 1965. *The Negro Family: The Case for National Action*. Washington, DC: The United States Labor Department.

Newport, J. 1989. Steps to help the urban black man. *Fortune Magazine* (December 18), pp. 164–166.

Peoples, J. & Bailey, G. 1991. *Humanity*. New York: West Publishing Company.

United States Bureau of Census. 1989. Washington, DC: Government Printing Office.

Woolf, H. B. (ed). 1974. *The Merriam-Webster Dictionary*. New York: Pocket Books.

# 7

# When White Americans Are a Minority

John Hartigan, Jr.

Throughout this country's history there has been an emphatic connection between whiteness and privilege. Whites, broadly speaking, have maintained and reproduced a powerful system of social status in which they occupy the most prestigious ranks. The mere fact of white skin color has long entailed a host of freedoms, priviledges, and assumptions of superiority that Americans with other skin tones have been systematically denied. As well, in a manner both mundane and routine, whites have long stood as the model of normative cultural experience in this country. In political contests, advertising, scientific studies, and popular cultural productions, whites have represented the norm in social matters, in contrast to which peoples of color have been regarded as "racial." Though whiteness has always been a racial identity, the cultural dominance that whites have achieved has been such that they seem simply "normal," while the differences of others are marked as "racial" in nature, with "race" referring to a complex of physiologically "permanent" features and differences linked to an assumed "inferior" status (Frankenberg 1993; Jackson 1993; Page & Thomas 1994). But for as long as whiteness has represented a dominant social order in this country, there have been whites that were not able to access or take advantage of the prestige and many privileges that this order entails. Whiteness, as a mode of social dominance, has always been unevenly inhabited. The upper-class status of certain whites, particularly those of Anglo-Saxon descent, belonging to Protestant faiths (WASP), long ago was established as a crucial factor in determining what counts as whiteness. Whites continually have been internally differentiated, and intraracial hierarchies based on class status have operated in this country since the English colonists first arrived. Amidst all of the internal means by which whites have drawn distinctions among themselves, the category of "poor white" consistently has been the most debased and contemptuously held position. But is the relatively disadvantaged situation of poor whites equitable with the condition of racial minorities in this country?

Before answering this question, we need to consider another aspect of how the status of whiteness and the position of whites as a majority population in the United States is being recast. This country is undergoing very broad and fundamental demographic changes. In all but three of the nation's ten largest cities, whites are now a clear minority. In the state of California, the most populous state in this country, whites will loose their majority standing by the year 2000. By 2010, the same situation will hold true in Texas as well. Linked with these demographic shifts, are the transformations of the popular culture and political landscapes in this country. While it may not be the case that the equation between whiteness and "mainstream" identity is forever sundered, the associations between minority status and social debasement or forms of systematic exclusion are being challenged. As a result, we have to begin thinking very specifically about what we mean when we talk about minorities and the majority in this country.

Before examining more closely the situation of whites in major urban areas or the cultural identity of "poor whites," we need to understand a key difficulty in considering any group of white Americans as a minority. Whiteness has long stood as the antithesis of being a minority. The vast, complex processes of "assimilation" in the United States have relied upon whiteness as both an implicit and, at times, explicit point of culmination (Higham 1988; Sollors 1986; Takaki 1993). As immigrant groups from Europe and Asia arrived here, their social and cultural differences from native-born Americans were manifold. In the process of adapting to the social mores in this country, members of these ethnic groups closely studied the manners, modes of language usage, and styles of dress of upper- and middle-class "successful" white Americans. Their "progress" at assimilation was measured by the extent to which these people managed to fashion a public persona that replicated many of the behavioral nuances of white, middle-class Americans. European groups were most facile at this process, largely because white Americans were more willing to recognize a shared cultural heritage or identity with these immigrants. But be aware that the ability to adopt a "mainstream," white persona was not equal for all Europeans. Irish, Italians, and Slavic immigrants each went through a phase in which their cultural differences from Anglo-Americans were regarded in racial terms (Saxton 1990; Roediger 1991, 1993). These phases, though, were not characterized by the duration of the racial regard for Asian immigrants, the currently arriving peoples of Latin American countries, nor for the African-American population at large.

In concert with the demographic changes mentioned above, the cultural identity of white Americans is being remolded as a declining emphasis is placed on maintaining whiteness as a homogeneous identity. The ideology that equated the process of Americanization with a "melting pot," by which people seamlessly became part of the "mainstream," is losing much of its efficacy. So-called "white ethnics" are reemerging from this "mainstream" as many white Americans articulate an interest in being recognized as members of subgroups (ethnic in origin) within the broader order of whiteness (Lieberson 1985; Alba 1990). Where whiteness once stood as a culmination of efforts by European Americans to blend into a background of similarly identified, unobtrusively characterized citizens, whites now find a greater diversity acceptable among those they recognize as similar to themselves. There are lines drawn and limits to this recognition, as we will examine next, but the point here is that if we are going to recognize some groups of white Americans as a "minority," it will have to be in this context where the connection between whiteness and a "mainstream" identity in this country is being reconfigured.

While the meaning and character of whiteness are changing, so, too, is the significance of the term "minority." The meaning of "minority" has developed through political contests and the formulation of public policy in this country. The term has been practically synonymous with "black," "Hispanic,"and "Asian" In public conversations, the term often has been used as a supposedly polite or inoffensive way to refer to racial groups generically. But as African-Americans, Hispanic Americans, and Asian Americans have become increasingly politicized, "minority" has gained recognition as a viable means of asserting and articulating a set of collective interests and for claiming self-representation for a group. That the term now might be applied equally to white Americans is indicative of the profound changes underway in this country.

Lest we trivialize the history and political significance of "minority," we need to be clear about what the term's connotations are. Two meanings are most frequently attributed to being a "minority." Primarily, a "minority" is disadvantaged socially and economically by being marked as a member of a group that has little status or is considered to be different and often "inferior" from members of the "mainstream." This definition, in turn, arises from the term's fundamental point of reference: the fact that a group is literally outnumbered in a society. The disadvantage that characterizes the conditions of a "minority" can be determined structurally through processes such as residential segregation and institutional racism, by which members of certain groups (African-Americans in particular) are denied jobs and access to capital in the form of loans. Or, this disadvantage can be composed by a cultural prejudice held by individuals throughout the country that effects the life chances of "minority" people they encounter. Most often, these two modes of disadvantage are intertwined, where cultural stereotypes of minorities consistently assure that they will be denied easy access to society's paths for success.

By these two definitions, we can posit a basic relevance of the term "minority" to the conditions of certain white Americans: when they are disadvantaged and/or when they are outnumbered. As noted above, these conditions are met in the lives of "poor whites" and whites in certain urban areas. In some cases, these categorical orders coincide. For the sake of clear and full elaboration, though, each will be examined here in turn.

"Poor whites" constitute a discernible presence in the history of European settlement of North America and in the growth of the United States. Indeed, many of the earliest English colonists, drawn from the ranks of the desperately unemployed as well as from the prison population, provide the archetype for the category of "poor white." In colonial records and travelogues attention is given to a subgroup of whites considered constitutionally distinct from the majority of colonists, either by their lack of hygiene or by their willingness to shed most remnants of European behavioral standards for being "civilized" (Cooke 1976; Saxton 1990). As the fortunes of a strata of European settlers developed at a less than successful remove from their fellow whites, the distinctiveness (and hence the cultural stereotyping) of "poor whites" was solidified. The terms for designating "them" vary from "white trash" and "cracker" to "linthead" and "coonass," but what remains consistent is the conviction held by a majority of whites that there are some people in their midst who do not measure up to social standards and, hence, are to be held in contempt, and discouraged or prevented from gaining access to social privileges (Hartigan 1996a, n.d.).

The disadvantage that comes with being a minority derives both from structural conditions (largely economic) that deny people access to the wider society and through the stigma of being stereotyped. The basis of any stereotype of a person and a group is a collection of certain recognizable features or characteristics. These are generated and motivated—whether or not they are "real" in any ostensible sense—as an antithesis of characterizations of "mainstream" life-styles. The social disadvantage that confronts "poor whites," primarily is derived from the tradition of stereotypes that have emerged over the centuries, during which some whites always occupied positions of social degradation due to their poverty, ill-health, or "alien" customs. To fully understand what we can refer to as the "poor white tradition" (Cooke 1976), we need to recognize both the source of the anxiety and contempt embodied in stereotypes of such whites and the serious effects that these stereotypes have produced.

The most obvious assumption is that these stereotypes are simply economically determined. Whether in systems of class or caste, the "lower orders" in all countries tend to possess distinctive features, traits, and life-styles; the "poor" have long been regarded as a cultural grouping (Lewis 1966). But in the United States, this demographic strata has attained perhaps a greater degree of coherence given the convoluted matter of racial identity. While the stigma attached to being poor are severe in this country, they are doubly so when the person mired in poverty is white. "Poor whites" have never "just" been poor; they have been used by other whites to mark a cultural boundary between themselves and blacks. Historically, this emotionally fraught function was derived quite literally. White overseers were the physical mediators between slave owners and their slaves. The job of the overseer, deemed distasteful by whites with greater social standing, was as much to preserve the status of their employers as it was to harshly drive black slaves in their labors (Jordan 1969). During and after Reconstruction, the role of sharecropper included both whites and blacks, and whites who burned their neck and arms working in the hot sun ("rednecks") were contemptuously marked by the indistinctness of their situation from that of blacks (Williamson 1984).

But the symbolic position of "poor whites" does not rest solely on such occupational positions that blurred the social clarity of the race line. The degradation of white poverty, at least superficially, resembles the living conditions of many poor blacks. The stereotypes of "poor whites" as lazy, licentious, unwilling to work, and prone to drink and violence, are quite resonant with derogatory characterizations of African-Americans. While it would be difficult, and perhaps unfounded, to assert a simple equivalence between whites and blacks living in poverty, it is clear that the differences between these groups are not substantial enough to match the huge intellectual and emotional investment by whites in their historical conviction of racial superiority. In other words, every image or instance of "poor whites" challenges or undermines a host of implicit assumptions held by whites of their advantaged position in society.

The symbolic "distinctiveness" of poor whites in the imagination of white Americans arose from very concrete, physical sources. The "body" of poor whites derives its stereotyped quality largely from the diseases that have disproportionately effected this group, particularly in the Southern states (Marcus 1988; Etheridge 1988). Parasitic diseases such as hookworm or nutritional maladies like rickets produce disturbing physical effects. Poor whites, who were prone to such diseases, developed characteristic bodily deformities: malformed skulls, extremely scrawny frames, and "listless" facial expressions. Though such diseases are now largely treatable and effectively managed by public health officials, the impression of such physical "distinctiveness" remains an animating feature in perceptions of poor whites.

Though a tradition of being stereotyped is a primary factor in being a "minority," the core definition of the term is that of a socially disadvantaged group. Though the stereotypes that comprise the "poor white tradition" are substantial cultural matters, does it follow that this group has been consistently disadvantaged in relation to the mainstream of American culture? Both historically and in contemporary terms, the answer is yes. Historically, we could focus on the way poor whites were exploited economically and socially by wealthy whites throughout the 1800s in all regions of this country, from the mills of the Carolinas and New England to the mines of Colorado and California. A record of these situations is gradually being assembled by social historians who are slowly recognizing the cultural heritage produced by poor whites as a response to their economic and social predicaments (McWhiniey 1988; Flynt 1989; Bolton 1994). But, perhaps the most compelling case of how poor whites have been disadvantaged is found in the Eugenics movement that swept this country in the early 1900s.

Eugenicists were influential in promoting and eventually passing legislation that limited the number of immigrants that could come to this country. They backed such legislation out of a fear and conviction that "foreigners" were corrupting the character of the United States. But they were not solely concerned with immigration policy. Researchers like Henry Goddard and Charles Davenport, leaders in the field of eugenics, also fretted over the "racial poisons" produced in the breeding practices of poor whites (Rafter 1988). In a number of research studies, eugenicists examined the tangled social and familial relations of poor whites living predominantly in rural areas. They found that the "white race" was being corrupted "from within," and they argued that the threat posed to the nation could be checked only via severe regulations on which whites can reproduce. Coining terms like "moron" and "imbecile" to describe the social ineptitude that they found among "poor whites," Goddard and Davenport, along with many others, successfully pushed for sterilization of "unfit" whites to be mandated by state laws. These laws were ruled constitutional by the Supreme Court in 1927 and they remain in effect and in use today (Philip 1991; Larson 1995).

The historical disadvantage that characterizes poor whites, however, is not as clear cut, nor as debilitating, as that confronted by African-Americans and other minorities in this country. But it is a "tradition" that continues to this day, though in a pattern somewhat unfamiliar to those who study the way minorities have been historically disadvantaged in this country. The cultural differences between whites that have provoked emotional intraracial distinctions have been more developed in certain regions than in others. This is the particularly the case with the Appalachian states. Since the end of the Civil War and throughout most of this century, travel writers, missionaries, and folklorists traversing the mountains of West Virginia, Kentucky, and Tennessee have described an "alien" and "foreign" people (McNeil 1989). Not surprisingly, the "features" these travelers found among "hillbillies" were an antithesis of popular notions of what it meant to be an American in various periods (Shapiro 1978; Batteau 1990). White Americans, enamored of the social religion of "progress" in all things commercial and national, were appalled to find that "hillbillies" in this region lived in a "awckward" condition in a land that "time forgot." Such dismissive characterizations of these poor whites made the inhumane acts of the lumber and mining companies that exploited the land in Appalachia for generations seem scant cause for social indignation or political redress. Is it a coincidence that just when the effects of strip mining and unfair labor practices in this region were most pernicious in the 1960s, a host of comic stereotypes of "hillbillies" in popular television shows such as "The Beverly Hillbillies," "Green Acres," and "Hee Haw" made the condition of these people seem laughable rather than tragic? As James Bransome has argued, during the 1960s and 1970s when these shows aired, "if similar programs even approaching the maliciousness of these were broadcast on blacks, Indians, or Chicanos, there would be immediate public outcry from every liberal organization and politician in the country and a scathing editorial in the *New York Times* about the programs' 'lack of taste'" (1978:203). What is it that made "hillbillies" seem an appropriate target of this kind of comic debasements?

Part of the answer lies in the historic population shifts that occurred in this country from the 1920s through the 1960s. As the economic and social basis of Southern agriculture was radically transformed—first by the Depression, then by government farm policies—blacks and poor whites poured from the South, seeking fortune or at least a better life in the Midwest and in California (Daniel 1985). Called "hillbillies," "oakies," and "trash," these whites, generally poor, were greeted with contempt by whites already living in these destinations (Gregory 1989). Denied jobs and good housing, these poor whites served primarily as an exploitable source of labor, and, again, as a means of drawing the line between better-off whites and blacks or other minorities. Especially in the automobile factories of the North, white "hillbilly" were scorned by native whites who surmised that the "lazy" or "violent" tendencies of these whites were no different than the habits of the Southern blacks whom they had also come to despise. Most of the chronicles of the Great Migration stress that black migrants to the Midwest were viciously received

(Lehmann 1991; Jones 1992). But it is clear that many of the poor Southern whites who also made this trip were scarcely treated much better.

The migration of Southern whites and blacks to the Midwest touched off a process that is central to understanding how a certain portion of white Americans, today, constitute a minority. The direct result of this migration was "white flight" from major cities. As Southern migrants arrived throughout the 1940s and 1950s, native whites poured out of the Northern cities, heading to the fast-developing green fields of the suburbs. This population shift was given further impetus by the urban insurrections that erupted in the late 1960s and early 1970s. The riots marked a culmination of two key developments in American political culture: one was the civil rights movement, the other the "War on Poverty." The link between these two developments brings us to the core of the complex of issues raised by positing some white Americans as a minority group.

The political discourse that gives credence to "minority" as an affirmative representational order derives primarily from the civil rights movement. African-American leaders and community organizers asserted the rights of "minorities" to proper and effective political representation. From this perspective, it is odd, then, to apply "minority" to the status of certain poor whites, even though, as was shown above, their lives are disadvantaged, historically and currently, in relation to the white "mainstream." The oddity of such an assignation is underscored further when we take into account the "War on Poverty" that was unleashed just as the civil rights movement was achieving its greatest inroads in the public consciousness of white Americans. The "War on Poverty," for the first time, politicized images of "poor whites," proposing to remedy their condition in a manner similar to the forms of redress proposed for minority groups. The effect, initially, was to distract whites from the concerns that African-Americans were stridently raising. The crux of the matter in the ensuing discussion of the "War on Poverty" is that promoting or insisting upon a "minority" status for poor whites adversely effects the way political discussion of racism and racial identity are pursued in this country.

Many white Americans in the 1960s assumed, unquestionably, that the affluence that characterized the postwar time economic boom in the United States had uniformly benefited everyone (Piven & Cloward 1979). In part, this perception was based on the skewed view of the country offered by the suburban tracts to which so many whites were then moving. The issue of poverty surfaced for white Americans largely through the efforts of John F. Kennedy. In his 1960 campaign for the presidency, Kennedy used a tour through Appalachia to illustrate how a portion of white Americans lived in conditions of economic deprivation. His notion for a "War on Poverty" was taken up and vigorously pursued by president Lyndon Johnson in 1964. Many white Americans rallied to this cause, but this effort was not simply well intentioned. As the noted sociologist Barbara Ehrenreich has noted, the "War on Poverty" served as a means of "changing the subject" from the emotional and desperate conflict over the civil rights movement (1990:42–48). The specter of poor whites provided a compelling alternate image and subject of concern that distracted many Americans from the articulate and militant challenge being raised by blacks against white supremacy. Extending the "same" regard for poor whites as for other disadvantaged minority groups achieved a leveling effect in which "race" seemed to dissolve. In effect, both in terms of federal policy and the interests of volunteers and supporters, white Americans were willing to extend a degree of redress to the poor broadly rather than contend with the specifically racialist politics that the civil rights movement entailed.

This proposed dissolution of racialized modes of political discourse and policy was illusory; the riots in America's cities assured that "race" would not simply go away. "Poor whites" faded from view as politicians and the media fastidiously constructed an image of poverty that bore a black visage. Both in the 1960s and today, that image was ill-founded. Whites, then and now, compose the majority of the poor in this country. Based on media coverage of the plight of impoverished families and youths, which consistently emphasizes African-Americans, it is easy to forget that 66 percent of people in poverty are white. Only 29 percent of poor people are black. What makes the condition of poor African-Americans so terribly distressing is that they represent more than 30 percent of the black population in this country; poor whites represent only 10 percent of the white population. The poor among these racial groupings are also each minorities, but in very distinct forms.

The significance of "minority" in the United States in the 1990s derives from the term's equivalence with races, "racial" categories, and groups. Many Americans are compelled by the image of a "color-blind" society, hence the investment in terms like "minority" that do not explicitly invoke a racial calculus. But the effectiveness of "minority" for covering the forms of social disadvantage that effects a range of Americans is questionable when it comes to the matter of poor whites. Two dangers are preeminent in considering poor whites as a "minority." The first was made manifest in the wake of the urban riots. Economic and political efforts to assist minorities regularly neglected—if not outright excluded—poor whites in urban areas (Greenstone & Peterson 1973). Poor whites, hence, were put at a social and economic disadvantage by the attempts to counter the effects of inner-city poverty on blacks and Hispanic Americans. However, were this situation to be remedied by including poor whites in such programs as another "minority" group, then the attention to racism and its enduring effects would be blunted or altogether lost. "Minority," as applied to poor whites, flattens an awareness of the continuing cultural significance of race in this country. But this application is not solely detrimental; indeed, the connection between whites and minority status can perhaps provoke a rather profound revision on the connotations that "minority" carries.

Once more, consider the meaning of "minority"; it carries both a burden and a benefit: It implies "race" without reifying our assumptions of racial identities as static, timeless forms, inevitably hierarchist along a continuum of "superior" and "inferior." "Minority" gestures toward a future without "race" while refusing to neglect or negate the still-present effects of the racial history in this country. But the term is not a be-all and end-all category for conveying the scale or operation of social advantage and disadvantage in this country. One implicit assumption about "minority" groups is a carryover from racial stereotypes. "Minorities" are usually discussed as homogeneous cultural orders—they are all alike. The connection between whites and minority status, especially in the major cites, belies this assumption. The prime benefit of further exploring this connection could be that we develop a recognition of greater diversity within "minority" groups. Let us turn, finally, to the minority status of whites in the largest cities of the United States.

Whites who live in America's major cities today largely resisted the surge of "white flight" toward the suburbs. They are a diverse lot in terms of class and ethnic backgrounds. But to grasp fully the significance of their position as a minority, one more demographic phenomenon has to be factored in the 1990s version of white flight. Whites continue to pour in from urban areas. But the impetus for the current flight, one that often carries these whites from the state and region entirely, is the large influx of immigrants arriving in these cities on a regular basis. Where internal migration provided the catalyst for "white flight" in the 1960s and 1970s, today it is the arrival of foreigners that are impelling whites to leave altogether states like California, Texas, and New York.

There is an intriguing class distinction in this latter-day version of white flight. It is the less-affluent, less-educated whites that are leaving (Frey & Tilove 1995). In the past, upward mobility resulted in outward mobility as whites in the upper income brackets moved to typically more expensive suburban homes. This same class, though, forms a core of the whites remaining in urban areas today, while whites who are in direct competition with immigrants over jobs and social resources are deciding to pack up and leave. A significant portion of the whites who remain behind in these cities are those who can afford to hire cheap immigrant labor to tend their gardens, wash their clothes, and clean their homes in gated communities, or drive their children to and from private schools. This group seems an especially odd fit with the received connotations of "minority."

But such whites are in fact a minority. They are part of a spectrum of whites who have become a "minority" in the largest cities in this country. What of the other whites in this position? There is a great range of class diversity amongst whites in these cities, a diversity that is magnified by the distinctness of the regions where the major urban areas are located. The whites in New York, Miami, or San Jose, while all in the minority, are located in distinct cultural circumstances because of the characteristics of the immigrants who are flocking to each of these cities. The following sketch is drawn from Detroit, a city with the smallest percentage of whites of any major urban area in the United States. Whites in Detroit compose just 22 percent of the population of this city. While Detroit has not been significantly effected by recent immigration, the extent to which whites in this city are literally outnumbered is illustrative of the situations that constitute white Americans as a minority.

In Detroit, whites can be characterized as belonging to one of three groups: poor whites, middle-class whites, and affluent whites. The first group can be broadly characterized as those unable to leave as the city slid into economic distress and chaos. As jobs and factories left the city, not all whites were able to follow. Still, it is not simply the case that all of these poor whites wished to leave. There are neighborhoods in Detroit where poor whites have very developed familial and sentimental ties. They chose not to sunder these connections even though it meant enduring decreasing opportunities for work and economic security. Then there are the middle- and working-class whites. They may be typified as city workers such as firemen, police, or bureaucrats. In Detroit, city regulations stipulate that city workers must be residents. Hence, though many of these whites would prefer to leave, they are bound to the city by their generally well-paying jobs. This group tends to foster hostility toward the new "color" of power in Detroit and the way the face of racial politics has changed. Finally, there are the more affluent, generally liberal, whites who made a conscious decision to stay in the city because they did not want to live in highly segregated suburbs. All but a few of the suburbs that surround Detroit are over 90 percent white. These communities were unappealing to whites who felt committed to an integrated society. Their ability to remain satisfied with life in Detroit is, of course, partially dependent on the fact that they reside in more upscale, well-policed neighborhoods. These whites tend to not be as subjected to the dangers of urban life as are the other two classes of whites in Detroit.

Given this mixed social assemblage, what can we say about these whites who are clearly a minority in Detroit? Since their characterization, here, is already overly generalized, it would not be beneficent to typologize them further. Clearly, their diverse class positions severely stress the received definition of "minority" as socially disadvantaged. Should they then be exempted from such a designation? To decide so would be to add a qualification to "minority" that would deprive it of a fundamental point of reference in designating a group that is outnumbered. Also, we would lose sight of a fairly unique experience these whites do share in common: Many of them can relate instances of being the object of racial prejudice, bigotry, or discrimination. Such a situation is completely alien to the vast majority of whites in this country. In Detroit, whites across class lines have generally felt some degree of discomfort or alienation based on their skin color, an experience that resides at the core of being a minority. Instead of opting to exclude whites from this mode of social designation (as a "minority"), we can consider their situation as a means to update the significance of the term in the 1990s.

"Minority" is an effective way of referring to some modes of being socially disadvantaged. However, it is not the case that all members of a "minority" group are equally disadvantaged. There are class conditions that alleviate much of the social stigma or stress involved with being a minority. This is especially true when applied to whites.

What the case of whites as a minority should convey is that all terms of social or cultural designation refer to phenomenon that are influx, changing, and mutable. We must resist "naturalizing" such terms in the way the racial identities have long been naturalized, assuming a fixed and unchanging referent. As well, the communities that are labeled "minority" are always more diverse than this homogenizing term suggests. While such communities often articulate a collective set of interests in either countering the historical effects of racism or the political underrepresentation of their racial group, class divisions and differences internal to such communities never simply disappear or become irrelevant. "Minorities" may represent certain racially uniform groupings, but within these groups class distinctions continue to mitigate who among them is more truly disadvantaged (Wilson 1978, 1987).

One last note. Referring to some white Americans as a "minority" clearly muddies the political and social usage of this term that has developed over the last thirty years. One reason why this disorientation should be accepted is that in referring to whites as a "minority" we implicitly begin to assail the tendency in both social science literature, political debates, and media coverages to treat whiteness as a normative condition, as a social condition that is somehow not racial, against which all others are racially defined. There is no simple formula to suggest how the benefits and deficiencies of so labeling whites are to be weighed. The challenge in this usage is to keep in mind the conflicting modes of attention, one directed toward the primacy of racial disadvantage and, the other toward the fundamental role of class divisions in determining life chances in this or any other industrialized country. The status of white Americans as a minority is not a subject to be concluded here; rather, it should taken as a topic that initiates an ongoing discussion about the complexity of our social lives and the often fumbling efforts we make to find terms to define our social world.

## REFERENCES

Alba, R. 1990. *Ethnic Identity: The Transformation of White America.* New Haven: Yale University Press.

Batteau, A. 1990. *The Invention of Applalachia.* Tucson: University of Arizona Press.

Bolton, C. 1994. *Poor Whites of the Antebellum South: Tenants and Laborers in Central North Carolina and Northeast Missippi.* Durham: Duke University Press.

Branscome, J. 1978. Annihilating the Hillbilly: The Appalachians Struggle with America's Institutions. In *Colonialism in Modern America.* H. Matthews, L. Johnson, & D. Askins (eds). Boone, NC: Appalachian Consortium Press.

Cooke, S. 1976. *From Tobacco Road to Route 66: The Southern Poor White in Fiction.* Chapel Hill: University of North Carolina Press.

Daniel, P. 1985. *Breaking the Land: The Transformation of Cotton, Tobacco, and Rice Cultures Since 1880.* Urbana: University of Illinois Press

Ehrenreich, B. 1990. *Fear of Falling: The Inner Life of the Middle Class.* New York: Harper Books

Etheridge, E. 1988. Pellagra: An unappreciated reminder of southern distinctiveness. In *Disease and Distinctiveness in the American South.* T. Savitt & J. Young (eds). Knoxville: University of Tennesse Press.

Flynt, W. 1989. *Poor But Proud: Alabama's Poor Whites.* Tuscaloosa: University of Alabama Press.

Frankenberg, R. 1993. *White Women, Race Matters: The Social Construction of Whiteness.* Minneapolis: University of Minnesota Press.

Frey, W. & Tilove, J. 1995. Immigrants In, Natives Out. *The New York Times Magazine* (August 20).

Greenstone J. D. & Peterson, P. E. 1973. *Race and Authority in Urban Politics: Community Participation and the War on Poverty.* Chicago: University of Chicago.

Gregory, J. 1989. *American Exodous: The Dust Bowl Migration and Okie Culture in California.* New York: Oxford University Press.

Hartigan, J. 1996. Name calling: objectifying "poor whites" and "white trash." In *White Trash: Race and Class in American Culture.* M. Wray & A. Newitz (eds). New York: Routledge.

————n.d. Unpopular culture: The case of "white trash." Cultural Studies, (forthcoming volume). New York: Routledge.

Higham, J. 1988. *Strangers in the Land: Patterns of American Nativism: 1860–1925.* New Brunswick: Rutgers University Press

Jackson, E.1993. Whiting-out difference: Why U.S. nursing research fails black families. *Medical Anthropology Quarterly* 7(4).

Jones, J. 1992. *The Dispossessed: America's Underclass from the Civil War to the Present.* New York: Basic Books.

Jordan, W. 1969. *White Over Black: American Attitudes Towards the Negro, 1550–1812.* Baltimore: Penguin Books.

Larson, E. 1995. *Sex, Race, and Science: Eugenics in the Deep South.* Baltimore: Johns Hopkins University Press.

Lemann, N. 1991. *The Promised Land: The Great Black Migration and How it Changed America.* New York: Vintage Books.

Lewis, O. 1966. *La Vida: A Puerto Rican Family in the Culture of Poverty.* New York: Vintage Books.

Lieberson, S. 1985. Unhyphenated Whites in the United States. In *Ethnicity and Race in the USA: Towards the Twenty-First Century.* R. Alba (ed). Boston: Routledge & Kegan Paul.

Marcus, A. 1988. The South's native foriegners: Hookworm as a factor in southern distinctiveness. In *Disease and Distinctiveness in the American South.* T. Savitt & J. Young (eds). Knoxville: University of Tennesse Press.

McNeil, W. K. 1989. *Appalachian Images in Folk and Popular Culture.* Ann Arbor: UMI Research Press.

McWhiniey, G. 1988. *Cracker Culture: Celtic Ways in the the Old South.* Tuscaloosa: University of Alabama Press.

Page, H. & Brooke, T., 1994. White public space and the construction of white privilege in U.S. health care. *Medical Anthropology Quarterly* 8 (1).

Philip, R. 1991. *The Surgical Solution: A History of Involuntary Sterilization in the United States.* Baltimore: Johns Hopkins University Press.

Piven, F. F. & Cloward, R. 1979. *Poor People's Movements: Why They Succeed, How They Fail.* New York: Vintage Books.

Rafter, N. 1988. *White Trash: The Eugenic Family Field Studies, 1872–1922.* Boston: Northeastern University Press.

Roediger, D. 1991. *The Wages of Whiteness: Race and the Making of the American Working Class.* London: Verso.

————1993. *Towards the Abolition of Whiteness: Essays on Race, Politics, and Working Class History.* London: Verso.

Saxton, A. 1990. *The Rise and Fall of the White Republic: Class Politics and Mass Culture in Nineteenth-Century America.* London: Verso.

Shapiro, H. 1978. *Appalachia on Our Mind: The Southern Mountains and Mountaineers in the American Consciousness,1870–1920.* Chapel Hill: University of North Carolina Press.

Sollors, W. 1986. *Beyond Ethnicity: Consent and Descent in American Culture.* New York: Oxford University Press.

Takaki, R. T. 1993. A Different Mirror: A History of Multicultural America. Boston: Little, Brown & Co.

Williamson, J. 1984. *The Crucible of Race: Black and White Relations in the American South Since Emancipation*. New York: Oxford Press.

Wilson, W. J. 1978. *The Declining Significance of Race:Blacks and Changing American Institutions*. Chicago: University of Chicago Press

———1987. *The Truly Disadvantaged: The Inner City, The Underclass, and Public Policy*. Chicago: University of Chicago Press.

# 8

# The Illusion of Ethnic Identity: An Introduction to Ethnicity and Its Uses

## Frank A. Salamone

> If ethnic alignments persist, it is because ethnic divisions are maintained by the efforts of their members as part of a pattern of social interaction (Banton 1986: 11).

Immanuel Wallerstein defines ethnic groups as interest groups who assume an identity grounded within a system of relationships (Gates 1992:295). Such groups frequently go into and out of existence depending on socially and culturally mediated circumstances. Henry Louis Gates logically attacks the notion of tradition as a long-lasting and constant cultural heritage (1992). Groups draw boundaries around selected symbols that serve as identity markers in order to emphasize their contrast with other similar group/categories and mask differences among their own members. They do so to present a united front so that they gain political advantages not otherwise perceived as attainable. E. J. Hobswam and T. O. Ranger (1983) remind us that cultural "tradition" is whatever a group says it is. Other scholars remind us that boundaries have meaning and are flexible (Fernandez 1982; Handler & Segal 1990; Barth 1969). People invent traditions to suit occasions and conform with relevant identities. Therefore, it is not unusual to note that people claiming the same identity, for example, "American," may fill that identity category with a different content. Certainly, those in the core area of that identity, the mainland United States, will have a different configuration of core symbols to signal their identity than those on the periphery.

Ethnic groups are political, economic, and social action groups. A number of theorists in ethnicity appear to agree that they are formed for some purpose: in order to obtain something that is more easily attained as a member of an ethnic group than as an individual or member of some other group. By their very nature, then, ethnic groups are ever-changing. Their membership changes as people enter and leave. Their ideology changes as historical eras fade into one another or as the total social and cultural ecological setting mutates. Only in its need to distinguish itself from other similar groups does an ethnic group remain constant.

In order to distinguish itself from other similar groups, ethnic groups promote an ideology that claims permanence. That ethnic ideology asserts a common ancestor for all members, a common set of values, behavior, and ideology—in essence, creates culture. The myth of uniformity leads to the belief that members, for many purposes, are interchangeable. The myth also helps structure social life and the interaction of members with others within their own group and between members of different ethnic groups. In order to ease ethnic interaction, groups exploit symbols. Thus, clothing, language, behavior—in fact, anything that comes within human range—are used to mark the boundaries of ethnic groups and signal group membership. People seeing these symbolic uniforms or boundary markers come to ethnic engagements with certain expectations. Life is predictable within tolerable limits and interaction programmed. That person is an enemy. That other one is a joking partner. So go the interactions of social life.

Of course, these relationships are not eternal. Ethnic groups come into being, mutate, split, merge, and even disappear. The circumstances under which these processes ensue form the bases of many investigations and require empirical representations. The meaning that ethnic groups have for one another is another area worthy of further investigation. Certainly, one such meaning has been as the other against which one's own identity is formed. Everything that one is not is what is found in the ethnic groups that form a group's ethnic interaction network (Salamone 1985). On the other hand, a person's own ethnic group contains what other ethnic groups lack. It defines itself in the process of interaction and continues to do so over time, in a never-ending game of hide and seek. Nor is its identity ever static, for it changes with each interaction depending on the total context of that interaction. Each ethnic group in the interaction network becomes a different group in its identity with other groups. Of course, the network of each participant group is not isomorphic with that of every other group. Ethnic identity is situational. It is situational in that it varies according to the context. But, it is also situational in that people and groups often change their ethnic identities according to the circumstances in which they find themselves.

Gunn (1992:254) discusses effects that the "problematization of the concept of culture" and the related postcolonial critique have had in liberating thinking regarding the relationship of culture and context. He also directs our attention to the arbitrary nature of boundaries and their use in relationships of power. Attending to the significance of constructing and maintaining boundaries, borders between identities and access to power, alerts us to the political uses to which they are put. Identities are never merely givens. They also are texts not works, processes not products. Michael Banton (1986) cuts to the heart of the controversy regarding the nature of ethnic groups. Whatever else they may be, they are not isolated survivals of some idyllic past; neither are they colorful "cultural" groups, unless, of course, presenting themselves in such light serves their general purpose. As Banton indicates, ethnic groups exist in conjunction with other similarly organized groups to achieve certain purposes for their members. Members of these groups believe that those self-defined purposes can be achieved most effectively in their field of social interaction through an organization defined in terms of a myth of a common origin and culture.

Ronald Cohen has noted that in "13 of the leading textbooks of anthropology from 1916 to 1971," there were no index listings for "ethnic" or "ethnic group" (1978:350). Clearly, things have changed since 1971. A number of factors forced anthropologists to deal with the fact that older units, mainly "tribes," perceived, or at least, presented as living in splendid isolation no longer could be defended intellectually or in any other manner. Realities of the postcolonial world, compelled a switch to presenting units in ethnic terms, in terms that stressed the mutability and permeability of boundaries in the process of social interaction of self and others. Frederik Barth (1969) correctly noted the political nature of ethnic groups as well as the use individuals made of these groups. Following the lead of Raymond Firth (1954), Barth focused on the manner in which individuals organize their lives in an economizing manner. He viewed ethnic boundaries as open. Individuals can and do cross them, changing their identities to effect the change. Far from treating ethnic groups as fixed through time, moreover, Barth viewed them as rather ahistorical, created as the occasion warrants in order to enable people to get the best possible deal. Anticipating Hobswam and Ranger on tradition, Barth treats culture as mere "flotsam and jetsam," arguing that people use cultural symbols to construct ethnic boundaries so that ethnic groups can function in social networks that are ethnically defined. However, he spends little time on the nature of these cultural symbols, implying that their content really does not matter and that any objects can serve just as well to symbolize a group's identity and serve as its boundary marker.

Joan Vincent has developed the concept of the political nature of ethnic groups and the manner in which their study aids in understanding the jockeying for power within the state (1974, 1982, 1990). Following the lead of Max Weber (1961), she views ethnic identity in situational terms. As the situation warrants, actors can widen or narrow the boundaries of an ethnic identity. Vincent's more recent works provide intelligible examples of the usefulness of her original theoretical position. However, as with Barth, there is a general lack of concern with culture except as it provides boundary markers to structure social interaction.

In contrast to Vincent, Richard Alba addresses that aspect of ethnic identity that he refers to as "expressive" (1985). This aspect includes ethnic parades, cooking, festivals, and other occasions when members play at being "ethnic." Such "occasional" expression appears to mark a declining culture. It may provide some emotional and psychological support but appears to have little significance otherwise. For Alba, this expressiveness appears to mark the end of an ethnic group's existence. He does predict the end of Italian-American ethnicity and cites the recent efflorescence of ethnic markers in the community as a sign of its imminent termination as a viable group. Alba's work has made one of Barth's key ideas explicit; namely, the use of cultural elements as boundary markers and symbols of ethnic membership. Alba and Vincent are not the only ones to examine ethnicity. Thompson and Ronen (1986) discuss a number of alternative perspectives that have been taken in the study of ethnicity. They point to the attempt to combine the ethnic concept with class analysis (Alba 1985), ethnicity, and regional analysis

(Hechter 1983), as well as others who attempted to examine the interaction of ethnicity with the interests of the state. Each of these attempts holds some potential for developing a better understanding of the nature and power of ethnic concepts.

Consequently, Ronald Cohen's (1978) concept of "situational ethnicity," which holds promise for integrating these various approaches, offers a potentially very powerful concept. According to Cohen,

Ethnicity is first and foremost situational...the interactive situation is a major determinant of the level of inclusiveness employed in labeling self and others...In one situation it may be occupation, in another education, in a third, ethnicity...The scale level of confrontation in the situation generally determines the scale level of ethnic inclusiveness. The label used provides self and/or others with a set of features that explain what to expect, where such behavior comes from, and often as not how one should react to such a syndrome (1978:388).

Cohen acknowledges a debt to Hoetnink (1967), who termed ethnic relations "segmentary," that is, triggered off by the level of opposition between self and other (1978:389).

Situational ethnicity provides a means for managing multiple identities, for understanding that an individual has use of layers of personalities, each one activated according to purpose. What Ronald Cohen neglects is the range of purposes that ethnic identity can serve. The concept of situational identity, to be truly useful, must account for cultural, political, social boundary, "occasional," "ethclass," "ecoeth," and various other types of ethnic identity. Moreover, it always must leave room for the strategizing individual who can and often does move from one identity and one group to another, changing "masks of identity" in the process. Cohen appears to be absolutely correct in stressing the subjective/objective nature of ethnic groups. Certainly, they are based on some sort of myth of common descent. But these myths can be created, and often are, in *ad hoc* situations. Neglect, relative or absolute, of cultural elements, treating them as epiphenomena, moreover, misses an essential aspect of ethnic groups—their emotional claims on group members, and even those who may have opted out.

A true concept of situational ethnicity requires appropriate attention to political, social, economic, cultural-symbolic, ecological, and other aspects of the interactive network in which people find themselves. It is "subjective/objective" in its focus. It focuses on the individuals who comprise a group as well as on the objective situation in which groups in a network interact, keeping in mind the need to perceive individuals under their multiple identities. It must answer the "why," "what," and "what for" questions central to a truly situational perspective in the study of ethnicity. In other words, a situational perspective must examine the psychological factors involved in the creation of ethnic groups, the cultural elements inherent in the content comprising the group's "baggage," and the social nature of their interactions with other similarly constituted groups. The concept "ethnicity" is, in fact, part of the broader concept of "identity." Identities are masks that we use to confront the world. All identities are situational and shift according to circumstances. National identities are no exceptions to the general predicament. They are epiphenomena, donned according to the needs thrown up by historical vagaries.

Any particular identity is the result of a process akin to a play in which the actor assembles bits and pieces from the masks of other identities, taking these "shreds and patches" and weaving them into a mask of identity used to confront other similar masks. The myth of national identity hides the more complex reality, but that reality is quite different from the ideal. The presence of strong competing ethnic identities, which are much stronger than the national identity, leads to cultural strain often expressed in aggressive or even hostile behaviors. There is a pressing need to tease out and confront the implications of the fact that identities, even those that appear most ascriptive or are largely achieved. It is essential to remember that identities are categories for sociocultural interaction and the content of what goes into those categories is situational, depending upon factors of time, place, setting, social actors, and audience. In fact, we need to grapple with the fact that which identity or set of identities individual social actors choose to use depends on the situation. Moreover, these identities are never fixed. Rather, social actors continually redefine them through their actions and transactions. An integral factor in the negotiation of these identities is the choice and use of salient symbols in defining identities and delineating their boundaries. Those whose actions are not in conformity with negotiated identities are "ungrammatical" in some way; they provoke hostile responses *simply because* they threaten the prevailing negotiated social order. Their very existence forces people to consider that what is apparently fixed is in reality in flux and, furthermore, that what is perceived as "natural" is in truth "artificial." As Abner Cohen (1974) indicated, ethnic enclaves serve as incubators of identity formation in which particular symbols become salient for interethnic negotiations and transactions. Frederick Barth and his disciples (1969) examined this idea in a number of different situations. It is the universality of the process in which shared symbols promote group coherence in intergroup transactions that is the most interesting.

Groups draw boundaries around selected symbols that serve as identity markers in order to emphasize their contrast with other similar group/categories and mask differences among their own members. They do so to present a united front so that they gain political advantages not otherwise perceived as attainable. Hobswam and Ranger remind us that cultural "tradition" is whatever a group says it is. People invent traditions to suit occasions and conform with relevant identities (1983). There is little need for a native-born person to prove that she/he is entitled to a core ethnicity in his/her homeland. Those on the periphery, however, must take greater care to present a particular, and consequently selective, version of what it is to be a member of a particular ethnic grouping. Studies of immigrant groups to the United States and elsewhere must keep this point in mind. It does illustrate the cogency of Cohen's (1974) remark that ethnic identity defines itself through competition and conflict. It also supports Barth's (1969) perception that the content of that identity changes over time and circumstance. Moreover, behavioral change, that is, acting like a member of another group, precedes ethnic identity change and eases it. It is suggestive that when the ethnic group exercising political power is in a numerical minority, there is a strong inducement to recruit members from another group similar to itself.

In areas where society is basically organized on principles of ethnic diversity or pluralism, as in the modern political situation in the United States, ethnic groups are political ones. An important reason for using ethnicity as a principle of organization is historical; that is, different ethnic groups entered an area at different times. Ethnicity is a principle of organization that cross-cuts all other ties within a group. Changes in ethnic group membership, therefore, also involve changes in interaction patterns and in self-identification. It is not surprising, therefore, that in order to validate their hold to a piece of the political pie, ethnic groups in America with relatively new identities began to stress tradition, defined in terms of religious identity, as an ethnic boundary marker. As Michael Crowder states, speaking of the Fulani in Nigeria, a newly formed political ethnic entity:

in the earliest interwar period, any emirs and chiefs ruled as "sole native authorities," a position which gave them, for practical purposes, more power than they had in precolonial days, where they were either subject to control by a council or liable to deposition if they became too unpopular...There was thus a minimal undermining of the traditional sources of authority. The main change for the Fulani Emirs of Northern Nigeria, for instance, was that they now owed allegiance to the British Government rather than to the Sultan of Sokoto(1964:28).

Crowder's study offers an example of the manner in which an ethnic identity is fashioned in response to very real exigencies of the political situation.

Studies of the relationship of women and power also have vastly increased our appreciation of not only the wide variety of types of power and the exquisite subtlety of many of its modes, but also of the way ethnic relations develop in interethnic settings (Gilmore 1990; Cucchiari 1990). Karen Sacks (1989) suggests that the relationship between male–female power in a society is related to its racial/ethnic and class relationships. For example, as the Sicilian-American group changes its general relationship to American society, male–female relationships also will change. Further, as individual members change their own relationships both to their ethnic group and to American society, their behavior, including their gender behavior, will change (Mangione 1981). Just how much these relationships change and in what direction they vary has much to contribute to the debate on the salience of ethnicity in America.

Some researchers do not believe that the Italian-American ethnic identity is in decline or merely an expressive identity to be brought out on festive occasions to amuse the neighbors and children. In common with any identity, it is part of the ethnic's fabric of existence, a means for locating self in time, place, and circumstance. It enters many negotiations, often on a difficult-to-observe reflexive level. Even when it remains unnoticed, as it often does for those who have entered the mainstream in their work and residence, it is just below the surface, a constant reminder of one's difference, at times a source of pride and at other times a source of shame.

The opening words of Jerre Mangione's *Mont'Allegro* (1981) are, "When I grow up I want to be an American." This issue of dual loyalty and ambiguous identity has become a significant one, spilling over into Sicilian-American gender relationships.

Just because so much of Sicilian identity comes from the nuclear family, any change in definition of gender relations entails a change in one's total identity. Inevitably, circumstances in Rochester, New York, forced a redefinition of those relationships, first through praxis, then through a reflection on those behavioral changes.

Finally, the "why" of ethnic groups must be questioned. The answer is both simple and complex. Belonging to a group is both a psychological and biological need. Without constant care the human infant dies. The mother–child bond is as old as the human species. Groups formed around that bond appear to be as old as culture. Without intimate, face-to-face groups we are somehow less than human. Ethnic groups possess a nativistic appeal to humans. They harken back to groups from our primal past, nostalgically reminding us of the security of our primary groups. The perspective of "situational ethnicity," first formulated by Ronald Cohen, when expanded, is a powerful tool in examining the occurrence of ethnic invention, definition, and employment. Further investigation of the ecological nature of ethnic groups in the United States, including changing male and female relationships within those groups, and their own particular branches holds some promise for furthering our understanding of ethnicity.

There is insufficient space to discuss the overall question of immigration to the United States from colonial days to the present. The ecological situation into which a group entered influenced its mode of adaptation and the options open to it. The type of immigrants who were drawn from the general pool of people in the home country also influenced the type of adaptation open to the group members. For example, most German immigrants tended to be Republicans fleeing from the failure of the liberal movement in the German states and had skills deemed valuable to the development of the United States. Most Irish immigrants were poor, Catholic, and viewed with suspicion by the Protestant elite. However, these migrants tended to have great political skills and spoke English, so that quite quickly they controlled political machines in urban areas.

Until relatively recently in U.S. history, the pressure for "Anglo conformity" was virtually irresistible, at least for those who wished to succeed on any kind of public level. Although diversity on a private level was allowed and even paid lip service, the public sector demanded conformity and assimilation from immigrants. English facility was assumed and "Americanism" was proudly taught in the public schools. Indeed, a major impetus for the growth of public education in the United States was the assimilation of immigrants. The "new immigration" of the 1880s, throuth the early 1900s, frightened the old white Anglo-Saxon Protestant (WASP) elite and eventually led to a strong racist anti-immigration policy that lasted until the Kennedy reforms of the 1960s. The "new" immigration has raised serious issues regarding pluralist and assimilationist models. Multiculturalism has become the order of the day, leading many to fear that it will lead to a fragmented America in which no common culture or society will be found. The *old* new immigrants, such as the Italians, generally oppose this policy. They argue in favor of ethnic pride and private pluralism, but they oppose a multilingual country in which "ethnic cheerleading" has become the order of the day. The general availability of welfare payments and affirmative action, moreover, has acerbated ethnic rivalries and often has caused the true plight of Southeast Asian and Central American immigrants to be overlooked in what, in comparison, are trivial arguments.

Although a large number of Italians continue to migrate to the United States, such immigrants are overlooked in general studies of Italian immigration. The experience of recent Italian immigrants is largely shaped by structures and perceptions formed in the early decades of the twentieth century. They enter an ecological niche carved out by the hordes of largely southern Italians and Sicilians who fled the poverty of the Mezzogiorno, seeking to make their fortune before returning to Italy. Millions stayed in their adopted country, forging a new identity with the aid of a Church they did not always trust. Similarly, recent Irish immigrants, many of whom are illegal aliens, smoothly ease into niches that the earlier migrants created with the aid of priests they did not trust.

Religion, as a cultural artifact, is more than a system for arranging people in groups to address the supernatural and perform appropriate rituals. It is a boundary marker that is useful as a means for political mobilization and self/other identification. It can, in other words, be used as a symbolic means for arranging people in groups to address political and economic issues that are vital to their perceived interests. It can become part of a master identity. Erving Goffman provides a classic explanation of the concept.

Society is organized on the principle that any individual who possesses certain social characteristics has a moral right to expect that others will value and treat him in an appropriate way. Connected with this principle is a second, namely, that an individual who implicitly or explicitly signifies that he has certain social characteristics ought in fact to be what he claims he is. In consequence, when an individual projects a definition of the situation and thereby makes an implicit or explicit claim to be a person of a particular kind, he automatically exerts a moral demand upon the others, obliging them to value and treat him in the manner that persons of his kind have a right to expect. He also explicitly foregoes all claims to be things he does not appear to be and hence foregoes the treatment that would be appropriate for such individuals. The others find, then, that the individual has informed them as to what they ought to see as the "is" (1959:27).

The movement in cultural analysis, then, has been from mechanistic models of objectified reality to semiotic inquiry into evolving processes, involving a shift from deterministic to possibilist paradigms. These paradigms concentrate on open rather than closed boundaries and on the two processes of definition and redefinition. Performative, action, interpretative, deconstructive, praxis, play, and other current anthropological approaches to the analysis of culture as a meaning, or semiotic, system share a number of assumptions about the nature of culture and social life. They view culture as created, not given. They use the distinction of Claude Lévi-Strauss between nature and culture as a point of analytic departure. These studies, moreover, concentrate on the manner in which the boundaries shift according to context, including the requirements of cultural performers as well as performance. Symbolic anthropologists, therefore, deem culture a relational process rather than an object. As such, meanings ooze out of one's grasp just like the mango in the Hausa proverb, "The world is just like a mango. When you think you have grasped it, it squirts out of your hand!" (Salamone 1975, 1979, 1985). The subversive nature of play in these perspectives lies in its ability to offer an alternate reality while drawing attention to the cultural, that is, the *created* and *negotiated* aspects of current social reality. For that reason, the literal-minded resist the anarchic frolic of play or confine it to marginal aspects, the so-called time-out periods, of their lives. Similarly, "serious" people with a stake in maintaining the current definitions of reality that empower them resist those outsiders whose very presence may question the permanence and correctness of the *status quo*, for they perceive these outsiders as merely playing with culture.

Ultimately, all of the current analytic approaches to ethnicity are about power and methods of retaining or obtaining it. As Raymond Firth, himself a progenitor of current approaches, observed, to be effective, subversions of reality must belong to the same category of reality as those they seek to reorganize it. In the current terminology, subversions, or competing interpretations, of reality must belong to the same universe of discourse as those they seek to replace. There is, therefore, a dialogic aspect to cultural negotiation, in which people seek to reinterpret even "agreed-upon" rules. Ethnic redefinition resembles a competitive dance in which the participants seek ever more bizarre ways in which to define themselves from each other. There is a playfulness present even when the competition is most severe, or maybe *when* it is most severe. If one participant ceases to play, there is no point in continuing the dance.

Ethnicity, then, has a game-like nature. It teases those who seek hardest to comprehend it. When it appears most serious, it is at its most playful. As Hobswam and Ranger (1983) have indicated, "ancient traditions" can be invented to suit any occasion. What matters is the occasion and those who do focus on the appropriate "occasion" for it to fit. Those who ignore the total context and concentrate on the tradition, delightful as it undoubtedly is, find themselves watching the hole instead of the doughnut. This magical slight-of-hand of ethnic groups serves a substantial purpose; namely, separating collections of people from similar collections of other people in the competition for scarce and desired resources. The more closely the people, in fact, are culturally, the greater the creative slight-of-hand required to separate them categorically. Ethnicity, in common with culture itself, is a thing of "shreds and patches" as Alfred Lowie, the anthropologist, said, echoing Gilbert and Sullivan. People form groups out of *this* and *that* emphasis as the circumstance warrants. What is important is the formation of groups to achieve desired ends. Individuals may or may not use their personal ethnicity in order to affiliate with an ethnic group. It is of empirical interest to find out which people do so and under what conditions.

## REFERENCES

Alba, R. 1985. *Italian Americans*. Englewood Cliffs: Prentice-Hall.
Banton, M. 1986. Ethnic Bargaining. In *Ethnicity, Politics, and Development*. D.L. Thompson & D. Ronen (eds). Boulder: Lynne Reiner, pp. 11–24.

Barth, F. (ed). 1969. *Ethnic Groups and Boundaries*. Boston: Little, Brown & Company.

Cohen, Abner (ed.). 1974. *Urban Ethnicity*. A.S.A. Monograph no. 12. London: Tavistock.

Cohen, Ronald. 1978. Ethnicity: Problem and focus in anthropology. *Annual Review of Anthropology* 7:379–403.

Crowder, M. 1964. *A Short History Of Nigeria*. New York: Frederick A. Praeger.

Cucchiari, S. 1988. Adapted for heaven: Conversion and culture in western Sicily. *American Ethnologist* 15:417–441.

————1990. Between shame and sanctification: Patriarchy and its transformation in Sicilian Pentacostalism. *American Ethnologist* 17: 687–707.

Fernandez, J. 1982. *Bwiti: An Ethnography of the Religious Imagination in Africa*. Princeton: Princeton University Press.

Firth, R. 1954. Social Organization and Social Change. *Journal of the Royal Anthropological Institute* 84:1–20.

Gates, Jr., H. L. 1992. *Ethnic and Minority Studies: Introduction to Scholarship*. J. Gibaldi (ed). New York: Modern Language Association of America, pp. 288–302.

Gilmore, D. 1990. Men and women in southern Spain: "Domestic" power revisited. *American Anthropologist* 92: 953–970.

Goffman, E. 1959. *Presentation of Self in Everyday Life*. New York: Doubleday.

Gunn, B. 1992. *Redrawing Boundaries*. New York: Modern Language Association.

Handler, R. & Segal, J. 1990. *Jane Austen and the Fiction of Culture*. Tucson: University of Arizona Press.

Hechter, M. (ed). 1983. *The Microfoundations of Macrosociology*. Philadelphia: Temple University.

Hobswam, E. J. & Ranger, T. O. (eds). 1983. *The Invention of Tradition*. Cambridge: Cambridge University Press.

Hoetinik, H. 1967. *The Two Variants in Caribbean Race Relations: A Contribution to the Sociology of Segmented Societies*. New York: Oxford University Press.

Lowie, A. 1937. *The History of Ethnological Theory*. New York: Farrar and Rinehart.

Mangione, J. *1981. Mont' Allegro*. New York: Columbia University Press. Original, 1942.

Sacks, K. 1989. Toward a unified theory of class, race, and gender. *American Anthropologist* 16:534–550.

Salamone, F.A. 1975. Becoming Hausa—Ethnic identity change and its implications for the study of ethnic pluralism and stratification. *Africa* 45:401–420.

————1979. Hausa ethnicity in Ibadan. *Afrika and Ubersee* 56:115–125.

————1985. *Gods and Goods in Africa*. Salem: Sheffield Press.

Thompson, D. L. & Ronen, D. (eds). 1986. *Ethnicity, Politics, and Development*. Boulder: Lynne Reiner.

Vincent, J. 1974. The structuring of ethnicity. *Human Organization* 33:375–379.

————1982. *Teso in Transformation: The Political Economy of Peasants in East Africa*. Berkeley: University of California Press.

————1990. *Anthropology and Politics: Visions, Traditions, and Trends*. Tucson: University of Arizona Press.

Weber, M. 1961. Ethnic groups. In *Theories of Society*. T. Parsons, E. Shills, K. D. Naegele, & J. Pitts (eds). New York: Free Press, pp. 301–309.

# PART III

## Ethnic Cultures in the United States

This section introduces the reader to the some of the vast diversity to be found within the United States based on ethnicity. As demonstrated in the last chapter by Frank Salamone, the term ethnicity has undergone substantial change since it was initially conceptualized and popularized in terms of tribal groupings. The term tribe now has been replaced with the term ethnic group which is used as an expression of diversity both within and across modern nation-state boundaries. Ethnicity as presently used in anthropology expresses this shift to the ethnic group as an entity with some commonality and as part of multiculturalism or cultural diversity. Others tell us that ethnic identities have become the paradox of the times, as globalization of the market-exchange systems spreads and populations continue to move across national boundaries while still maintaining much of the cultural tradition they take with them. Based on this constant movement, some scholars even suggest that ethnicity now transcends the context of diversity. Others now see it as a segment of a larger community of shared beliefs, common origins, and shared activities. In today's world, ethnicity means commonality, but with growing social importance and tied to many issues of cultural diversity. Despite these differing views that have occasioned a great deal of debate, for most Americans the idea of ethnic group continues to persist much as it always has, as does its relationship to the diversity that characterizes countries. Although ethnic and ethnicity have lost much of their original meanings, as people in greater numbers now move about the world as never before and maintain much of their traditional cultures, the concepts still have value in distinguishing a category of diversity, and denoting specific and unique cultural groups that have evolved in newer contexts that are unlike any other in the world. As has been pointed out, ethnicity has become contextual, the result of the historical experience of a group in a social context and intricately tied to the group's self-identification, serving many social, economic, and political purposes.

Each of the chapters in Part III focus on one of the major ethnic categories of diversity generally recognized by Americans, while also providing some basic information on a representative cultural group from within the categories. Cultural categories are different from the cultural groupings that make them up. Categories are just means of classifying things together, usually according to some common denominator or traits that they all may share. As you might recall from Michael D. Lieber's discussion of "thingies" in Chapter 4, categories are "thingies" that generally do not reflect the actual complexity exhibited by all those being classified in the same category. Most ethnic categories are based on some perceived cultural trait(s) (real or imaginary) shared by those being grouped together: customs, foods, dress, and so on. In some cases, ethnic categories are established on no more than the fact that people share some variation of the same language (e.g., Spanish for all those characterized as Hispanic Americans, Hispanics, etc.). In some cases, groups are formed on the basis of these things being combined with physical similarity and perhaps some consideration of geographical origin (e.g. Asian Americans, African Americans, South Asian Americans, etc.). In the case of the aboriginal inhabitants of the United States, all of these things are used to categorize the Native Americans into a single grouping. Some categories are created on the basis of religion with only a nominal recognition of geographic origin or physical appearance (e.g., Muslims, Jews, etc.). Unfortunately, the end result of these kinds of categorizations is to obscure more than they clarify. Not only do they obscure the many cultural differences among the peoples overgeneralized into them, but they also hide the actual diversity that exists within such groupings themselves, and within the country itself. The practice also leads to more stereotyping, discrimination, and prejudice. In actual fact, each of these commonly used categories of diversity is made up of a great many specific cultural groups with their own beliefs and practices, a diversity within diversity as it were. Other than the fact that they might speak a similar language or that they originated in similar parts of the world, or that they share a religion or look physically quite similar, they may share little else.

Most Americans tend to view diversity on the level of categorization, preferring to deal with the diverse group of "Hispanics" rather than all of the unique cultural groups that might be generalized into the category (e.g., Mexican-Americans). The practice obscures the real cultural differences that do exist and must be dealt with in the context of diversity if we really want to come to grips with that. Each author addresses the problems of overgeneralization, defining or characterizing people in this way. Each focuses on a specific cultural group within the board category to emphasize the problem(s), providing some sense of the historical forces that have impacted upon and shaped that specific cultural group in the American context. Each author also conveys a little something of what the readers should know to begin to develop a greater awareness or understanding of that particular group. The number of diversity categories is actually not very large, but the number of actual cultural groupings that are combined within them is exceedingly large. It would be almost impossible to treat all the specific cultural diversity in the United States that exists by virtue of ethnicity. One would have to address each and every group that has come to the United States and combined some of their traditional customs with those of the country, resulting in the unique culture they evolve in the American context. The latest census lists some 42 such groupings, but the actual number is more than twice that. Space simply precludes attention to each and every one of the specific ethnic groupings that actually are represented in the United States. But it is hoped that with a specific example from each of the major ethnic categories, readers will gain some appreciation of the problem(s) of ethnic categorizing and some feeling for the actual ethnic diversity of America, as well as some basic knowledge of at least one specific grouping contained within each category. It is a start.

In Chapter 9, Seamus Metress focuses on the European American category before narrowing down his discussion to the Irish-Americans, who have had a long and somewhat turbulent history in America. In Chapter 10, Mikel Garcia conveys something of the problems associated with the category of African American and some of the specific beliefs and practices that have come to set the African-American group ethnically apart from all of the others. Alicia Re Cruz discusses the Hispanic (Spanish-Speaking) American category in Chapter 11, with a particular focus on the Mexican-American community in the United States. The author emphasizes the role of history in the development of their identity, perspectives, and culture as well as perceptions of them by others. Chapter 12 focuses on the category generally referred to as Asian Americans. Jonathan Okamura focuses his discussion on Filipino-Americans, a group even more marginalized than most other specific cultural groups of this category (e.g., Korean-Americans, Japanese-Americans, Chinese-Americans, etc.). In Chapter 13, Charles Cambridge, himself a member of the Navaho tribe and trained anthropologist, examines the historical context for the American Indian (all those included in the Native American category) and reminds us of the legacy of history, particularly with regard to identity and the very special problems experienced by so many Native American cultures.

# 9

## The Irish-Americans: From the Frontier to the White House

Seamus Metress

### EUROPEAN AMERICANS AND IRISH-AMERICANS

Americans of European origins came from a variety of cultural geographic areas. The very earliest immigrants to America came from northern and western Europe and included the English, Dutch, French, Germans, and Irish. Later immigrants came from Scandinavia, Germany, and Ireland, while in the late nineteenth and early twentieth centuries they were joined by eastern and southern Europeans such as the Poles, Italians, and Russians. According to many historians most of these groups especially the earlier groups from northern and western Europe, lost their identity in the American "melting pot." However, in the 1960s and 1970s the myth of the melting pot was challenged and replaced by a "salad bowl" model (Glazer & Moynihan 1963). First African Americans, and then Hispanic Americans and Native Americans began to reaffirm their own cultural heritage and refused to melt. After Michael Novak (1973) lashed out against American society for robbing him of his history, a new interest developed in one's sociohistorical roots and there was a call for more sensitivity to others and their roots. Many individuals began a personal, conscious effort to understand their cultural and family history.

### THE IRISH-AMERICANS

Denis Clark has said that "the Irish Americans could well be the ethnic group that best reveals the extraordinary extent and variations of acculturation in the United States" (Clark 1986). The Irish-American ethnic identity has its beginnings in the colonial period of American history. However, most people tend to associate the Irish-Americans with the massive influx during the potato famine of the 1840s. The category of Irish-American includes both Irish Protestants and Irish Catholics, although most Americans associate the Irish with Catholicism. The categorization of Irish Protestants as Scotch Irish is not helpful, since early Irish Protestants like

Andrew Jackson referred to themselves as Irish and joined Irish social groups such as the Friendly Sons of St. Patrick. In the 1990 Census, over 40,000,000 persons identified themselves as Irish-Americans, but the vast majority so identified were Protestants. Some of these Protestants are derived from early populations of Irish Presbyterians and Irish Quakers, while many are the descendants of those who were Catholic but became Baptists in the South and Methodists on the Western frontiers because of the absence of an institutional Catholic Church in these areas.

The Irish-Americans are a widespread group, geographically stretching from coast to coast and north to south. Most historians tell us that they settled in urban areas, but rural Irish communities are dispersed throughout America. In some areas the rural Irish Americans outnumbered their urban counterparts. The widespread distribution of the Irish-Americans results in differences in religion, family life, occupational history, and their attitude toward other social groups. The regional experiences of Irish-Americans have indeed created distinctive varieties of Irish-Americans. Therefore, it is difficult to generalize about this group because of its long and widespread existence in the United States. However, for convenience, this chapter will concentrate on the most identifiable aspect of "Irishry" in America, the Irish-American Catholic. Such a choice does not mean to deny the significance and contributions of those of the Irish Protestant heritage. The Irish Catholic community throughout its history was influenced and integrated by the Catholic Church, the big-city political machine and democratic party, and Irish nationalist organizations involved in the struggle for freedom in Ireland. None of these factors or anything comparable served to integrate the experience of Irish Protestants, making them more difficult to generalize about.

## SOCIOHISTORICAL DEVELOPMENT

The Irish diaspora has been one of the most extensive movements of people in world history. Ten times more people of Irish ancestry live in the United States than in Ireland itself. Ireland was Britain's first colony, and its history has been one of political and economic exploitation. Irish people left Ireland for the United States for a wide variety of reasons, including religious persecution, starvation, political oppression, and economic underdevelopment. However, the causes, extent, and composition of emigration differed markedly during different historic periods.

### Stages of Emigration

It is useful to survey Irish emigration utilizing a five- stage historical model. The five stages consist of: the colonial period prior to 1815; the pre-famine period from 1815 to 1845; the Famine years, 1845 to 1855; the post-famine years from 1855 to the 1920s: and the post-independence years from the 1920s to the present (Clark 1986; Duff 1971; King & Fitzgerald 1990; Miller 1925). The history of emigration has contributed significantly to what the Irish-American is today in the context of the American culture. For example, during the colonial period, Irish emigration was dominated by the artisans, small shopkeepers, and small farmers from an Ulster Protestant background. However, the actual number of Catholics was considerable, consisting of possibly 40 percent of the total Irish migration. About 400,000 to 500,000 Irish came during this period, including a substantial number of indentured servants and slaves brought here after the seventeenth-century Cromwellian War. Commercial restrictions placed on Irish economic development and religious persecution of both dissenters and Catholics were the primary causes of emigration. This particular wave of immigrants settled mainly in the middle Atlantic states of Pennsylvania, Maryland, Virginia, and Delaware and the southeastern states of Georgia, North Carolina, and South Carolina.

The pre-famine emigration began at the conclusion of the Napoleonic Wars in 1815. The end of hostilities resulted in a partial loss of English markets for Irish agricultural products, and further restrictions on Irish industrialization led to greatly diminished economic opportunities. At the same time a shift from tillage to grazing encouraged estate clearance by the eviction of small farmers and peasants. At this time more and more American ships were carrying raw materials to England and on the return voyage offered cheap passage to America. Instead of returning empty, the ship captains could use the emigrants as paying ballast. At the same time Agrarian secret societies were also beginning to use violence and intimidation to deal with oppressive landlords and their agents, as well as resisting the tithes payable to the Anglican Church. Fear of becoming caught up in such violence encouraged some people to emigrate. A combination of these factors led to about 1,500,000 Irish emigrants going to America. At first, many of these emigrants were Protestant dissenters from Ulster, but later Catholics from the South came to dominate. They settled in the eastern urban centers, especially Philadelphia and New York, and later extended inland, first along the canals and later along the railroads. But, significant numbers did settle in agrarian settings where they attempted to make a living as farmers.

The period most associated in the popular mind with Irish emigration is the famine years. From 1845 to 1855, about 1,500,000 people came to the United States largely from the west and southwest of Ireland. A massive failure of the potato crop due to a fungus, *Phytophora infestans*, combined with British inaction and the colonial socioeconomic structure to produce more massive death, destitution, and emigration. These emigrants left hurriedly by any means the could, including overcrowded unseaworthy "coffin ships." These ships were characterized by a death rate similar to that of the slave ships from Africa. This group was the most destitute yet, the most aggressively Irish and Catholic of all of the emigrant waves. They, too, settled in the eastern port cities as well as Akron, Toledo, St. Paul, and St. Louis located along the inland transportation routes.

During the post-famine years from 1855 to the 1920s, emigration became an institutionalized part of Irish life. Over 2,500,000 plus people came to America and settled largely in the previously settled areas. Emigration during this period was generally the result of deteriorating economic conditions and increased political repression. Evictions began to increase, and agrarian violence and disobedience intensified. These emigrants came largely from the economically impoverished areas of west and extreme southwest Ireland. It was this group that sent back massive amounts of money to Ireland in order to improve the conditions of those left behind or to pay for further emigration of relatives.

From the conclusion of the Anglo-Irish War in 1921 and the partition of Ireland into the two units of the present, the Irish-American emigration pattern has been one of spurts and lulls. Shortly after the founding of the Irish Free State, emigration slowed dramatically. However, most of the nationalist emigration from the six northeastern counties still under British control continued. The discriminatory nature of the partitioned statelet, with respect to employment, housing, and civil rights, encouraged greater nationalist emigration from the Northeast. Recent emigration, legal and illegal, especially among the young, has increased again in the Republic of Ireland due to the disastrous economic situation at home.

The arrival of the Irish in America throughout history has been characterized by much prejudice and exploitation. The Irish were viewed with suspicion by Anglo-Americans since the majority of them were poor, anti-English and Catholic. They were subjected to high rents and crowded, unsanitary living conditions. From the famine until the mid-twentieth century a "No Irish Need Apply" attitude was commonplace (Metress 1981; Miller & Wagner 1994). Although largely a rural, peasant people, the Irish easily urbanized in the United States. The urbanization of the Irish peasant was the result of many different factors. Farming was a symbol of oppression characterized by poverty, rack rents, eviction, starvation, and foreign masters. However, the city offered opportunities of two types: unskilled jobs and the chance to develop political power. In the urban ghettos there was safety in numbers from hostile nativist attitudes toward emigrants, as well as less religious discrimination than in the predominantly Protestant rural areas. Nativist reactions included anti-Irish riots, job and housing discrimination, and even anti-Irish political parties, e.g., the Native-American Party and the Know-Nothings.

The major institutional impacts of the Irish in America were in the areas of politics, labor, and religion. It is in the area of politics, especially big-city politics, that the Irish have achieved the most recognition. The Irish who came to America were familiar with the techniques of representative government and they were skilled at manipulating the democratic process, especially those who emigrated after Daniel O'Connell's Catholic Emancipation struggle (Duff 1971). They knew how to organize rallies, prepare and deliver political oratory, and employ the art of pamphleteering. From the start, it was clear that the Irish would aggressively use their experience to seize political power. By the 1850s they had gained much local and neighborhood power, and from the 1860s to the 1890s they gained control of many of the big cities, e.g., New York, Buffalo, Philadelphia, St. Louis, San Francisco, Kansas City, and some others. As machine politics declined during the depression, the Irish became active participants in the New Deal and remained the bulwark of the Democratic Party until the nomination of George McGovern. Irish big-city politics was based on a pragmatic view of what people wanted. The Irish did not expect their leaders to be saints, so to them some degree of corruption was inevitable. They differentially conceptualized graft at the top helping a few, and graft at the bottom working for everyone. Loyalty and responsiveness to the needs of constituents were more important than honesty. It was loyalty in the face of personal setbacks that held the organization together. If you stand by your own and wait your turn, you will be rewarded eventually. To the Irish, self-righteousness would not win elections since most people are not ideologues. The machine politics of the Irish have been criticized as being corrupt and contrary to social progress. In reality, the machines were more successful as reformers than most liberals and may have created the climate for later social programs. The reasons for their success in politics were multifactorial. In addition to their familiarity with the Anglo-American democratic system, their Catholicism served as an ethnic organizing force while the ghetto institutions, e.g., saloons, social clubs, and athletic clubs, were used for political organizing. Further, politics, unlike most of the professions, was open to self-made individuals with little formal training. Finally, many of the Irish exhibited a gregarious verbal nature that lent itself well to political campaigning.

In the field of labor, many historians have portrayed the Irish influence as conservative or reactionary. But this stereotype is not supported by an examination of the labor movement. It was the Irish and their descendants who first attempted to organize the miners, longshoremen, and iron workers. In fact, the Irish and Irish-Americans provided much of the labor movement's early leadership with men and women such as Mother Jones and T.V. Powderly. Radical Unionism never really flourished in the United States because of state repression and fragmentation of the working class. But the Irish were important in two of the most radical unions, the Industrial Workers of the World (IWW) and the Western Federation of Miners. By the early years of the twentieth century Irish-Americans politically controlled a majority of the unions in the United States.

The Irish had an enormous impact on the American Catholic Church. For the emigrants, the church was a source of identity and psychic support, and its priests often helped fight the "system." The Irish were not interested in accommodation with their old enemies, the Anglo-Saxons, and thus stirred up nativistic animosities that resulted in convent burnings and physical attacks on their neighborhoods. The great numbers of Irish Catholics, with their demand for an Irish clergy, simply overwhelmed the early church. The Catholic Church in America changed from a predominantly quiet, subdued rural institution to an aggressively Irish and urban one. Because of that change, by 1870, a conflict developed within the church between the liberals, led by Bishops Ireland, Gibbons, Keane, O'Connell, and Spaulding, and the conservatives led by Bishops McQuaid and Corrigan. The liberals viewed the church as an agent for Americanization, stressed the melting pot concept, and supported the public school system and social justice. Conservatives felt that it was necessary to preserve Catholic ethnic identity and loyalty, stressed parochial education, and supported capitalism against labor unions while they made other calls for social justice. It is also important to note that it was during this time that the Irish church leaders created the parochial school system as well as most of the Catholic colleges and universities. However, these schools Americanized the students, and their "Catholicity" replaced their Irishness. Charges of inferiority of the parochial schools have not been supported by the facts, either historically or contemporaneously. The schools were important in the transition from immigrant status and greatly aided social and occupational mobility. Irish Catholics today send a higher percentage to college than any other ethnic group, excluding Jewish-Americans.

From the early 1800s the Irish immigrants have supported a variety of political movements aimed at freeing their homeland from British domination. They have contributed their money, time, and political influence to the repeal movement, the Fenians, the Young Irelanders, the Land League, the Sinn Fein party, and the Irish Republican Army (IRA) (Metress 1995). They have organized American support groups such as the Fenian Brotherhood, Clan na Gael, Friends of Irish Freedom, and Irish Northern Aid. After the Irish Free State gained nominal independence for 26 of Ireland's 32 counties in 1921, the level of involvement diminished. But with the violent destruction of the nonviolent Northern Ireland civil rights movements by loyalists in the early 1970s, Irish nationalist activity in the United States again surged. Led by more recent immigrants from the northeast of Ireland, as well as old veterans of the Anglo-Irish War of Independence of 1919–1921, a new support network has emerged.

Irish emigration to the United States established the base for a very large Irish-American population. But Irish-America is extremely variable with respect to its identification with its Irishness. Identification can be one of name only or limited to the gaudy, comic, superficial "St. Patrick's Day Irish" image. However, for a significant number it involves participation in Irish cultural activities: dancing, music, theater, courses and lectures, and Gaelic sports. For others, it involves active participation in the struggle for freedom and social justice in northeast Ireland today.

## THE STATE OF IRISH AMERICA TODAY

Except in South Boston and New York, Irish-Americans do not live in ethnic neighborhoods. However, ethnic identity is still significant for many who identified themselves as Irish-American in the Census. During the 1960s, coincident with "ethnic revival" in the United States and the outbreak of hostilities in Northeast Ireland, a resurgence of interest in Irish roots has occurred. Trips back to Ireland, genealogical studies of familial roots, membership in Irish organizations, and interest in Irish history and culture are commonplace. Beyond this, it is also the case that significant numbers of people now attend and participate in Irish cultural activities and language classes. A large number of Irish publications now flourish: *The Irish Echo, The Irish Edition, The Irish Herald, The Irish Voice, The Irish People,* and *Irish America.* All of the publications carry local Irish-American news, news from Ireland, Gaelic sports results, ads, and obituaries. *The Irish People* is primarily the political voice of Irish republicanism in America and *Irish America* is a magazine with fine feature stories. Cultural organizations such as the Ancient Order of Hibernians, Chomhaltas Ceoltoiri Eireann, the North American Feis, Irish cultural centers, and local Irish clubs have experienced a growing membership.

Many people belong to Irish-American nationalist organizations such as the Clan na Gael, Irish Northern Aid, and the Irish American Unity Conference. These organizations have carried on political education, lobbying, and fund raising associated with the struggle in Northeast Ireland over the last 25 years. Such support has included financial support for the families of Irish political prisoners and intensive lobbying efforts in the U.S. Congress. Those involved have done so in the face of public criticism from other Irish Americans, media apathy and hostility, and direct harassment from the FBI. Many traveled to Northeast Ireland to observe first hand the war between Irish nationalists and the British and their loyalist allies and have become articulate spokespersons. The effectiveness of Irish nationalists is highlighted by the attention paid to them and their activities by both the British and American governments. A good example can be seen in the McBride Principles, an American-based proposal similar to the Sullivan Principles in South Africa. Promoted by a variety of Irish groups, the principles attempt to force American companies in Northeast Ireland to not participate in the systematic job discrimination against Irish nationalists. The campaign has been a major source of public education and political pressure that has forced the British government to spend millions of dollars to counteract them and defeat legislative attempts. However, McBride legislation has been passed in over 13 states and a number of cities.

## Sociocultural Characteristics of the Irish-American

The family is still the most important aspect of Irish-American social dynamics. Family loyalty is very intense. While they may squabble among themselves, Irish families present a united front to outsiders. Siblings visit often and try to help each other whenever possible. Even if separated by great distance, phone contact is frequent and regular visits common. Some feel stressed when their relationship is disturbed and many experience feelings of social loss. Extended family outings are still common, and participation in weddings, baptisms, first communions, and wakes is intense and frequent (Greeley 1981). Within the Irish-American family, the mother has a stronger role than probably is the case with any other American ethnic group. Irish mothers, contrary to the belief of many outsiders, have much power and are rarely subordinate to the male. Mothers often control family finances and are major decision-makers. It is still common for Irish-Americans to practice a no-nonsense system of childrearing with specific attention to schooling and career development. Higher education is highly valued, but often getting a good job is more important than the education itself.

Economically, welfare is still a major concern among Irish-Americans, who came from a history of poverty and economic instability. From their very beginnings, poverty, thrift, and saving for the future have been important. It's no different today. Home ownership still remains an important, significant mark of social advancement and economic security. Irish-Americans tend to seek jobs or professions with security and a good retirement plan. Most of them prefer pragmatic professions, e.g., medicine, teaching, law, criminal justice, and politics, rather than the more esoteric ones such as philosophy, music, and art.

For Irish-Americans, marriage outside the group is common. Even today, 30 to 40 percent still choose mates from the Irish-American community. However, 68 percent of all Irish-Americans report some mixed ancestry. The most common admixture is German/Irish especially among Irish Catholics. The Irish-Americans have the largest families among European ethnic groups, averaging 2.28 while they express the ideal size to be 3.37, compared to the national average of 3.1. Irish-American women expect 3.5 children while males expect 3.3. This is the reverse of the national picture, where males expect more children. Irish-Americans today are experiencing a decline in the percentage of non-marriage choices and an increase in late marriages. Among males, non-marriage is about 14 percent, while among females it is 12 percent. Irish-American males today marry at about 24.5 years and females at 22, compared to earlier averages of 34 and 31, respectively (Greeley 1981).

In the area of education, Irish Catholics tend to send a higher percentage of their children to college than any other ethnic group, except for the Jews. Many come through the parochial school system built by their ancestors, which was branded inferior and clannish by jealous white Anglo-Saxon Protestants (WASPs). However, parochial students surveyed in Greeley's research were not more clannish and actually performed more liberally than their public school counterparts (Greeley 1969). Today, parochial school graduates go on to elite non-Catholic universities as well as Notre Dame, Boston College, Fordham, and Georgetown. In fact, these same parochial schools today are a refuge from the poor quality and chaos of urban public schools, especially for minorities in the inner city.

### Sociocultural Dynamics

Irish-Americans still worry about what the neighbors will think. This is perhaps an artifact of virulent anti-Irish nativism of earlier times when the Irish were not very welcome in many communities and social circles. To many Irish-Americans, embarrassing your family group in view of outsiders is a serious social concern. This has possibly affected the involvement of many in the modern Irish nationalist struggles, which the American media has regularly demonized. For a number of the "respectable" middle-class Irish-Americans, the struggle is an embarrassment, or worse, would get them branded as supporters of "terrorist" thugs by friends, family, and neighbors. The Irish-American sociologist, Father Andrew Greeley, noted that the National Opinion Research Center (NORC) survey uncovered some interesting data that tend to counter the accepted myth that Irish-Americans are conservative on sociopolitical issues. The NORC found that they are more likely than any other ethnic group, except Jews, to approve of female careers, vote for a female president, and reject the idea that a female's place is in the home. There is also little difference in male or female support for feminism.It was also found that Irish-American life satisfaction was high with low feelings of alienation. There is little or no evidence of alleged sexual repression, and no apparent differences from the national average on both premarital and extramarital sex, and they are 13 percent less likely to condemn homosexuality. Only 17 percent disapprove of birth control, while only 28 percent disapprove of divorce. Based on this data, It would seem that the sexual morality of Catholicism has been greatly modified by today's Irish Catholics (Greeley 1981).

Problem drinking remains an area of concern. However, Greeley's work seems to indicate that although many Irish drink, and their religion does not curb drinking, their problems are no worse than urban English Protestants and less than those of Polish-Americans, Slavic-Americans, and African-Americans. But common Irish social drinking can turn dysfunctional and lead to alcoholism. It is unfortunate that some Irish-Americans link drinking with their identity, while others turn to drink because of a self-fulfilling prophecy based on societal stereotypes.

### The Catholic Church

Irish-Americans continue to participate in the Church and its activities. Since Vatican II, participation includes both traditionalists and liberalized modernists. However, the number of Irish-Americans entering vocations as nuns, brothers, and priests has declined since Vatican II, contributing to a shortage of clergy. After World War II, the Irish moved to the suburbs and left overbuilt churches in the inner cities, which are harder to finance, staff, and maintain. The parish is still important in the life of Irish-Americans, but it is not the identifying feature of the urban church it once was. In the suburbs, many other alternatives exist to detract from the parish as a focal point. Loyalty to the church has not diminished since Vatican II loosened traditional church discipline. In spite of a decline in many traditional religious practices, Irish-American Catholics remain the most devout on almost all measures of religious zeal. The Irish outrank other Catholics in mass attendance, weekly communion, approval of religious vocations in the family, membership in religious organizations, and spiritual reading. According to Greeley, on a scale of "Catholicity," differences between Irish Catholics and other Catholics in religious devotion have actually increased since 1963 (Greeley 1981). Vatican II did not force the Irish away from Catholicism as many intellectuals predicted or at least hoped. If fact, Irish-American Catholics are the least likely of all Catholics to abandon their religion for an alternative.

## INTERGROUP RELATIONS

The Irish were the first unwanted immigrants to the United States and became the targets of much hate and violence. Their experience in urban America was a preview for those to come; Jews, Italians, Poles and African-Americans. It was the Irish who led the way for other ethnics to reach accommodation with the WASP establishment. However, their own oppressive experience did not often lead to championing the cause of other ethnics (Clark 1986). Among European Americans, the Irish had their battles with the German-Americans, Italian-Americans, Polish-

Americans, and Jewish-Americans. Conflict with the German-Americans occurred in the 1840s and 1850s, and involved competition for jobs and political positions. German-Americans were opposed to the Irish domination of the Catholic Church. They wanted national parishes based on language, which the Irish opposed, fearing that they would dilute the political power of the church. German/Irish rivalry disappeared quickly and a generally cooperative situation has prevailed into the present day (Dolan 1975).

Jewish-Americans provided the more serious threat to the Irish. Jews desired the same jobs and were intent on gaining positions of political power. Irish-Americans tended to associate Jewish-Americans with rising communism, and tensions became most acute during the Spanish Civil War. As Jewish-Americans moved into Irish neighborhoods, street fights were not uncommon. However, by World War II the Irish and Jews had adjusted to each other and began to come together on many political and social issues (Bayor 1978).

Italian-Americans presented other problems for Irish-Americans. They began to move into traditionally Irish neighborhoods and compete for construction jobs and housing. Job sites often were disrupted by fights between the Irish and Italian workers. The Italians thought that the Irish-dominated Catholic Church was strange and inhospitable. The Irish thought the Italian brand of Catholicism as worldly and not very devout. Even lay groups split along ethnic lines. For example, the Irish-dominated Knights of Columbus was passed up for the Sons of Italy. Irish/Italian accommodation took longer than that with the Jews, especially in the city. However, as both groups moved to the suburbs after World War II, the old feuds were forgotten and intermarriage became a common sign of middle-class status for both.

Polish/Irish conflicts were common to midwestern cities such as Detroit, Toledo, Chicago, and Milwaukee. The focus of the conflict in large part was associated with the Irish control over the Catholic Church. Polish Catholics resented this situation and often clashed with their Irish bishops. In a number of instances, Polish/Irish confrontations resulted in physical violence. Even today there are hints of the old animosities, especially within the context of the church.

Irish interaction with Asian Americans was largely limited to the Chinese. They were seen as a threat to jobs and improved wages. The Irish often supported exclusionary immigration policies against Asians, and in a few cases, especially on the West Coast, violently attacked the Chinese. Such interaction was intense but relatively short-lived. Today Chinese/Irish contacts, while not intense, are generally harmonious.

The Irish and the African-Americans were the first two mass immigrant groups to populate the United States. Both have had long histories of oppression and exploitation in this country. African-Americans were brought here in bondage, as slaves against their will, while most Irish were driven from their homeland by British oppression and starvation. Both groups shared a number of sociohistorical characteristics that set them apart from other immigrant groups. Some of these characteristics are tied to their lower class experience in America, while others are related to experiences in their homelands. Both have been victims of exploitive colonialism, from rural peasant backgrounds, victims of derogatory behavioral by the directive role of a church, and victims of disruption of the basic family structure and minority status with much alienation and discrimination. However, the two groups had a number of important differences, some of which greatly affected group mobility. The white skin of the Irish allowed them the luxury of anglicizing their name and assimilating into the dominant Anglo-American majority. The Irish church was more organized and authoritarian than the African-American church, and they were able to use it as a resource in the form of education, jobs, and social welfare services. The African-American family was disrupted by slavery, while the Irish family was stabilized under the authority and watchfulness of the church.

The Irish were actually the pioneers of ghetto living while the African-Americans ghettoized much later, following the Civil War. The Irish ghetto became the power base for the Irish rise in city politics and ultimately national power. For many blacks, the ghetto has proved to be more permanent and less a source of political power. The Irish used public jobs provided by the political machines for economic gain. But recent research reveals that the rewards of urban politics in the pre–New Deal period were modest, and the most significant gains of the Irish were concentrated in areas where they had less political strength. It is also possible that the relative security of blue-collar jobs in public works, fire and police departments, may have hindered the rise of an Irish-American middle class. The security of the occupations encouraged long tenure at low-status jobs.

### Interaction of the Irish-American and African-American

The nature of Irish-American and African-American interaction has varied from one time period to another. It changed from a rather benign interaction in colonial times to one of violence and antagonism during the industrialization of the country. In colonial times, the numbers that had any opportunity to interact were small, and both groups lived in a subordinate relationship to the Anglo-Americans. After the Irish immigration following the Napoleonic Wars, they began to compete with the small free African-American population. It was during this period that the Irish-American and African-American began to develop a more antagonistic relationship and violent clashes occurred in Philadelphia in 1832, 1834, 1842, and 1849. The African-American response to the Irish invasion paralleled that of the anti–Irish-American nativists. But black nativism lacked the racism and anti-Catholicism so characteristic of the Anglo-American nativists, and many black leaders were outwardly disappointed that the Irish did not join them as allies.

Antagonism grew throughout the mid-1800s, reaching an apex during the growth of the abolition movement. As the country moved toward civil war, the Irish were torn between a desire to prove their patriotism and a dislike for the Abolitionists. They were seen as anti-Catholic, anti-prohibitionist, and anti-labor. Freed slaves could compete with the exploited white working class for their low-paying jobs, many of which were in Abolitionist-owned factories. The Catholic Church provided very little leadership for the Irish on the question of abolition. Despite this, Irish-Americans joined the Union Army in great numbers (300,000 +) and fought bravely to preserve the union. They proved their allegiance to America with their blood at Bull Run, Fredericksburg, and Gettysburg. However, the Conscription Act of 1863 was resisted violently, as the Irish felt it placed the greatest burden on the Irish and German poor. In New York, they rioted and attacked African-American sections of the city.

A brief period of improvement in relations after the Civil War deteriorated in the 1880s as racial tensions increased and continued on into the 1920s. Irish and African-Americans clashed over jobs, housing, and voting rights in such places as Philadelphia, Memphis, New York, Jersey City, and Chicago. With the rise of the New Deal, the Irish helped to organize and develop its coalition politics that included blacks, Jews, and newly arrived immigrants from Eastern and Southern Europe. As a group, many Irish politicians contributed to the establishment of a government role in the economics and social welfare of the individual. African-Americans began to make some minor advances as a result of New Deal politics, while the growing Irish-American middle class was beginning to be more concerned about the demands of African-Americans. However, the war in Vietnam and the anti-busing campaigns of the 1970s shattered the growing cooperation in a few areas of the country. The virulence of these local clashes, with race often playing a somewhat marginal role, has tended to obscure the important contributions of many Irish-Americans to the cause of social justice for African-Americans. It also ignored the observations of many public opinion surveys which indicated that the Irish-American Catholic wass the most liberal of all gentile groups with respect to issues important to African-Americans.

It is also interesting to note that throughout the whole time period of negative Irish/African-American interaction, a great many African-Americans supported the nationalist struggles in Ireland. Black leaders from Frederick Douglas to Jesse Jackson have understood and supported the just demands of the Irish people in Ireland for an end to British oppression on Irish soil. Black intellectuals, the black media, and many ordinary black people have openly supported the cause of Irish freedom (Metress 1990).

### Sociodynamics of Irish-American/African-American Relations

If Irish-Americans and African-Americans had become allies in the nineteenth and twentieth centuries, American history might have been quite different. But these two large groups interacted antagonistically during much of that time period. The reasons for this were not really racist, for there is no evidence that the Irish were preconditioned toward anti-black bias in Ireland. Rather, the exploitive nature of American capitalism resulted in both groups competing for the same unskilled jobs. Both struggled to overcome their marginal sociopolitical status, and each developed a highly protective attitude toward perceived threats to any gains. The exclusionary nature of most of the Irish-dominated unions did not help improve relations, and spatial relationships played a significant role in clashes over housing and public facilities. The propinquity of the two groups with similar needs created a situation that invited conflict. Of course ethnocentrism and a lack of understanding on the part of both groups also played a role. Both groups seemed to use the other as an opportunity to look down on a group that they perceived to be inferior. It is also possible that each group may have recognized a little of themselves in the other oppressed, degraded group and thus reacted with contempt and disgust. However, throughout the history of the black and green interaction, it is highly probable that members of both groups were indifferent to the problems of the other rather than actively antagonistic. The majority of Irish immigrants were so busy struggling for just basic subsistence that the plights of others was simply irrelevant to them. Likewise, African-Americans who were the victims of fulminant Anglo-Saxon racism, economic exploitation, and deprived of their absolute freedom had little time for the problems of others.

## EPILOGUE

Young Irish-Americans who seem to be concerned with their Irish roots are now socially secure. It is possible that it will be easier for them to nurture their Irishness than their parents. Pride in their own ethnic background will allow them to feel more comfortable with themselves. A group that is sociopsychologically secure will feel less threatened by others or the remnants of anti-Irish Catholicism that still survives in America today. Irish-Americans as a group are more informed and assured about their own sociohistorical experience. This will encourage them toward a greater acceptance of differences in others and promote more toleration. If anything, the appreciation of similar shared experience and the nature of cultural variation may promote intercultural understanding and sensitivity to the needs and aspirations of other groups. More importantly, outsiders must understand the oppressive historical roots of the Irish-Americans in both Ireland and nineteenth-century America to appreciate their concern with socioeconomic status. The influence of Catholic values on personal values and social attitudes is deep and significant. Further, the role of Democratic party politics and union struggles must be appreciated to understand the sociopolitical attitudes of Irish-Americans toward contemporary problems.

## REFERENCES

Bayor, R. H. 1978. *Neighbors in Conflict: The Irish, German, Jews and Italians of New York City 1929–1941.* Baltimore: Johns Hopkins Press.

Clark, D. 1986. *Hibernia-America: The Irish and Regional Cultures.* Westport, CT: Greenwood Press.

Dolan, J. P. 1975. *The Immigrant Church: New York's Irish and German Catholics 1815–1865.* Baltimore: Johns Hopkins Press.

Duff, J. B. 1971. *The Irish in the United States.* Belmont, CA: Wadsworth.

Glazer, N. & Moynihan, P. 1963. *Beyond the Melting Pot: The Negroes, Puerto Ricans, Jews, Italians, and Irish.* New York: Cambridge, MIT Press.

Greeley, A. M. 1969. *Why Can't They Be Like Us: Facts and Fallacies About Ethnic Group Differences and Group Conflicts in America*. New York: Institute of Human Relations Press.

————1981. *The Irish American: The Rise to Money and Power*. New York: Harper & Row.

King, J. A. & Fitzgerald, M. F. 1990. *The Uncounted Irish in Canada and the United States*. Port Credit, Ontario: P. D. Meany.

Metress, S. P. 1981. *The Irish American Experience: A Guide to the Literature*. Lanham, MD: University Press of America.

————1990. Black on the Green: A Historical Perspective. *The Irish People* 14:6.

————1995. *The American Irish and Irish Nationalism*. Lanham, MD: Scarecrow Press.

Miller, K. 1985. *Emigrants and Exiles: Ireland and Irish Exodus to North America*. New York: Oxford University Press.

Miller, K. & Wagner, P. 1994. *Out of Ireland*. Washington, DC: Elliott & Clark.

Novak, M. 1973. *The Rise of the Unmeltable Ethnic: Politics and Culture in the 70s*. New York: Collier.

# 10

# African-Americans as a Cultural Group

## Mikel Hogan-Garcia

### INTRODUCTION AND DEFINITION OF TERMS

The United States commonly is referred to as a nation composed of immigrants.Yet, immigration is only one source of its cultural diversity. Colonization of the Native Americans, who had migrated from Asia approximately 15,000 years ago, and the forced immigration and enslavement of Africans are two other sources of the cultural diversity in the United States. It may be more accurate to say that the United States is a nation of *racial* and *ethnic* groups. I use the terms ethnic and cultural group interchangeably when referring to patterned beliefs and behaviors characteristic of members of a group that set them apart from other groups. The patterned beliefs and behaviors of cultural groups in the United States may be based on a common way of life in their country of origin, their immigration experience, and adjustment to life and work in the United States. At the individual level, cultural or ethnic *identity* refers to the extent to which a person feels a sense of belonging and loyalty to a group and shares in their way of life, which is evidenced by their spending time with other members of the group. It may also include feelings of pride or shame about one's membership in a group (Erchak 1992).

Relevant to the discussion of terminology is the term *racial group*. Race has been defined as a biological classification of human groups based on heredity and genetic differences. As a result of historical developments in social relations among groups in the United States, however, race is also a social construct that ascribes status to groups of people within the social system. The social meaning attached to the physical characteristics of African-Americans past and present results in economic, educational, social, and political obstacles to their full participation in mainstream society. Given these definitions, African-Americans are an ethnic or cultural group, and they are a part of that racial group also known as African American or black American). There are approximately 30.8 million, or 12 percent,

African Americans out of a total of 248 million people in the United states. The majority live in the South with smaller numbers in the north, central, northeastern, and western regions of the United States (Jones & Harrison 1994).

Misunderstandings and other problems result whenever African American is defined or perceived as a homogenous group. African Americans are very diverse. There are differences based on education, occupation, religion, generation, gender, region, sexual orientation, and their residence in urban, rural or suburban areas. In addition, individuals and groups of African-Americans will differ in relation to identity. To compound matters, further, a person may identify with more than one group because one's identity can involve race, ethnicity, and other social categories such as gender. Cuban-Americans from Florida who speak Spanish and participate in family and community events may also be African by race and participate in organizations such as the Urban League or the National Association for the Advancement of Colored People (NAACP) that promote equal opportunity policies for African-Americans. Moreover, if the Cuban-American is female, she also may be involved in women's rights organizations. In this chapter four historical contexts in which African-Americans constructed themselves as a cultural group will be described. Five specific institutions illustrating the traditions of African-Americans in providing mutual help, education, and their struggle for equal opportunity also will be discussed.

## DEVELOPMENT OF AFRICAN-AMERICANS AS A CULTURE GROUP

Four historical time periods combine to provide some valuable insights into the broad situational context in which African-Americans have developed a sense of group identity that is distinct from other groups within the United States: forced immigration and slavery, emancipation and institutionalized segregation, the great migration and development of urban ghettos, and the civil rights movement of the twentieth century.

### Forced Immigration and Institutionalized Slave Labor

The violent removal of Africans from the West coast and Central Africa and their subsequent life of chattel slavery was the foundation for the formation of African-American culture. Sterling Stucky, a culture historian, provides a description of this process.

During the process of their becoming a single people, Yorubas, Akans, Ibos, Angolans and others were present on slave ships to America and they experienced a common horror...As such, slave ships were the first real incubators of slave unity across cultural lines, cruelly revealing irreducible links from one ethnic group to the other, fostering resistance thousands of miles before the shores of the new land appeared on the horizon—before there was mention of natural rights in America (1987:1).

Tales of the traumatizing experience of the slave trade and "mid-passage," the name given to the voyage of the slave ships, have been retained in folklore to this day in certain areas of the South. The story of "King Buzzard" is one whose themes recall treachery, suffering, and loss of their African way of life when they were enslaved. Other stories, such as "Gullah Joe" and "Old Man Rogan," tell of their painful life in slavery. The themes tell of feelings of loss for one's African family and homeland as well as the grief felt when members of one's slave family were physically abused and sold to other slave owners (Stuckey 1987).

By the end of the seventeenth century, the servitude of African slaves took precedence over indentured servants. Slave labor had become the mainstay of the agricultural economy producing such crops as; tobacco, cotton, rice, sugar, hemp, and indigo (used in making dye). The system was one of chattel slavery because the slaves were socially defined as legal property, not people. Being property, slaves had no legal rights, and masters could use any type of physical coercion to maintain control. The virtual control exercised by owners was legally sanctioned by a system of laws called the Slave Codes. Although most slaves were owned by the upper class in society (three out of four Southerners did not own slaves, for example), a system of race hierarchy in social relations and an ideology of white supremacy became entrenched in American mainstream culture, particularly in the South and the North (Morgan 1975; Fredrickson 1965).

Slaves survived chattel slavery by developing their own family and community in their quarters "from sundown to sunup" (Genovese 1974). Meier and Rudwick suggest:

Whether one views Southern servitude as harsh or paternalistic, the older view that slavery virtually denuded Negroes of a culture of their own has now been discredited. Instead, it is universally recognized that, within the slave regime, blacks demonstrated a striking resiliency and found enough "social living space" to develop a community and subculture, which enabled them to maintain group identity and to cope with the oppressive institution in which they found themselves. Nowhere has this new perspective of historians produced more important results than in analyses of the slave family and slave religion. White culture and the masters' actions played a role in shaping both, it is true, yet it is just as true that what emerged was as much or even more a product created by the slaves themselves (1976:76).

Since incidents of slave resistance and rebellion were perceived by whites as caused by the presence of the free black population, legal restrictions called the *Black Codes* were imposed on free blacks. Free blacks were those who had purchased their freedom, had run away from their owner, or whose owner had freed them. Altogether, the racial laws imposed second-class citizenship on free blacks in southern and northern states (Berlin 1974: Litwack 1961). For example, in some states they were required to carry a certificate of freedom or be claimed as a slave. Occupations, travel, and freedom of assembly were restricted in addition to segregated public facilities such as parks, cemeteries, theaters, and opera houses. In some states they could not testify in court against a white person and their voting was restricted or outlawed altogether. Some northern states, such as New York, New Jersey, Connecticut, Rhode Island, and Pennsylvania, who had freed their slaves during the American Revolution and allowed them to vote, outlawed their voting between 1807 and 1837 because of pressure from white immigrant workers who perceived free blacks as competing for their jobs and voting against their political interests (Meier & Rudwick 1976).

The prejudice and discriminatory treatment of the free black population in the North and South during slavery times was the context in which the institutional infrastructure of African-American communities was built and their status as a minority assured. Since that time, various political organizations have worked for equal rights while church, mutual aid, education, and independent newspapers worked toward the formation of the culture and institutions that would come to characterize the African-American communities (Curry 1981:240–242), as well as their responses to the status imposed upon them by the powerful white majority.

The national conflict over slavery increased in the decades preceding the Civil War. Conflict increased when Congress passed the Fugitive Slave Law of 1850. A story told by an African American whose family migrated to Wisconsin before the Civil War reveals how the law impacted both black and white residents of the state:

Most Wisconsonites disagreed with the Fugitive Slave Act, which permitted slave catchers to cross state lines for the purpose of returning escaped slaves, and in some cases to kidnap free blacks. In 1854, Joshua Glover, an escaped slave from Missouri who had been working in Racine for two years, was apprehended by his former master and imprisoned in Milwaukee. A band of men from Racine and Milwaukee broke open the jail, freed Glover, and sent him safely to Canada. The case eventually led the Wisconsin supreme court to defy the federal government by declaring the Fugitive Slave Act unconstitutional (Cooper 1977:4).

### Emancipation and Institutionalized Segregation

When President Abraham Lincoln took office in February of 1861, the conflict over slavery had resulted in seven states seceding from the union. In April of the same year, the Civil War started when Confederate forces attacked Fort Sumter. On January 1, 1863, President Lincoln issued the Emancipation Proclamation freeing slaves in rebellious Southern states, and in 1865 the Thirteenth Amendment to the Constitution abolished slavery altogether. Black leaders, however, saw this as just the beginning of their work in obtaining rights of citizenship since racial segregation by custom and an ideology of white race supremacy was deeply entrenched in both slave and free states.

Martial law was imposed on the Southern states during the Reconstruction period. The Freedman's Bureau was established in 1865 by the Department of War with the responsibility to protect and provide for the welfare of the freedmen. The work of the Freedman's Bureau was thwarted, however, by other political and economic forces such as the Black Codes. The laws were "a system of social control that would be a substitute for slavery, fix the Negro in a subordinate place in the social order, and provide a manageable and inexpensive labor force" (Meier & Rudwick 1976:170). In addition, the former slave labor system survived in the development of sharecropping and the crop lien system. Freedmen were not paid a wage, but instead rented a plot of land and paid to the owner a certain proportion of the crop, sharecrop. In the crop lien system, the freedmen who paid on credit at the plantation store for the farming supplies (seed, mules, and tools) were supposed to pay the debt when the crop was sold, "the croppers paid heavily for the purchases they were compelled to make at the plantation store. Buying food and clothing on credit with the crop as lien, they were charged high prices, outrageous interest rates, and were forced to depend on the planter's rendition of accounts. After the crop was sold, they were likely to end up in debt to the planter, particularly in a poor year. Out of this arose the system of debt peonage, whereby insolvent croppers, unable to repay debts from one year to another, were required by law to work indefinitely for the same unscrupulous planter" (Meier & Rudwick 1976:173). In 1877, martial law was ended and federal troops were withdrawn from the South in a compromise between Southern Democrats and the Republican administration of Rutherford B. Hayes over a disputed election with Democrat Samuel J. Tilden. Racial restrictions on African-Americans increased and in 1896 segregation was legitimized by the Supreme Court in *Plessy vs. Ferguson*. Legal segregation thus became the law of the land until it was overturned after decades of political battles in the 1954 Supreme Court ruling in *Brown vs. Board of Education.*

### The Great Migration and Development of Urban Ghettoes

The great migration refers to the Northern relocation of about one million African-Americans at the time of World War I. There were economic and social crises in the South, such as the boll weevil infestation of the cotton crop, floods in Alabama and Mississippi, and widespread lynching of blacks. In the North, industry needed unskilled and semiskilled labor because the war had stopped immigration. The migrants to the urban areas were faced with life conditions of poverty coupled with the continued animosity of white workers who saw African-Americans as economic rivals for their jobs. They were also seen as political opponents because working-class white men (women did not get the franchise until 1920) voted Democratic, while African-Americans voted Republican (Lincoln's party). "In 1917 the fears and suspicions of whites erupted into race riots in Philadelphia and Chester, Pennsylvania, and at East St. Louis, Illinois, where the most serious racial outbreak in the twentieth century cost the lives of at least thirty-nine blacks. Friction also resulted from competition between Negroes and whites for limited housing. Yet, despite resistance both during and after the war, the ghettoes expanded block by block" (Meier & Rudwick 1976:236).

In addition to racial conflicts, blacks faced residential and school segregation, and hotels and restaurants increasingly barred black customers. Racial restrictions also extended to black men in the armed services. After World War I, "Returning soldiers in 1919 found themselves in a situation that if anything was worse than the one before they left: a revived Ku Klux Klan, loss of job opportunities due to demobilization, and an extraordinary outbreak of race riots—over twenty in that

'Red Summer' of 1919. They ranged from Washington, DC, to Elaine, Arkansas, from Longview, Texas, to Chicago. The basic cause of most riots lay in white fears of economic competition and voting power of urban black migrants" (Meier & Rudwick 1976:239).

In addition to these external pressures from whites, there were internal forces within the black communities that contributed to the increasing ghettoization. Blacks found mutual protection in their separate communities, and the institutional structure of black communities was centered in the ghettos—the churches, clubs, mutual aid, educational, and political organizations. Additionally, the concentration of blacks in specific sections of the metropolitan cities supported a black business and professional class (which included political leaders) whose careers were rooted in the support of a concentrated black population. As living conditions worsened after World War I, intragroup conflict arose in some black communities because some older residents blamed the Southern migrants for the increased racial restrictions. Furthermore, black leaders had to negotiate different interests based on the diverse social classes developing within the community.

### Civil Rights Movement of the Twentieth Century

The urbanization of African-Americans in ghettoes formed the urban basis for the civil rights movement of the twentieth century that culminated in significant equal opportunity legislation in the 1950s and 1960s. The goals, strategies, and tactics of the civil rights movement were preceded by a long tradition of political work by African-Americans. For example, from colonial times there are records of slave petitions to legislatures for their freedom (Grant 1968). In the eighteenth century, blacks held mass meetings, public speeches, and also petitioned legislatures for civil rights. For instance, in 1787, Prince Hall, a free black in Massachusetts, petitioned the state legislature for equal education facilities for free black children. Unsuccessful, in 1798 he established a school in his home (Aptheker 1973:19-20). In the nineteenth century African-Americans continued their struggle for equal opportunities in the free states and the abolition of the hated institution of slavery. Moreover, African-American women in the middle and upper classes also worked individually and collectively for race and gender equality (Loewenberg & Bogin 1976). One example is Ida B. Wells' "Crusade for Justice" (Duster 1970). Ida Wells' investigations and newspaper editorials about the circumstances of 728 lynchings of blacks resulted in the looting and burning of her Memphis, Tennessee, newspaper and her "permanent banishment from the South" (Giddings 1984: 28–29). In the twentieth century, black men and women continue their political work for rights of citizenship and equal opportunities.

A number of African-American organizations were involved in the twentieth-century civil rights movement. The National Association for the Advancement of Colored People (NAACP), was originally founded as an interracial organization in the tradition of the Abolitionist movement by W.E.B. DuBois in 1909. In the past and present, the NAACP works on numerous projects, from an antilynching bill that was passed by congress in the 1920s (but was never enforced) to voting rights and the elimination of segregation in housing, occupations, and education. The National Urban League was founded in 1910 with the mission, "to assist African-Americans in achieving social and economic equality. The league implements its mission primarily through advocacy, bridge building among the races, program services, and research" (Tidwell 1994). The Congress of Racial Equality (CORE) was founded during World War II at the time of a threatened march on Washington of 50–100,000 black men by A. Philip Randolph (Meier & Rudwick 1976:243–268). The Student Nonviolent Coordinating Committee (SNCC) is another organization whose activities included demonstrations for desegregated schools.

In addition to the strategy of nonviolent demonstrations and legal challenges to racial restrictions, some black leaders advocated more militant strategies in the 1940s and 1950s. Some researchers interpret the movement as a response to the growing poverty and unemployment of urban African-Americans. In 1952, for example, the median black family income was 57 percent of white family income. In 1962 income had fallen to 53 percent of whites, "due to automation and other technological change black unemployment rose steadily. In 1962 it was two and one half times that of whites and in some cities higher. It was during the economic recession that a black nationalist organization called the Nation of Islam, originally founded in the 1930s, became nationally prominent" (Meier & Rudwick 1976:285). Important black leaders in this group were Malcolm X and, more recently, Louis Farrakhan. Another militant nationalist organization operating in the 1960s was that of the Black Panthers.

Although there were differing ideologies, strategies, and tactics being used by African-Americans in the civil rights movement, it succeeded in influencing some national policies aimed at opening opportunities to African-Americans and other excluded groups. The many successes of the movement were the result of several developments: blacks' political organizing, such as was outlined above, combined with national and international developments. Two examples are the federal policies of President Franklin Roosevelt's appointment of the Fair Employment Practices Commission to open occupation opportunities to blacks in the war industry in the 1940s, and President Truman's desegregation of the armed forces and establishment of the commission to study race relations. In addition, the civil rights movement was helped by the expanding economy following World War II and international developments such as the independence movements against colonial powers in Africa, Asia, and Latin America that influenced a growing respect for people of color. In 1954, the Supreme Court ruled against segregated schools in the *Brown vs. Board of Education,* thus overturning *Plessy vs. Ferguson* of 1896. In 1964 and 1968 the Civil Rights Acts became law, creating a legal foundation of equal opportunity for African Americans and members of other traditionally excluded groups. In 1965, the Voting Rights Act was enacted by Congress and President Lyndon Johnson. It sought to end discrimination and allow all citizens to participate in the political process by outlawing literacy tests, complicated registration forms, and intimidation tactics at the polls. In the 1970s these laws were amended and expanded, and some effort was made to enforce them. Since the 1980s, however, implementation of these laws has been weakened. Equal opportunity has yet to be implemented in spite of the passage of the previous laws mentioned above and the passage of the 1991 Civil Rights Act, which was aimed at strengthening the right of victims of discrimination to sue. Today, African-Americans and other groups continue their efforts to halt the weakening of the civil rights legislation.

## AFRICAN-AMERICAN INSTITUTIONS

In addition to a long tradition of political organizing aimed at securing equal opportunities, there are four other institutions that date back to slavery times. These African-American institutions are discussed to provide a glimpse of the traditions, values, and means by which this group survived as a minority in the United States: family, church, education, and community service (or self-help) institutions. Three common values embodied in these institutions include mutual help, education, and equal opportunity (Williams 1974; Gwaltny 1980).

### African-American Family

The roots of the African-American family lie in Africa among the cultures of West Africa, Angola, and the Congo. Although each had their own language, beliefs, customs, and histories, they shared some common patterns. In each of these cultures from which American slaves were taken, integral to community life was the extended family. The key characteristic of the extended family is its flexibility and support of family members through pooling resources and caring for other family members and their children.

Marriages among slaves were not legally recognized, yet slave marriages and family formations in the slave quarters was common. The custom of slave marriage was "jumping over the broom" (Rawick 1972). Slave marriages were long lasting despite separation due to owners' sale of mates. For example, Herbert Gutman surveyed family data on 40,000 ex-slaves and concluded, "We have examined briefly decisions made between 1864 and 1866 of about forty thousand different adult ex-slaves, men and women who were still together in families and who registered slave marriages at the end of this process" (Gutman 1976:34). In addition, Gutman says the records of the Freedman's Bureau reveal many family members re-united after traveling across the southern states after the Civil War.

A predominant family form since slavery is the husband and wife nuclear family, in which both partners are employed. In 1990 the nuclear family accounted for just over one third of African-American families. Single-parent households were 53 percent of African-American families, with 88 percent of these being headed by women. Another family form is the extended family. It consists of a married couple, or a single parent, and their children or grandparents and their grandchildren, as well as another relative or relatives (nieces, nephews, aunts, uncles, cousins, etc.). Augmented families are similar to the extended family but instead of relatives a boarder or friends co-habitat (Henderson 1994).

This tradition of flexible and supportive family forms has provided one of the means for African-American survival. My personal data on the black community of Los Angeles from 1883 to 1919 suggest mutual support and the pooling of resources within the families was common. Furthermore, as racial discrimination in occupations and housing increased in Los Angeles after 1910, the family data suggest an increased reliance on family members for housing and economic support (Hogan-Garcia 1985). In a more recent study of a six-generation African-American family in south-central Los Angeles, a similar pattern of mutual support exists. The oldest member in the family, Grace Phillips, was born in Los Angeles in 1891. In the 1940s she and her husband purchased a home adjacent to one of her son's so that "granny," as she is called, could care for her grandchildren since her son's marriage had ended in divorce. They lived next to each other for about fifty years, during which time she helped raise the two grandchildren and cared for her ailing mother and later her ailing husband; and, later still, when she was ailing, she was cared for by her son and his second wife. Her grown grandchildren who lived elsewhere in the Los Angeles area also made regular visits. For example, one granddaughter made weekly visits to help with the housecleaning and gardening. At 98 years old Granny comically commented on the role of her son in her life: "I took care of him in his childhood and now he's taking care of me in my second childhood, and if I live much longer he'll be taking care of me in my third childhood" (Phillips 1989).

Granny's mutual support system extended into the neighborhood when in the 1950s she founded several clubs, one being "Granny's cleanup committee," in which she organized the children on her block whose parents worked (*Los Angeles Times* 1977). She taught them manners in addition to supervising the local neighborhood cleanup projects—raking leaves, picking up trash, and taking food to neighbors who were sick. Granny says the success of her children's project lies in an obvious social fact: "there is not a child on earth that can't be bribed with candy" (Phillips 1989). It is important, however, not to romanticize the support pattern of extended families, African-American or those of other cultural groups. Although mutual support in extended families confers benefits on family members, there are also substantial costs: economic, emotional, and costs to physical health. Anthropologist Rayna Rapp refers to the sharing in poor extended families as similar to walking on a "tightrope." "Pooling is a norm in family behavior, but it's a hard norm to live with, to either meet or ignore. To comply with the demands of the extended family completely is to lose control over material and emotional resources; to refuse is very dangerous, as people know they will need one another" (1987:229).

Today the extended family in African-American communities continues to be a strength despite its strain on the African-American family structure. The primary strain is the pervasiveness of poverty and its attendant problems. Economic changes in the last twenty-five years have produced major employment shifts and the loss of opportunities for all African-American males and females. With the reduction of some manufacturing and white-collar employment as companies have downsized, automated, and relocated to other countries, there has been a decline in black working-class jobs, an expansion of poor blacks, and an increasingly unstable black middle class. Medium family income in 1990 was $21,423, or 58 percent of white income of $36,915. Moreover, black family income has remained 55 to 60 percent of white income since the 1950s (Feagin & Feagin 1993:234). According to economist Edna Bonacich, the income gap between African-Americans and the white population, "reflects the impact of discrimination, and the concentration of African Americans in jobs that offer minimal pay and few benefits" (Gonzalez 1993:309). In 1990, 10.2 percent of the employed African-Americans were in managerial and professional occupations, and 9.3 percent were in technical and sales positions. The remainder were in working-class jobs: service occupations, operators and laborers, cleaners, servants, maids, nurses, orderlies, cleaning and building services. According to the U.S. Census figures on unemployment in 1992, which, by the way, researchers agree reflect an undercount, African-American unemployment was 13.3 percent, whereas white unemployment was 5.8 percent. In 1992, furthermore, the poverty rate for African-American families was three times higher than for white families, with 31.1 percent of the African-Americans living in poverty (Gonzalez 1993:292). The economic strain on black families is also reflected in the increase in the divorce rate and decrease in two-parent families. For example, in 1970, 68 percent of black families had two parents, compared to 50 percent in 1990, an 18 percent decline in twenty years. In 1990, the number of two parent families was 83 percent for whites (Lawson & Thompson 1995).

### African-American Churches and Mutual Benefit Institutions

Slaves brought their African religions to the colonies where, for the first one-hundred years of slavery, they blended with the religious beliefs of European Americans and Native Americans. The reason for the development of a unique hybrid religious belief system among U.S. slaves was the openness of African religions to adapt and blend with other religious belief systems. Furthermore, because their religion did not distinguish between secular and sacred activities (all activities were seen as potentially sacred), religion was a space of creativity and social strength, and it became central in the creation of African-American communities (Raboteau 1978). In the middle of the nineteenth century, slave owners and missionaries changed their policy on the religious practices of slaves by attempting to shape and control slaves' religious lives. Slaves were successful in "maintaining considerable religious autonomy," however, because they had their own slave preachers, or assistants to missionaries. Baptists and Methodists were especially successful among slaves because they encouraged the development of a black clergy. For example, it was common for slaves from several plantations to hold their own "hush arbor" prayer meetings late at night in a cabin or in the woods. When their master refused them permission to attend, they oftentimes met in secret. Ex-slaves told of their regular prayer meetings, at least once a week. "The nighttime prayer meetings and sings made daily lives bearable, kept alive in them the struggle for freedom," and "the religious ceremonies emphasized and tightened the social bonds among slaves" (Rawick 1972:34, 37).

The black churches established in the free black communities were interrelated with community service organizations. The tradition of African-American churches has been to integrate secular and sacred concerns. They provide religious functions but also community services, "a source of economic cooperation, an arena of political activity, a sponsor of education, and a refuge in a hostile world" (Rawick 1972:50–51). In addition to churches, free black communities formed community service organizations such as mutual aid, fraternal organizations, and educational services. Sometimes mutual aid societies and educational services preceded the founding of a church, and at other times, they were outgrowths of church activities. Two examples illustrate this. On the East Coast in Newport, Rhode Island, an African-American mutual benefit organization called the African Union Society formed in 1780. Community services included maintaining birth, marriage, and death records as well as providing for "decent burials," apprenticeships for black youth, and resources for people in crisis. In 1807, the African Union Society merged with another organization, the African Benevolent Society, and established a school—free of charge to children of the free black community. In 1824, the first black church was formed under the auspices of the African Union Society (Meier & Rudwick 1976:99).

In the Los Angeles black community, educational organizations were outgrowths of church activities. For example, in the 1880s "laymen" in the Los Angeles black community established the first churches in the community, the Second Baptist and First African Methodist Episcopal. Both churches served spiritual and secular needs: "The churches were headquarters for meetings concerning labor and politics, as well as for religion. It was not uncommon at Sunday morning service for the church clerk to announce that a brother who was an experienced plasterer had just arrived in the city and needed employment, or that a woman, a good cook, needed a job" (Bass 1960:20). In addition to the two churches founded between 1885 and 1890, each church had "literary societies," which provided weekly forums for public education in the form of discussions of books and poetry, study clubs, and debates on the current issues. These educational events, participated in by all age groups, served as a community support to education since their children attended public schools. The Los Angeles Odd Fellows Lodge was formed in 1885. Affiliated with the churches, fraternal orders such as the Odd Fellows provided sickness and burial money to its members. Later some fraternal societies developed into black insurance companies ( Hogan-Garcia 1985).

Today's African-American churches continue to demonstrate the  values of mutuality, education, and equal opportunity  by serving  as community centers that focus on spiritual needs, political action, and community service (which includes education). For example, when referring to black communities as being in a "state of chaos," W. Franklyn Richardson, in the National Urban League's  recent report on black America,  says, "Today, when one in four black males is incarcerated or on parole, and where a disproportionate number of black men is addicted to, or sells drugs, not to mention teenage pregnancy, single parenting, divorce, unemployment, poverty, and the overwhelming sense of hopelessness and helplessness, the African-

American church must once again rise and provide the catalyst for change necessary for the revitalization of the African-American community" (1994:115).

In addition, the tradition of mutual support continues in the 1990s in the "self help" development initiatives in Black communities. For example, quoting again from the National Urban League's 1994 report:

Despite sharp and devastating declines in federal assistance to cities in the last 12 years, many of these initiatives mobilize citizen resources: churches, corporations, foundations, and nonprofit institutions; they adamantly confront a range of complex and ominous challenges including violent crime, housing shortages and deterioration, environmental justice, education, employment development, business and commercial development, and the development of physical infrastructures. This light flows from a dynamic, restless, stirring, spiritual reservoir deep within those who care not only within the African American community and about African Americans but also, ultimately, themselves (Henderson 1994: 22).

### Education

As we have now seen, during slavery times black churches and mutual benefit societies founded schools for free blacks. For example, The Brown Fellowship Society of Charleston, South Carolina, in 1790 established a school for free blacks. Later in the nineteenth century, in 1834, it became "legally mandatory that a white person attend each class" (Meier & Rudwick 1976:111), as race restrictions were increasingly placed on free blacks due to fear of slave insurrections. Blacks also attended public schools in some states. In the north, free public schools for whites "was the rule by the 1830s, but it did not include blacks;"—they were usually segregated (1976:111). Throughout the North the pattern at these schools was similar: overcrowded in rundown buildings with limited supplies and equipment. Blacks responded by working with school districts to improve their children's school and blacks organized desegregation protests. The school desegregation efforts of the twentieth century were thus foreshadowed by many such efforts dating back to the times of slavery (111–115). Today, segregation and inadequate schools continue to be problems as African-American students are the majority in many urban schools, and there is a decrease in financial and professional support to education (Henderson 1994:18).

### CONCLUSION

In order to promote better understanding of African-Americans as a cultural group, an overview of four historical time periods has been presented and five African-American institutions that reflect the way of life they constructed within the context of the United States have been discussed. Furthermore, three traditional values embodied in all of their institutions; mutual support, education, and equal opportunity, also were addressed. Given the current statistics on the poverty rate and incidents of discrimination experienced by African-Americans (Tidwell 1994), the words of John Gwaltney on the "core of Black culture" are as relevant today as when he wrote them in 1980:

This is not...another collection of street-corner exotica but an explication of black culture as it is perceived by the vast majority of Afro-Americans who are working members of stable families in pursuit of much the same kind of happiness that preoccupy the rest of American society. Almost all of the men and women whose thoughts are represented in this volume think well of themselves and are well thought of by their relatives, friends, and neighbors. Their feelings of personal and communal satisfaction are rooted in the astonishing reality of their civil, principled survival in spite of the weight of an empire that rests upon their backs (1980:xxii).

## REFERENCES

Aptheker, H. 1973. *Afro-American History*. Secaucas, NJ: The Citadel Press.
———1969. *To Be Free: Studies In American Negro History*. New York: International Publishers Company Inc.
Bass, C. 1960. *Forty Years: Memoirs From the Pages of a Newspaper*. Los Angeles: Charlotta Bass.
Berlin, I. 1974. *Slaves Without Masters: The Free Negro in the Antebellum South*. New York: Vintage.
Cooper, Z. 1977. *Black Settlers in Rural Wisconsin*. Madison, WI: The State Historical Society.
Curry, L. 1981. *The Free Blacks in Urban America, 1800–1850: The Shadow of a Dream*. Chicago: University of Chicago Press.
Duster, A. (ed). 1970. *Crusade for Justice: The Autobiography of Ida B. Wells*. Chicago: University of Chicago Press.
Erchack, G. 1992. *The Anthropology of Self and Behavior*. New Brunswick: Rutgers University Press.
Feagin, J. & Booher Feagin, C. 1993. *Racial and Ethnic Relations*. Englewood Cliffs: Prentice-Hall.
Frederickson, G. 1965. *The Inner Civil War: Northern Intellectuals and the Crisis of the Union*. New York: Harper & Row.
Genovese, E. 1974. *Roll, Jordan, Roll: The World the Slaves Made*. New York: Pantheon Books.
Giddings, P. 1984. *When and Where I Enter: The Impact of Black Women on Race and Sex in America*. New York: William Morrow & Company, Inc.
Gonzales, J. 1993. *Racial and Ethnic Groups in America*. Dubuque: Kendall / Hunt Publishing Company.
Grant, J. 1968. *Black Protest: History, Documents and Analyses, 1619 to the Present*. Greenwich, CT: Fawcett Publications Inc.
Gutman, H. 1976. *The Black Family in Slavery and Freedom:1750–1925*. New York: Pantheon Books.
Gwaltney, J. 1980. *Drylongso: A Self-Portrait of Black America*. New York: Vintage Books.
Henderson, L. 1994. African Americans in the urban milieu: Conditions, trends, and developing needs. In *The State of Black America*. B. Tidwell (ed). New York: The National Urban League, Inc., pp. 11–30.

Hogan-Garcia, M. 1985. Adaptation Strategies of the Los Angeles black community: 1883–1919. Ph.D. Dissertation. University of California, Irvine.

Jones, D. J. & Harrison, G. 1994. Fast facts: Comparative views of African American status and progress. In *The State of Black America*. B. Tidwell (ed). New York: The National Urban League, Inc., pp. 213–236.

Lawson, E. & Thompson, A. 1995. Black men make sense of marital stress and divorce. *Family Relations* 44:211–218.

Litwack, L. 1961. *North of Slavery: The Negro in the Free State*, 1790–1860. Chicago: University of Chicago Press.

Loewenberg, B. & Bogin, R. (eds). 1976. *Black Women in Nineteenth-Century American Life:Their Words, Their Thoughts, Their Feelings*. University Park: Pennsylvania State University Press.

*Los Angeles Times*. 1977. The garden Grace built. (January 18), Section B, P. 41.

Meier, A & Rudwick, E. 1976. *From Plantation to Ghetto*. New York: Hill & Wang.

Morgan, E. 1975. *American Slavery, American Freedom.*. New York: Hill & Wang.

Phillips, G.1989. Personal interview, November 17.

Raboteau, A. 1978. Slave religion: The "Invisible Institution." In *The Antebellum South*. New York: Oxford University Press.

Rapp, R. 1987. Urban kinship in contemporary America: Families, classes, and ideology. In *Cities of the United States*. L. Mullings (ed). New York: Columbia University Press, pp. 219–242.

Rawick, G. 1972. *From Sundown to Sunup: The Making of the Black Community*. Westport, CT: Greenwood Publishing Company.

Richardson, F. 1994. Mission to mandate: Self development through the black church. In *The State of Black America*. B. Tidwell (ed). New York: The National Urban League, Inc., pp. 113–126.

Stuckey, S. 1987. *Slave Culture*. New York: Oxford University Press.

Tidwell, B. (ed). 1994. *The State of Black America*. New York: The National Urban League, Inc.

Williams, M. 1966. *The Strange Career of Jim Crow*. New York: Oxford University Press.

# 11

---

# The Mexican-American Community
# in the United States

Alicia Re Cruz

## INTRODUCTION

Defining the Mexican-American community, that is, those individuals of Mexican origin living in the United States, is not an easy task. Members of this population usually have been referred to as "Chicanos," "Mexicanos," "Hispanos," "Spanish-Americans," and "Spanish-speaking people." It seems that the most generalized level used to identify themselves is that of "Mexican-Americans" (Garcia 1981). However the usage of this term requires a hard revision when trying to incorporate the undocumented immigrants of Mexico who, although living in the United States, are not American citizens. Demographically speaking, although there have been major shifts in the way this population has been defined in the U.S. Census (Moore 1976), the current term in use by the Census Bureau to ethnically categorize this group is "Hispanics." This ethnic label has become the most convenient way to refer to Americans of Spanish heritage. However, "Hispanics" (sometimes Hispanic American) is an umbrella label that masks a broad variety of ethnic, national, and cultural backgrounds concentrated in different geographical areas in the United States: Puerto Ricans in New York and other Northeast and Midwest cities; Cubans in Florida and the Northeast: and Mexicans in the Southwest. To complete the diversified ethnic mosaic of the entire Hispanic group, we also need to include the increasing number of individuals coming from Spanish-speaking countries in the Caribbean and in Central and South America.

The term "Chicano" was adopted by U.S. citizens of Mexican descent during the *Chicano* movement in the 1960s and 1970s. This label implies an active awareness of their Mexican heritage. After the 1970s, "Chicano" as an ethnic label charged with political activism connotations lost strength, but it remained as an identifier of the Mexican-American community, that is, those who have significant cultural and social roots in the United States, as opposed to the Mexican immigrant community, those with more profound roots and recent origins in Mexico. The succession of generations of Mexicans in the United States, and their different socioeconomic and ideological circumstances according to their historic contexts, is an important factor to take into account for the understanding of other ethnic label usages for certain groups within the Mexican-American community. As such, those who were already settled for two or three generations in Texas preferred to be labeled as "Latin Americans" as opposed to the new immigrants from Mexico, while in New Mexico they preferred to be identified as "Spanish-Americans." Yet, among the Mexican-Americans, there is a faction that considers themselves as homeland people; others prefer to enhance their purely Spanish ancestry, and some others do feel more identified with the Anglo culture. These ethnic preferences are at the core of the existence of such a broad spectrum of ethnic labels for self-ethnic identity or to identify the Mexican-American group. This prolific ethnic terminology yields many shadows in the image of the Mexican-American community as a single entity. Each of these ethnic denominations has a different usage that denounces the speaker's particular cultural stereotype, and the choice of the ethnic label expresses the family, group, and/or the culture with which the individual wishes to be identified. This battle of ethnic identifying terms for the Mexican-American community also evidences the socioeconomic disparities and differences between earlier and more recent Mexican generations and their regionalization in the United States. Bearing in mind the intradiversity of what we call the Mexican-American community, I will use the "Mexican-American" label to refer to the people of Mexican origin, residents for two or more generations, and citizens of the United States.

### Mexican-Americans in Time and Space

Any time that we have to define a particular community, we try to place it in both time and space. How should we consider the Mexican-American community? How is it related to the Mexican nation? Is it an immigrant ethnic community within the broader multiethnic social composition of the United States.? These questions address the important issue of considering Mexico as a nation itself, and the historical processes involved in its transformations in relation to those of the United States. The analysis of this historical dynamism is relevant for the understanding of the differences within the Mexican-American community from which the current stage of diversity within the ethnic group emerges. The diversified mosaic that the Mexican-American population displays today can be traced back to the colonial makeup of Mexico. Mexico is a *mestizo*-state, biologically and culturally based on joint European–Indian ancestry. As such, the ancestral nation-state from which the Mexican-American community was born is a melding formation of Europeans and Indians who also exhibit great cultural diversity (e.g., Pueblos, Yaquis, Navajo, Nahuas, Mayas, etc.). Within this Mexican *mestizo* social tapestry, certain superior cultural and social qualities are attributed to the white group, while the Indian dark skin is undervalued.

In defining the Mexican-American community, the degree to which Mexican-Americans perceive themselves as living within an extension of their Mexican homeland needs to be examined. History helps us illuminate the interpretations of many Mexican-American groups who consider the Southwest as their homeland. Certain Mexican-American groups assert that the mythological homeland of their *Aztec* ancestors was *Aztlan* (Aztec comes from this term used for the ancestral land), located in the area known today as the Southwest. This is the myth of origin that stands for the birth of the entire Mexican nation. According to the myth, a group of people left their homeland in *Aztlan*, guided by their god *Hummingbird-on-the-left* (Wolf 1959:130). In their migration toward the South, the people were told that they would come to a place where they would see an eagle devouring a serpent, at the top of a cactus plant. This would be their "promised land," which later would become the capital for their empire, *Tenochtitlan,* in the fourteenth century. The myth of *Aztlan* constitutes the ideological legitimation for those who claim the Southwest as the origin of the Mexican nation. As such, the myth has become an important ideological device, particularly for the Chicano movement of the early 1970s in attempting to raise ethnic consciousness among Mexican-Americans.

Since the end of the sixteenth century, when people from Mexico began settling the area, settlement continued until the arrival of the "Americans," or "Anglos." Those who defend the Mexican rights and claim the Mexican cultural heritage of the Southwest, interpret the Anglo presence in the area as an "invasion" of these territories (Acuña 1981; Steiner 1979). Others focus on such things as the Mexican political negligence to justify that "people dwelling in the area turned toward the United States as a more responsive political authority than Mexico City" (Weber 1982). History then can be revised or interpreted for ideological purposes that may mask political interests. Undoubtedly there is also a psychological dimension behind the historical right of belonging to this region. Place names (San Antonio, El Paso, San Francisco, Los Angeles) and names given to natural phenomena (Colorado River, Guadalupe River, and Sierra Nevada Mountains) are constant reminders of the Mexican origin of this region. For most ethnic groups, the attachment to land becomes synonymous with culture, religion, and the main features of their ethnic identity. Thus, the Southwest has become an area of dispute between the Anglo population, who assert that they were the developers of the area, and the people of Mexican origin, who claim their ancestry to be rooted in the Southwest. This debate emerges from different perceptions of interpreting the historical process and stamps the different cultural stereotypes used to characterize Mexican-Americans, which also marks the selection of ethnic terms to refer to certain groups within the Mexican-American community. For example, today, the popular eschewing of the adjective *illegal* refers to those who have crossed the border without U.S. authorization, the term ratifying the complete and undiscussed Anglo sovereignty over all of the territory that the Mexican-Americans claim was originally Mexican. The Mexican-American community favors the description of this group as *undocumented,* which leaves the discussion on the historical rights upon the Southwest still open by just stressing the legal status of the individual.

This introductory sketch attempts to convey the idea that the Mexican-American community represents a far more heterogeneous group than might be suggested by any single term of identification that currently may be in general use. The following is an overview of the historical Mexican-American experience in the United States. It is not a study of the community itself, but a historical account of the roots and divergent cultural and socioeconomic development of what is today referred to as "The Mexican-American community." Two frameworks will be used to dissolve the most common assumption that undocumented immigrants, Hispanics, Mexicans, and Mexican-Americans, are all the same. First, by combining socioeconomic and cultural information, a holistic comprehension of the variation of groups within the Mexican-American ethnic community will be reached. Second, the integration of a historical perspective will provide the information to contextualize the reasons and implications of the relationship between Mexico and the United States, which is closely related to the different ways of self-identification among the Mexican-American community. The integration of this historical perspective will highlight the origin and development of various cultural stereotypes and assumptions that underlie the individual American's normal perceptions of the Mexican-American community as well. This will assist us in uncovering all of the socioeconomic and political nuances in the origin of the stereotype portrait of Mexicans as just lazy, illiterate, and unable to get politically organized. This perception of the Mexican-American that emerged prior to the Mexican-American War has continued right on up to the present, although it has been redefined according to various community transformations. History and its intrinsic socioeconomic, cultural, and political frameworks mark not only the geographic dynamism of the United States/Mexican border, but the salient features of the social and ideological boundaries of these two distinctive cultures, which will account for the changes in ethnic identities that have accompanied U.S. and Mexican relations.

## A BORDER NOT "THE BORDER"

With the first Spanish contact on the American continent around 500 years ago, the New World already was inhabited by a large number of indigenous populations that exhibited a great variety of socioeconomic and cultural characteristics, from complex sociopolitical systems such as those of the Maya or Aztec to the more simple social structures of the Navajo, Comanche, and Apache, among many others. Eventually, the Spaniards took control, although limited in some areas, of all Mexico, Central America, and the southern part of the United States. Few Spanish women came to the New World. In general, there was a physical as well as a cultural blending of widely diverse Spanish backgrounds within the variety of Indian cultures. The result was the emergence of a new cultural system, that of the *mestizos*. With the assistance of the Nahua Indians, the Spanish expansion toward the northern areas started during the second half of the sixteenth century. Very little of the desired mineral wealth was discovered in the north. Christianization then became the driving force for the colonizers, who were represented by the numerous *missions* established in Arizona, California, and New Mexico. Missions established at such places as Santa Fe, El Paso, Tucson, San Diego, and Los Angeles became key settlements in the Spanish exploration of the west during the seventeenth and eighteenth centuries. By the early nineteenth century, the Spanish colonizers had occupied areas of New Mexico, Arizona, California, and Florida, and they left sheep, horses, and cattle ranches, irrigation, new crops, mining techniques, and adobe construction as their legacy in the Southwest. After obtaining independence in 1821, the former Spanish territories in the southwestern United States became a part of Mexico. This was the time of the first significant migration of Europeans into the area. These immigrants, driven by an expansionistic spirit, as settlers-to-be, and by virtue of their need for land, clashed almost immediately with the resident Mexican population that already was well established in the territory. This was a politically transitive and turbulent time for Mexico, as it struggled with changing from a Spanish colony to an independent nation.

The cultural and ideological confrontations between the resident Mexicans and Americans, and their competition for land, resulted in the creation of cultural stereotypes to legitimize the Anglo dominance in the area. The stereotype view of the Mexican as backward and lazy was vigorously nurtured during the period of Texas independence (1836–1845). The following, which is from that period, exemplifies the stereotyped description of Mexicans held by most Americans:

The character is quite peculiar. The half-breed, as might be expected, exhibits much of the Indian character; the dull suspicious countenance, the small twinkling piercing eye, the laziness and filth of a tree brute, using freedom as the mere means of animal enjoyment...The intelligence of these mestizos, as they are called, is quite limited; and what little they do possess, is of very doubtful utility. For it seems to be used chiefly in directing their choice of shade trees, under which they shall spend the day in sloth, or in stealing a bullock's hide on which to throw their lazy carcass at night (Farnham 1976:60).

The everyday life of those individuals was actually quite different. The extended family was the center of the social system. Depending on the family's economic status and its urban or rural setting, the household might have included parents, children, grandparents, grandchildren, maiden and other relatives, headed by a male patriarch. Most social interactions are centered around the church (weddings, celebration of saints' days), sometimes accompanied by festive activities (Meier & Ribera 1993:44). For most of the areas in Latin America colonized by Spain, the Catholic tradition provided the ideological coverture for the social activity of the community, and the protection of the community was one of the most important colonizing devices that Spaniards used to their advantage. Economic and political control was more efficiently exercised when the Indians were congregated together rather than dispersed across the countryside. By the same token, the congregation of the Indian community also facilitated the continuation of native culture, although intensively transformed by Spanish influences and impositions. When a particular Indian community was taken, one of the first things that the Spanish conqueror did was to destroy the native temples, the locations of which were then used for the building of the Catholic churches, the ultimate statement of ideological dominance. The goal was to destroy the native ideological apparatus that then was supplanted by that of the conqueror. The same metaphor easily can be applied to the native community; the structural basis was kept alive, but without the traditional native leadership. The traditional notions of community and family became the foundation of the Mexican social apparatus; they were kept alive and nurtured through social interaction tied to religious ceremonies. However, the resulting cultural heritage of the now Mexican people has always been strongly criticized by the Northern Europeans, who are motivated more by the Protestant work ethic and a strong spirit of individualism. The Protestant work ethic has contributed significantly to the stereotype image of Mexicans as inferior simply because of their historically different economic development. The cultural images of Mexicans based on this difference have been extensively nurtured in American newspapers, where they have consistently spoken of Mexicans as "savage, barbaric, immoral, and corrupt" (Brack 1976:102). Mexicans, aware of these "ideological sketches" toward them, promoted ideological confrontation by portraying the Americans as eccentric and religiously fanatical individuals who proclaimed liberty and humanitarian principles while driving the Indians from their lands or virtually annihilating them (Brack 1976:100). Even an article in *La Aguila Mexicana* expressed suspicions about the ultimate goals of the Americans in Mexican territories. The article pointed directly to the Americans' disdain for Indians, whom they referred to as "savages," and suggested that this was as a sign that Mexicans were envisioned in the same way because of their cultural differences with Anglo-Saxon culture (Brack 1976:102).

These particular cultural portraits originated and emerged for both Mexicans and Americans in a very particular historical context. From the point of view of the Americans, Mexico lacked leadership, was unable to organize politically, was full of ethnic conflicts, and faced many financial problems. This image still survives today. This was also the time of the "Manifest Destiny" for Americans, the peculiar Anglo-American version of the concept of the chosen people. It focused around their ferrous faith that they were being guided by "divine providence" to control all lands from the Atlantic seaboard to the Pacific Ocean. Mexican territories were simply perceived as an obstacle to satisfying these goals, much as the Native-American territories were previously viewed (Alvarez 1985:37). Mexican-Anglo political relationships became much more tense in the preliminaries of the Mexican-American War of 1846, just as the cultural images of the two respective ethnic stereotypes were being hotly debated in newspapers in both countries.

### One Border, Two Cultures

By the Treaty of Guadalupe Hidalgo, which was signed at the end of the Mexican-American War of 1846, Mexicans of the newly acquired U.S. territories suddenly found themselves with a different and rather ambiguous national identity. Although Mexican by birth, language, and culture, the war's end transformed them into U.S. citizens. These Mexicans who suddenly were transformed into American citizens constitute what is referred to today as "the Creation Generation" for the Mexican-American community (Alvarez 1985:37). By the treaty, Mexico was forced to yield almost half of its land, all that north of the Rio Grande River, to the United States. The Protestant/Anglo ideology was to then impregnate the way the socioeconomic order was to be established in the area. Within this new social order, Mexicans (perceived as "colored people") were clustered in a subordinated social position. This experience of political subjugation provoked resistance against the Anglo community. Resistance movements quickly gained in popularity, as is evidenced in folk productions such as *el corrido de Gregorio Cortez* (Paredes 1958), and even social banditry was viewed positively as a strategic maneuver against the American society.

Following the war, the social dominance of the Americans differed from territory to territory. Mexican leaders in New Mexico established alliances with Anglos in ranching, railroading, and banking. This, the subjugation of the Apaches in 1886, and the completion of the railroad in 1881 opened the territory to a larger number of Anglo settlers, so that by the first decade of the twentieth century, a considerable number of resident Mexicans were forced into the status of a dependent minority (Moore 1976:16). In California, with the discovery of gold, the Anglo settlers quickly outnumbered the native Mexican population or *Californios*, so that by 1850 Mexicans represented only some 15 percent of the total population in the region (Cortes 1980:705). Under a new socioeconomic order that was instituted by the Anglo community, many of the original *Californios* landowners lost their lands while others were pushed into work as ranch hands or unskilled laborers.

Ultranationalism and anti-foreigner sentiments characterized the people of the United States by the time Texas became a state in 1845. Within the context of these sentiments, ethnicity, and skin color became prime criteria for social ascription, while economic developments in Texas during the second half of the nineteenth century significantly impacted the resident Mexican population in the Southwest. The cattle boom of the 1870s and 1880s, the expansion of sheep raising, and the developments in cotton production all became possible because of cheap Mexican labor (Acuña 1981; Cockeroft 1986; Meier & Ribera 1993). This economic boom attracted a new group of immigrants into the area during the period of the 1880s and 1890s. Among these immigrants came a large number of poor white migrants from the Old South. They brought not only their labor, but also ideological baggage that was highly focused on color prejudices. Out of this came discrimination toward the resident Mexicans, and this resulted in increased racial tensions between the Mexicans and the Americans (Meier & Ribera 1993:86).

All of this brief history, particularly in the Southwest, up through the end of the nineteenth century, reveals an complicated web of socioeconomic, political, and ideological processes that influenced the ultimate development of the Mexican-American community. The Treaty of Guadalupe Hidalgo, which drew the geo-political "border" with Mexico also marked one of the last chapters in the creation of the United States as a "nation." It also represented the beginning of a long and complex chapter on the multiethnic and cultural diversity that would characterize that country. It is not accidental that the ultranationalist ideology of the Americans during the second half of the nineteenth century coincides with the definition of the U.S./Mexican border and the rise of the United States as an "ethnic mosaic." The treaty became a symbol of military conquest and the differentiation between the Anglo-Self and the Mexican-Other. "Mexican-Other" included all who were not

"Anglo." The cultural differences based on skin color still are used by Americans to keep Mexicans in a frozen caste, politically and economically isolated within mainstream American society (Acuña 1981:121).

### The First Flood of Mexican Migrants

In the early days of Texas as part of the United States, there were few significant differences between the Mexican immigrants and the existing resident Mexicans who became citizens of the United States as a result of the treaty of Guadalupe Hidalgo. The following period was also marked by waves of Mexican immigration into the United States, only to be interrupted by the Mexican Revolution of 1910 that forced even more Mexicans to cross the border. As it is today, the border was an imaginary line through which labor flowed. Because of the social and economic crises experienced by Mexico following the Mexican Revolution and the dictatorial regime of Porfirio Diaz, Mexicans migrated north in even greater numbers. These migrants who crossed the border after 1900 constitute the "Migrant Generation" of the Mexican-American community in the United States (Alvarez 1985:39). Some came with their families, and all brought with them the Mexican culture that was to be injected into that of those already settled in the region. Rich mineral deposits in Arizona and New Mexico, agricultural development, expanding railroads, and other communication networks attracted large numbers of migrants. Entire families migrated only to end up harvesting fruits, vegetables, or cotton and live in company housing barely fit for human habitation. Landowners preferred tenant families with "at least eight children and a wife who worked in the fields "like a man" (Amott & Matthaei 1991:75). This also meant that their children were exposed to extremely unsanitary conditions and an almost total lack of educational opportunities. Some scholars have estimated that these migrations during the 1910s to1930s, shifted approximately one-eighth of Mexico's population northward (Acuña 1981:123).

Already familiar with exploitation at home, these migrants accepted the grievous economic conditions in the United States. Being representatives of a culture that still was viewed as an enemy by the Americans in the Southwest, their acceptance of the social and economic conditions with which they were faced only revitalized and reinforced the old stereotypes of Mexicans as childish, dirty, dishonest, and irresponsible. Such stereotypical images totally disregarded the tremendous effort and difficulties that these immigrants had to endure in adjusting to American culture with its economic and social environments ruled by mechanization.

World War I represents another milestone in the experience of the Mexican-Americans. The war and an emergent American patriotism reawakened the negative feelings against Mexicans that continued to exist from earlier Mexican/American confrontations. The participation of the United States in the war also brought most European immigration to a total stop. A scarcity of labor pulled first-generation Mexican-Americans into the northern areas of the country. Consequently, in the Southwest a need for new cheap Mexican labor fostered still another migratory exodus out of Mexico. With this new wave of immigration, the Mexican-American population started drawing lines among themselves, between the original Mexican inhabitants of the area, and the more recent immigrants who were simply called "Mexicans." As American institutions became established in the area, the original Mexican inhabitants accelerated their assimilation to the American social system. This is most clearly seen in the creation of community groups and other types of associations just for Mexican-Americans.

### The Big Depression. Greasers Go Home!

The economic recession of the United States in the 1930s also influenced the migratory movements of Mexicans and their social and economic positions in the United States. The severe scarcity and competition for jobs led the U.S. Congress to pass legislation in 1929 that considered it a felony for a migrant to illegally cross the border. Mexican-Americans in Texas already had to endure the lowest level of educational opportunity, employment, health, and living conditions (McLemore & Remo 1985:14). Underemployment and low wages characterized both Mexican-Americans and Mexican immigrants. The economic crisis pushed many of them into becoming completely dependant on local and state relief for their survival. This inevitably led to the overgeneralization of Mexicans as a burden for the American taxpayers, a stereotype that continues right up to the present (Meier & Ribera 1993:152). Working in agriculture or in the "informal economy," most Mexican-Americans and Mexican immigrants were summarily excluded (and still are) from unemployment insurance, industrial accident insurance, and other social entitlement programs. Deportations of Mexicans became quite common, and the general social anxiety being experienced by most Americans revitalized the old stereotype of Mexicans being dishonest. Both Mexican immigrants and Mexican-Americans were blamed for many of the social ills of American society at that time; the Americans reacted with "Greasers go home!" (Acuña 1981:123). The League of United Latin American Citizens (LULAC) evolved and began to articulate a self-conscious sense of Americaness among Mexican-Americans. To differentiate themselves from the newer Mexican immigrants, members of this organization began to use the self-identifying ethnic label "Latin Americans." The Mexican-American community in New Mexico preferred the label of "Spanish-American" for self-identification. The LULAC and a number of other Mexican-American organizations opposed more Mexican immigration, alleging that their presence in the labor market would have very negative impacts on the already established Mexican-Americans (Balderrama 1982). This served to reinforce the distinctions between the incipient Mexican-American middle class and the immigrant Mexican groups. It was at this point that the differentiations and variations between and within various groups of Mexican-Americans began to take on increased significance.

### The *Bracero* Program

The labor shortages of World War II caused still another wave of Mexican immigration in the United States and the birth of the *bracero* program. *Bracero* means manual worker. This program, which was tantamount to an official call for labor assistance by the American government, lasted from 1942 until 1964. Under the *bracero* program, Mexicans were recruited as workers by the U.S. government. Under an agreement between the two governments, workers were guaranteed a minimum wage. A U.S. Department of Labor employee called it "legalized slavery, nothing but a way for big corporate farms to get a cheap labor supply from Mexico under government sponsorship. The *braceros* were hauled around like cattle in Mexico and treated like prisoners in the United States" (Amott & Matthaei 1991: 79). Although the *braceros* came from a broad range of social backgrounds, the average *bracero* was an unmarried male from a rural background who might have moved from the village to the closest town or city in Mexico just prior to moving to the United States. The financial rewards did provide them with the strength to cope with the family separations they would experience and the inhumane treatment and hard working conditions they were to face in the United States (Cockcroft 1986).

### World War II — Test for Mexican-American Patriotism

The participation of Mexican-Americans in World War II awakened their hopes and brought significant transformations to the Mexican-American community. According to Alvarez, this period promoted a sense of cultural loyalty to the United States and a state of collective consciousness to Mexican-Americans that the author encapsulates in "the Mexican-American Generation" (1985:44). Certainly, military service tended to distance Mexican-Americans even further from their traditional Mexican life and values. Promoting their "Americanization" throughout the war experience, the young Mexican-American generation differentiated themselves from their elders who were more attached to their Mexican traditions. This constitutes the "Mexican-American Generation" for Alvarez (1985:44). Their service in the war boosted an awareness of their patriotic contributions to winning the war effort and gave them new status and respect. In short, the Mexican-American participation in the war had a marked impact on their identity as Americans rather than on their Mexican past. As participants in the war, they were to feel a part of the American mainstream, and this contributed to the distinction they increasingly made between themselves and Mexican immigrants.

### The Undocumented

The question of illegal immigration looms large in any assessment of recent Mexican immigration into the United States and its impacts. They are persons who cross the border without documents or authorization. In looking at the historical development of the heterogeneous Mexican community in the United States, it is clear that a pattern of movement was perpetually motivated by the closeness of the border. Moving back and forth, documented and undocumented workers have filled the labor needs of southwest economic development. However, the Mexicans have always been deported when jobs grow scarce. Although the *Bracero* program slowed illegal immigration during the war, by the 1950s the domestic labor supply increased and "Operation Wetback" was quickly initiated to stop the flow of illegal immigration into the country. Operation Wetback had serious impacts on the undocumented workers and their families. Some families were broken up as the head of the household was forced to leave. Those who stayed were at high risk of becoming additional financial burdens on the state. Thus illegal immigration was practically guaranteed by the end of the *Bracero* program in 1964.

The term *mojados* or "wetbacks" was generated to refer to those who swim the Rio Grande River as their means of entering into the United States. The smuggling of undocumented individuals has become a lucrative business along the border. This kind of activity demands a highly complex system that includes the *coyote,* who makes the arrangements, and the guides (called *polleros* or *pateros),* who actually take illegals across the border. The difficulty in obtaining entry visas by Mexican nationals has facilitated the continued existence of this type of network, which has become institutionalized in Mexico and across the border (Conover 1987).

The stream of Mexican immigrants, both legal and undocumented, continues to grow even at the present time. Undocumented migration has become the source of heated social debates (Cornelius 1978). Proposition 187 in California, restricting undocumented immigrants from social entitlement programs, is a recent example. People justified this policy on the premise that Mexican immigrants lowered American wages and displaced American workers (Weintraub & Ross 1980). Numerous studies have contradicted the underlying assumption of this premise by pointing out the immigrants' service in opening up additional jobs for both black and white English-speaking citizens in education, health, and other social services. Further, the studies have shown that the immigrants have added to the consumption system that contributes to the local economy and creates even more jobs (Muller 1984). Since 1981, Mexico has experienced a profound economic depression, and its resulting poverty has only fueled even more Mexican migration to the North, providing an "escape valve" for the internal pressures brought on by the mass impoverishment being experienced by Mexican nationals. Another factor of undocumented Mexicans entering the United States comes with their cultural and economic contribution to the already established Mexican-American community. Culturally, they "refreshed" the already existing Mexican traditions and community. Economically, they become the major clientele for Mexican-American economic enterprises. Lacking cars, seeking anonymity, and unable to afford the expensive shops, they become the patronizers of Mexican-American businesses in the local neighborhoods. In turn, Mexican-Americans provided them with a needed social network through which they could obtain information about medical services, education, and legal advice (Rodriguez & Nuñez 1986:139).

It should be pointed out that most of the research on the Mexican migration has focused on men. Because of this, there is a decided lack of information on female Mexican migration. This circumstance is the result of two faulty assumptions. First, it has been assumed that the number of female migrants is small. Second, it has been presumed that women migrate only as part of a family or to follow migrating men (Kossoudji & Ranney 1985). Studies have shown that from 35 to 50 percent of the illegal migrants from Mexico have been women (Simon & DeLey 1985). During the last decade, female Mexican immigration has increased substantially. Although it is not our place to analyze female Mexican migrants here in this context, it must be pointed out that understanding the female migrants from Mexico would lead to a better understanding of the acculturation process among Mexican-Americans, the transformation of family that was being experienced, and perhaps the development of economic patterns among Mexicans once they settle in the United States. The female Mexican migrant is an active economic member of the household and as such represents an important departure from Mexican tradition. This, in turn, has important repercussions on female/male power relations and the female/male roles within the family.

Although the Southwest has been one of the traditional destinations for illegal immigrants, once in the country many now find their way as far north as Detroit or Chicago in search of a job. Throughout the Southwest, on the West Coast, and now in areas far removed from these, undocumented immigration continues to be a vexing problem for the political agenda of the United States.

### Emerging Self-Ethnic Consciousness and Political Activism Among Mexican-Americans

The brief historical overview of the Mexican-American community and its development has highlighted a broad spectrum of Mexican experiences in their efforts to accommodate to the American culture and society. It also has highlighted the very close linkage between the U.S. economic demands and the continued waves of Mexican migrants. All of this is intrinsically related to the cultural images and representations Americans have generated and use to portray and perceive the Mexican-American group. Although the combination of all of these factors may portray the Mexican-American community as an ethnically victimized one, born of the political and economic subjugation by the dominant North American society, Mexican-American resistance and consciousness needs to be addressed for a complete understanding of Mexican-Americans.

Mexican reaction to the loss of land and subservient position in the United States led to a type of social banditry, as represented by Joaquin Murieta, who robbed rich Anglos, and Juan Cortina, who organized armed attacks on Anglo landowners in the 1860s. During the first quarter of the twentieth century, a number of organizations began to appear in many major Mexican-American urban neighborhoods. These *mutualistas* associations tried to provide some assistance to people within the Mexican-American community (e.g., for burial, employment, disability insurance, etc.) (Klor de Alva 1988:113). Serious union activity among Mexican laborers also started during the first decade of the twentieth century, parallel to the development of large-scale industrial and agricultural enterprises in the Southwest. Hundreds of Mexicans went on strike in 1903 against two Los Angeles' street railways. Strikes erupted among agricultural workers in the 1930s, who were especially hard hit by the depression, defaults on the payment of wages, deterioration of housing, and poor sanitary facilities. California experienced over half of the agricultural strikes that were to hit the country in the 1930s. One of the most famous strikes came against the southern Pecan Shelling Company of San Antonio, Texas, in 1930. Although the 1930s was a decade of economic distress for Mexican-Americans, it also inspired their search for an identity. Children of the immigrant waves of the 1920s, referred to as "gangs" by the Los Angeles newspapers, came to characterize Los Angeles' *barrios.* Teenage members of these gangs affected a distinctive way of dressing that included the "zoot suit." This consisted of a flat-crowned, broad-brimmed hat, lengthy draped coat, and high-waisted, baggy-legged trousers with tight-fitting pegged cuffs. They also originated customs that included the long-tailed coat, high boots, ducktail haircuts and ankle-length watch chains, called *pachucos.* Their self-identification also provided for a cross with three dots to be tattooed on the left hand, just above the thumb (Acuña 1981:325).

World War II brought the economic and social plight of Mexican-Americans into sharp focus, and this led to various attempts to foster an appreciation of both Mexican and Latin-American history and culture in public schools as a way of reducing the prejudice being experienced by Mexican-Americans. World War II, like World War I, boosted the "Americanization" of the Mexican-Americans in the United States. However, continuing links to villages in Mexico, the revitalization of Mexican values and culture accompanying ongoing Mexican immigration, the many Spanish-language newspapers, magazines, and radio stations all combined to preserve the Mexican tradition. By extending themselves into the towns and cities of America, young Mexican-Americans were taking the first steps into the working-class culture. Furthermore, their reawakened consciousness as U.S. citizens drove them to revindicate their civil rights. This represented a starting point for Mexican-American political power development. La Alianza Hispano-Americana, founded in the early nineteenth century, and the League of United Latin-American Citizens (LULAC) (active since 1929) are the real predecessors of the politically active organizations created after World War II. The Community Service Organization (CSO) was founded in California with a goal to combat discrimination and educate the Mexican-American community to participate in the political process by voting. As the movement of Mexican-Americans to the cities increased during and after World War II, civil rights issues took on greater importance for the Mexican-American community. The American G.I. Forum was founded in Texas to promote civic and political action among the Mexican-Americans (Allsup 1982). The Mexican-American Political Organization (MAPA) and The Political Association of Spanish-Speaking Organizations (PASO) were all created during the 1950s (McLemore & Romo 1985:21). The 1960s saw the peak of Mexican-American political activism. El Partido de la Raza Unida (The Party of the United Race) was founded to control elections in South Texas. Cesar Chavez, Rodolfo "Corky" Gonzalez, Reyes Lopez Tijerina, and Jose Angel Gutierrez, major leaders of the Mexican-American community, all created different organizations. The most widely known of these leaders, particularly because he got the most national attention, was

Cesar Chavez, whose goal was to organize migrant agricultural workers under the National Farm Workers Association (NFWA). The members of this organization supported and participated in a strike against the owners and operators of the grape vineyards in California. It became the social movement known as La Causa or El Movimiento. This movement spread to other cities as representatives of it spoke at schools, universities, and in other public arenas, often presenting their case in the form of corridos or folk ballads, and in traditional Mexican style. The members of many of these new organizations began to refer to themselves as *Chicanos*. Chicano cultural activism found expression in *El Grit—Journal of Contemporary Chicano Thought* in 1986 (Acosta Belen 1988:99).

Generally, *Chicanism* argued that *Chicanos* had the right to cultural autonomy and self-determination. They related themselves to ancient heritages associated with the Aztecs and other pre-Columbian peoples. By the end of the 1960s, the *Chicano* movement had made a substantial impact on many public high schools, colleges, and universities throughout the country. The movement was very successful in generating a new generation of scholars, intellectuals, and activists as well as a proliferation of organizations for educators, engineers, businessmen, lawyers, and *Chicanas*. During the 1960s and 1970s, larger and larger numbers of *Chicanas* participated in and presided over various *movimiento* groups (Amott & Matthaei 1991:84). In general, *el movimiento* had great influence in organizing the enlarged Mexican-American community. By claiming their Mexican heritage as symbol of their identity, they infused into American society a broader respect for Mexican-Americans. As a result of such efforts, more than fifty universities and colleges initiated some Chicano/Mexican-American studies departments and programs. An important element in the legacy of the *Chicano* movement was the Voting Right Act of 1982, which prohibited electoral practices that resulted in denying a citizen's right because of race, color, or language status.

### Cultural Development Among Mexican-Americans

Until 1930, the cultural rhythm of the Mexican-American community was orchestrated by the upper classes. The LULAC broke this tone by integrating the ideals of the middle class (Meier & Ribera 1993:233). Some have characterized this change as the "Americanization" of Mexican-Americans. The search for the ethnic identity of *el movimiento* in the 1960s led to a cultural explosion during the 1960s and 1970s. Inspired by their Indian background and their diverse experiences with the American culture, *Chicano* artists reached recognition in the theater, painting (particularly murals), music, literature, poetry, and the plastic arts. In their cultural development, Mexican-Americans have emphasized their heterogeneity as a group. Differences in occupations and professions, levels of education in Spanish and English, degree of assimilation into American culture, regional Mexican cultural differences, and the cultural climates in Mexico and the United States at the time of migration reinforce this group heterogeneity. Language, country of origin, historical experiences in both Mexico and the United States, and their minority position in the United States all have served to help unify the Mexican-American community. To document the ways Mexican-Americans have moved toward the American mainstream or to examine the degree to which they have been able to maintain their distinctive Mexican identity would require far more space than is available here, but no treatment of the Mexican-American group would be complete without some mention of certain aspects of their social and cultural life.

Retention of the Spanish language has characterized Mexican-Americans in comparison to other non-English languages that have been declining significantly. This has important political implications. Before 1975, Spanish monolinguals had great difficulties participating in the electoral process because voting materials were only presented in English. The current translation of this material into Spanish has contributed to a much higher rate of Mexican-American participation in the voting process (de la Garza 1985). Bilingual education has been supported vigorously by the community. Supporters have argued that a much more effective education of Mexican-American children has resulted, and this provides for their integration into the societal mainstream. They also argued that bilingual programs strengthen the American appreciation for Mexican culture, just as recent immigrant arrivals from Mexico reinforce the Mexican traditions within the Mexican-American community, despite the different social, economic, and ideological components. Mexican culture constantly is being infused into American society. In addition to their supply in labor, Mexican-Americans have enriched American culture with their architecture, literature, art, music, theater, and cuisine. Their murals decorate hundreds of walls in dozens of U.S. cities. Their music can be heard in many American households. Celebrations like Cinco de Mayo in the Southwest have become major holidays.

Although underrepresented in high-prestige, high-paying jobs, the proportion of Mexican-Americans engaged in professional occupations has risen substantially (McLemore& Romo 1985:25), but unemployment continues to be 30 to 40 percent higher than for Anglos (Meier & Ribera 1993:273). The unemployment rate for Chicanas is 50 percent higher than for Anglo women. Discrimination and a lack of educational opportunities are important reasons for the current underrepresentation of Mexican-Americans in higher paying occupations.

## CONCLUDING REMARKS

This study on the definition and characterization of the Mexican-American community as a component of the ethnically diverse mosaic of the United States shows an intricate historical development that, starting with a *mestizo* social order in the colonial Mexico, gets more socially, economically, and culturally diversified once it becomes part of the United States. A review of the different processes that have created such a diverse spectrum of identities within the Mexican-American ethnic community revealed how these identities are linked to the labor market and economic rhythms of the United States and the various stages of a continuing Mexican economic crisis. This economic crisis has become the integral mark of the Mexican and U.S. economies since the late 1960s. However, economic conditions began to change in the early 1980s, converting the crisis into a global phenomenon. Certainly this "globalization" has affected the migration patterns and impacted the dynamics of Mexican-American identity. An interesting consequence of Mexican migration is that language has been retained because of the supportive nature of their extended families in both the United States and Mexico, their divided sense of community between their residence in the United States and their "home" in Mexico, and because of the generally unskilled jobs they tend to occupy do not require English.

In short, this brief look at the Mexican-American community reveals the diverse conditions for persons of Mexican origin who came to the United States. Given this diversity, it is not surprising that variation would come to characterize this group as they followed their subsequent paths of adaptation to American life. Perhaps the most important insight from this discussion is precisely that the Mexican-Americans are not a single, homogeneous group—not ethnically, socioeconomically, nor politically. The different ethnic terms or labels used either to refer to Mexican-Americans, or for these to refer to themselves, reflects the intriguing intragroup heterogeneity of Mexican-Americans as a group. In the study of cultural stereotypes and overgeneralizations, the social, political, and ideological implications for the Mexican-American's diversified experiences in the pluralized-ethnic arena of the United States are illuminated. According to the 1990 Census, 13.3 million persons of Mexican descent now live in the United States. Most of these are immigrants and their descendants. The continuous elective immigration has historically shaped, and will continue to shape, the Mexican-American community as it will continue to affect the American sociocultural landscape and their mutual interaction for many years to come (Meier & Ribera 1993:273).

## REFERENCES

Acosta-Belen, E. 1988. The Hispanic Legacy. In *The Hispanic Experience in the United States*. E. Acosta-Belen & B. Sjostrom (eds). New York: Praeger.

Acuña, R. 1981. *Occupied America,* 2nd edition. New York: Harper & Row.

Allsup, C. 1982. *The American G.I. Forum: Origins and Evolution.* Austin: Center for Mexican American Studies, University of Texas Press.

Alvarez, R. 1985. The psycho-historical and socioeconomic development of the Chicano community in the United States. In *The Mexican American Experience: An Interdisciplinary Anthology*. R.O. de la Garza, et al (eds). Austin: University of Texas Press, pp. 33–56.

Amott, T. & Matthaei, J. 1991. *Race, Gender and Work.* Boston: South End Press.

Balderrama, F. 1982. *In Deffense of La Raza*. Tucson: University of Arizona Press.

Brack, G. 1976. Mexican opinion, American racism, and the War of 1846. In *Three Perspectives of Ethnicity*. C. E. Cortes, A. I. Ginsburg, A. W. F. Green, & J. A. Joseph (eds). New York: G. P. Putnam's Sons, pp. 94–103.

Cockoroft, J. D. 1986. *Outlaws in the Promised Land.* New York: Grove Weidenfield.

Conover, T. 1987. *Coyotes.* New York: Vintage Books.

Cornellius, W. 1978. *Mexican Migration to the United States: Causes, Consequences, and U.S. Responses.* Cambridge: Center for International Studies, MIT.

Cortes, C. 1980. Mexicans. In *Harvard Encyclopedia of American Ethnic Groups.* S. Thernstrom, A. Orlov, & O. Handlin (eds). Cambridge: Belknap, pp. 697–719.

Cortes, C. et al. 1976. *Three Perspectives on Ethnicity.* New York: G. P. Putnam's Sons.

de la Garza, R. O. et al (eds). *The Mexican American Experience: An Interdisciplinary Anthology.* Austin: University of Texas Press, pp. 33–56.

Farnham, T. 1976. The indolent, mixed race of California. In *Three Perspectives on Ethnicity.* C. Cortes, A. I. Ginsburg, A. W. F. Green, & J. A. Joseph (eds). New York: G. P. Putnam's Sons, pp. 60–62.

Garcia, J. 1981. Yo Soy Mexicano...:Self-identity and sociodemographic correlates. *Social Science Quaterly* 62:88–89.

Klor de Alva, J. 1988. Telling Hispanics apart: Latin sociocultural diversity. In *The Hispanic Experience in the United States.* E. Acosta-Belen & B. Sjostrom (eds). New York: Praeger.

Kossoudji, S. & Ranney, S. 1985. The labor market experience of female migrants: The case of temporary Mexican migration to the U.S. *International Migration Review* 18(4): 1121–1143.

McLemore, D. & Romo. R. 1985. The origins and development of the Mexican American people. In *The Mexican American Experience: An Interdisciplinary Anthology.* R. de la Garza et al. (eds). Austin: University of Texas Press, pp. 3–32.

Meier, M. & Ribera, F. 1993. *Mexican Americans, American Mexicans,* 4th edition. New York: Hill & Wary.

Moore, J. 1976. *Mexican Americans.* Englewood Cliffs: Prentice-Hall.

Muller, T. 1984. *The Fourth Wave: California Newest Immigrants.* Washington, DC: The Urban Institute.

Paredes, A. 1958. *With His Pistol in His Hand.* Austin: University of Texas Press.

Rodriguez, N. & Nunez, R. T. 1986. An exploration of factors that contribute to differentiation between Chicanos and Indocumentados. In *Mexican Immigrants and Mexican Americans.* H. L. Browing & R. de la Garza (eds). Austin: Center for American Studies, University of Texas Press.

Simon, R. & DeLey, M. 1985. The work experience of undocumented Mexican women immigrants in Los Angeles. *International Migration Review* 18(4):1212–1229.

Steiner, S. 1979. *The Mexican Americans.* London: Minority Rights Group.

Weber, D. 1982. *The Mexican Frontier, 1821–1846: The American Southwest Under Mexico.* Alburquerque: University of New Mexico Press.

Weintraub, S. & Ross, S. 1980. *The Illegal Alien from Mexico: Policy Choices for an Intractable Issue.* Austin: Mexico–United States Border Research Program, University of Texas Press.

Wolf, E. 1959. *Sons of the Shaking Earth.* Chicago: University of Chicago Press.

# 12

# Filipino-Americans: The Marginalized Minority

Jonathan Y. Okamura

Filipino-Americans are an ethnic minority with a distinct culture and identity who are part of the larger Asian American racial category in the United States. At 1.4 million, they are the second largest (20%) and one of the fastest growing Asian American groups, largely as a result of ongoing immigration from the Philippines. Filipino-Americans share many historical experiences with other Asian American groups such as Chinese-Americans, Korean-Americans, and Japanese-Americans, particularly recruitment as "cheap" agricultural labor to California and Hawaii and racist exclusionary discrimination as they attempted to participate in the larger society in the pre–World War II period. Rather than mere geographical origin in Asia, these shared historical and more recent experiences of subordination in the United States provide the structural basis for Filipino-Americans being considered Asian Americans since there is no one primary Asian culture, language, religion, or value system that is common to all or most Asian American groups. Indeed, cultural and social diversity is a major characteristic of Asian Americans insofar as they include, besides the groups mentioned above, Koreans, Vietnamese, Cambodians, Laotians, Asian Indians, and a number of smaller groups (e.g., Hmong, Thais). In 1990, Asian Americans together numbered 6.9 million and represented only 2.8 percent of the U.S. population (U.S. Bureau of Census 1993:8).

Although Asian Americans have been present in what eventually became the United States long before its formal establishment, Asian American identity is of far more recent origin given its social construction and emergence in the late 1960s. During this period of tremendous social, cultural, and political change in American society, Asian American community activists, university students, and faculty representing several cultural groups, including Filipino-Americans, perceived the organizational advantage of forming such coalitions among themselves to pursue common economic and political interests and objectives. Given the relatively small population of individual Asian American groups, they realized that combining their numbers, resources, and leadership under their newly created common identity of

Asian Americans would be to the strategic advantage of all groups. Defining and asserting themselves as Asian Americans also served as a means of reclaiming their identity, history, and social position in American society since Filipinos, Chinese, Japanese and other Asian immigrants had been collectively categorized by whites as "Orientals" along with a variety of demeaning stereotypic traits such as dirty, immoral, treacherous, and unassimilable.

Since the 1980s, some Filipino-American community leaders have questioned a continuing alliance with and support of other Asian American cultural groups. These leaders, who represent social service, legal, and educational organizations, maintain that while Chinese and Japanese Americans have attained considerable socioeconomic mobility and political representation at least partially by establishing coalitions with Filipinos and other Asian Americans, the former have not benefited to the same extent and continue to be a socioeconomically disadvantaged and politically marginalized minority. In this regard, Filipino-Americans have been victimized by the usual "model minority" stereotype of Asian Americans who are portrayed as economically successful, educationally gifted, and able to advance themselves through their own hard work, perseverance, and family sacrifice. Because they have been categorized as Asian Americans and therefore presumably not requiring special consideration, Filipino-Americans have been denied access to equal opportunity and affirmative action programs, particularly in higher education, despite being underrepresented as both students and faculty.

At least one Filipino analyst has contended that Filipino-Americans should dissociate themselves from the generalized Asian American identity and "assert their ethnic uniqueness" (San Juan, Jr. 1994:119). He maintains that since the Philippines was on the verge of independence when it was colonized (unlike China and Japan) by the United States, between 1898 and 1946 Filipinos in America were not conventional immigrants but "colonial subjects." As another alternative, some Filipino-Americans have proposed that they identify themselves as and collaborate with Latin Americans given the nearly four-hundred years of Spanish colonization of the Philippines, the Spanish ancestry of some Filipino-Americans, and their general familiarity with Spanish culture. However, this proposal has not been seriously advanced by the Filipino- American community.

## FILIPINO-AMERICAN CULTURE, IDENTITY, AND DIVERSITY

As an ethnic minority, Filipino-Americans are distinguished by their distinctive culture and identity, and their culture provides the basis for the expression and maintenance of their ethnic identity. Cultural norms and values centered on family and kinship relations especially serve to distinguish Filipino-Americans from other ethnic and racial groups in American society, although these are differences of degree and emphasis rather than of kind. Certainly for Filipinos, one's family (including extended family members) is the primary source of individual and social identity and of material and emotional support and security. The family and kinship norms and values that Filipino-Americans consider especially important include respect for and deference to parents and older relatives in general, maintenance of close family relations, including those with extended family kin, and love and concern for their children. These family values and norms are evident in the obligation to and care and support for parents in their old age, monetary assistance provided to relatives in the Philippines, including helping them to immigrate to the United States, and the efforts and sacrifices that parents make to ensure their children's well being and future economic security. In this case, a very significant value among Filipino-Americans concerns providing an education, particularly higher education, for their children. Education is valued because it is viewed as a means of socioeconomic mobility for their children, and thus Filipino-American parents believe that it is the best legacy they can bestow to them. The Filipino value on higher education can be seen in the encouragement and material support that parents provide to their children, even though they themselves may not be college graduates.

While Filipino-Americans share certain cultural norms, values, and a common ethnic identity, there is considerable sociocultural diversity within the community, primarily as a result of ongoing immigration from the Philippines since 1965, when U.S. immigration laws were liberalized. The newer immigrants have contributed to the revitalization of Filipino-American culture in language, values and beliefs, religious rituals, and other social and cultural activities in the communities where they have settled. As a result, substantial social and cultural diversity has developed within the Filipino-American community based on some correlated differences in language, generation, class, cultural values, and behavioral norms. For example, third- and fourth-generation Filipino-Americans generally are unable to speak any Philippine language, have a higher socioeconomic status than first-generation immigrants, and are more familiar with "American" than Filipino cultural values and norms.

As for the linguistic diversity among the Filipino-Americans, the three major ethnolinguistic groups in the Philippines, e.g., Ilokanos, Visayans, and Tagalogs, are all well represented in the Filipino-American population as well as smaller language groups such as Pampangans, Pangasinanses, and Ilonggos. Philippine language usage is very prevalent among Filipino-Americans, particularly immigrant families; two-thirds (66%) of Filipino-Americans (five years old and over) speak an Asian or Pacific Islander language, presumably a Philippine language, at home (U.S. Bureau of Census 1993:8). American-born or American-raised Filipinos may not be able to speak the language of their immigrant parents or grandparents, but they generally do know their Philippine ethnolinguistic background.

Generational differences among Filipino-Americans also are important insofar as they imply American or Philippine birth and upbringing, and thus cultural differences between native-born and foreign-born Filipinos. The former can include those born before World War II and their third- and fourth-generation descendants, who are very much assimilated into American culture and society, and also the children of post-1965 wave of immigrants. First-generation immigrants include the remaining "old-timers" or "*manongs*" (literally older brother in Ilokano) who came as labor recruits through the early 1930s, post–World War II arrivals, and the "newcomer," post–1965 immigrants who continue to arrive in substantial numbers each year. The extent of immigration is such that almost two-thirds of Filipino-Americans are foreign-born, and it has contributed to what is very likely the most significant social cleavage in Filipino America, e.g., between its immigrant and American-born or -raised segments. While this division has been manifested in occasional conflicts between native-born and Philippine-born male youth, it generally takes the form of avoidance and negative perceptions of and attitudes toward each group. Immigrants maintain that the American-born are disrespectful of traditional cultural values and resent their brash, impolite interpersonal style, while the U.S.-born contend that immigrants are overly concerned with events in the Philippines and are too status conscious (Ciria-Cruz 1994:44). In many ways but especially through language use, interpersonal networks, and various cultural practices, American born and immigrant Filipinos express and affirm somewhat distinct identities as Filipino-Americans.

Filipino-Americans can be found in all fifty states, but a majority resides in California (732,000), where they are the largest Asian American group (Barringer et al. 1993:112). Other states with significant Filipino populations include Hawaii (168,000), Illinois (65,000), New York (62,000), and New Jersey (53,000). These states also receive the greatest number of Filipino immigrants and in the same rank order as above. Filipino-Americans are concentrated in the western United States (71%) and, unlike during the pre–World War II period, are a predominantly urban group. Metropolitan areas with sizable Filipino populations include Los Angeles–Long Beach, San Francisco–Oakland, and San Diego in California; Honolulu, Hawaii; and Chicago, Illinois. Daly City, which is about fifteen miles south of San Francisco, is especially recognized as a Filipino-American community in northern California.

Distinctly Filipino-American communities are evident in California, Hawaii and a few other states where there are significant population concentrations. These communities can be discerned by the presence of a variety of Filipino-owned, small business establishments, oftentimes clustered together in mini shopping malls, such as video rental shops featuring recent Philippine films, restaurants, travel agencies, bakeries, and remittance sending shops. Particularly in Hawaii, Filipino-American residential communities are distinguished by two-story houses decorated with various Spanish-style embellishments such as balustrades, red-tile roofs, heavy *narra* wood front doors, and wrought-iron fences and railings. As manifestations of Filipino-American identity and culture, these commercial and residential areas signify and demarcate the ethnic boundaries of Filipino communities within the larger context of multiethnic cities and towns.

## IMMIGRATION AND HISTORICAL DEVELOPMENT

### Early Arrivals

Filipinos were first present in what eventually became part of the United States over 400 years ago. It is known that in 1587 Filipino sailors were aboard a Spanish ship that landed at Morro Bay near San Luis Obispo, California. This ship was part of the galleon trade between Manila and Acapulco (the Philippines and Mexico then being Spanish colonies) that went on for 250 years beginning in 1572. Thus, in 1781, Antonio Miranda Rodriguez, perhaps a former crew member on a Spanish ship, was a member of a forty-four person expedition sent by the Spanish colonial government in Mexico that founded what eventually developed into the city of Los Angeles. Shortly before then, Filipino sailors, later called "Manilamen," deserted their ship and settled in the bayous around Barataria Bay south of New Orleans in 1763, a year after Spain gained possession of what later became the state of Louisiana. The Filipino-American community in Louisiana is believed to be their oldest continuously settled community in the United States.

Filipinos were present in Hawaii when it was still an independent kingdom. The 1853 government census recorded the presence of five Filipinos who again were probably sailors who had been aboard European (including Spanish) or American trading ships that had been to the Philippines. It also is known that in 1888 a troupe of twelve Filipino musicians and acrobats from Manila decided to stay in Honolulu rather than continue with their tour of the United States following a salary dispute with their manager.

After the annexation of the Philippines by the United States in 1898 as a result of the Spanish-American War, the first Filipinos to come to America were college students. This group of students were called *pensionados* because of the colonial government scholarships they received and began attending American colleges and universities in 1903. The program ended in 1910 when all of the *pensionados* returned home; nonetheless, thousands of Filipinos continued to enroll in American higher education institutions at their own expense.

### Immigration to Hawaii

As a result of the American annexation of the Philippines, Filipinos were free to enter the United States, including Hawaii which also was annexed in 1898, as "nationals" although they lacked the full benefits and privileges of American citizenship. Accordingly, they were recruited by the Hawaiian Sugar Planters' Association (HSPA) to work on the plantations with the first group of fifteen Ilokanos from the northwest of the Philippines arriving in 1906 for a tour of plantation conditions. After a few unsuccessful efforts to organize in the next two years, Filipino labor recruitment was firmly established in 1909, hastened by a major strike organized by Japanese workers. The first group of Filipino laborers were primarily Visayans from the central Philippines and these were followed by Ilokanos, who eventually emerged as a substantial majority of the Filipino-American population in Hawaii.

Philippine immigration to the United States continued until 1934 when the Tydings-McDuffie Act restricted Filipino entry to an annual quota of fifty persons. This act, which also provided for eventual Philippine independence in 1946, allowed for the importation of Filipino agricultural workers in the event of a labor shortage. Concerned about the ongoing unionization of plantation workers by the International Longshoremen's and Warehousemen's Union and a possible strike, the HSPA in 1946 requested and was granted approval to bring in another 6,100 Filipino men who would be the last plantation labor recruits, and they were accompanied by 450 women and 900 children. Thus, between 1909 and 1946, about 126,000 Filipinos immigrated to Hawaii, the great majority of whom were single young men from rural villages with little or no formal education. Most of these men came with hopes of saving some of their earnings in order to purchase land upon their return to the Philippines. Almost half of them (61,000) did return home, while about 19,000 moved on to the continental United States, and the remainder stayed on in Hawaii.

Life on the plantations in Hawaii was quite a struggle for Filipino and other workers because of the terrible working and living conditions. Filipino labor recruits signed a three-year agreement which stipulated that they would receive free transportation to Hawaii, housing, medical care, and wages of $1 a day in 1915. On their part, the recruits agreed to work a ten-hour day in the fields or twelve hours in the mill for six days a week. As the last group of recruited laborers, Filipinos received the lowest wages, which discouraged them from bringing their families to Hawaii. A former field worker described the drudgery and pain of plantation labor:

So hoe hoe hoe is what we did for four hours in a straight line and no talking, resting only to sharpen the blade and then walk to the next lot...After one week of hoe *hana* [work], I felt as if I had been kicked and beaten all over. My body was tight and my back ached like it does now that I'm old and weak with a broken body (Melendy 1977:86).

The plantation maintained strict paternalistic control over the daily life of workers through abusive field overseers, particularly to prevent them from engaging in labor organizing activities. By 1922 Filipinos had become the largest ethnic group (41%) on the plantation work force, and in the 1930s they represented 70 percent of the workers (Lind 1980:82).

Filipinos had an especially difficult period of adjustment to Hawaii society due to the general lack of alternative employment opportunities besides plantation labor. The immigrant groups that had preceded them on the plantation, the Chinese and Japanese, had established economic niches for themselves in Honolulu in wholesale and retail trade sectors, and in skilled and semiskilled work by the 1920s. The Depression severely restricted Filipinos to agricultural labor. In consequence, Filipinos were unable to develop a significant urban population; less than 8 percent of the 63,000 Filipinos in Hawaii in 1930 resided in Honolulu, where they found seasonal work in pineapple canneries and hotels (Cariaga 1936). The preponderance of men over women (5 to 1 in 1930) as a result of labor recruitment and their primary employment as plantation laborers resulted in much negative stereotyping of Filipinos as violent, criminally inclined, uneducated, and temperamental. One Filipino anthropologist noted that, "Newspapers have tended to play up their misbehavior so that the public has been constantly made conscious of the Filipino in a bad light. Whenever a serious crime is committed by a Filipino, his nationality is designated" (Cariaga 1936). Another disadvantage of their gender imbalance was the much slower and smaller development of the second generation of Filipino-Americans who were born and educated as American citizens, which retarded their socioeconomic mobility as a community.

## Immigration to the Continental United States

The Filipino-American historical experience in the continental United States differs in some respects from that in Hawaii. Since there was no organized labor recruitment agency similar to the HSPA, most of the early arrivals in the western states were former plantation laborers from Hawaii. As late as 1924 there were only 6,000 Filipinos in the entire mainland United States. After passage of the 1924 immigration act that excluded entry of certain Asian and other groups, between that year and 1929 about 24,000 Filipinos were recruited or arrived on their own for unskilled work in California such that there were over 30,000 of them by 1930. Unlike in Hawaii, there were no established Filipino communities comparable to the plantation "Filipino camps." Filipino laborers on the West Coast traveled for most of the year following the ripening crops in pursuit of work. At the start of the year, they harvested asparagus, an activity for which Filipinos became especially noted. In the spring and summer some Filipinos went to Alaska and Puget Sound in Washington to work in salmon canneries, while others picked lettuce in the Salinas Valley and various other fruits throughout California. In the fall Filipinos made their way to the Yakima Valley in Washington to harvest apples. During the winter months, some of them moved to cities and worked in hotels and restaurants as service workers.

Another significant difference between the Filipino-American experience in Hawaii and the continental United States was the far harsher treatment to which they were subject on the mainland, although there also was substantial racism and discrimination against them in Hawaii. As Filipino-American novelist, poet, and labor organizer Carlos Bulosan wrote in his well-known autobiographical novel:

I came to know afterward that in many ways it was a crime to be a Filipino in California. I came to know that the public streets were not free to my people: we were stopped each time these vigilant patrolmen saw us driving a car. We were suspect each time we were seen with a white woman (Bulosan 1973:121).

Between 1928 and 1930 in several farming towns in California, Washington, and Oregon there were outbreaks of "anti-Filipino race riots" as a culmination of the bigotry and hostility toward them. The most publicized of these riots occurred in Watsonville, California, in 1930 when a mob of several hundred whites attacked Filipino farmworkers and killed one of them.

Because of their willingness to work for lower wages, Filipino laborers were viewed as "unfair competition" by white agricultural workers. Filipinos also were despised because of their supposed immoral character, involvement in crime, and their relationships with white women, the latter an outcome of their especially unbalanced sex ratio (14 males to every female in California in 1930). As a result, a backlash movement to exclude Filipinos from continued immigration to the United States was initiated by organized labor and other conservative groups. Antimiscegenation laws (ruled unconstitutional in 1948) also were passed in several states in the 1930s to prohibit Filipinos from marrying white women.

Besides California, pre–World War II Filipino immigrants settled in other parts of America. Some went to Washington state and Alaska, while others moved on to cities in the Midwest and East. In Chicago, Filipinos obtained civil service positions in the postal service or were in the U.S. Navy, as also were those in Philadelphia. Filipinos in Detroit, New York, and Washington, DC took temporary jobs as service workers in restaurants and hotels or as domestic servants.

### Post–World War II to 1965 Immigration

With immigration limited by a 100-person annual quota established when the Philippines gained independence, between 1946 and 1965 only 34,000 Filipinos entered the United States. Almost one-half of these immigrants (16,000) were the wives of American servicemen, including Filipino-Americans, who had served in the Philippines during and after World War II. Following the war and through the 1950s, many former labor recruits returned to the Philippines because of the great difficulty in having their families join them. During this period, most Filipino-Americans still were restricted to unskilled and semiskilled work, especially in agricultural labor. In California as late as 1960, agriculture remained the largest employer of Filipinos (31%) even though its share had declined considerably from 1950 (55%) (Melendy 1977:96). As for the small urban Filipino population, the findings of a Seattle study in 1948 were fairly representative of the West Coast situation. They indicated that two-thirds of the Filipino-Americans surveyed were service workers in hotels and restaurants, while smaller numbers were factory workers (18%) and unskilled laborers (14%), and none were in managerial or professional positions (Melendy 1977:96). In 1960 the largest Filipino-American communities in the continental United States were in Los Angeles (7,700), San Francisco (7,500), and New York (4,300), where former farmworkers lived in inexpensive rental housing in "Little Manilas."

In Hawaii Filipino-Americans faced a similar restricted employment structure. In 1950 a majority of working Filipino males still were classified as unskilled laborers (53%) with minimal percentages employed as professionals (1.2%) and managers (3.0%) (Lind 1980:85–89). Partially due to their entry into defense industry jobs during and after World War II, significant proportions of Filipino men worked as operatives (20%) and craftsmen. On the sugar plantations, Filipino-Americans still comprised almost one-half of the employees (47%) in 1965 (Lind 1980:82). However, Filipinos were able to establish a much larger urban presence than on the U.S. mainland. In 1960 there were almost 22,000 Filipinos residing in Honolulu, and ten years earlier more than one-half of their city population was clustered within a half-mile radius of the intersection of King and Liliha streets in a working-class district near the downtown area (Lind 1980:67). Another significant difference with the mainland situation was the election to political office of Filipino-Americans in Hawaii beginning in 1954 with three of them serving in the territorial legislature in the late 1950s.

### Post–1965 Immigration

The tremendous growth in the Filipino-American population from 340,000 in 1970 to 780,000 in 1980 and to 1.4 million in 1990 is due largely to immigration from the Philippines as a result of the 1965 immigration act. This act allowed for the reunification of families and the entry of skilled workers needed in the United States. In the first five years after the immigration law was passed, more than 7,300 Filipino doctors, surgeons, engineers, and scientists were granted legal entry as professionally skilled workers needed in the United States along with teachers and accountants, resulting in a "brain drain" from the Philippines. However, after changes in the law, since the 1970s the great majority of Filipino immigrants have been admitted under the family reunification provisions.

Since 1965, one million Filipinos have immigrated to the United States, with about 500,000 coming in the 1980s. In the early 1990s about 60,000 Filipinos have been arriving each year such that by 1994 they comprised, at one million, the second largest immigrant group (after Mexicans) in the United States. Almost two-thirds (64%) of Filipino-Americans are foreign-born and, among those immigrants, another two-thirds (66%) have arrived since 1975 with almost one-half entering between 1980 and 1990 (U.S. Bureau of Census 1993:8). With an estimated backlog of 600,000 visa applications pending review at the U.S. Embassy in Manila, it is very likely that Filipinos will continue to immigrate at their relatively high level unless immigration restrictions are imposed. At current immigration levels, the Filipino-American population is projected to increase to 2.1 million by the year 2000, when they will be the largest Asian American group. Despite their majority foreign-born population, Filipinos lead all other immigrants in becoming naturalized American citizens. For the ten-year period between 1983 and 1992 nearly 270,000 Filipinos were naturalized, and they represented about 14 percent of the annual number of naturalized citizens.

It needs to be asked why there are such great numbers of Filipinos immigrating to the United States. There is a widespread assumption that Filipino and other immigrants from developing countries come to America primarily for economic reasons, e.g., having a higher standard of living, a higher income, or a better job. However, Filipino immigrants have a different understanding of their migration intentions and their own behavior. Surveys and other research indicate that Filipino immigrants report joining family members as their primary reason for immigrating to the United States (Carino et al. 1990:57; Lasman et al. 1971; Okamura 1983). A representative sample survey of almost 2,100 adult Filipinos who were issued immigrant visas to the United States in 1986 found that the reason most frequently given for immigrating was family affiliation (42%), which as followed by "work/livelihood/income" (29%) (Carino et al. 1990:57).

Filipino immigration to the United States is a classic example of a "chain migration," or the process in which family members in the home country are assisted in immigrating by their relatives who had gone before them. Previously settled family members generally provide the air fare, initial accommodations, and information and assistance on obtaining a first job for their newly arrived relatives (Okamura 1984). This support and assistance is an indication of the strong value placed on family ties among Filipino-Americans. Besides influencing their decision to immigrate, the presence of relatives also is the determining factor as to where newly arrived Filipino immigrants usually settle in the United States. The immigrant survey noted above found that over 90 percent of the respondents gave the presence of relatives as the primary reason for selecting their intended destination in the United States (Carino et al. 1990:63). Economic factors (6%), e.g., availability of work, are of much less significance in immigrants' choice of where to settle. Kinship and family relations contribute significantly to the increasing concentration of Filipino-Americans in the western states, especially California, and in particular towns and cities within those states, despite regional or local economic trends.

Due to its substantial immigrant component, the Filipino-American community represents a diaspora as evident in the transnational relations between it and the Philippine homeland (Okamura 1995). While Filipino-Americans can be viewed as an ethnic minority within the political and economic structure of the United States, they also can be conceived as a diaspora community that maintains strong linkages with their country of origin. These relations are evident in transnational circulations of capital and consumer goods, people, and information between Filipino America and the Philippines. Each year Filipino-Americans send back well over $1 billion to their relatives and friends in the Philippines for their support and assistance. In the first half of 1994, they remitted almost $800 million through official bank transfers (*Filipinas* 1994:53), and that amount does not include cash carried back by returning Filipinos on visits home that may total twice the official remittance figure. An overseas Filipino returning home for a visit is called a *balikbayan* (literally, returnee to the nation), and she/he invariably returns overladen with various consumer goods to be distributed to relatives and friends. The giving of these highly desired and appreciated gifts serves to affirm and maintain kinship relations between relatives separated by time and space. Increasingly more accessible long-distance telephone communication contributes to the same purpose by conveying timely information that enables Filipino-Americans to participate quite actively in ongoing family decision-making and other family matters that require their advice and assistance. Thus the Filipino-American diaspora gives new meaning to the notion of the "extended" Filipino family as the diaspora transcends spatial, cultural, and national boundaries.

## SOCIOECONOMIC STATUS

Data from the 1990 United States census on various socioeconomic indices, e.g., educational, occupational, and income status, indicate that Filipino-Americans have achieved minimal overall mobility since 1980 and remain a subordinate ethnic minority in American society. While they tend to have higher family incomes and educational attainment levels than whites, their educational status would lead one to assume that they should have made greater progress in occupational status. It has been argued that the gains which have been made are primarily due to "immigration, not empowerment over time" through the progressive "accretion of economic and political power by earlier waves of Filipinos" who arrived during the first half of the century (Ciria-Cruz 1994:41). As shortly will be made evident, Filipino-Americans continue to encounter significant resistance in the employment market.

**Educational Attainment**

Filipino-Americans have a very high level of educational attainment (among persons 25 to 64 years old), particularly in terms of earning a bachelor's degree or higher (43%), compared to whites (25%) (Barringer and Liu 1994:44). Filipino women have an especially high percentage of college graduates (42%) and rank second to Indian-American women (from South Asia) (49%), who perhaps have the highest level of educational achievement among American women (U.S. Bureau of Census 1993:8). Filipino-American men (36%) also tend to have an above-average percentage of bachelor's degrees or higher recipient numbers. These high levels of educational attainment are attributable primarily to the arrival of college-educated immigrants, which has been referred to as Philippine "foreign aid" to the United States. The 1986 survey of Filipino immigrants cited above found that almost one-half (47%) had attended or graduated from college, with another 10 percent having studied in or finished graduate school education (Carino et al. 1990:28). However, in California, Filipino-Americans have the highest high school dropout rate (12%) among Asian Americans. Most second- and third-generation Filipino-Americans continue to be underrepresented in colleges and universities, and are not achieving the same high educational level as their Philippine trained counterparts (Azores 1986–87; Okamura 1991).

Thus there is somewhat of a contradiction in Filipino-American educational attainment. While immigrants arrive with relatively high levels of education, their children and other American-born Filipinos generally are unable to replicate these high levels. Given the strong cultural value placed on college education among Filipino-Americans, the primary explanation for the underrepresented status in higher education of American-born and/or American-educated Filipinos pertains to institutional barriers that restrict their access to and persistence in college rather than to any academic deficiencies on their part.

**Occupational Status**

Occupational distribution among Filipino-Americans in 1990 indicates only slight mobility since 1980 despite their continued relatively high educational status.

Less than two-thirds of working Filipinos (16 years old and over) are employed in white-collar positions as managers and professionals (27%) or as technical, sales, and administrative support workers (37%) (U.S. Bureau of Census 1993:9), while the corresponding percentages in 1980 were at 25 percent and 33 percent, respectively. The proportion of Filipino-Americans who hold managerial and professional positions is comparable to that for whites (26%) but less than for Asian Americans (31%). Filipino women (18%) are employed more so as professionals than their male (11%) counterparts, perhaps due to the significant numbers of women who work as nurses and other health professionals (Barringer & Liu 1994:56).

At lower levels of the occupational scale, a substantial percentage of Filipino-Americans are employed as service workers (17%) at a proportion higher than for Asian Americans (15%) and the total American population (13%) (U.S. Bureau of Census 1993:9). Service work continues to be the largest occupational category for Filipino men and the second largest for Filipino women (Barringer and Liu 1994:56). In 1980, the same percentage of Filipino-Americans were service workers as in 1990, and the combined proportion of skilled craft workers (7%) and semiskilled operators and fabricators (11%) in 1990 is only four percentage points less than in 1980 (22%) (U.S. Bureau of Census 1988:12). Service work employment is especially prevalent among Filipinos in Hawaii with its tourism-based economy.

Filipino-Americans are particularly distinguished by their very high labor force participation rate (75%) among persons sixteen years old and over, which is the highest among Asian Americans (67%) and is much higher than for the United States as a whole (65%) (U.S. Bureau of Census 1993:9). Filipino-American women (72%) perhaps have the highest rate of labor force participation among American females. This high employment rate can be attributed to a strong work ethic among post-1965 immigrants who describe themselves as being willing to accept a job even though it may not be equivalent to their previous occupation or work experience in the Philippines.

Despite their relatively high educational qualifications, Filipino-Americans appear to receive less economic returns in terms of occupational status and income compared to other racial and/or ethnic groups, which is very likely the result of discriminatory employment practices (Barringer et al. 1990:31, 40; Cabezas et al. 1986–87:13). This unequal treatment particularly affects professionally trained and college-educated immigrants who encounter occupational downgrading from their previous positions in the Philippines. The 1986 survey of Filipino immigrants reported that while substantial percentages of employed men (20%) and women (34%) held professional or technical positions during the year just prior to their immigration, these proportions had declined dramatically after two years in the United States for both employed males (9%) and females (15%) (East-West Population Institute 1990:12–14). Occupational downgrading also is evident in the tremendously increased number of 1986 immigrants in blue-collar work. While relatively small percentages of male (6%) and female (9%) immigrants had service jobs before immigrating, these figures had increased considerably two years later for both men (33%) and women (24%). The cumulative result of these various forms of employment discrimination is that Filipino-Americans are distinguished by "low income and occupational status, poor occupational mobility, and minimal economic and political empowerment" (Cabezas et al. 1986–87: ), a description that unfortunately also would have applied to them prior to World War II.

## Family and Individual Income

The high labor force participation rate of Filipino-Americans contributed to a higher median family income ($42,600) in 1989 than that of Asian Americans ($41,600) and whites ($35,100) (Barringer and Liu 1994:76). However, per capita income among Filipinos ($13,600) was lower than for Asian Americans ($13,800) and all Americans ($14,100) (U.S. Bureau of Census 1993:9). This discrepancy can be attributed to Filipino-American families having more working members on average than other families and to their greater prevalence of extended family households, which results in their higher family income. A far greater proportion of Filipino families (30%) have three or more workers compared to Asian American (20%) and all American families (13%), which may be necessitated by their lower individual incomes. Another factor in the higher median family income of Filipino-Americans that needs to be considered is that a majority of them resides in California, where income levels (and the cost of living) are higher than for the country as a whole.

The overall socioeconomic status of Filipino-Americans as indicated by their educational achievement, occupational distribution, and income levels may obscure significant disparities within the population. Filipinos in New York and New Jersey have a much higher socioeconomic status than that of their counterparts in Hawaii (Liu et al. 1988:509). More than two-thirds of Filipino immigrants in New York and New Jersey who came in 1973 and 1979 and 50 percent who arrived in 1985 were health and other highly trained professionals, especially medical doctors and nurses, in the Philippines. In contrast, Hawaii Filipinos remain very much a working-class group with only limited upward social mobility, especially into managerial and professional positions since the beginning of the 1970s (Okamura 1990). The largest employment category for both Filipino-American men (25%) and women (30%) in Hawaii is service work, particularly in the tourist industry. Substantial numbers of Filipinos are employed in tourism as hotel room maids, food service workers, gardeners, and maintenance workers.

## Social and Economic Problems and Concerns

A continuing problem for Filipino-Americans is employment discrimination that severely restricts their hiring and promotion, and thus their socioeconomic mobility. In 1988 several Filipino-American organizations filed a class action lawsuit with the U.S. Equal Employment Opportunity Commission (EEOC), which maintained that the San Francisco city government systematically discriminated against Filipinos

(Feagin and Feagin 1993:390). The suit noted that while Filipino-Americans comprised 12 percent of the city's professional employees, they were only 1 percent of the administrative and supervisory staff. The organizations leading the lawsuit argued that whites in city government stereotyped Filipino-American professionals as incapable of holding leadership positions, and that they were not promoted because of their accent.

A Filipino-American, Manuel Fragante, was discriminated against and denied a clerk's position with the city of Honolulu in 1987 specifically because of his "accent," despite scoring the highest among the over 700 applicants who took the civil service examination for the position. With the support of several Filipino-American community organizations, Mr. Fragante filed a suit against the city government that ultimately was unsuccessful after six years of litigation (Forman 1991:6). In another case in San Francisco, in 1992 five Filipino-American security guards were either fired or reassigned from their posts at the U.S. Treasury Department after complaints by government administrators of their "funny English." An employment discrimination lawsuit was filed on their behalf by the Asian Law Caucus and other groups shortly after the EEOC ruled that they had been unlawfully discharged from their positions "because of their race and national origin." The case was settled out of court in 1994 with financial compensation to the guards.

Language discrimination also has been a source of employment problems for Filipino-Americans. In 1991 a federal court upheld a "speak English only" rule instituted by a southern California hospital that prohibited its Filipino nurses from speaking Tagalog, the Philippine national language. By the court's ruling, the hospital could legally continue its ban against conversing in Tagalog even when the nurses were on break. As a result, other health care facilities in California, which employ thousands of Filipino and Latino immigrants whose first language is not English, have established similar language prohibitions and harassed Filipino workers for allegedly violating them (*Philippine News* 1995a:A15). These various forms of employment discrimination against Filipino-Americans are symptomatic of the increasing immigrant bashing and hostility in the 1990s.

Very much a contributing factor in employment discrimination is the widespread stereotyping of Filipino-Americans, even in the national media. In a November 1994 broadcast of the highly rated situation comedy "Frasier," his father in the cast made a supposedly humorous remark, "For an extra five grand, you could have bought a whole new wife from the Philippines," that made reference to so-called "Filipino mail-order brides." Filipino-American organizations and individuals expressed outrage at such a blatant racist and sexist comment by demonstrating at National Broadcasting Corporation (NBC) studios in San Francisco and New York with signs stating "Racism is not funny." The Philippine consul general in Los Angeles, where the series is produced, wrote a letter of protest to the local NBC affiliate which stated that, "This remark...perpetuates the kind of blindly negative stereotyping of other peoples and cultures reminiscent of a less enlightened period in American television and media" (*Philippine News* 1994: A15).

In Hawaii, Filipino-Americans have become the favorite target of "ethnic jokes" by Waikiki comedians concerning their supposed culture and behavior, particularly their accent, dietary habits, and color preferences. In light of the Fragante case and others involving job discrimination, these sorts of inaccurate remarks should not be treated lightly as being expressed in jest, meaning no offense, and having no real consequences for Filipino-Americans. An obvious danger of the jokes is that they disseminate and reinforce derogatory stereotypes of Filipinos, but the far greater damage they inflict extends beyond the specific stereotypes depicted in them. Every time such a joke is repeated, it reinforces the notion that such actions against Filipino-Americans are permissible, and therefore they can be maltreated without fear of sanction or reprisal. For those who find these jokes funny, it may be a short step for them to reject a Filipino-American job applicant or to demean a Filipino-American coworker because her/his accent or behavior is similarly considered "funny."

Another problem area for Filipino-Americans concerns their being victims of hate crimes and other forms of violence. Almost every issue of the larger Filipino-American community newspapers contains an article about a Filipino who was killed or seriously injured in a violent confrontation, e.g., domestic abuse, drive-by shooting, car jacking, or robbery. In 1994 Filipino-Americans had the second highest number (39) of reported incidents of anti-Asian hate crimes, according to a report of the National Asian Pacific American Legal Consortium (*Philippine News* 1995b:A12). In Hawaii, young Filipino males have been seriously injured in gang violence against Samoans and Vietnamese. These hate crimes are reminiscent of the anti-Filipino race riots of the 1930s, except that they are more frequent and more violent.

### Political Participation

Filipino-American political status is even less well established than their socioeconomic status. It has been estimated that there are only about 100 Filipino-Americans have been elected or been appointed as public officials in the mid-1990s (Ciria-Cruz 1994:41). This lack of political representation significantly contributes to the perception that Filipino-Americans are still an invisible minority,...[out of sight, out of mind] to the centers of power and purveyors of influence. Similarly, they have been described them as "one of the most marginalized and most misrecognized ethnic and racial constituencies in America (San Juan, Jr. 1994: 25).

Hawaii is the only state in which Filipino-Americans have attained a significant degree of political representation, and many "first Filipino-American" distinctions in politics were achieved in the islands. In 1994 the first Filipino-American governor in the United States was elected in Hawaii. The first Filipino-American legislator, mayor, state cabinet member, and state supreme court justice all were elected or appointed in Hawaii. However, there are no, and perhaps never have been, any Filipino-Americans elected to the governorship of any other state or to the U.S. Congress. Filipinos are best represented at the local level of electoral politics as town mayors (e.g., Delano and Vallejo, California) and in city councils (e.g., Daly City, California and Kodiak, Alaska) and local boards of education, and their strongest showing is again in Hawaii. Following the 1994 elections, there were two senators and four representatives, all of whom were Democrats, in the Hawaii state legislature. But in the remaining forty-nine states, the situation is far more dismal. In the mid-1990s only three states (Washington, Maryland, and West Virginia) had Filipino-Americans in the state legislature and notably not in California, where a majority of their population resides and where they have the highest naturalization and citizenship rate of any immigrant group in the state.

In non-electoral politics, because there were so few who could vote, Filipino-Americans historically have used labor organizing as a collective means for advancing their political and economic interests. In Hawaii, Filipinos led and participated in numerous strikes on the sugar and pineapple plantations and organized their own labor unions, such as the Filipino Federation of Labor led by Pablo Manlapit, beginning in the early 1920s. As the largest ethnic group on the plantations since the 1920s, Filipinos made great sacrifices during strikes and the labor movement in general for the ultimate benefit of all working people in Hawaii. Filipino-Americans have held prominent leadership positions, including the directorship long held by Carl Damaso, in the International Longshoremen's and Warehousemen's Union, the union that finally succeeded in organizing all plantation workers in 1946.

In California, agricultural growers withstood the larger labor organizing efforts of field workers until the 1960s. But Filipino farmworkers in the Salinas Valley formed their own union, the Filipino Labor Union (FLU), in 1933. Led by Rufo Canete, the FLU organized several strikes in the 1930s including a victorious strike in 1934 when it won recognition as a union and wages of forty cents an hour after violent opposition from the white lettuce growers. Another union, the Filipino Agricultural Laborers Association, by 1941 had won several strikes and obtained wage increases and better working conditions.

Filipinos along with Chicanos comprised the bulk of agricultural labor in California until the 1960s, and together they led the movement to organize farmworkers and established a joint union, the Field Workers Union, as early as 1936. Later, in 1959, a Filipino-American, Larry Itliong, led the Agricultural Workers Organizing Committee (AWOC), a multiethnic but predominantly Filipino union. In 1965, AWOC organized a strike against grape growers in Delano in the San Joaquin Valley, California and soon was joined by the National Farm Workers Organization, headed by Cesar Chavez, a Chicano American. After seven months the strike ended in victory for the workers, and the two unions merged in 1966 as the United Farm Workers Organizing Committee, of which another Filipino-American, Philip Vera Cruz, served as vice president. As leaders and members of these and previously organized unions, Filipino-Americans played a major role in enhancing wages and working conditions for agricultural workers in California and Hawaii.

More recently, Filipino-Americans have organized various advocacy groups to promote their political and economic concerns and to protect their rights. Gabriela Network, named after an Ilokano woman leader (Gabriela Silang) in the revolt against Spain in the late nineteenth century, is a women's rights organization that has sought to eliminate bride trafficking agencies. Other groups and agencies, such as Filipinos Against Proposition 187 and Filipinos for Affirmative Action, have been established to challenge the conservative political shift in the 1990s that would deny Filipino-Americans equality of opportunity. There also are more mainstream associations such as the National Filipino-American Council, which includes 3,000 community and civil rights groups, that has lobbied for fair immigration laws. In addition, Filipino-Americans have been leaders and active participants in various Asian American advocacy agencies and organizations such as the Asian Law Caucus and the Asian Pacific Islander American Health Forum.

## CONCLUSION

Filipino-Americans represent another dimension of the cultural and social diversity of American society. As discussed above, they have brought and maintained their cultural values and beliefs, expressed their distinct ethnic identity, established recognizable commercial residential communities, and organized their own labor unions and advocacy organizations. They also have sought to participate actively in the economic, political and educational institutions of the larger society. However as we have seen that in doing so, Filipino-Americans have encountered substantial prejudice, stereotyping and discrimination. In many ways they have found it extremely trying and at times threatening to maintain their culture and identity as Filipino-Americans. Even to speak their own language can result in severe sanctions such as losing their job or being made fun of.

It is these conflict situations of cultural diversity that provide the most significant challenge to multiculturalism in American society, and on occasion they seem to threaten the very survival of our society. But it is precisely in this context that Filipino-Americans and other racial and ethnic minorities make their greatest contribution to the United States by reminding the American people of our most cherished principles and values of liberty, equality and justice for all. Far from threatening the quality of life in the United States with their different beliefs, values and behaviors, immigrant minorities such as Filipino-Americans reaffirm for us what it means to be American.

## REFERENCES

Azores, T. 1986-87. Educational Attainment and Upward Mobility: Prospects for Filipino-Americans. *Amerasia Journal* 13(1):39–52.
Barringer, H. R. & Liu, N. 1994. The Demographic, Social, and Economic Status of Native Hawaiians. Report prepared for Alu Like, Inc. March.
Barringer, H. R., Gardner, R. W., & Levin, M. J. 1993. *Asians and Pacific Islanders in the United States.* New York: Russell Sage Foundation.
Barringer, H. R., Takeuchi, D. T., & Xenos, P. 1990. Education, occupational prestige, and income of Asian Americans. *Sociology of Education* 63(1):27–43.
Bulosan, C. 1973. *America is in the Heart.* Seattle: University of Washington Press. Original, 1943.

Cabezas, A., Shinagawa, L., & Kawaguchi, G. 1986–87. New Inquiries into the socioeconomic status of Pilipino Americans in California. *Amerasia Journal* 13(1):1–21.

Cariaga, R. R. 1936. The Filipinos in Hawaii: A Survey of Their Economic and Social Conditions. Master's thesis, University of Hawaii.

Carino, B. V., Fawcett, J. T., Gardner, R. W., & Arnold, F. 1990. The New Filipino Immigrants to the United States: Increasing diversity and change. *Papers of the East-West Population Institute*, No. 115.

Ciria-Cruz, R. P. 1994. How far have we come? *Filipinas* 3(10):40–44.

East-West Population Institute. 1990. Recent Filipino Immigration to the United States: A Profile. Honolulu: Population Institute, East-West Center.

Feagin, J. R. & Feagin, C. B. 1993. *Racial and Ethnic Relations*, 4th edition. Englewood Cliffs: Prentice-Hall.

*Filipinas.* 1994. Signed, Sealed, Delivered. December, pp. 16–18.

Forman, S. M. 1991. Filipino Participation in civil rights policies and practices in Hawaii. In *The Filipino-American Experience in Hawaii*. J. Y. Okamura, A. R. Agbayani, & M. T. Kerkvliet (eds). *Social Process in Hawai* 33:1–11. Honolulu: University of Hawaii Press.

Lasman, L., Buluran, O. J., Nolan, J., & O'Neil, L. 1971. A Study of Attitudes of Filipino Immigrants about Hawaii. Master's thesis, University of Hawaii.

Lind, A. W. 1980. *Hawaii's People*. Honolulu: University of Hawaii Press.

Liu, J. M., Ong, P. M., & Rosenstein, C. 1988. Dual chain migration: Post-1965 Filipino immigration to the United States. *International Migration Review* 25(3):487–513.

Melendy, H. B. 1977. *Asians in America: Filipinos, Koreans and East Indians*. Boston: Twayne Publishers.

Okamura, J. Y. 1983. Immigrant Filipino Ethnicity in Honolulu, Hawaii. Unpublished doctoral dissertation, University of London.

———1984. Kinship and community: Filipino immigrants in Honolulu. *Dialogue* 20(1):27-43.

———1990. Ethnicity and Stratification in Hawaii. *Operation Manong Resource Papers*, No.1.Operation Manong Program, University of Hawaii.

———1991. Filipino educational status and achievement at the University of Hawaii. In *The Filipino-American Experience in Hawaii*. J. Y. Okamura, A. R. Agbayani, & M. T. Kerkvliet (eds). *Social Process in Hawaii* 33:107-129. Honolulu: University of Hawaii Press.

———1995. The Global Filipino Diaspora as an Imagined Community. Paper presented at conference on Contemporary Diasporas: Focus on Asian Pacifics. Los Angeles, CA, February.

*Philippine News.* 1994. Prime Time TV Slurs RP, Filipinas. December 7–13, pp. A1, A15.

———1995a. Union Rep Will File Suit for Language Prejudice. March 1–7, pp. A1, A15.

———1995b. Hate Crimes Against Asian Americans Rising. August 6–12, pp. A1, A12.

San Juan, Jr., E. 1994. Configuring the Filipino Diaspora in the United States. *Diaspora*, 3(2):117–133.

U.S. Bureau of the Census 1988. We, the Asian and Pacific Islander Americans. September.

———1993. We the American...Asians. September.

# 13

# American Indians: The Forgotten Minority

## Charles Cambridge

## INTRODUCTION

The history of American Indians is a confusing maze of different opinions and perceptions. Our purpose in this chapter is to illuminate the reader's mind of an almost forgotten history concerning the aboriginal peoples of the United States (Brophy & Aberle 1966). Our purpose is not to present a total picture of historical and current events, but to introduce a compressed description of truthful events that have shaped American Indians and their culture. Indian people are found from the cold regions of the Intuit in northern Alaska to the Yahgan, who fight the great winds in southern Tierra del Fuego. The Indian tribes represent the only inhabitants of the Western Hemisphere otherwise known as the New World at the time of Columbus. Despite the impressions that arise from the term "the New World," native peoples represented cultures that are of a great age. Some of these old Indian cultures developed to a very high degree in social complexity and technological development. Within these cultures, the native sciences became highly developed, leading to the sciences of astronomy and mathematics. However, Americans have not viewed American Indians as a people within their own cultural reality, but instead have viewed and measured Indians by existing stereotypes. The noble savage again has become the ideal stereotype, moving away from the image of the drunken and brutal savage. A spirit of the noble savage is clear in the movies, *Dancing with Wolves* and Disney's *Pocahontas*.

Indian cultures are unique in America. Some Indian tribes have survived, while other tribes have been destroyed. Many have maintained their traditional cultures, while others have lost their cultures and communities. The history of American Indians in their relationship with Europeans and Americans is full of brutality and intent destruction. The unique history of tribal people can be told in several images with distinctive political, social, and cultural focuses. What follows is a blend of several viewpoints woven into a narrative.

## THE BEGINNING OF HISTORY: THE COLUMBUS
## AND THE EUROPEAN EXPERIENCE

A continuous burning issue is the claim that the "history" of tribal people in the Western Hemisphere did not begin until Europeans discovered the Americas. Europeans have argued that Indian people did not have a written language and, therefore, no history. This argument is based upon the fact that Europeans believed that oral traditions could not serve as a valid indicator of history. Therefore, the history of Indian people could only begin with Columbus and his writings .

Two hours after midnight land appeared, at a distance of about two leagues from them. ...waiting for day, a Friday, on which they reached a small island of the Lucayos, which is called in the language of the Indians "Guanahani." Immediately they saw naked people, and the admiral [Columbus] went ashore in the armed boat...When they had landed...The admiral called the two captains and the others... and said that they should bear witness and testimony before he, before them all, took possession of the island, as in fact he did, for the King and Queen, his Sovereigns...I, he says, in order that they might feel great amity towards us, because I knew that they were a people to be delivered and converted to our holy faith rather, by love than by force, gave to some among them some red caps and some glass beads, which they hung round their necks, and many other things of little value. At this they were greatly pleased and became so entirely our friends that it was a wonder to see...Our Lord willing, at the time of my departure I will bring back six of them to Your Highnesses, that they may learn to talk...All these are the words of the admiral (Washburn 1964:3–5).

Columbus did not realize initially that he had sailed into unknown lands. New lands had been discovered, and shortly this would became a well-known fact. This vast unclaimed land laid open for European powers to exploit. It was not a question of negotiating issues or events with the savages. Europeans wanted to exploit the wealth of the New World with only other jealous European powers to stand in their way.

### Civilizing and Christianizing the Savages

Europeans rationalized the need to Christianize and civilize native people soon after Indians were declared human beings. The thought that Indian people were actually animals stemmed from the fact that they were not mentioned in Christian literature as deriving from Adam and Eve, let alone from Noah. The discovery of the Americas rocked the foundation of European Christianity. Was Christianity true doctrine, or did God just forget to tell various European religious leaders about Indian people? These questions and other questions  created many debates and conflicts within the intelligentsia and political leaders of Europe. It eventually was decided that Indians were human. Nevertheless, many today still disagree with this old religious decision. Eventually, this created the need to assure that the newly discovered Indians actually became civilized Christian people. The Pope assigned this responsibility to the royalty of Europe and they became the guardians of the native people of the New World. Under this European guardianship, the idea of native people as wards of the Europeans became reality. This religious relationship established a long-lasting approach to Indian policy. Today at the highest level of government, the United States reflects the European association with American Indians. As with Europeans, Indians became wards of the U.S. government. For the European, civilizing the Indian people meant taking the savages from an uneducated and brutal state and elevating them to civilized behavior. With a belief that native religion was associated with evil and Satan, European missionaries swarmed into the interior of the continent seeking to convert the new humans. These attempts eventually became known as the "Whiteman's Burden." Death was the result for those who resisted. With the discovery of gold, Christianity took a deadly direction. Europeans would rationalize that Indians were beyond redemption and had to be killed (Spicer 1969; McNickle 1973).

### Divide and Conquer

The area now known as the United States had more than 500 different tribes at the time of its "Discovery." These tribes had their own sovereignty, territory, government, culture, religion, and language. After "Discovery," the people of these tribes helped many initial European settlers survive by providing protection and food. However, as the population of Europeans increased and their settlements grew in number, their demands for Indian land and resources greatly increased. Conflict and war resulted. Quite often, Indians became involved in the conflicts among European powers. European wars began to decimate the Indian populations of these tribes. No matter the participants, senseless killings filled with inhuman cruelties were common. Battlefields became fields of rotting bodies that would lie under a sacred sun. Many countless battles have been lost in time and history. Each European country wanted a share of the Americas. So, through means of warfare and competition, they divided the Americas into vast European colonies. The native people, who were culturally attached to the land, fell under the domain of the European power. Furthermore, beside war, European diseases began to take its toll on native populations.

The most pressing issues for American Indians across the history of the United States have been the loss of land and the death of many people during the centuries of treaties and wars. The population of native people in the U.S. area at the time of discovery is unknown. Some anthropologists estimate a population of 250 million Indians, while others estimate a population of one million. A tense debate has occurred over the historical population of Indian people. The question becomes how bad was the genocide of American Indians?

## THE AMERICAN EXPERIENCE

When the American revolution was successful, the tiny and newly formed government was quickly aware that Indian people still formed a threat to their continual existence. Disease and warfare had taken its toll within Indian tribes, but the Eastern tribes were still strong in their population and military might. Many tribes found in the East are familiar to the reader. The Delaware, the Iroquoian tribes, the Algonquian tribes, and many others lived in the Eastern Woodland cultural area. With these and other tribes, relationships were defined by treaties with Europeans. Treaties fulfilled the need to legalize and legitimize the transfer of land title from the Indians to the Europeans. With the formation of the United States, Americans accepted Indians as the occupiers and owners of the land that needed to be transferred through treaties and purchases. This was an absolute recognition of the sovereignty of Indian tribes. Nevertheless, in 1828, Andrew Jackson became the president of the United States. Under his administration, his goal was the complete removal of the Eastern Indian tribes to the West. In 1830, Congress passed the Indian Removal Act that gave the President of the United States the authority to remove Eastern tribes to lands west of the Mississippi River. Between 1832 and 1843, most of the eastern tribes lost their lands and then were forced to the West. As Americans moved west, Eastern tribes, given lands initially in Arkansas, Kansas, Iowa, Illinois, Missouri, and Wisconsin, again were forced to move into Oklahoma, which became known as the Indian Territory. With the discovery of gold in California, many demanded the removal of Indians from their lands throughout the United States. Most Americans believed that gold was buried on remaining Indian lands and territory.

### The End of Treaties and the Loss of Sovereignty

The Indian treaty period ended in 1871, when the U.S. Congress decided that the government would no longer continue the practice of recognizing Indian tribes as independent nations. They were no longer a military threat. Federal policy turned from conquering the independent Indian tribes to the problem of managing all of the conquered Indians. The Indian relationship with the federal government became a dizzy succession of paternalistic Indian agents, who in several cases, exploited the tribes under their jurisdiction, and a succession of federal legislation all aimed at "solving the Indian problem."

Several pieces of legislation, out of several thousand, are worth commenting upon because of their significant impact on American Indian tribes. The Dawes Act of 1887 (General Allotment Act) established the framework under which large tracts of Indian land were declared surplus properties and reverted to the United States. Each Indian male received a tract of land, a wagon, and seed. If the Indian farmer proved industrious and competent, he would receive U.S. citizenship and legal title to his land. In a later setting, the tribes represented an alien problem that refused to go away. To resolve this problem, Indians were made citizens of the Untied States, certainly without the approval of the Indian tribes. The American Citizenship Act accomplished this in 1924. The Meriam Report of 1926 was an analysis of federal Indian policy. The report was very blunt in pointing out the failure of Indian programs in the United States. This report caused a massive change in Indian policy. A result of the Meriam Report was the passage of the Indian Reorganization Act of 1934 (IRA). The passage of the IRA turned American Indian policy in an opposite direction by slowing the policy of assimilating the Indians into American society. Carrying out this new federal policy was Commissioner of Indian Affairs, John Collier, who appointed several anthropologists to help in the new policy. Under John Collier, tribes began to enlarge their reservations and stop the constant loss of land. He also encouraged the development of tribal governments and the political structures of tribes. This was the complete opposite of previous government policy.

In the 1953, the United States attempted to get out of the Indian business. At this time, Congress began to terminate federal programs and control over several Indian tribes by virtue of House Concurrent Resolution 108, otherwise known today as the Termination Act. The Termination Act ended a tribal legal existence. The tribe's status as wards ended and their tribal members were given American citizenship. More than 100 tribes were selected for termination, which ended the tribe's legal existence as a sovereign entity. Under termination, the tribe's resources were sold and distributed among the tribal members. The reservation's land base was divided among tribal members or sold to outsiders. The tribes ceased to exist and tribal members no longer were considered Indians.

### Stealing Indian Kids and the Boarding Schools

Since most Indians were not standing in line to become Americans, forced assimilation became the answer. Many assimilative policies were initiated through the centuries, but an extreme method was the Indian boarding school. Education provided a means of destroying tribal culture. The beginning of Indian education in the United States was the federal funding of the Civilization Fund in 1819. The Fund began with a $10,000 federal allocation and was controlled by members of Christian organizations. The feeling of government officials was that missionaries were ideal to educate Indian children. Later, the Fund was formalized into the Civilization Division in the federal bureaucracy. In 1884, the Civilization Division became the Indian Educational Division. The basic logic of these boarding schools was the civilizing of Indian people by taking their children away from their homes and tribes. In 1879, the first Indian boarding school was founded in an abandoned army base in Carlisle, Pennsylvania. This school was known as the Carlisle Indian school. Indian kids were taken usually by force and sent to a boarding school. The school was far from their home, and visiting their children was difficult for parents. If parents did arrive to see their children, they were treated rudely or ignored. The school officials stated that Indian children would become visibly upset and moody after their parents' visit.

The boarding schools seem more like military installments or even prisons instead of schools for the education of Indian children. When some children became disgusted with the boarding school, they ran away. The school staff identified these kids as absence without leave (AWOLs). The school staff then would hunt the

AWOLs like escaped convicts. Many Indian kids died running away from boarding school in their attempt to go home. The most appalling and unjust of all of these boarding schools was the Bureau of Indian Affairs' (BIA) Chilocco Indian School in Chilocco, Oklahoma. Many children in Chilocco were expelled from other BIA schools. Among boarding schools, Chilocco was known as the end of the line. As a disciplinary measure, occasionally, young children were handcuffed to overhead beams and flogged. Others were placed in solitary confinement comparable to the sadistic discipline in penal institutions. When asked what he would do if given more money, the superintendent of Chilocco said he would build a jail and hire more guards.Within the boarding school setting, Indian children were not allowed to use their tribal language. English Only was the rule inside the walls of the boarding school. The children were taught that their native language was vulgar and only English was proper. When a child did use their native language, school employees punished them severely. Another policy of the boarding schools was the ease of obtaining a diploma. Teachers would give promotions if the student failed and was too old to remain in the grade. Boarding schools never held back school students for academic failure. As a result, most boarding-school seniors graduated with approximately a ninth-grade education.

## MORMONISM, THE NEW AGE, AND SPACE ALIENS

Many theories exist to explain the existence of Indian people. Europeans and Americans have thought that Indians were the Ten Lost Tribes of Israel, Celts, Egyptians, Phoenicians, Irish, people from Atlantis, and, finally, pace aliens. This is certainly not a complete list. A popular origin theory argues that Indians were peopled and influenced by Atlantis, the legendary island. First mentioned by Plato, he writes that Atlantis existed in the Atlantic Ocean west of Gibraltar and sunk beneath the sea during massive earthquakes. With the discovery of the Americas, this almost forgotten myth was revived to provide an explanation for the origin of Indian people. Atlantis was the ideal civilization that reflected all of the desires of a "Utopia." With its destruction, Atlanteans sailed to the Americas to begin new cultures.

At the turn of the nineteenth century, another origin myth was created that reinforced the attitude of pagan, brutal, and evil Indians. This was the beginning of Mormonism. By some means, God chose a wanting character by the name of Joseph Smith to receive a visiting Angel Moroni. During this close encounter, the Angel gave Joseph Smith gold tablets written in God's own's personal language that required translation to English. The gold tablets represented the history of the ancient people of the Americas. With the translation finished, the Book of Mormon came into being. In short, the Book of Mormon describes the journey of Hebrew tribes from Jerusalem to the east coast of North America. This new religious twist reflected an earlier origin theory that Indians were the original Ten Lost Tribes of Israel and actually Jews.According to Mormonism, two competing groups emerged from the Hebrew immigrants in the New World: the Nephites and Lamenites.

Naturally the white Nephites were the good, industrious, and true believers in the faith. The Indian Lamenites were weak and degenerated to a heathen state that perpetuated a sinful and pagan culture. Naturally, war broke out between the Nephites and Lamenites. The Lamanites destroyed the Nephites, except for a few. Shortly afterward, a new migration of Hebrews from Jerusalem sailed to the Americas and revived the Nephite's culture. The Nephite nation gathered in the mountains known as Cumorah and were destroyed in a final battle with several hundred thousand Nephite troops and families killed. History repeated itself and again the evil Lamanites destroyed the good Nephites. They also believed that the modern-day Lamanites have to be civilized so that the ideal past civilization with a true religion may be restored. Smith defined the duty of the Mormons as restoring Jesus' holiness to American Indians and to bring redemption. Mormon missionaries were sent into all parts of Indian country. Tens of thousands of Indians embraced the Mormon religion and allied themselves to the modern Nephites. Yet as the Nephites increased in strength, their purpose remained the same. The Nephites had to destroy the culture of the Lamanites.

History is filled with non-Indians creating new religions and cults based upon Indian religions. Today, we have a New Age invasion of Indian reservations. These New Age individuals seek sacred Indian knowledge and life ways. For many, they take a little bit from here and a little bit from there, creating a unique mixture of religious and philosophical thoughts. Today, several whites have claimed that, usually by accident, they came across an Indian elder who recognized them as lost relatives or as a person who is special. By this holy induction, the Indian elder tells these honored whites all the tribal secrets during this encounter. In one case history, in a serene forest setting, an Indian elder gave a white lady his ancient tribal truths and secrets. Her personification to Indian status occurred when she was walking though the forest during a time of mist. She came upon an old Indian in a clearing as the sunlight broke through the clouds and struck the old Indian. As their eyes met and locked, he said, "Welcome granddaughter." She was told to sit and face the Indian elder, and he began to introduce her to the tribal religious ways and secrets. With this knowledge and being adopted as an Indian, she began to spread the sacred words to a growing following. As her religious membership grew, her religious income also grew. Many of these pseudo-Indians have become famous for bringing the true word of Indian salvation to the world's non-Indian population for a slight fee. However, money became the driving force instead of the salvation of individuals.

Yet, these social phenomena take a different, but related, form among Indian individuals who want to participate in the growing business of Indian mysticism and occultism. Without the traditional education and religious training, many of these people have lived on the very fringe of traditionalism. Without or limited in their traditional knowledge, they will invent a new religion by borrowing tribal rituals of several tribes. Occasionally, their tribal religion becomes their focus and reflects in the new religious occult. One Indian, by using illegal drugs, became a medicine man because "I had a vision." His decision was not based upon the request of the Indian spirits, but was a merely a manifestation of drugs upon his body and mind. He is now successful with a non-Indian clientele who seeks Indian secrets and cure. These pseudo-Indian medicine people have developed a high degree of deceptive skills to con the non-Indian patient. Indian fakes exploit gullible people who are searching for absolute truth and knowledge. Because of the opportunity to cycle and recycle a fraud, such New Age Indians can become quite well off financially. Through his religious con, substantial money will continue to flow. The financial possibilities have created a rush to become a New Age Indian religious leader. Unfortunately, with the increased market for Indian spirituality, traditional medicine people are not immune, and the sadness of these comments becomes clear given the flood of traditional medicine people toward non-Indian exploitation of their religion. As non-Indians begin to provide a higher source of income, traditional medicine leaders move away from their communities to serve non-Indian outsiders, forsaking their sacred duty of maintaining the health and well being of their tribal members. These serious sacrileges are major threats to the tribes as they continue to struggle to maintain their traditions. However, some have argued that real value is possible by allowing the New Agers access to Indian traditions. They argued that New Age folks provide economic support of Indian people and serve as allies in supporting Indian issues.

A movement is afoot among American Indian groups to return to the passion of good old-fashioned traditionalism (Steiner 1968; Josephy 1971). The religious servitude of Indians to New Age non-Indians has become a serious topic among tribal religious leaders. These Indian religious caterers increasingly have come increasing under fire from traditional Indians. Only recently have traditional Indians attempted to reinforce the traditional belief that "outsiders" must not participate in traditional ceremonies. Blacklisting and the denial of aid to those who have, or are abusing the religious order of the tribe have become serious responses to the loss of religious values. Some medicine men are demanding proof of tribal enrollment from persons whom they do not know, before they provide religious and medical services. Other traditional medicine people will only doctor tribal individuals who are known members of a tribal community. However, revival of Indian traditional authority becomes difficult to enforce given the renegade tradition leaders, who for profit, will only cater to non-Indians off the reservation.

Indians are really space aliens is an origin theory that is beginning to grow in popularity. In the view of some of my friends, this seems like a reasonable thought. Instead of being descendants of lost earthly civilizations such as Atlantis, many argue that Indians are space aliens or the result of their scientific experiments. A few Indians who claim to be scholars advocate a belief that Indians have a space alien connection. They have been lecturing to very attentive audiences about the Indian and extraterrestrial connections. For example, Venus, the second planet from the sun, is considered the home of the ancestors of Indian people. However, because of a catastrophe, Indians had to leave Venus and travel to earth. The narrative in their explanations is long and complex, but interesting. A similar story involves the Pleiades, and again an interstellar catastrophe occurs; Indian ancestors are forced to journey to earth from the Pleiades. Evidence for such assertions is plentiful if one picks and chooses from several different sources. From reconstructed history and mythology, many can argue any type of extraterrestrial origin for any tribe. Stories of worlds, journeys to earth, star people, and aliens exist in most tribal mythologies. Many reported sightings of space ships on Indian reservations reinforce the alien connection. Pictures of aliens and secret symbols from Indian religious arts and crafts also support this belief.

## THE CASE OF THE NAVAHO NATION

The Navahos and the closely related Apaches, contrary to the traditional images of their desert, mesas, and Hollywood, are not originally from the southwestern part of the Untied States. The Navahos, Apaches, and Southern Athapaskans are related to the Athapaskans of northwestern Canada, Alaska, and the northwest coast of the United States. However, the traditional name for both tribes is Dińe, meaning "The People." During the fourteenth century, the first peoples of the Dińe tribes began migrating into the long-established southwest territory of the Pueblo Indians and their Anasazi ancestors. With their arrival into the Southwest centuries before the Spanish, the Dińe met and contacted with the highly developed and complex Pueblo Indian culture. Their association brought complex cultural changes to the Navaho people. The Pueblos introduced several new elements such as farming and weaving into traditional Navaho culture. As these and other cultural elements drifted into the Navaho cultural matrix, a new and different Navaho cultural sophistication began to develop. Beginning in the sixteenth century, contact with the invading Spaniards introduced additional Navaho cultural changes, such as the introduction of horses, sheep, silver working, and new crops. Most importantly with the introduction of horses, the Navaho revolutionized their trading and raiding abilities. Of the many alien cultural items absorbed into the Navaho cultural matrix, the horse was of major and critical importance. The horse, with its mobility, made a high degree of contact with others and increased the range for hunting and raiding. This points out an important Navaho cultural ability to assimilate elements from foreign cultures without disrupting their traditional cultural core. The Navahos constantly selected whatever suited them from alien cultures and then adapted each item into the traditional Navaho mold. This redefining of the Navaho matrix has allowed the Navahos through the centuries to survive on their own terms. In this manner, the Navahos could avoid assimilation into alien cultures and to maintain their traditional culture throughout the centuries.

### The Navahos and The Americans

Warfare and slavery become the fundamental relationship of the Spaniards and later the Mexicans with the Navahos. In the years immediately following the U.S. war with Mexico, the Navaho conflict with the Americans became similar to the physical and social conflict the Navahos had with the Spanish and Mexicans. The Navaho raiding patterns continued against the inhabitants of the Southwest. During these conflicts, Navaho slavery became a traditional aspect of the Navaho struggle with the Spanish, Mexicans, and, eventually, the Anglos.

Indian slavery differed little from black slavery with all its horrors and implications. Although the figures are at best rough estimations, probably five thousand Navaho were held as slaves in 1860...I know of no family which can raise one hundred and fifty dollars, but what purchases a Navajo slave, and many families own four or five—the trade in them being as regular as the trade in pigs or sheep. Previous to the war their price was from seventy-five to a hundred dollars; but now they are worth about four hundred dollars...I have been conversant with the institution of slavery in Georgia, but the system is worse here, there being no obligation resting on the owner to care for the slave when he becomes old or worthless. Fortunately for the Navajos, they generally got the better of the Mexicans in their warfare until the Americans came to their rescue (Wrone & Nelson 1973:317).

Another interesting result of warfare against the Navahos included the taking of their scalps. Navaho scalp prices varied among the legal authorities throughout the Southwest. Still, a 150 dollars for a Navaho warrior's scalp and a 100 dollars for a Navaho woman's and child's scalp were about average. The primary use for Navaho scalps was to prove to legal authorities that a Navaho was killed and to serve as proof for the payment of a bounty. For many unsavory Mexican and American characters, it was a means of employment. The scalps became a sale item for the tourist trade and were imported to the East for sale as a curio and souvenir. However, scalp entrepreneurs wishing for a quick profit and wanting to avoid going in search of Navahos to scalp began to look closer to home. Eventually, scalps brought in for the bounty and sent east for souvenirs obviously were not Navaho, but from individuals with red and blond hair. So when scalps started to appear that obviously which were not from Navahos, the scalp business came to a grinding halt. However, many entrepreneurs wanted to continue receiving an income by killing Navahos. Since scalps were not being accepted as proof of the killing of a Navaho, bounty hunters would then bring the head of a Navaho victim to the authorities. So, the logical step from scalping was to become a head hunter. Even for the sun-harden bounty hunters, the reality of caring for rotting Navaho heads until they reached civilization for the collection of the bounty proved nearly insurmountable. Still, toward the end of this policy, several heads with their distorted features and drying skin seem not to be a Navaho or members of surrounding tribes. The suspicion grew that some heads were actually non-Indians who were unlucky enough to come across the bounty hunter's greed.

In the 1850s, the Navahos faced the U.S. Army as both American and Mexican citizens wanted to exterminate the Navahos. However, with the upheaval of the Civil War, military commanders were hard-pressed to deal with the Navahos and the Apaches. The regional military commander for the New Mexico Territory, Brigadier General James H. Carleton, instructed his command to kill every male Navajo and Apache Indian old enough to bear arms. This extermination policy did little to stop the Navahos from raiding deep into Mexico and far into the Plains. Eventually, the Civil War ended and battle-hardened troops were ordered west to subjugate the Indians. Indian wars began to spread throughout the West as the United States, in their belief of Manifest Destiny, moved into the West.

When the Anglo conquest of the Southwest began in earnest in the mid-nineteenth century, the Navaho raids and other basically socially unacceptable behavior became intolerable. The Anglo army, always a part of any social interaction between Whites and Indians, enlisted the organized support of the Mexicans, hired the Utes and other Indian tribes, and finally succeeded in building enormous odds against which the Navaho stood alone (Leighton & Leighton 1944:6).

The result was inevitable. The U.S. Army gave the legendary Kit Carson the chore of pacifying and subjugating the Navahos by any means. The Americans gave the Navahos until July 20, 1863, to surrender. Some Navahos who knew of the threat complied, while most did not. With the passing of the surrender deadline, Colonel Carson invaded Navaho country with a scorched earth policy. He destroyed Navaho homes, fields of crops and orchards of fruit trees to starve the Navahos. Under these conditions, the Navahos began to surrender. Carson exterminated those refusing to surrender. Finally defeated, 8,000 Navahos were forced to walk 400 miles from their homeland to Bosque Redondo, also known as Ft. Summer, in eastern New Mexico. With high emotion, the Navahos refer to the march and imprisonment in Bosque Redondo as the "Long Walk." However, many Navahos hid in the isolated desert and mountain regions of the Southwest and escaped capture.

During their internment, the Navahos faced the possibility of removal to Indian Territory in Oklahoma or Florida. However, the wish of several Americans and Mexicans was to have the U.S. Army kill the captured Navahos. However, removal to an unknown land or absolute extermination did not occur. Yet, with the total defeat by Carson and the consequent removal from their homeland, the Navahos became dispirited and homesick. After years at Fort Summer, the captivity of the Navahos ended in failure. In 1868, a new treaty was forced upon the Navahos after which the Americans allowed them to return to a new reservation created from part of their homeland. Besides seed, the federal government furnished each member of the tribe with a few sheep and goats. For the Navaho, this marked an end to their former life-style and the beginning of a new way of life.

After the initial shock of reservation life, Americans could not easily enforce their demands because of the isolation and vastness of the Navaho reservation. The Navahos used the rugged terrain of the reservation to isolate themselves from the outside American influences. Left alone, the Navahos on their own terms began to enjoy a time of relative prosperity. Beneath this appearance of prosperity, however, lurked an ecological disaster that came to a head in the 1920s and 1930s. Given the great number of herd animals, the reservation's land base was simply insufficient to support the animals and their increasing numbers. The traditional Southwestern lack of water reinforced by periodic droughts and severe overgrazing stripped the Navaho rangeland of its natural grass and vegetation. It was this ecological disaster that produced conflicts between the Navahos and federal officials. Stock reduction ordered by the federal government led to confiscation and the killing of herds of animals. This policy pushed the Navahos into poverty and direct confrontation with the U.S. Government. Yet, the policy failed to take into account the Navaho cultural factors. For instance, the Navahos did not understand the practical concerns of the

Americans and the ecological realities involved. For the Navahos, the changes in the landscape with the loss of grass and soil was attributed to a disregard and lack of respect for the proper behavior and ceremonies. In other words, a failure in the harmony of the world was causing all of the difficulties. Furthermore, the Navahos believed that their livestock were not merely a source of food, but also a source of pride, prestige, and wealth. A sense of well being for the Navaho was the intimate feeling stemming from the ownership of his herds. Stock reduction was imposed upon the Navahos through force. These events reinforced the Navahos' thoughts that whitemen were indeed mad. The whitemen failed to understand and appreciate the Navaho resistance and defiance. Distrustfulness and skepticism became the hallmarks of the American and Navaho relationship.

World War II brought sweeping and profound changes to the Navaho people and their reservations. With their traditional warriors' roles suppressed since their defeat by the Americans, the Navahos were drawn into the war's fervor and enthusiasm. Despite treaty provisions against renewing the military power of the Navaho people, the United States allowed the Navahos to respond to the demands for labor in the U.S. military and war industry. As Navahos enlisted and became industrial workers, they left the reservation in masse for the first time. Navahos by the thousands entered the U.S. military with others moving into cities off the reservation to work in the war industry. Navaho men served in every branch of the Armed Forces during the war and saw action in every military theater. They were loyal troops and received every type of military honor and decoration. Perhaps the most unique contribution of the Navaho to the military and the war effort involved several members of the tribe who were members of the U.S. Marine Corps. During the war, the U.S. Marine Corps capitalized on the linguistic peculiarities of the Navaho language. A new military code was developed that was based upon the Navaho language. Utilizing Navaho Marine volunteers, this unbreakable Navaho code was used successfully in the Pacific theater and in other areas of the conflict. Besides the usual military communications training, the Navaho Marines were trained in a code based on their own language. The Japanese were unable to break the Navaho code throughout the war, although they had captured a Navaho soldier during the surrender of the Philippines. This Navaho facing torture and other threats could translate the Navaho language but not the accompanying military code. Other Japanese code-breaking attempts ended in failure. The Navaho code was a highly guarded secret in the U.S. military. Each Navaho code talker was assigned non-Navaho bodyguards who were under orders to kill the Navaho code talker if any threats of capture by the enemy were real. Today, the Navaho code talkers have an organization that meets periodically and keeps the history of their military efforts and contributions alive.

As a result of the military and war activities by members of the tribe, the economic structure of the Navahos moved from traditional herding and farming to wage earning that was based on a war economy. Large amounts of earnings from soldiers and industrial workers began to flow into the Navaho reservation. Buying consumer products became infectious, and changes in the Navaho culture were inevitable. The Navahos became optimistic of further wealth and greater growth as the war continued. However, with the ending of the war, jobs and the new wealth disappeared. In the decade following the conclusion of World War II, the Navahos became immersed in a period of frustration, confusion, and poverty. Even with increased federal appropriations in the late 1940s and the Navaho-Hopi Long Range Rehabilitation Act passed in early 1950, the federal support failed to duplicate the war economy. The federal efforts during this time only increased the misgivings of most Navahos. During this economic confusion, the Peyote Church began to take hold on the Navaho reservation. Considering the Navaho's war-time experiences and the chronic failure of new federal legislation to generate effective and practical economic development on the reservation, their willingness to turn to a new religion was not surprising.

In the 1952, the Bureau of Indian Affairs (BIA) began a series of national Indian employment relocation programs. These relocation programs attempted to place Navahos in cities for employment training and placement. Federal officials hoped that relocation would result in assimilation since the reservation was viewed as a barrier to integration into American society. Thousands of Navahos took part in the relocation program and moved into the cities. Many Navahos sent to the city were provided training in such vocational fields such as welding, cooking, clerical and secretarial training. Once in the city, the BIA provided short training programs that introduced the Navahos to the realities of urban life. Pamphlets concerning the use of gas stoves and telephones, and how to catch a city bus, were a few of the topics dealt with. The one dealing with the telephone was interesting. The phone was animated with a smiling face and bubbles of explanation as to how to talk to a telephone operator, and other useful information. Nevertheless, the life of the relocatee was a lonely life in an unfamiliar and strange city. The failure rates for this program were extremely high. One Indian agency had an 85 percent return rate because their tribal members were unable to deal with urban life.

In 1956, a massive push by American companies began to exploit the vast oil and gas reserves on the Navaho reservation. The actions of the oil and gas industries brought about an economic boom that resulted in short-term economic gorging. In a short time, increases in economic development with high employment occurred. These oil booms created major fluctuations in the Navaho and white populations as they responded to the demands of increased employment. In 1950, for example, only 3,573 people lived in Farmington, New Mexico, the largest city in San Juan County. In the spring of 1958, the oil and gas boom had caused such a large immigration of oil workers that the Farmington population increased to 65,000 people. When the oil boom ended, Farmington's population dropped to 17,000 people. Many Navaho people who could find work found themselves with wages inadequate to meet the high costs of living in a boom environment. Employers established high standards for work skills that eliminated the poorly trained and uneducated. Anglo employers and workers built work and social barriers against the Navahos so that it became difficult for them to get a job or obtain a promotion. Many employers pointed to the Navahos' lack of training, skills, and education as factors for unemployment or underemployment. Yet, job discrimination was a reality and must not be excluded in any review of Navaho culture.

One solution to increase employment on the Navaho reservation was to increase industrial development on the reservation by the creation of industrial parks. However, because of the isolation of the reservation and an unskilled labor force, the industrial parks never achieved a high level of success. Still, in the early 1970s, the Navaho tribal government was successful in luring the Fairchild corporation to the reservation. With federal and tribal funds, a large plant was constructed for Fairchild Corporation in Shiprock, New Mexico. However, in 1974, the American Indian Movement occupied the Fairchild semiconductor plant with the argument that the Navahos were being exploited. At this particular time, Fairchild was the largest employer of Navahos from the reservation. During the occupation, the American Indian Movement extensively damaged the semiconductor facility. After the plant was held for a long period, Fairchild decided not to reopen it. Fairchild came to the decision that the response of the federal and tribal authorities was inadequate, and further operations would be jeopardized, so Fairchild moved their operation to Southeast Asia. More than 900 Navahos employees, most of whom were women, were left unemployed. With the reality of high unemployment on the reservation, the Navahos were quite upset with the American Indian Movement and their supporters. Without a paycheck, most lost their cars and other items purchased on credit. This event still burns in the memory of many Shiprock Navahos. Even today, the Fairchild building in Shiprock is mostly empty.

### Navahos, American Indians, and the Year 2001

Today, there are some 800,000 American Indians in the United States. Over 100,000 of them live in the urban environment, while most continue to live on the 200 reservations set aside just for them across 26 states. Three-fourths of them live below the poverty line. As the year 2001 approaches and a new century begins, what does the future hold for the Navahos and other American Indian tribes? The question is very difficult to answer. Recently, in 1995, the Disney Corporation subjugated American Indians and the world to their animation of Pocahontas. Lyrics from the song "Savages" from the film *Pocahontas*, modernize an old message: "What can you expect from filthy little heathens their whole disgusting race is like a curse, their skin's a hellish red. They're only good when they are dead" (Disney 1995). Perhaps in this we can find a prognosis about the future of American Indians.

The animated noble Pocahontas is an ideal red Barbie doll whose goal in life is to marry a tall, blue-eyed, blond, white man. For many contemporary young Indian males and females, this idealism speaks to the move away from their culture and the increase of intertribal and interracial marriages. Tribes now face a real threat to their existence. Unfortunately, we now have reached a stage where some tribes are unable to marry tribal members because they are all related. They now must marry outside the tribe, and so the tribe is genetically doomed. These two situations do not speak well of the future of American Indian tribes.

The only future truth in the movie, *Pocahontas*, is the character of Governor John Ratcliffe, which is a fairly accurate portrayal of a gold-hungry European.

Unfortunately, Disney has captured a true piece of Indian history that is reflective of future events. American Indians still have many things that Americans want, and they will take these items from the Indians. This reality sets in motion the mechanism working for the destruction of Indian culture. The future of the Navahos and other American Indian tribes is fighting for survival as cultures wanting to be left alone. This ideal will not take place, which is the sad part of this story.

## REFERENCES

Brophy, W. & Aberle, S. (eds). 1966. *The Indian: America's Unfinished Business.* Norman: University of Oklahoma Press.

Disney Corporation. 1995. *Pocahontas.* Feature film. Hollywood: Disney Corporation.

Josephy, Jr., A. M. 1971. *Red Power.* New York: McGraw-Hill.

Leighton, A. H. & Leighton, D. C. 1944. *The Navaho Door.* New York: Russell & Russell.

————1946. *The Navaho.* Cambridge: Harvard University Press.

McNickle, D. 1973. *Native American Tribalism.* New York: Oxford University Press.

Spicer, E. H. 1969. *A Short History of the Indians of the United States.* New York: Van Nostrand.

Steiner, S. 1968. *The New Indians.* New York: Harper & Row.

Washburn, W. E. 1964. *The Indian and the White Man.* Garden City, NY: Anchor Books.

Wrone, D. R. & Nelson, Jr., R. S. 1973. *Who's the Savage?* Greenwich, CT: Fawcett Publications, Inc.

# PART IV

## Special Interest Cultural Groupings and Scenes

Although most people immediately think of racial and ethnic groupings whenever the topic of cultural diversity arises, there are a great many other cultural groupings that make up the actual diversity of the United States. Dealing with these is a little more difficult and complicated than when the groupings are ethnically identifiable. These additional cultural groupings that combine with ethnic ones to complete the diversity of American culture come with all of those special interest groups that have accompanied the development of the complex society. Such groups are identified on the basis of the very specific beliefs and behaviors that distinguish them from other groups. It is also the case that many of these cultural groupings are frequently in direct competition with one another or, in the extreme cases, in direct conflicts with one another. For this reason alone, no discussion of diversity would be complete without taking these cultural groupings into account.

Some of the special interest cultural groupings may very well fall into what have been identified and described as *cultural scenes*. Cultural scenes bring people from all kinds of other cultural backgrounds together for specific purposes or in pursuit of specific goals. They represent viable cultures made up of people who share the same specific information and behavior expectations. Cultural scenes are tied to social situations, time-bound and contextual—they function or become active only at certain times and in certain places. These are also constituent cultural groups that contribute to the makeup of nation-states, and they are significant elements of the diversity of America. Recently, a number of these special interest cultures have even become internationalized and/or transnational, transcending national groupings or the specific cultural groupings that make them up.

Covering all of the cultural groupings that naturally would fall under this kind of diversity would be a tall order. Nearly every category of the cultural experience as it has evolved in the modern nation-state has spawned cultural groups of this kind. But, as with the ethnic categories already shown to be made up of many different specific cultural groupings, so, too, categories of special interest actually are composed of many specific groups. The special interest categories most readily recognized are those associated with sex and gender differences, politics and economics, age groupings, religion and churches, businesses and occupation. In addition to these, there are a whole host of other more specific interest groups associated with such things as education, ideas of conservation, animal and human rights, leisure activities, the physically challenged or handicapped, and so on—the list is almost endless. Because of the vastness of this kind of cultural category, some selection has to be made just to provide a small sense of what this diversity contributes to the multiculturalism (diversity) of America. There is probably no good justification for the categories and groups selected for presentation in this section other than to say that selection was based on relative importance—at least in the public's mind, because of the interest they generate across the United States. Some categories (and examples of the specific groups that comprise them) simply cannot be ignored. While a selection of categories and specific cultural groupings has been made, it should not be construed to mean that other groups and categories are not equally significant to the topic of diversity. Space prohibits attention to all of the groupings that naturally fall into this part of diversity. As with the discussion of ethnic categories and groups, the few representatives of this section represent only a beginning.

All of the chapters in this section of the volume are designed to give the reader some exposure to the diversity that comes with special interests and a greater awareness of some of the many specific cultural groups that in fact exist within this broad category. No discussion of diversity in the United States would be complete without some attention to the categories of gender and sex. In Chapter 14, Shari Neller Starrett addresses gender identity as it produces cultural groupings, focusing specifically on women's culture. The author raises the question of whether or not there is one women's culture or many different cultures that simply have been generalized into one in the minds of most people. In Chapter 15, Tiffany D. Rogers addresses sex cultures, those normally generalized into what most people refer to as the homosexual community. She makes the point that gay culture (that of male homosexuals) and lesbian culture (that of homosexual females) are quite different. She also discusses the historical context and sources for the perceptions Americans tend to hold regarding this community in general. This history and the actions of most people based on their perceptions have combined to account for the reactions of the American "straight" society and the homosexual community. It has helped the homosexual community, both gay and lesbian, to establish their identity, and it has resulted in a unified effort on the part of the homosexual community to pursue equal rights with other Americans. In Chapter 16, Gretchen Siegler focuses on new religious movements in America, cultural groups that usually are referred to as sects or cults. Focusing on one specific grouping, the author shows how such groups are actually quite innovative and frequently successful despite the general social climate in which they find themselves and the negative perceptions widely held about them by members of mainstream religion in America.

In Chapter 17, Danny Wilcox examines the whole "drug culture" in America, another category that obscures more than it clarifies. In his discussion, the author points out that most Americans belong to one or another of the actual "drug cultures" of America. While the illegal use of drugs gets most of the time time and attention of Americans, the author concludes that the conflict is not over drugs, but over the meaning of life and the role of drugs in the lives of every American. The category of the "physically challenged or physically disabled" has garnered increased attention recently with the passage of the American Disabilities Act requiring businesses, the schools, and nearly everyone in the society to make reasonable accommodations for those who fall under this legislation. This category actually includes many different cultural groupings, each quite distinct from the others based on their own particular circumstances, needs, and problems they face. In Chapter 18, Kathee M. Christiansen turns the tables on those who generally see people with "physical disabilities." She points out that it is not that the deaf who are "handicapped," but most Americans who are "sign language-impaired." In Chapter 19, Ann Jordan explores organizational and business cultures. In her discussion, she relates these cultures to all other kinds of cultural groupings, and points out how these diverse groups come together in the contexts of organizational cultures, themselves being globalized. She also suggests how anthropology can help in the management of this diversity.

# 14

## Gender Identity: Unity Through Diversity

### Shari Neller Starrett

The very idea of "women's culture" implies that there is something (cultural rather than biological) that defines and binds women, some basic set of things that women from all cultural contexts share. But is there? This is a far more difficult question than it may appear to be. In this chapter we will not be examining the biological designation of those human beings who are categorized as female, but instead we will try to reach a better understanding of the acquired social definitions of gender that contribute to the identity of women. We will discover that for women (and this is probably also quite true for men) the acquisition of a gender identity is deeply embedded in an extremely varied, complicated, and overlapping series of life experiences. This will mean that if you want to understand "women's culture," you must be able to develop an awareness and appreciation of the many ways in which any particular woman becomes gender-identified as a woman among other women, and as someone who will be recognized as a woman by other women and by men.

### GENDER AND SOME OF ITS COMPLICATIONS

Gender identity, of course, is not entirely separable from biology. In obvious ways, the sexual organs that we are born with contribute to what we learn and the way we are treated in the earliest stages of our lives—the ways in which we are diapered or toilet trained illustrate this point. You may think that it is equally obvious that there are readily identifiable ways in which, right from the beginning, we are taught and learn to express ourselves to others as gendered persons, as social beings who happen to come in bodies with specific sorts of parts. In fact, examples such as the effects of what or how we are taught to play are now so commonplace that pointing them out has become pretty close to unnecessary. But the development of the gender identity of "woman" consists of far more subtle and effective influences than whether or if we learn to like playing with dolls or cars.

In order to get a handle on some of these deep and sometimes hidden influences,

I will introduce a list of terms that will help us to start taking notice of some of the significant things that can contribute to the way any particular woman becomes a woman. This list is *not* meant to be rank ordered, nor is it meant to cover everything that is important in this process, but it is meant to help us start thinking about factors that many people may not have thought about as crucial to an appreciation of a woman's identity as a woman.

My philosophical training has taught me to appreciate both the value of carefully dividing up a complicated topic and the risks of doing so. It is possible to confuse a modest attempt at a clarification of complications with a fixed (and false) formula for successfully reducing something that just *is* complicated, and cannot or should not be oversimplified. No individual human or cultural group can or should be oversimplified or treated formulaically; and if someone tries to tell you otherwise, you should examine their assumptions or'motivations. With this in mind, in the next five sections I will try to convince you that if you want to understand the cultural identification of women, it is wise to consider the many ways in which women are effected by: (1) ongoing support units, (2) ethnic or racial focuses, (3) contexts of sexuality, (4) exposure to moral instruction or value-defining situations, and (5) abilities and disabilities (and how they are balanced). After the specific values and complications of these five areas have been discussed, we will go on to address the question with which I opened this section: Is there some basic set of things that women from all cultural contexts share?

## ONGOING SUPPORT UNITS

It is arguable that the term "family" could be used to characterize what actually needs to be considered in this section. In America today there is a renewed interest in the importance of the family. In choosing the title of this section, I am in no way dismissing the importance of this renewed interest. What this section draws to our attention is the presence or absence of continuing, supportive people during the period that leads up to a female child becoming identified as a woman—a period that I personally think probably lasts from birth to death, but how long it takes is not the issue here.

The twentieth-century philosopher Simone de Beauvior offered a number of reasons why a female person is not born a woman, but becomes one. She wrote insightfully about the defining importance of the significant people in our lives who see us, and in whose eyes we see ourselves. She was particularly interested in how women have come to see themselves, through the eyes of men, as "the other," that is, how women have not been separately defined, but defined in terms of how they differed from men (De Beauvoir 1953). This focus on the role played by significant people in the way women learn to understand themselves easily opens up to thinking about the interaction between family members. The term "ongoing support unit" is introduced to get us thinking about a wider set of significant people than is traditionally associated with the concept of a family. This wider designation can but does not necessarily involve genetic relatedness or providing food, shelter, and clothing. Instead, it draws our attention to the influences of various people in whose eyes we come, over time, to see ourselves, and who are continuous enough in our lives that, in large part, we decide or become who we are in response or in relation to them, for example, a long-time friend who may seem more of a sister than does a biological sister, to whom I want to provide unqualified support and with whom I identify with so strongly that if she experiences a life-altering event, I am also altered.

It is important to take note that people who are "there for us" can be not only traditionally or untraditionally related to us, but they can "support" our identity formation in positive or negative ways. A supportive person can be well-meaning but miss the mark entirely, or end up providing support that has effects they never intended—as for example, with overprotective or heavy-handed parents who pass on lessons of familial dependency relations or intrusiveness to their daughters, or religiously motivated friends who cite doctrine that does not inspire, but elicits shame in a young woman, perhaps deeply lowering her self-esteem. In addition to being an inspiring grandmother or a friend who helps us to grow, an influential person in a support unit could be a neighbor, nanny, nemesis, or an unavoidable nameless nitpicker whose focus on the apparently small details of our lives makes us self-conscious in some lasting way. Such people somehow make it easy or, over time, force us to open or to close up in ways that later can become characteristic of how we see ourselves as women. The amount of time we spend with such people need not be as significant as the impact of whatever time we do spend with them. We need not even remember their names to internalize their influences.

Labeling and appreciating this complex source of input into the development of a woman's identity teaches us to ask the question: "Can we identify specific ongoing support groups that have contributed to women's identities?" In some cases the answer will point us in the direction of looking at the influences of traditional family units but, given the decreasing numbers of such units, in very many cases that will not be the most likely direction in which to look.

To the extent that the concept of "a family" currently is being enlarged to include nontraditional support units (Blakely 1994), it will become more likely that examinations of family relations will provide insight into women's gendered identities. There is, for example, a growing body of literature on African-American women about the "mother-centered" families in which many grew up—where the mothering was frequently not done by biological mothers, or even by individual women, but rather in a shared, nurturing unit in which some variable cross section of women cared for others in the unit who needed caring for, whether or not any genetic link was present. Patricia Hill Collins, for example, distinguishes between "blood mothers" and "other mothers," and discusses the important role played by this latter category in many families (Collins 1994).

What counts as "the" unit in such a creatively expanded family is apparently very open-ended, with biologically unrelated people unofficially (that is, not through legal actions) being adopted as fathers, mothers, brothers, sisters, cousins, aunts, grandparents, etc., who can continue to be so identified, not just for many years, but through subsequent generations. It is important to note that this is not some new definition of family, but that it is a description of a practice that can be traced back through many generations of African-American families (Hooks 1990). Recently one of my African-American students told me that she believed that being raised this way had given her a much larger sense of what it could mean for her to be a woman or a mother. Such practices are, of course, not exclusive to just this ethnic group, but this illustration suggests that a wide variety of experiences in the support units with which women are identified for some significant period of time impact their sense of just who they are and what they can be in relation to others. In discussions of articles about various historical examples of creative extensions of the concept of "family," people from many different backgrounds do recognize analogous lessons. Do you?

Regardless of how a family is defined, some people will claim that among the basic set of things that it is to be a woman is being (or being somehow programmed to be) a mother, or a nurturing member of a family. Often this is thought to be a very simple point about women being defined by having the physiological capacity to  give birth and to establish a "natural" support unit for children (e.g., through breast-feeding). But the points raised in this section allow us to begin to see just how socially impacted concepts such as mothering and family can be, and how important it is to appreciate the many ways in which particular women have had significant variations of such concepts contribute to their self-definition. In some support units women have seen models of women who nurture alone, or together, or who designate nurturing to some specific people (perhaps some women and men),  and not to others (perhaps the biological parents). What comes naturally to these women may vary greatly.

## ETHNIC OR RACIAL FOCUSES

The illustration in the preceding section supplies us with a bridge to a second source of influences on women's  gender identities. If concepts as seemingly basic as "family" and "mother" can be interpreted and enlarged within ethnic groups, reason suggests that such groups could alter any number of concepts which would influence the gender identities of their women members. In obvious ways gender identity overlaps racial or ethnic identity—women can come from every sort of background, and their gender and ethnic interests often bump into each other in very difficult ways. But these overlapping interests are not easy to generalize about.

While we can learn a lot from the discussions of specific ethnically identified writers about their experiences and their proximity to or study of the practices of others within their ethnic group, no writer can (and few will want to) speak for all members of any group, regardless of how identified they are with that group. Alice Walker (1974) can get us thinking about "our" mothers' gardens, Amy Tan (1989) can introduce us to a cross section of women of Asian-American descent with whom we can identify, Annie Dillard (1987) can create a familiar vision of growing up female in America, and we can draw insights from all of them. But who draws what insight and how they draw it may or may not have anything to do with whether readers are ethnically identified with these women writers, or how accurate their remarks are, in general, about members of the ethnic group that they represent.

Ethnic identity is acquired unevenly, running the gamut from persons having deep, sustained exposure to having little or no sense at all about the facts or values of their ethnic heritage. Cases of mixed or obscured ethnicity abound. For example, European Americans (after the first generation) sometimes are identified ethnically and sometimes not (Italian-Americans, often; German-Americans, not quite as often; British-Americans, rarely). For the most part, the students that I encounter who consider themselves European Americans are only nominally inclined to identify themselves in terms of any specific ethnic/cultural heritage; and if pressed, they tend to identify with European culture in general, even if they are pretty sure, for example that their family, has no, e.g., French or Italian background. And, of course, there are European Americans of all racial groups, which complicates the problem even more.

What gender lessons have impacted the identities of European American women? Surely more than those directly attached to their specific (biologically licensed) ethnic, or racial cultures. In addition to a long history of activism for women's rights (Wollstonecraft 1792), women from European American cultural groups also have inherited extremely influential male-headed or "patriarchal" legal and religious institutions that have directly and indirectly codified what women can or cannot, should or should not, do. Can or should women fight in the front lines in battle? Can or should women who have children out of wedlock receive support? Although our inherited legal and religious institutions come from many different cultural groups and differ on such issues, they have addressed and continue to try to answer these questions in ways which imply that women's role in society needs specific and separate rules and regulations.

Are all women of the African American, Asian American, Native American, or Hispanic American categories in significantly different situations? Some of the specific laws and lessons that they have inherited may differ, but the effects of their ethnic heritage is similarly complicated. As Americans, they inherit all of the institutionalized (sometimes conflicting) lessons and practices of this country, and perhaps even more from their particular ancestors. They may or may not have had easy access to their own (biologically licensed) ethnic identity and its cultural lessons. Such information could have been intentionally or unintentionally blocked. Although there is a widespread, active attempt to appreciate the vast historical and cultural values associated with ethnic and/or racial groups, some people who acknowledge the value of ethnic identities continue to argue for a "melting pot" American mentality.

A version of this "melting pot" thinking frequently is raised in reference to women, for, despite the American inheritance of European patriarchal practices (and probably because of historical writers like Mary Wollstonecraft and American counterparts like Susan B. Anthony), there is the popular notion that American women have more possibilities to expand their identities than women who remain deeply linked to some ethnic or racial groups from other parts of the world. All

American women have to decide for themselves whether or not this is true, and all of us have to wade through the stated values and devalues of our ethnic or racial backgrounds, to the extent that we can become aware of them, or we risk missing the ethnic influences passed on to us through the people who raised us, and the people who raised them. Labeling and appreciating this ongoing and important source of input into the development of women teaches us to ask the question: Can we identify specific ethnic or racial focuses that have contributed to women's identities? And when we do ask this question, we have to be prepared for a time-consuming search for the answer.

Before going on we should pause on a complication that has been suggested in this section, but warrants closer attention. More and more American women are of mixed ethnic and racial backgrounds. If this is not already true of the great majority of American women, it is hard to imagine a future in which it is not true. I have had students with all sorts of mixed ethnic backgrounds, and nearly all of them have expressed disappointment that they have not been given the societal room to deeply identify themselves with all of the parts of their heritage, but instead have been pressed to identify with one group over another. Literature on biracial experience is just becoming available (Camper 1994) which promises to give a huge percentage of women insight into how to deal with the parts of their background that previously may have been minimized.

So the choices are not just whether to find our identity as women within an ethnic group or in an ethnic melting pot, but also whether we can affirm a number of distinct backgrounds at once. Reason suggests that, like the choices of finding one's identity as a woman through identification with one group, or discovering it in a homogenization of all groups, the third option of finding it by affirming specific links to different ethnic groups is not only available to persons of biologically identified ethnicities, but to any woman raised in or strongly influenced by some ethnic groups.

Establishing a gender identity in an ethnically complicated "ongoing support unit," can result in deep tensions between the various lessons that are internalized. When such units are ethnically rich, we can come to see ourselves in and through the eyes of people with dramatically different sorts of sensibilities about concepts such as "family" and "mother." But working through such tension, and having a wide variety of close  and inspiring role models, also can be exciting and liberating. When we do identify ourselves as women we find our own way through whatever complex mix of sensibilities we have encountered.

## CONTEXTS OF SEXUALITY

For some, adding sexuality to this already very complicated picture of how one becomes a woman may risk making the project of understanding women's culture in general seem almost delusional. For others, women's sexual development may seem to be such a "given," that they might think that a common form of sexuality is a  binding factor. This latter group is probably assuming what Adrienne Rich has called "compulsory heterosexuality" (Rich 1986). In fact, traditional notions of "family" and "mother" frequently assume women's heterosexuality as part of her gender identity. For example, it often is assumed that a woman is "built" to have intercourse with a man, and to bear "his" children. But just how good the assumption of women's basic cultural heterosexuality is depends on the extent to which options in sexual identity have become real options for women.

Most (if not all) women know that there are other historically common sexual practices beyond heterosexual practices, but a good number of women do not understand these practices as "live" or real options. The various social contexts in which women participate may or may not contain viable models of homosexual, bisexual, transsexual, or celibate practice. For many women the word designations for these various sexual possibilities might be available, but there has been no context in which to see these alternatives at work in identity-defining "on-going support groups." When this is the case, the overgeneralized cultural practice of heterosexuality among women is probably a fairly safe assumption. Whether or not biological factors (hormones, etc.) "determine" sexual preferences in women, or preferences follow from acquired tastes and a strong will, if such preferences are not understood as realistic possibilities, women (inner turmoil notwithstanding) will not be able to choose them and at the same time maintain some realistic goals and expectations. How many women today are in such a situation? While heterosexual practice is surely the dominant, socially reinforced, and most widely celebrated form of sexual identity, for many women a variety of "live" options are emerging.

Our previous discussions of the creative extensions of the concepts of "family" and "mother" suggest the possibility that "ongoing support units" can effectively reinterpret even these most familiar of practices. Many examples can be cited of "ongoing support units" that extend family and mothering practices to include women who are sexually identified as other than heterosexual ( Geldner 1994). Film depictions of these options are especially far-reaching (e.g., *Boys on the Side*). It is even arguable that these options have become "live" options not through immediate support units, but through media representations of such units. Sexual practices often, if not mostly, remain implicit in more traditional families, but frequently get very explicit exposure in the movies, not to mention the nightly news.

One might ask what worries people who believe that other forms of sexual practice are not properly identified with the concept of "woman," and who also believe that women's heterosexuality is part of what really defines women's culture. For if this is the case, even when "live" options are present, it would logically follow that "real" women would not be inclined to pursue them. Such people are in a bind, of course, if more and more adult females do chose other options. Statistics on this possibility will continue to be collected, but in the meantime, if we want to understand the cultural dimensions of being a woman in America in the latter part of this century or the beginning of the twenty-first century, we must learn to ask: *Can we identify specific and different contexts of sexuality that have contributed to women's identities?* " That is, we need to look not only at heterosexual modeling, but whatever sexual options were opened by the people who effectively contributed to the way any particular woman came to see herself.

But women who breathe life into "dead" options also need to be considered. Alternative forms of sexuality with different sorts of partners is not the only category here. Women, for example, who choose to live celibate or to be artificially inseminated can be seen as choosing options that may not have been modeled for them in any viable way. The first women to engage in artificial insemination were, in many ways, sexual pioneers. It may have seemed an interesting idea, but until fairly recently it was only an idea. It always has been possible for women to engage in sexually self-gratifying behavior, but now it has become possible for women to define a very singular form of sexual existence that can be extended to include childbirth without ever having had "sex."

Learning to put the concept of "sex" in quotation marks is part of what is necessary to begin to understand how many ways women can be defined in contexts of sexuality. When I grew up (in the 1950s and early 1960s) I understood having "sex" in only one way. It was also euphemistically called "going all the way," and specifically referred to a penis penetrating a vagina. It took me an embarrassingly long time to recognize that this was only the tip of the sexual iceberg, so to speak, and that remaining focused on only this could be roughly analogous to being stuck on the tip of an iceberg. Doing "it," as we thought of "it" then, was to do a very limited act or, to be a bit more to the point, something extremely goal-oriented and not very time-consuming. The late 1960s and early 1970s served to stretch the imaginations of many young women on this score—mainly through an emphasis on small-group subcultures (e.g., communes, love-ins like the famous "summer of love" in San Francisco in 1967, as well as in more politically defined groups). Whether or not people really succeeded in challenging the hypocrisy of the day or in raising people's consciousness about sexual issues in this period (which were expressed goals) is beside the point. What did happen was that many young women began thinking about their sexuality in expanded ways, particularly in regard to learning to experience sexual pleasure themselves, regardless of what kinds of partners they had or whether they had one.

Today, having "sex" can mean any number of things, although this may be somewhat more true for women than for men. Still, our task is to try to understand women's cultural identity, and to do so we must examine the ways in which women's sexual self-understanding has developed, and be prepared to try to understand the appeal of sexual behaviors and experiences that we might not have personally experienced or considered. This frequently depends on not only a willingness to spend time understanding these things, but also a willingness to recognize and think about one's own sexual preferences and prejudices.

## EXPOSURE TO MORAL INSTRUCTION OR VALUE-DEFINING SITUATIONS

Here we want to learn to pay attention to the way women have learned to assess right and wrong, good and bad, and what counts as an excellent and as a minimally acceptable action. The work of psychologist Carol Gilligan and the responses that people have had to her work have been very helpful in getting me started in this project (Gilligan 1982). Through a series of interviews with young women and a study of theories of moral development that presumably have been focused on men (e.g., Piaget, Kohlberg), Gilligan concludes that women learn to place and affirm value differently than do men. She goes on to discuss the emergence of women's more relational, people-based (and men's more individualistic, rule-based) moral responses.

Without denying the importance of Gilligan's insights, we need to remind ourselves that conventional "wisdom" about how men and women respond in morally sticky situations commonly suggests that women think more about those closest to them while men are supposed to move quickly to more abstract (and allegedly more weighty) considerations. Most of the familiar fairy tales and story lines that I am aware of which are supposed to impart moral lessons seem to underscore these moral gender differences. Snow White is good because she cares for and worries about the dwarfs, and her Prince is good not because he cares about her, but because he rights the wrong done to her, and symbolizes the (princely) power to do so. The murderous young female exec in *Fatal Attraction* is bad because she becomes obsessed with a particular man, and the man is bad, because he breaks his marital vows, and then (eventually) good not because of his feelings or lack of feelings, but because he recognizes that his interests and responsibilities are at issue, and must be separated and reaffirmed, and because he learns (the hard way) the male version of the *Scarlet Letter* lesson (which, arguably, Hester Prynne herself did not learn).

Of course there are many stories that convey various moral lessons, but which are the ones that have had the most influence on our gender sensibilities? Notice that the stories that I have chose to use as illustrations turn on romantic and erotic relationships. Such stories are at least as effective, and arguably more effective, than other kinds of stories at getting or keeping our attention when we are becoming sexually aware and learning to specify our gender sensibilities. Women audiences are often named as "target audiences" for such stories (consider the marketing of romance novels, romantic "screwball comedies," as well as the marketing of (not to demean their talent) Julio Iglesias, Demi Moore, or Brad Pitt (cf. in the 1950s: Fabian, Doris Day, and Rock Hudson)).

But stories, films, and celebrity images that convey moral and gender lessons are only one source of value-defining influences for women. Instruction sometimes occurs in the real-life episodes at home, in specifically religious settings (e.g., church, temple, or informal gatherings of believers), at school, at work, at play, or wherever we are with people who contribute to the way we come to see ourselves as women. Although all of these value-providing-contexts should be examined, I will briefly discuss only two of them, home and school.

What we are taught at home generally is thought to be a major source of our gender sensibilities. In fact, the first category of analysis of women's gender identity that I introduced ("ongoing support units") was chosen, in a large part, to stress the (human) influences established at home (understood in a wide sense). But when discussing how women's identities are related to lessons learned at home, too often our focus is drawn only to "positive" moral lessons that are said to have been directly modeled for women in this context. Whether or not we think the lessons that have been taught intentionally were positive or not is  not the issue so much as whether we think that the lessons that are thought to be positive are the only ones that are taught. For example, if we attend only to what parents *say* to daughters, and not what they *do*, we miss much of what their daughters learn. Similarly, if we attend only to what parents say or do in the presence of their daughters and not to what they say or do when they think their daughters do not hear or see them, we also miss a lot. Or consider what lessons are overlooked if we attend only to what parents say or do in relation to their daughters, and do not consider whether or not their daughters learn that there are significant differences in what their parents say or do with the boys in the family.

Girls and boys can be explicitly taught "positive" values in a thoroughly loving manner and still learn many negative lessons. In order to make sense of this often obscured context of moral learning we must learn to ask the question: *Can we identify implicit as well as explicit moral lessons that have contributed to women's identities?*" Often this requires speculating on lessons that may have remained implicit or internalized and never spelled out by particular women themselves. Each of us can be unaware of the variety of ways that meaningful people and events have effected us. The questions we must learn to ask about implicit and explicit moral lessons, as with all the questions I suggest in this chapter, are often just as important and as difficult for women to ask about themselves as they are for others to ask about them. The need for everyone interested in understanding women's gender identity to try to answer these questions cannot be minimized.

There is also no minimizing the importance of appreciating the defining role of school or formal educational contexts in establishing the values associated with women's gender identity. Distinguishing between school and formal educational setting is important because so many kinds of schools are informal. The phrase "school of hard knocks" helps to illustrate this point, as does pointing out things like televised schooling (e.g. "Sesame Street"), "Sunday school," and a variety of kinds of teaching and learning toys that are manufactured to maximize consumer response (e.g., to home school products)  and for commercial profit.

The impacts of this more informal variety of education on the development of women's moral identities are complicated in ways similar to the complications of the impacts felt at home.  In both cases, the obvious or expressed lessons are not the only ones that are learned. In fact, the casual, relaxed, or informal atmosphere associated with both home and school contexts that are linked with leisure time may be the most effective places for implicit messages to be received. The idea of subliminal learning is based on a similar assumption. Some young women may be on guard and reflective when they know they are being instructed, but isn't everyone a bit more vulnerable to accepting things  uncritically when they are presumably simply relaxing, hanging out, or just enjoying the company of friends or family?

Formal education, of course, can also suggest values to women in less than obvious ways. Negative expectations about the mathematical abilities of girls is a well-known example of this point, as are teachers' recorded tendencies to call on and to ask more questions of male students, sending even more subtle messages of their lower expectations of female students. Perhaps even more pernicious is the often unmarked absence of women among the writers to be read or studied in various disciplines. Many of my Women's Studies students have told me that they were not even aware that women writers had not been included in many of their literature courses until they took a Women's Studies course where a majority of women authors were intentionally assigned, and only then recognized the contrast to other classes. Several students have even said that in some classes when one or two women writers were included, they were used as illustrations of "lesser" or limited talent because the sorts of things they concentrated on were too focused on women's interests. What sorts of values does that lesson provide?

Apparently, in a number of formal educational contexts, even today, a "good" woman, or a woman who is thoroughly identified as a spokesperson for woman's sensibilities or women's culture, cannot be understood as both a good woman and a good example of great or unlimited talent—if she reveals a woman's interests, she reveals her limitations.

## ABILITIES AND DISABILITIES
## (AND HOW THEY ARE BALANCED)

There are all sorts of limitations that women perceive themselves to have, and which others take them to have. When I first began taking note of the importance of understanding perceived abilities and disabilities in women, I was thinking mainly about things that were measurable or widely acknowledged as assets and liabilities—women with high IQs, or women who were blind, for example. I soon came to realize that regardless of how measurable such things were, they were only controversially called assets or liabilities. Women with high IQs could perceive themselves as handicapped when dealing with men or women who did not want to work with women who might be smarter (in some measurable way) than they were. Blind women could perceive themselves as having a substantial advantage when confronted with situations in which an expanded reliance on senses other than sight was exactly what was called for—being able to read at night during a massive power failure, for example, or, for that matter, if they had a book, being able to read much more readily than could sighted women who depended on glasses that easily could be misplaced or broken.

I came to appreciate the interplay between abilities and disabilities mainly by reading the work of women who were identified as "disabled" (Saxon and Howe 1987). A number of these women are particularly interested in how disabilities can impact who they are as women (Mairs 1992). They sometimes contrast themselves to "able-bodied" women or evaluate the way that others have contrasted them to "able-bodied" women. Or they may discuss and illustrate the many ways in which bodily disabilities and other of the most obvious or measurable sorts of disabilities are not simply limitations, but also can be sources of growth, humor, and creative redefinition of everyday life that establish new links to other people.

But despite this ability to put a positive spin on disability, most women who are, in some official way, labeled "disabled" resist the euphemism "differently abled." This alternative description is thought to go too far in trying to describe a capable image, and tends to obscure the obvious fact that they live in a world that all too often ignores or dismisses the importance of what they require (e.g., access ramps, specialized educational materials, equal opportunity for employment) if they are to turn limitations into resources. This is an especially sensitive issue for physically disabled women who are ignored or dismissed in regard to what they need to realize their gender possibilities. This should not need to be said, but far too many people fail to appreciate that disabled women have, and need to be given the opportunity to realize, as many possibilities for developing as women as other women have. For example, if conventional assumptions about women as the ones who are the primary care givers are not backed up by a willingness to supply what a physically disabled woman needs (e.g., books in Braille that can be taught to children, kitchens lowered for use from a wheelchair), she is unable to creatively take up this traditional care-giving option if she is inclined to do so. Women must find a way to strike a balance between their own disabilities and abilities, but if they cannot get access to what they need to strike this balance, their own creative potential can be deeply damaged.

Despite the importance of attention to measurable or widely acknowledged "disabilities" and the abilities with which they are supposed to contrast, we also need to learn to consider hidden or internalized factors that can be powerfully disabling or enabling. Particularly relevant here are the economic advantages or disadvantages that can enhance ability or deeply hamper not just a woman's sense of who or what she is, but her sense of whether there is anything she can do outside of whatever limited choices she has been shown. Consider the case of a young girl who grows up with only the bare opportunity of going to school, coupled with a life of turmoil and poverty, and perhaps even close observation of domestic abuse. The damage done to her, although perhaps not measurable, could be disabling in such intensely complicated ways that discovering how this affected her gender identity, and what were necessary to help her turn her disadvantages into advantages, would take the deepest sort of commitment. But in this case, if we wanted to understand how she understood herself as a woman, and whether or not others would recognize her as such (or would see her gender development as having been blocked), this sort of commitment is exactly what would be required.

When considering what goes into making a woman a woman we must learn to ask the question: Can we identify abilities and disabilities (and the extent to which they have been balanced or intensified) that have contributed to women's identities? And when we set about asking ask this question, we have to be ready to respond with a commitment that might draw on all of our emotional, physical, intellectual, and material resources. Appreciating disabling as well as enabling factors in a woman's sense of self forces us to accept responsibility for at least trying to make sense of the real or apparent failures and cruelties of others, and perhaps of society in general, which may be very painful for us to even think about, much less to try to understand.

# IS THERE SOME BASIC SET OF THINGS THAT WOMEN FROM ALL CULTURAL CONTEXTS SHARE ?

My guess is that at this point an answer to this question of, "well, yes and no," will not be too surprising. And this is my answer. But, of course, I still have to say how yes and why no. After having read the five preceding sections, it may be tempting to conclude that what women share is the form of their experiences, but not necessarily the content. That is, one might suggest that the five areas which I have just argued should be considered when trying to understand women's gender identities are areas in which all women are, in some way or other, affected, and they differ only in specifically how they are affected. It may make you doubt the aptness of these five areas in regard to an analysis of women if I now say that these areas can as easily be thought of as indicating the form (but not the content) of what men have in common, too.

But it is not the form of these five areas of concern that is most important. What is important are the ways in which these forms direct our attention specifically to the great variation in  the contents of women's lives. Women are unified only through their diversity. This may seem like a contradictory claim, but it is not. "Women's culture" becomes sensible as a subject of study through a close appreciation of the various overlapping possibilities for living life as a woman.

There are many ways in which women's lives can and do overlap.Women obviously differ significantly, but since the units, focuses, contexts, and situations in which they participate can cut across any particular group of women, the odds are very high that women within different groups will share something with women out of their group. An Asian American woman might not share ethnicity with a Latina but could easily share family similarities, sexual preference, significant value-defining experiences, or a sense of abilities and disabilities. One of the reasons that so many women readers identify with Alice Walker's *In Search of Our Mother's Gardens* (Walker 1974) is not that they identify with the lack of cultural history about African-American women, but because they recognize that their own foremothers (biologically related or not) also lived with limitations that forced them to find their own ways of blossoming, or of surrounding themselves with growing things, when little could be grown in the outside world.

Women cannot be grouped into a single culture because there are infinitely many ways for any one of us to be grouped and to differ within our groups. But just as groups can break apart from differences, new groups can reform from cross-group similarities. Like my Grandmother's old lace tablecloth, made many years ago and brought out now for special occasions, threads may continue to break apart, but I can find any number of ways to tie together other loose threads to make sections hold together for awhile. Women's culture holds together in a similar fragile but reinforcing way.

## REFERENCES

Blakely, M. K. 1994. *American Mom*. Chapel Hill, NC: Algonquin.

Camper, C. 1994. *Miscegenation Blues: Voices of Mixed Race Women*. Toronto, Ontario: Sister Vision.

Collins, P. H. 1994. Black women and motherhood. In *Living With Contradictions*. A. Jaggar (ed). Boulder: Westview.

De Beauvoir, S. 1953. *The Second Sex*. New York: Knopf.

Dillard, A. 1987. *An American Childhood*. New York: Harper & Row.

Geldner, L. 1994. A lesbian family. In *Living With Contradictions*. A. Jaggar (ed). Boulder: Westview.

Gilligan, C. 1982. *In a Different Voice: Psychological Theory and Women's Development*. Boston: Harvard University Press.

Hooks, B 1990. Homeplace (a site of resistance). In *Yearning: Race, Gender, and Culture Politics*. Boston: South End.

Mairs, N. 1986. On Being a Cripple. In *Plaintext*. Tucson: University of Arizona Press.

Rich, A. 1986. Compulsory Heterosexuality and Lesbian Existence. In *Blood, Bread, and Poetry: 1979–1985*. New York: W. W. Norton.

Saxton, M. & Howe, F. (eds). 1987. *With Wings: An Anthology of Literature By and About Women with Disabilities*. New York: Feminist Press/CUNY.

Tan, A. 1989. *The Joy Luck Club*. New York: Ballantine.

Walker, A. 1974. *In Search of Our Mothers' Gardens: Womanist Prose*. New York: Harcourt Brace Jovanovich.

Wollstonecraft, M. 1792. *A Vindication of the Rights of Woman*. (Reprint) New York: W. W. Norton, 1988.

# 15

# Of Prejudice and Pride

Tiffany D. Rogers

## INTRODUCTION

The homosexual community, represented by the lesbian and gay cultures, creates important issues for the United States as other issues of cultural diversity become increasingly important. Within the context of the heterogenous U.S. nation-state, the problems of cultural diversity are far reaching. The breadth of this problem imposes a need for flexibility and foresight in defining both culture groups and their status in contemporary American society. The difficulty in identifying lesbians and gays, because homosexuality crosses all cultural lines, as well as the emphasis on the sexual aspect of homosexuality, has led to a narrow perception of what defines lesbian and gay cultures. These groups, as with any other minorities, are threatened with both institutional and social discrimination. As the concept of cultural diversity increasingly shapes approaches to culture groups in education, community service, and public policy, the issues associated with them take on increasing importance for all minority groups, but particularly those that historically have been faced with much discrimination and marginalization.

The decision to address the issue of lesbian and gay culture rests in my being a lesbian and a curiosity about myself and others like me. This interest also has been sparked by the discrimination and hatred that I and others have experienced because of our particular sexual orientation. Whispers, snickers, and other responses to me as a stereotypical looking lesbian—meaning the short hair, male clothing, and masculine mannerisms—led me to a feeling of responsibility to the *gay cause,* that is, to force heterosexuals ("straights") into accepting myself and fellow gays, and to fight against both the institutionalized and covert forms of discrimination. This desire has evolved from one that was aggressive and militant to one that seeks to ideologically define who and what gays are about, and from this intellectual foundation approach the issues of equality of rights and understanding that I feel are critical to the survival and health of my cultural group. Therefore, it is with this intention that I approach the issues of gay culture within the context of cultural diversity.

Prior to the discussion of the cultures of the homosexual community, it is necessary to discuss some of the terminology inherent to the group. Admittedly, this discussion will be overgeneralized on both lesbians and gay men, and it will exclude bisexuals altogether. Although lesbians, gays, and bisexuals face similar issues of discrimination, socialization, and life-style, they each have issues that are specific to their own groups, particularly those associated with gender roles. Bisexuals are excluded not because of a failure to recognize their role and contribution to the homosexual community, but because they represent a unique culture group within the homosexual community that must deal with some very specific issues. Throughout this chapter, both lesbians and gay men are referred to as *gays*, only as a means of simplifying the discussion. It is a misnomer, however, and the reader should be aware that the generalization serves only to deal with an already broad and difficult to define group. The use of the term *straight* is used to refer to heterosexuals when used within the homosexual culture context.

## CULTURE

Culture is the ultimate human adaptation, the means by which human beings adapt to a natural world that is less than hospitable toward their biological makeup. Humans are not likely to survive naked in the woods. However, armed with culture and its material objects, they do have a fair chance for survival. As it was described previously (see Chapter 1), culture is the complex system of beliefs, behaviors, and the material and sociocultural products thereof. Within this broad definition are the specific values, norms, social structures, social organizations, material products, and phenomenological beliefs that are unique to the individual culture group. These things are shared by all of the members of a culture group, and are transmitted to new members through various forms of enculturation. The history of a group, its physical adaptation, and its subsistence are among the factors that work to shape the formation of a cultural identity. Through the use of language, symbols, supernatural beliefs, and the assertion of cultural identity, groups maintain a cohesiveness that works to ensure their survival and preserve their identity.

## THE HISTORICAL CONTEXT

To understand the actual history of lesbians and gays in the United States, it is important to understand some significant aspects of the development of Western culture and its consequent beliefs, philosophies, norms, and values. For example, it can be argued that the overriding influence in the development of the United States is Christianity. Christianity has provided the philosophical foundation for the social and institutionalized beliefs and values of the United States. Ideas about appropriate sex and gender behavior have evolved (and been justified) through the manipulation and interpretation of the Christian Bible. At different times, and for different reasons throughout the course of Western civilization, the Bible has been called upon to evidence the dominant group's position on the topics of gender and sex. This interpretation has changed over the course of time to accommodate social norms as the needs and circumstances of the dominant group have changed. But biblical interpretation always has been the prime tool of legitimization, particularly with regard to homosexuality. Within the social structure, different expectations and restrictions are placed upon the behaviors of the sexes, be this in terms of labor, social position, or domestic responsibility. As with other aspects of society, this genderization and the concomitant expectations serve the functional purpose of meeting the basic needs of the larger social group.

The distinction between sex and gender is significant in discussing contemporary lesbian and gay cultures and what has shaped them in the United States. It is also important for the sake of a philosophical understanding of the historical attitudes and enculturation processes of males and females. Sex refers to the biological makeup of individuals. Although it has been argued that males and females are not the only two biological or chromosomal sexes, this discussion will be limited to just the broad categories of male and female. Gender is the assignment of behavioral norms and expectations to the sexes. In this there are three primary components. The first is *core gender identity*, which is an individual's self-concept of male or female as defined by the individual's cultural group. The second component is that of *gender role,* which defines the set roles that males and females are assigned by their cultural group. The final component is *sexual orientation*, which defines the erotosexual attraction of individuals to either others of the same sex, opposite sex, or to both sexes. The term *gender transposition* refers to the degree of adherence to culturally assigned norms of gender behavior (Blumfeld & Raymond 1993). It is from the culturally determined sex roles and ranges of gender behaviors that societies dictate what is appropriate or inappropriate behavior for both females and males. The roots of Western ideology about such behavior stretch back to Aristotle, who argued that nature had dictated the roles of men and women by virtue of their biological makeup. He held that males were naturally superior and females inferior, and thus males should dominate and females should submit. Freud argued that the aggressiveness of males and the passivity of females was attributable to the biological behavior of their sex cells, with the male sperm being active and the female ovum being immobile. He also cited the penetration of the male into the female during the sex act as part of this biological justification (Blumfeld & Raymond 1993). Such arguments as these have served to further legitimize the biblical arguments about appropriate sex and gender behavior, although they are in reality different approaches to the same ideological perspective.

The Age of Discovery and the Industrial Revolution added two notable factors to our contemporary ideas about gender behavior. The Age of Discovery brought forth the miracles of technology and science. Herbert Spencer and Charles Darwin argued for the evolution of humanity and an approach to the natural world that not only contradicted accepted Christian doctrine, but also threatened the Christian phenomenology altogether. The majority of the scientists and philosophers of the nineteenth century viewed the world as if it were a great clock that functioned according to discernable laws of nature. This threat to Christianity resulted in a struggle between the scientific community and the religious community over the sense of purpose and teleology that they perceived from different perspectives. The scientific revolution rattled the "Great Chain of Being" that placed God at the head of a continuum in which humanity reigned over the natural world. The scientific approach, although it did not necessarily prescribe an atheistic philosophy, certainly it undermined much of God's authority with its discoveries. Although attempts were made on the parts of both groups to find a middle ground, as with the development of the "Divine Watchmaker" theory which held that God created the world like a clock and then left it to run, the general tendency was toward an ever-widening schism between science and religion. The threat to religious authority exacerbated the hard-line approach to appropriate and inappropriate behavior of individuals, and this consequently affected the rigidity of social norms about gender behavior.

The Industrial Revolution further intensified the tension between females and males as each group worked to define their roles in a society that saw women and men faced with changing roles. Social norms and expectations had to change to respond to the shift from basically an agriculturally dominated subsistence to one of greater industrialization and urbanization (Miller 1995). This need to stabilize sex roles increased intolerance toward deviance in sexual behavior. Although laws forbidding homosexuality had existed for centuries, it was not until the nineteenth century that homosexuality became a legitimate topic for study (Blumenfeld & Raymond 1993), and the first "scientific" approaches appeared to deal with the basic issue. Although still condemned, Western societies were beginning to ask the question of why it existed. Most of the investigations that followed, particularly from psychology, were influenced by the ideological and cultural histories from whence they came. It seems readily apparent from this brief historical account that there is a discernable evolution of western ideology that explains the foundation for many attitudes concerning homosexuals. It also helps to explain why homosexual history so often is defined by persecution, prosecution, prejudice, and rejection. Not only does homosexual behavior threaten society by not conforming to expected ranges of gender behavior, it also defies the scientific beliefs about sexuality that are born of this ideology.

## THE CONTEMPORARY CONTEXT

History and culture are involved in a dialectical relationship in which historical events work to shape a culture's development, and, conversely, culture works to shape the way in which groups respond to historical events and circumstances. Understanding contemporary lesbian and gay culture in America requires at least a cursory understanding of the history of homosexuals in the United States, where they historically have been viewed as outcasts and have had to face more difficult obstacles than other minorities easily identified by color or language. Homosexuals have had to face the problems of legitimacy and identity. Through an examination of political and legal history, religion, psychiatry, the emergence of the gay civil rights movement, and the AIDS crisis—all of which have contributed to the development of a homosexual sensibility and a cohesive cultural identity—we can gain some insights into the current social circumstances of homosexuals and the status of gay identity in contemporary American culture.

The prejudice and discrimination that homosexuals in the United States have faced since colonial times has been the result of religious ideology, political expediency, and a set of Western values and norms defining appropriate gender and sex behavior that were brought from Europe and translated through the dominant Puritan ethic. During the colonial period, sodomy was a crime that was punishable by death. In fact, the etymology of the slur "faggot," which commonly is used to denote a gay male, finds its roots in the practice of tying together gay men to be burned, as one would bind sticks of wood together for burning. Thomas Jefferson later reduced the punishment for acts of sodomy to castration (Blumenfield & Raymond 1993). The outlawing of homosexual acts was common in almost all of the states up to World War II. By the end of World War II, homosexuals were actually perceived as a national threat because of their susceptibility to blackmail. This perception resulted in not only a legal response against homosexuality, but exacerbated a growing social malevolence toward homosexuals. Although penalties against homosexual acts rarely are carried out, they have continuously posed a serious threat to active homosexuals and, probably more importantly, have been used to justify discrimination against them. The institutionalized condemnation of homosexual activity has been used to legitimize the condemnation of same-sex activity in cases of child custody, housing, and employment. Although little legal harassment of homosexuals occurs, the presence of the sodomy laws leaves open the potential for legal reprisal as attitudes change and personal security erodes still further in the United States.

Politics has played heavily in discussions of "family values." Such discussions rarely accommodate the generated family structures of homosexuals. The political manipulation of "family" has only further undermined the status of lesbians and gays in America. It has been used to justify withholding certain rights from the homosexual community—the right to marry, equal rights, and equal opportunity under the law. It also allowed the government to avoid any serious efforts to stem the spread of by AIDS until it reached into the heterosexual community (Crimp 1991). Homosexuals and others have simply been made into scapegoats for a whole host of social issues. As the United States becomes increasingly conservative in its political and social outlook, there is every indication that lesbians and gays will become increasingly marginalized and their identities manipulated.

### Religion and the Homosexual Community

Another element that has figured prominently in the development of lesbian and gay identities has come directly from religion. Religion has played a vital role in both institutionalized and covert acts of discrimination against gays. The stories of Sodom and Gomorrah and the laws of Leviticus and Deuteronomy both have been used consistently to justify the abomination, punishment, and discrimination of gays. The emphasis of religions on the moral aspects of homosexuality delayed significant scientific study of homosexuality until the last half of the nineteenth century. Investigations into the "crime against nature" emanate from either those who viewed it as an inborn characteristic, or from those who viewed it as an acquired one (Bayer 1981). The Judeo-Christian community always has viewed homosexuality as a sin against nature and a sickness of the soul. Because religious ideology so often reflects social attitudes, it should come as no surprise that religious positions so often are reflected in the political scene where homosexuals have been identified and treated as outcasts. This status of outcast, as well as the necessary mechanisms to survive and overcome this, have played a significant role in the foundation of the homosexual cultural identity.

The homosexual response to their expulsion from the mainstream churches and the religious community was to establish their own church. In 1969, the Reverend Troy Perry established the United Fellowship of Metropolitan Community Churches (UFMCC) in Los Angeles, California. The motivation of Reverend Perry was to provide for the religious and spiritual needs of lesbians and gays that had been taken away from them. The UFMCC has become a powerful force in gay community solidarity, and has established churches throughout the world. Reverend Perry's personal religious background is charismatic, but in recognition of the diversity of religious denominations represented by individuals who attend the UFMCCs, each individual church has the freedom to develop an identity inclusive of differing religious backgrounds. Although the UFMCC does have a specific discipline—that God is omniscient, omnipotent, and omnipresent—vows are only necessary for those seeking membership, and all religious groups are welcome to participate in the life of the church without extreme pressure to conform to a particular set beliefs. Understandably, the UFMCC maintains that individual spirituality is unique to the individual, and individual expression must be respected. Although this is contained within the ideology of the UFMCC, in actual practice this may or may not be the case, depending on the specific church. The ideal, however, does appeal to many and has created a religious institution within the homosexual culture that is capable of meeting the religious needs of its diverse members. Currently, in an attempt to gain mainstream legitimation, the UFMCC is petitioning to become a part of the World Council of Churches. While the petition is experiencing strong resistance, it is indicative of a unified gay initiative that seeks the acknowledgment of the dominant and heterosexual religious establishment.

### Psychiatry and the Homosexual Community

Psychiatry has been active in discussing homosexuality since its beginnings with Sigmund Freud. Freud described the condition of homosexuality as "inversion" and characterized it in three categories: *absolute*, identifying those who are exclusively oriented towards same-sex partners; *amphigenic*, identifying those whose attraction could go either way, and *contingent*, identifying those whose attraction is based on environmental factors (Blumenfield & Raymond 1993). Although Freud considered heterosexuality to be "normal," he did not classify homosexuality as degenerate or the result of gender confusion. It was his professional colleagues, psychiatrists and psychologists, who later would pronounce homosexuality as abnormal and curable. The causes of homosexuality have stressed stage fixation, which is associated with the psychoanalytic school that began with Freud. Others have described it as neurosis, a castration complex (fear of women by men), and the result of guilt issues (Blumenfield & Raymond 1993). Albert Ellis, one of the giants of early-twentieth-century psychology, described lesbians as being either overtly or covertly psychotic (Cory 1964). This tradition of viewing homosexuality as a psychological disease was institutionalized up until the 1973 decision of the American Psychiatric Association to remove homosexuality from the *Diagnostic and Statistical Manual of Psychiatric Disorders* (Bayer 1981). However, removing homosexuality from the manual has not ended the treatment of homosexuality based around such beliefs. Enormous controversy still persists over the decision to remove homosexuality from this list, and it has created a schism in the psychiatric profession (Bayer 1981). The important point to remember is that there are a number of historical factors that embody the western view of appropriate behavior and values that are manifested in the response toward homosexuals in the United States. It is from these social expectations, and the responses made to them, that the identity of lesbian and gay America has been shaped, stereotyped, and presented in the form that most people recognize. These historical factors are important when discussing aspects of lesbian and gay cultures, in particular how these cultures respond to the changing perceptions of heterosexuals.

## Civil Rights Movements

A lesbian and gay civil rights movement in the United States emerged during the 1950s. The Mattachine Society in Los Angeles and the Daughters of Bilitis in San Francisco basically were established as a consequence of expanded opportunities resulting from World War II and the elimination of those opportunities after the war. World War II expanded the roles of men and women throughout American society as the needs of a wartime economy required the use of women in industry, and the need for soldiers enabled many homosexuals to serve in the military with little harassment, at least during first part of the war. At war's end, an ambiguous situation developed as these groups were expected to return to their formal marginal roles in society. The Mattachine Society and the Daughters of Bilitus both were organized to actively pursue equal rights for gays and lesbians and protection under the law (Miller 1995). These early groups sought to establish that homosexuals were the same as heterosexuals while accommodating the heterosexual establishment at the same time. The early activists believed that, by showing the straight world that lesbians and gays were fundamentally the same as them, apart from their sexual orientation, they could achieve acceptance from that group. The consequence of this was a tepid assertion of identity that failed to solidify a cohesive homosexual identity. Although both of these groups were vital in the emerging homophile movement of post–World War II, it is the Stonewall riots of 1969 that served as the catalyst for the gay civil rights movement that mobilized lesbians and gays throughout the country and changed the face of homosexual culture and community. The raid on the Stonewall Inn in New York precipitated days of rioting that sparked protests throughout the country and gave rise to the emergence of the Gay Liberation Front and other activist groups. The first gay pride parade was held in New York City in 1970 (Dubberman 1991). Since the Stonewall days, increasing solidarity and organization have characterized the gay civil rights movement.

A large part of homosexual solidarity has focused on the unique qualities of lesbian and gay culture, and the unwillingness to accept heterosexual assertions that homosexuality is a sin or a sickness. Although internal issues surrounding feminism and lesbian separatism have made alliances between lesbians and gay males some-what difficult, there has been an increasing unity of cause established between the two groups. Since the late 1960s, efforts to seek equal rights and protection from discrimination have been focused on the legal system, in the form of lawsuits against the military, and against heterosexist discrimination in employment and housing. Gay newspapers, neighborhood organizations, tavern associations, and organizations at work and church have created a solid movement that resists violence from the state and gives the gay civil rights movement an ethnically based quality (Miller 1995).

The period of the Reagan–Bush Era in American politics represents a particularly difficult time in the gay civil rights movement. During the 1970s, the movement was largely aligned with feminist and ethnic minority movements, and enjoyed many of the successes of these groups in terms of obtaining some protection under civil rights laws. However, with the conservative trends of the 1980s and the resurgence of the Christian Right, these efforts to gain legal and social tolerance were hindered (Miller 1995). Social issues associated with the AIDS epidemic exacerbated the tendency of the state to ignore civil rights claims, and in many respects were used to justify more laws and discriminatory behavior toward homosexuals, particularly men.

## AIDS CRISIS

The AIDS crisis in the homosexual community is fundamental to understanding the situation of lesbians and gays in contemporary America, and a contributing factor to the emergence of a more unified gay identity. The issue of AIDS, and the consequent political and social reactions to it, as well as the attempts to deal with the epidemic, have done much to shape the homosexual community in the present. The first cases of AIDS in the gay male population were identified in 1981, with 244 known dead from the disease by November of that year. This number evoked no response from the state. A year later, the body count was at 1,123, with still no response from the state. By November of 1987, 25,644 individuals were known to have died from AIDS. At this point, Ronald Reagan asked the Department of Health to determine the extent of the virus in American society, but it was not until the AIDS virus had spread into the heterosexual community that the state made a concerted effort to fund or undertake research and education programs to combat the disease (Crimp 1991).

Some of the justification for this stance came from other sectors of society, particularly the Religious Right, who proclaimed AIDS as "God's gift to the gays." The response to the AIDS crisis on the part of the state was inaction, in and of itself a form of marginalization. The opportunity for AIDS to be used to ideologically legitimize the condemnation and discrimination toward gays resulted in a stagnation of the civil rights movement. Groups such as ACT UP emerged to deal with the crisis, and groups oriented toward the procurement of equal rights had to refocus in order to contend with the political and social struggle to combat the disease (Crimp 1991). The gains made from the 1960s to the present for at least a mild tolerance of homosexuals were undermined by the resurgence of hatred based on fears generated out of the enormity ans seriousness of this worldwide epidemic. Within the homosexual community itself, the emergence of militant groups such as ACT UP and QUEER NATION now have redefined the approach to equality of rights. The approach of the homosexual community to the dominant culture has become increasingly hostile.

Another consequence of the AIDS crisis has come with its internal toll on the homosexual community itself. Homosexuals have had to deal with internal factors on two fronts: the acceptable range of sexual behaviors and divisions created within the cultures themselves. In the transformation of sexual norms, homosexuals historically had enjoyed significant freedom in sexual behavior. There seemed to be an attitude associated with social rejection that ideologically gave homosexuals, particularly men, license to engage in whatever sexual activities they chose with whomever, whenever, and wherever they chose to do so. This reflects both the sexual revolution of the 1970s as well as a belief that gay sexual behavior was outside of the moral strictures of mainstream society. With the AIDS epidemic, the picture has changed significantly for gay males. The promiscuity, cruising, and informality of their sexual conduct has been tempered by the fear of contracting and spreading the virus. From this has come an emerging set of ethics for gay behavior. Whereas the former philosophy held that if it feels good, do it, there is now a growing condemnation of unsafe sexual practices as well as a conservativism with regard to the range of acceptable sexual behavior.

Another internal issue focuses on the split between the gay men and women cultures. Lesbians were largely believed to be immune from contracting AIDS, and this increased already existing difficulties in perceptions between lesbians and gay males as to the focus of the gay civil rights movement. Because lesbianism has been aligned with the feminist movement historically, a significant lesbian isolationist trend has emerged in the homosexual community. Some of this separatism began with the perception in the 1950s and 1960s that lesbians were being marginalized by their gay male counterparts in addressing issues in the homophile movement. This separatism and the differing agendas of gay males and lesbians has caused division in the gay civil right's movement since its inception. Because of the political and social pressures, the AIDS crisis has caused a realignment within the homosexual community on the role of its groups to combat the consequences of the disease. Increasing incidences of AIDS among lesbians have aligned the two sexes in a united front in efforts to combat the disease. The result has been that lesbians and gays both have focused on issues that deal directly with AIDS in response to the threat that this disease poses for the survival of both groups.

The history of gays is a complex one that overlaps the emergence of feminism, the black civil rights movement, the sexual revolution, the Vietnam War, and the new conservatism of the 1980s and 1990s. The overlapping of historical events is reflected in gay culture. The response to shifting social attitudes has shaped both the homosexual response to the United States and the dominant heterosexual culture's response to homosexuals. Throughout the history of the United States, the attitudes of acceptance and intolerance have fluctuated with the overall social trends of the times.

## LESBIAN AND GAY CULTURES

Anthropology historically has made little effort to study gay cultures, much less as it exists within the United States (Blackwood 1986). Whether this exclusion has been the product of ethnocentrism or simply a reflection of a lack of awareness on the part of anthropologists, the ethnographic record of gay cultures is sparse. Within the homosexual culture in the United States, the tremendous diversity of its members creates great difficulty in identifying specific beliefs and behaviors that characterize this culture group as a whole. Homosexuality cuts across many other cultural identifications, leaving sexual orientation as the only readily identifiable binding factor. Out of this biological circumstance, however, has arisen the need of this group to survive within a dominant cultural context that is largely hostile toward its members. From a biological commonality and the constant threat from the dominant heterosexual group, the gay cultures have emerged and merged. Culture establishes an identity that transcends sexual orientation and takes on characteristics that loosely and very generally define processes of enculturation, acceptable behaviors, and the range of ideology that will be associated with it. Homosexuality embodies much more than the specific sexual practices of those who identify themselves homosexual. For the average lesbian or gay, their primary homosexual identities will be arrived at long after other cultural identifications have been acquired already. Ethnic, class, gender, and religious cultural affiliations will be acquired before they ever recognize their homosexuality or "come out of the closet." This tendency for gays to be enculturated at a later age creates particular problems in defining clearly what constitutes gay culture.

Homosexuals are not identifiable because of their ethnic background, socio-economic status, age, gender, language, or any other of the factors that have been used to distinguish members of other culture groups within the American context. Homosexuality exists on all strata of American society and with all of its other cultural groupings. It cannot be correlated to any single factor (Kinsey 1948). In fact, sexual orientation may be the only shared characteristic of individuals as they initially enter into the homosexual community. Despite the vast differences, there are some shared characteristics that can be used to define these groups as culture groups. For example, being lesbian or gay is quite different from being homosexual. Homosexuality refers to sexual orientation and erotosexuality, however the terms "lesbian" and "gay" are peculiar to specific culture groups. One may be homosexual in orientation without acting upon it sexually, or one may be sexually active with same-sex partners but not have contact with the larger "gay" context, thereby not being *culturally* lesbian or gay. Although this distinction is minor, it is significant in the differences between the biological aspects of human sexuality and the cultural aspects of human sexuality.

In defining gay culture, the enculturation process, the social organization, networking, ideas of "family", language, and other symbolic forms of gay identity can be used. The enculturation process for homosexuals begins with the recognition of a same-sex orientation. This process is deeply personal and often privately very painful for the individual, but it does manifest some general characteristics that are exhibited among all homosexuals. First of all, lesbians and gays are as subject to the same stereotypes, overgeneralizations, representations, and misrepresentations experienced by most other people. Coming to terms with a homosexual orientation can cause shame, fear, loneliness, alienation, depression, a sense of helplessness, and anger. The pressures of "coming out," can result in self-destructive behavior, alcoholism, and substance abuse; in the worst case scenarios, it can result in suicide. Once an individual has reached the point of recognizing their homosexuality and they seek others of their kind, their enculturation begins. One model of the "coming out" process posited by Vivienne Cass describes the process in six stages.

The first stage is referred to as *identity confusion*, the point at which an individual recognizes same-sex attraction and begins to question who they are. Feelings of alienation accompany the growing awareness of the differences between themselves and their heterosexual peers. At this point, the danger of suicide is greatest, evidence of this in the fact that most homosexual suicides occur between the ages of sixteen and twenty-one. In the second stage, referred to as *identity comparison*, the homosexual begins to rationalize their feelings; arguing that it is either temporary or just a stage, or by acknowledging that they may be bisexual. It seems to be less abhorrent to think of oneself as bisexual than homosexual at this stage. But feelings of alienation may be heightened and intensified at this point. In the third stage, *identity tolerance,* homosexuals come to better terms with their orientation and begin to counteract their feelings of alienation by seeking out other homosexuals, while they move toward a greater self-acceptance of their identity. Feelings of isolation from the heterosexual group become stronger during this stage of the process. *Identity acceptance* comes in the fourth stage. Individuals begin to develop friendships with other homosexuals, and they begin to answer the question of who they are. The fifth stage is referred to as *identity pride,* and it is a time during which homosexuals begin to immerse themselves in the lesbian and gay culture, in its art, books, literature, and other aspects of the culture. It is also the point at which there is an increasing awareness of the incongruity between the proud self-identification and the rejection of the larger society, and this awareness is followed by an intense anger and rejection of heterosexuals.

The sixth and final stage of the process of "coming out" is called *identity synthesis*. The hatred of stage five softens and the person develops a balanced position between self-pride and heterosexual rejection. At this stage, homosexuals usually begin to differentiate between the attitudes of heterosexuals and those who are supportive. Homosexuality then becomes emphasized and integrated into the person's personality (Blumenfeld & Raymond 1993). There is a general uniformity of experience that leads homosexuals into the active gay culture.

Through the relationships established in the fourth stage, the process of learning the norms, language, history, and values of lesbian and gay culture begins. As exploration begins into what these cultures mean, the friendships formed between homosexuals ensure some level of emotional security. It is important to remember that homosexuals have to overcome the negative stereotypes that accompanied their enculturation into other culture groups. In addition, the world in which emerging lesbians and gays find themselves may be starkly different from the world they knew before. They must learn to speak, act, and perceive as a lesbian or gay; this process can be awkward and difficult. Visits to gay bars, involvement with women's groups, participation in gay pride parades, activist marches, and gay churches all provide models of behavior and atmospheres that allow gays to socialize in relative safety as they also help build a sense of cultural cohesiveness.

A lover of mine once described sex between women as being akin to the sharing of a secret with your best friend. There is an intensity and intimacy that aids in the narrative passage of information. One author describes our history as largely an oral one that is transmitted from first lover to first lover to first lover. These words define who we are as lovers and as people with unique characteristics (Grahn 1984). It is in this environment, and under ideal conditions, that an individual's sexual identity emerges and that their place in the gay culture is defined. At this point in the experience, the individual's gay identity becomes more cohesive, integrated, and articulable. The idea of being gay begins to take on specific meaning as the individual's likes and dislikes begin to be defined and the individual's personality within the context of gay culture begins to take form. Where before there may have been the complete acceptance of everything homosexual, now there is a greater syncrety between a person's previous experiences and cultural identities, and their choices in the gay culture.

## GAY LANGUAGE AND OTHER SYMBOLS

Important elements for the members of any culture are the language and cultural symbols used for expressing their ideas. Different ideas and symbols have specific meanings and significance for those who share them as part of a group. This exists within the gay culture as well and is referred to as *gay speak*. Words such as *butch, femme, dyke, fairy, queer, straight, mainstream, breeder, fag, fag hag, queen, flaming,* and *camp* all have meanings that communicate specific ideas that are easily understood by other gays. These words can have very different meanings for non-gays or no meaning at all. The language used by gays expresses their situation in society and their sense of self-perception within a rejecting society, but it also encompasses an empathy for other culture groups who face similar prejudice and discrimination. For example, the language emphasizes inclusive words, or language that does not emphasize a disparity between groups, as with the word "man" to describe humanity or "his" to indicate multiple or unknown gender. Ideologically, this removes the emphasis on male and the implied white domination. Terms such as *butch, femme,* and *dyke* (females), and *fairy* and *queen* for males, are terms that identify the gender of the individual and their degree of femininity or masculinity. This use of such language about someone or by someone communicates both internal and external perceptions of the speaker or the one spoken of, and it helps to define the identity for the listener. For example, if I approach a gay male friend and tell him he's flaming, he understands it to mean that I perceive him as engaging in a particularly feminine and silly behavior. The connotations may be positive or negative, depending on the circusmstance. Although limited, this listing does provide some insight into the use of language among lesbians and gays.

Words are powerful, and the ways in which groups use words—along with what words are used toward them—are important. One way in which groups who are discriminated against appropriate the power of negative words used against them is to use them in self-reference. As a consequence, there is a movement among younger lesbians and gays to refer to themselves and their culture as *queer.* By taking this word and attaching it to positive self-identification, gays are reducing the negative implications of the word. The same is true with other derisive slang terms such as *fairy, fag, dyke, faggot,* and other terms of equal or greater offensive value.

Beyond language, there are other symbols that gays have appropriated and transformed into positive identifiers, in much the same way that the Christians appropriated the cross as a positive symbol. Up until contemporary times, the most prevalent and popular symbol used to represent gays has been the pink triangle. This symbol had its origins in Nazi Germany during the regime of Adolf Hitler. At that time, the triangle was used to identify homosexuals who were persecuted and slaughtered in Nazi concentration camps. The pink triangle emerged in the 1960s as a symbol of the gay rights movement (Crimp 1991) and now is considered a positive symbol of pride, one that is used throughout homosexual representations.

Another symbol that has emerged with prominence in the past fifteen years is the "rainbow flag," which is used to symbolically represent the diversity of the lesbian and gay cultures. The function of this symbol is to ideologically combat the difficulties that different groups face in dealing with cultural diversity. Because of discrimination against homosexuals, it is vitally important that there be cohesion within the group. The cohesion must transcend potential culture conflicts that easily could emerge from the diversity within their own ranks. The rainbow flag sends a strong signal to members of gay culture to respect their diversity, and a strong symbol to detractors that homosexuals represent a united front.

Colors have different meanings cross-culturally, and the primary colors of the gay community are pink and lavender. Pink is associated more with males and lavender more with females. These two colors have a long history in western culture. The color lavender can be found in Greek myth, in the story Apollo who accidently killed his male lover Hyacinthus and in honor of him turned his body into a purple flower. The color also figures prominently in the poetry of Sappho in his references to same-sex relationships, and it has been used to symbolize, power, royalty, spirituality, and transition for people across the historical spectrum from Rome to medieval witches to Native Americans (Grahn 1984). The significance of the color purple has been transmitted through the ages from one homosexual to another. Pink is a color that figures more prominently in modern times, and it is associated almost exclusively in the Western tradition with women and feminity. This is why Hitler chose the color to designate homosexuals in Nazi Germany, and why it has been symbolically appropriated in contemporary times.

### Family and Networking

The concept of family is an important one in the homosexual community and its cultures. The ideas of fictive kin (the arbitrary assignment of biological kinship status to persons not related by blood) serves multiple purposes. Family among homosexuals emerged as a term to differentiate between sexual and non-sexual relationships. After World War II, and the emergence of a greater community solidarity, the term has come to designate all individuals along a continuum that runs from friend to lover. The concept of family also has acted as a mechanism to ideologically establish responsibilities and rights among homosexuals. By asserting a kinship designation for other homosexuals, there is an inherent responsibility to provide and care for each other, much as would be expected in a biological family. It also provides an effective means of networking, which is particularly important when individuals are faced with crisis. Furthermore, there is a sense of security attached to this idea which is important because of the frequency of disownment by biological kin. The very idea of "family" designates more intimate and involved relationships than does the concept of "friend."

Networking in lesbian and gay culture involves both informal and formal systems of behavior. Informally, the symbols, kinship, and word of mouth communication enable gays to identify areas that are either dominated by gays or are hospitable to them. Networking enables various organizations in the community to reach out to individuals and groups to accomplish group goals or to provide aid. In the more formal networking sphere, there are newspapers, political and social organizations, bars, churches, and businesses frequently advertise homosexual-oriented activities and resources. The *Gay Yellow Pages* tells gays and lesbians what businesses are run by other gays, lesbians or supportive heterosexuals. There exist a large number of newspapers, magazines, political and social organizations that help keep people abreast of group activities and issues of concern to the homosexual community. All of this makes it possible for members of the lesbian and gay cultural groups to locate much needed resources and information as well as provide for social activities.

## CONCLUSION

Within this discussion it was pointed out that homosexual culture represents a threat to many traditionally held beliefs about appropriate gender roles, sexuality, and the formation of society's units. Representing a threat to the dominant ideology, homosexuals have been placed in an adversarial position in which their struggle for tolerance and legitimacy. To accept homosexuals as a normal facet of contemporary American life will require a dramatic change in the historically based Western ideas of appropriate behavior and norms, as well as an expansion of the gender concept. In the current political and social environment in which other minority groups such as Jews, immigrants, and welfare mothers are being attacked and assigned the role of scapegoat, there is little likelihood that this change will occur. The focus on "family values," a return to traditional morals, and the assertion of the dominant heterosexual white male power in this country likely will worsen homosexual problems associated with cultural diversity. Lesbians and gays will be rejected right along with other minority groups, perhaps even more so. It is from this circumstance that an approach to cultural diversity that is actualized in education and community becomes increasingly important. The pain of ostracism and ridicule is all too common for homosexuals who express their identities, and it threatens their ability to be healthy and functional not only within lesbian and gay culture, but in the American culture at large.

## REFERENCES

Bayer, R. 1981. *Homosexuality and American Psychiatry.* New York: Basic Books.

Blackwood, E. 1986. *The Many Faces of Homosexuality.* New York: Harrington Press.

Blumenfeld, W. & Raymond, D. 1993. *Looking at Gay and Lesbian Life.* Boston: Beacon Press.

Cory, D. 1964. *The Lesbian in America.* New York: Citadel Press.

Crimp, D. 1991. *AIDS, Cultural Analysis, Cultural Activism.* Boston: MIT Press.

Dubberman, M. 1991. *Stonewall.* New York: Plum.

Grahn, J. 1984. *Another Mother Tongue.* Boston: Beacon Press.

Kinsey, A. 1948. *Sexual Behavior in the Human Female.* Philadelphia: Saunders.

Miller, N. 1995. *Out of the Past.* New York: Vintage Books.

# 16

## Drug Culture: Everybody Uses Something

### Danny Monroe Wilcox

A common scene in America today is the politician in a loud, critical panic about the "rise of the drug culture." When mentioned, a lot of us automatically assume that the use and trade of illicit drugs is the primary focus. Yet most Americans have only a vague awareness of the traditional and historical uses of medicinal plants. Nor is much attention given to the use of psychoactive substances to achieve spiritually significant, ecstatic visions since prehistoric times. No connection is made with drugs such as alcohol and tobacco, which are permitted by social and legal convention. Absolutely no account is taken of the over-the-counter drug industry or the business of prescription medicine. Most Americans are totally oblivious to the origin and development of these practices, but still manage to distinguish between the good drugs and bad drugs. The term *drug* has been too narrowly defined for popular understanding. Americans tend to perceive drugs as substances that are illegal, used despite legal and social prohibitions. This restricted description is not the result of any informed research, but a concept generated and accepted through the active process of culture. The term *drug* should be employed to refer to any non-food substance that is used for medicinal, spiritual, or even recreational purposes. The concept of culture also is quite misunderstood by most Americans, used to mean something exotic or even alien. Therefore, the popular interpretation of *drug culture* generates a narrow, restricted image of people unlike ourselves who engage in illegal and immoral activity. This image reflects beliefs that are magically conjured to the surface upon hearing the phrase.

An adequate description of drug culture depends on an awareness of the early human use of medicinal and psychoactive substances. It must be based on the fact that virtually every culture has its own complex system of substance utilization. The most basic interaction between substance, culture, and the individual is best understood in a pan-human context. The most fundamental meaning of drugs among human beings must be appreciated to correctly apply the concept of *drug culture* to our current social problem. In addition to understanding such broad similarities, particular groups make specific adaptations to natural and social environments. It is important to consider the distinctive drug culture groups in America. Various scenarios can demonstrate the wide variation in competing beliefs and behaviors that are culturally patterned. We also must look at the aspects of specific drug cultures that profoundly affect people beyond the boundaries of the American nation-state. It is important to know how various substances have meaning within the cultural context, how these meanings are conceived in the idealized value system of the culture, and how they actually are operationalized in the reality of daily existence. Through such an approach, the specific category of *drug culture* in American diversity could be examined using factual, rather than cultural knowledge.

## THE RISE OF DRUG CULTURE

Human beings have used pharmacologically active substances from prehistoric times to the present. The healing properties of specific plants have been known for millennia. Ethnobotanical and archaeological work have clearly shown the great extent and antiquity of such knowledge (Furst 1976). Substance use in all cultures has meaning. The most basic reason people have used, and continue to use, medicines is for healing. Both physical maladies and mental conditions can be treated by various agents. Many effective pharmacological substances are used, but whether or not the medicines achieve the desired result is frequently of secondary importance. The culturally patterned belief that certain drugs actually work can be just as meaningful. The most fundamental meaning of drugs to the user is that they can affect health and well being. Mental, emotional, or spiritual states are directly related to the well being of the individual. Such problems also may be treated with certain substances. The psychological benefits of being administered a drug that the user believes will be effective can be substantial. In traditional societies where most substances must be prepared and utilized according to social, ceremonial, and ritual prescriptions, this is particularly true. The ritual and ceremonial contexts for healing ensure that what people believe has a significant impact on behaviors associated with the particular medicines. The ritual basis for much healing is as important as the pharmacological efficacy of the medicine (Radcliffe-Brown 1952).

The medicinal use of substances is an important part of the adaptive process of culture. Over thousands of years, people have learned that certain plants prepared in specific ways have a predictable effect on people's health. They believe these things heal them. At the same time, they may believe the use of substances that are ritually, ceremonially, and socially prohibited may lead to illness, madness, or death. While these beliefs often may be correct, cultural knowledge frequently can be at odds with the facts. Psychoactive substances are used because people believe these drugs are endowed with specific properties that can affect a person's physical health or spiritual well being. Such experiences, mediated through altered states of consciousness, have important meanings. Traditionally, this type of experience is sought as an integral part of the spiritual essence of life. The ecstatic visionary has the ability to "see" what explains the world more thoroughly, what makes it comprehensible, and how to manipulate unseen forces for the adaptive benefit of all members of the group. Substances with psychoactive properties have been used for the purpose of achieving spiritually significant, altered states of consciousness for thousands of years (Furst 1972). Shamans are ritual specialists who often are associated with specific knowledge about healing and visionary experience. These medicine men and/or women have specialized information concerning the ritual preparation and administration of different substances. Healing, in many traditional societies, is properly sought through the shaman's direction, as are vision quests. Shamans were probably the first real specialists to appear in foraging societies. The particular roles of physicians and priests in the modern world have developed from shamanistic origins. But early peoples did not distinguish between the two roles. Healer and spiritual advisor could not be separated. This double role continued in most cultures until relatively recent times. At present, scientific medicine and religious prescriptions generally are considered mutually exclusive. Although some religious traditions stress the healing power of the spiritual life and some doctors advocate "holistic" medicine, our rational, scientific approach to health and religion is noticeably dualistic. People in traditional cultures usually do not make such hard distinctions between material reality and the spirit life.

Just as the curing of physical ailments is adaptive, the use of psychoactive plants also can be considered adaptive. If the realm of human life cannot be separated from that of various spirits, visions that are catalyzed by psychoactive substances can be made an integral part of the overall decision-making process. Social and subsistence behavior can be affected by this type of substance use. It would seem obvious that the meanings of various medicinal and psychoactive substances are probably different for members of traditional cultures as opposed to the meanings ascribed to recreational drugs commonly used in American society. However, the primary importance of the medicine or drug is not only associated with the specific cultural meaning attached, but with the pan-human fact that substances have meaning and are useful in relation to the health and welfare of the individual user and the group.

Generally speaking, we can say with confidence that human beings have been using various substances for medicinal, spiritual, and recreational purposes for thousands of years. We also can be fairly certain that, although the cultural meaning of various substances may differ greatly between specific cultures, the one common fact is that these substances always have meaning. Drugs are sometimes sacred, sometimes profane, but always meaningful. The individual's view of the particular meaning of a given substance is culturally determined. Through the belief and world view of the group, the individual will be fairly certain of the truth regarding the use of drugs. Whether comparing traditional cultures in different parts of the world, traditional cultures to modern nation states, or different cultural groups within modern American society, this seems to be the case. Although the meaning of drug use will vary according to the cultural membership of the individual user or abstainer, drug use will always have a meaning attached. The specific group will believe their own interpretation is the correct view.

No matter the interpretation, the one general fact is that there are very few, if any, human groups that have not used drugs in meaningful ways. This includes psychoactive substances. The very old and near worldwide, native production and use of alcohol (Marshall 1979) and the pervasive use of hallucinogens clearly show that just about everyone uses drugs. Whether medicinal, spiritual, or recreational, everybody uses. The most essential meaning of drug use is to affect the health and welfare of the user. The ceremonial context of use contributes to this basic meaning and gives it ritual and social importance. The only real difference between them lies in the complex of substances and beliefs about the proper way to use them. The "rise of drug culture" has definable roots and patterns in ancient human experience and has occurred a very long time ago. For millennia, traditional human cultures mediated the meaningful use of drugs through ritual, ceremony, and belief. This continued to be the case in contemporary life and is not likely to change anytime in the near future.

## DEVELOPMENT OF DRUG CULTURE

The humble, indigenous beginnings of drug culture gave rise to a variety of drugs, and after the development of human civilizations it also gave rise to further specialization in religious institutions. The ritual and religious leaders maintained knowledge and the authority to sanction the use of various substances. As state-level organization developed, this authority was no longer based primarily on the ecstatic shaman's spiritual leadership, but became codified in law. Historically, religious specialists, such as priests in western Europe, became the official dispensers of medicines. Others who had some special knowledge of plants and potions were considered witches. During inquisitions, these illegal practitioners of medicine often were prosecuted as devil-worshipers. The penalty for such unsanctioned drug pushing was often death.

The period of Enlightenment and Age of Reason elevated scientific explanation to a prominent position and contributed to the dualistic separation of medical versus religious knowledge. Eventually, doctors became the sole legitimate authority in the use of drugs. Priests and preachers were restricted to spiritual healing without the benefit of medicines or other substances, but they still were recognized as the sole legitimate authority on spiritual knowledge. Those who practiced either one without the expressed consent of the established medical or religious institution were considered quacks and heretics and persecuted accordingly. Szasz (1987) clearly demonstrates this dynamic interaction. Ritual, ceremony, and social relations are important to the meaning of drugs in the context of cultural knowledge. A drug is considered positively and its use encouraged in some instances. Other drugs may be considered physically and spiritually harmful and culturally prohibited. Often in recent history it is possible to look at the major psychoactive substances and see the development of prohibition after a period in which use of the drug was tolerated, if not embraced, as some kind of wonder drug. By looking at the use, development, and eventual prohibition of most naturally occurring, traditionally used drugs for healing and recreation, we can see how cultural knowledge determines people's beliefs about drugs. The development of synthetic substances over the past century also impacts the cultural knowledge we have, which determines people's beliefs about drug control. A historical perspective illuminates the actual role of cultural knowledge in the decisions to permit or prohibit various substances and ultimately leads to a description of contemporary drug culture.

## THE USE AND CONTROL OF DRUGS

The most basic psychoactive, pharmacopeia that traditionally has been available to various cultures in different regions of the world consists of alcoholic beverages, tobacco products, opium, coca, marijuana, and hallucinogenic plants. No culture utilizes all of these substances, but almost all cultures permit or encourage the use of at least one of them. These drugs have been used by a wide variety of cultures for thousands of years. For example, alcoholic beverages have an almost worldwide distribution. Indigenous North America is the major exception, but even though there are a few cultures that had no knowledge or prohibited the use of alcohol, most utilize some form of alcoholic beverage. Ethnohistorical work and modern ethnography demonstrate not only the widespread use of alcohol, but also the invariably ceremonial context of most drinking in traditional societies (Mandelbaum 1965; Heath 1981).

Anthropological studies of traditional cultures have caused many to conclude that "addiction" per se is not observed in these cultures (Heath 1983). Even in cultures where heavy drinking occurs, it appears that the ceremonial context of the drinking somehow mitigates against the debilitating, recreational, excessive use found in modern societies (Heath 1984). After the development of the distillation process and the introduction of hard liquor, problems with alcohol became more apparent. Benjamin Rush, one of the signers of the Declaration of Independence, wrote a paper called "The effects of ardent spirits on the human mind and body" in 1786. This early work outlined basic differences in acute and chronic drunkenness, and suggested that some drunks were a product of the environment and others simply inherited the problem (Levine 1978). The introduction of whiskey to the Native American populations caused well-known problems, and many concluded that the problem was genetic. But Leland (1976) thoroughly discredited "the firewater myth," and MacAndrew and Edgerton (1969) demonstrated that Native Americans drank the way they did because they had learned it from hard drinking, hard living, and cutthroat European trappers and frontiersmen. These researchers also showed that even abnormal behavior under the influence of alcohol was not the result of the pharmacological effects of alcohol, but learned behavior. In other words, drunken comportment was determined by cultural rules just as normal behavior.

But drunkenness increasingly became perceived as a threat to society in the late nineteenth and early twentieth centuries. Various temperance groups and religious institutions agitated for the prohibition of alcoholic beverages in this country and drinking ultimately was outlawed. Most people are familiar with the results of the experiment to make drinking alcohol illegal, but most do not realize that, ironically, it probably contributed significantly to the development of increasingly serious alcohol and criminal problems in this country (Levine 1984). Since the failure of that experiment, alcohol has received the blessing of American culture as a legally approved, highly psychoactive, recreational drug. Most Americans drink some form of alcoholic beverage, and the ceremonial and social importance of participation can be observed at bars, restaurants, business meetings, and Super Bowl parties. The social context of most drinking is a reflection of the basic meaning of alcohol for Americans who drink (Douglas 1987). The acceptance of a drink on a dare by the adolescent serves as a rite of passage to adulthood. Workers gather after hours to ceremonially celebrate the end of the day. Business people share the ritual of a drink or a glass of fine wine in order to demonstrate that they are suitably refined. Embraced by cultural approval, alcohol is still legal despite its being the most extensive drug problem in the United States.

Opium was first grown in the Near East. People have utilized opium for at least 2,000 years as the greatest pain killer the world has ever known. Many people also smoked opium recreationally, but it is erroneous to assume that opium smoking is something pushed upon western civilization by indigenous cultures of the East. Most Americans are vaguely aware of the "Opium Wars" between Great Britain and China in the last century. However, many mistakenly think it was fought because the Chinese were trying to extend the opium trade to the west. Ironically, imperial Britain wanted to force them to accept the sale of opium to its people. It was a great, money-making product and considered worth the military costs. The subsequent immigration of Chinese to the United States in the nineteenth century ensured that Americans would be introduced to opium smoking. Most Chinese claimed that it was an important aid to the heavy labor in which they were employed. Numerous opium dens operated in San Francisco. These businesses were closed down as racist attacks on Chinese immigrants were intensified. At the beginning of the twentieth century, the attacks were so visceral and effective that the U.S. Congress prohibited further immigration by the Chinese. They also prohibited opium smoking, which had been effectively associated with the Chinese as a particularly bad habit in order to justify the racism (Inciardi 1990). In the West, opium smoking was recognized as a health problem. Morphine was refined from opium and hailed by all as the wonder drug that could effectively cure the habitual opium smoker. The product, while a great analgesic, did not live up to its billing with regard to opium smokers because a morphine habit was even harder to kick. Heroin was refined and hailed as the "wonder drug" to cure morphine addiction, but again, the same problem. Propagandists effectively associated all of these problems with racial minorities (particularly the Chinese), determined that they were dangerous to the individual's health and spirit, and outlawed their unprescribed use in the early twentieth century. Since the drugs are so effective as pain killers, their use under the care of a bona fide, licensed physician was and still is permitted. All other use is subject to criminal prosecution.

Coca leaves have been used by the Native Americans of the Andean highland regions for thousands of years. Chewed in combination with other substances, it is a stimulant and provides a mild increase in heart rate, oxygen exchange, and wards off fatigue. These are important adaptive effects for people living and working at extremely high altitudes. In the late 1800s cocaine was refined from coca and identified as the new wonder drug for the treatment of other addictions and even of some mental illnesses, including depression. Coca was an active ingredient in Coca Cola until the early 1900s when it was outlawed. Some of the physicians and others who had touted the potential benefits had discovered some of the debilitating effects of chronic use (Inciardi 1991), but this health hazard was not the overriding concern of those who agitated for its prohibition. The harmful effects of the drug were associated with a racial minority. This time African-Americans were the example of what could happen if the substance was not strictly controlled. Particularly in the South, people were presented propaganda that depicted drug-crazed, black males engaging in such violent acts as rape (usually of white women) and murder. The campaign was successful and the drug was prohibited by law (Park & Matveychuk 1986).

Marijuana is a euphoriant used by traditional people for ages. The Bantu peoples of Africa use it and claim that they get more energy for work. Americans use it and say that it slows them down. This is an excellent example of the different ways that cultural knowledge can mediate the negative effects of any substance. Perfectly legal in this country until the 1930s, marijuana was used by many people, but most frequently it has been associated with the Mexican migrant farm-workers in the Southwest. Again, the propaganda machine effectively associated the Mexican-Americans and African-Americans with reefer madness, and these ethnic minorities became the focus of arguments to prohibit its use. Violence and terminal laziness were said to be the most predictable side effects. These racist arguments succeeded once again, and the use or possession of marijuana was prohibited by law (Lyman & Potter 1991). Interestingly, with the rise of the counterculture and the conversion of a large majority of the white, middle-class, young people to the hippie, flower child movement, marijuana began to gain enormous popularity. Suddenly, the majority of white, middle-class kids were criminalized by their use of marijuana. Laws in most states called for stiff, felony prosecution. Almost overnight millions of members of the predominant cultural group in this country were at risk for being punished as criminals. Shortly thereafter, most states relaxed their marijuana laws. But cultural resistance to the decriminalization of marijuana has kept it a prohibited and illegal drug.

The 1960s also introduced many Americans to the use of hallucinogenic substances. Mushrooms were the most frequently encountered, but others such as peyote had a brief, if somewhat limited, tenure. Along with the discovery of the development of LSD-25, a lot of young Americans were bombarded by suggestions to "turn on, tune in and drop out." This message was totally unacceptable to mainstream American culture. Federal and state governments moved quickly to outlaw these substances, and dirty looking, hippie dropouts were used as the characteristically other and alien examples of what would happen if one used such hallucinogens. Madness and self-induced death were the predicted outcome. People were mobilized to outlaw these drugs through a basic fear of alien cultures they did not understand.

Tobacco first was used by Native Americans as a hallucinogenic. This was not your regular filter smoke, but a powerful and extremely potent form of tobacco. It was smoked, chewed, and even administered as an enema for quick and efficient absorption into the bloodstream. It also was smoked or chewed chronically in some cultures. For Americans, tobacco use is a failed experiment. In the early part of the century, tobacco companies began to manufacture pre-rolled cigarettes in order to make it more convenient to smoke. Somewhat later, tobacco companies came up with the filter tip. This enabled a great many individuals who otherwise could not tolerate the strong smoke in their lungs to successfully smoke cigarettes. "Light" cigarettes increased the population of smokers. Advertising, such as Virginia Slims for the ladies, the Malboro Man, the freshness of menthol, and Charly Camel, has been enormously successful. The downside for the business is that they also have contributed to enormous health-care costs related to smoking. Still, there is no evidence that any of the sacred, spiritual species has ever passed into secular use. Tobacco use is perfectly legal and, although attitudes currently are changing in America, it is almost universally condoned by American culture. At the moment, tobacco companies are extremely nervous and upset about recent moves to have tobacco regulated by the Federal Drug Administration (FDA) as a habit-forming drug. Tobacco-related illnesses will be responsible for as many as one-half a million deaths this year in the United States. That is roughly four or five times the 100,000 deaths that will be attributed to alcohol, which is roughly four or five times the 25,000 deaths that can be demonstrated to be caused by all other illegal and legal drugs that are available in the country (Zimring & Hawkins 1992).

Obviously, our priorities are culturally conditioned rather than being based on whether or not a substance is good or bad, innocuous or dangerous. Our cultural knowledge actually leads us to permit the use of alcohol and tobacco despite tragic consequences. Our cultural assumptions lead us to prohibit the use of other psychoactive drugs despite the sometimes modest problems associated with their use. Our culturally determined beliefs assure us that we know the "truth" about drugs.

Synthetic drugs, such as barbiturates and depressants, amphetamines and other central nervous system stimulants, seem to have a similar history. Upon discovery they were hailed as new wonder drugs and later it becames obvious that there were side effects, at which time the controls were reinforced. The more possible it is to use a drug recreationally, the more intense the pressure to control. These drugs can be prescribed only by a physician and are otherwise illegal to possess or consume. Despite the illegality of taking a prescription drug that has been specifically provided to someone else, almost all of the students in my drugs and culture class have taken someone else's prescription drug. It is often the parent who provides the drug to the child in order to affect health. Furthermore, a huge black market exists. The trade of prescription drugs, particularly sedatives and stimulants, is substantial. Even though our legal system does all it can to restrict these substances, success is only partial.

We can observe the difference between the idealized value of the strict control of prescription medicine and daily reality. For example, the parents who give their child some tranquilizers to medicate the effect of some personal trauma are not considered deviants, but good and caring parents. If that same child takes a few of the pills to school and gives them to  friends for the same reason, that child is breaking the law and can be prosecuted as a criminal, a drug pusher. The over-the-counter drug industry is one area that does not actually provide many drugs for recreational use. But in the day-to-day reality of the drug business, the over-the-country industry has an enormous impact on what we believe drugs are all about. While "take only as prescribed" is commonly written on packaging and even stated in some broadcast advertising, there can be little doubt that many individuals determine for themselves what might be the proper dosage. So there is some reason to think that there are inherent, potential dangers in some over-the-counter drugs, even though the FDA assures Americans that these minor drugs are harmless, "if taken as directed."

The most culturally pervasive aspect of the over-the-counter industry is the massive amount of advertising. No matter what the product, the most basic message to the potential customer is that a product means relief, is available, and can profoundly and positively affect the user. The healing can be expected to take place immediately, if not sooner. The user gets "safe, quick, and easy" relief from pain and suffering. The idealized cultural value concerning the over-the-counter and prescription medicines is one that is consistent with the most basic meaning of all drug use, namely, that these substances can heal us or improve our state of being. The reality of the legal drug business is that people increasingly believe that it is some substance or drug they need in order to feel better. Importantly, in this respect, they are readily available at the corner drugstore. The positive value of drugs as operationalized in our culture leads directly to experimentation and the use of illegal substances. If all of these advertised remedies work, and someone tells a friend about experience with an illegal drug, and they attest to the efficacy of that remedy for improving one's state of being, and thus it is not too far a leap to try it out. The ceremonial necessity of sharing a cure or mind-altering drug with a cohort extends to all aspects of drug culture, legal or illegal.

The basic and traditional human pattern of drug use was one in which medicinal and psychoactive substances generally were used in a ritual and ceremonial context. The shaman or witch usually was consulted as the legitimate healer within the culture. The recreational use of substances was likewise confined by social and ceremonial prescription. Certain drugs were prohibited and considered profane. Culturally determined drug use produced beliefs about drugs. The significance of belief with regard to healing and curing agents is not restricted to traditional cultures, but is also manifest in modern American society. Most Americans believe that their prescription for antidepressants, valium, or librium will help them to cope. They believe prescribed antibiotics will help heal their viral infections. They believe that the sinus, hemorrhoid, headache, or stomach medicines they buy over the counter will be effective in alleviating minor problems. Sometimes these beliefs are appropriate, and at other times they reflect the superstitious and magical thinking we are so quick to criticize. While the unmistakably deleterious effects of alcohol, tobacco, and some illegal drugs can be demonstrated, people often take these drugs in the belief that they positively affect their well being. Recreational drugs relax them and help them to deal with everyday life in a more pleasant context than otherwise would be possible. They believe that they need help and they believe that a drug helps.

## MAJOR CONSTITUENT DRUG CULTURES
## IN THE UNITED STATES

Virtually everyone in this country is a member of a drug culture. They may participate in more than one specific cultural group. In each culture, members use a range of drugs based on their cultural knowledge and belief. Each culture utilizes a particular set of substances according to these beliefs. Each discourages the use of drugs it believes are really harmful or dangerous. Each is in competition with the other: economically, politically, socially, and morally. It is necessary to separate the different drug cultures that are major constituents of what might be called the American drug culture. At present, two primary classes of drugs are used; legal and illegal. There are three categories that are legally permitted: alcohol products, tobacco products, and pharmaceutical products that are dispensed legitimately. These pharmaceuticals include prescription drugs and over-the-counter remedies, only some of which are psychoactive; the remainder are medicinal.

Almost all Americans are members of the over-the-counter and prescription drug culture. Doctors prescribe and most responsible people participate in order to positively affect their health and well being. They buy these drugs in the belief that they are ill, they need them, and they will be healed by them. None of these drugs is to be used recreationally, only medicinally. Economically, it is big bucks and politically, it is correct. The two-thirds of the adult American population who drink some form of alcoholic beverage constitute the drug culture of alcohol. While user behavior is widely variable, they generally claim that alcohol promotes a spirit of conviviality and togetherness, relieves anxiety and inhibitions, and positively affects their well being. They consume alcoholic beverages in the belief that these results actually will occur. The drug is used ceremonially, recreationally, and medicinally. Economically, it is big bucks. Politically, it is correct in most cases. Over one-half the adult population smokes or chews tobacco. This drug culture is a self-described group of drug "addicts." While their behavior may appear irrational, they seem to believe that they have to keep doing it, and are in constant competition with nonmembers for space and air. They believe that it calms their nerves, even though the drug stimulates the cardiovascular system. The drug is only used recreationally and not medicinally. Economically, it is big bucks. Politically, it is now incorrect, despite the fact that it used to be sexy and cool.

The other primary class of drug culture is the illegal drug culture. This includes the medically and legally unauthorized use of prescription drugs, as well as the use of substances that are prohibited by law. The common thread in this culture is the illicit nature of the use, but this group is also widely diverse. Marijuana smokers, pill poppers, cocaine snorters, heroin shooters, speed freaks, and vision seekers all believe that their state of well being will be meaningfully affected in some way as a result of their drug use. Members of this particular drug culture are in belligerent competition with nonmembers. This competition can result in disagreements over the meaning of drugs and the incarceration of hundreds of thousands of individuals. These drugs are used recreationally and also as self-prescribed medicines. Heroin junkies frequently may refer to the drug as "my medicine." Economically, it is big bucks. Politically, it is dangerous. Legally, it is prohibited. Socially, it's rejected. Morally, it's wrong. Criminally, it's a big boost. Practically, it is tough to study. Tragically, it is a mess.

One of the most instructive examples of the confusing relationship between meaning, drugs, culture and the individual is revealed by the problems associated with the use of crack cocaine. In the late 1970s and early 1980s, cocaine began to gain notoriety as a fashionable and trendy drug associated with fashionable, trendy, and wealthy people. At the time, the cost of the drug was prohibitive to potential middle-class consumers. A perusal of media coverage in the late 1970s and early 1980s demonstrates that cocaine was not initially seen as a broad-scale threat to American society. The cost of the drug seemed to preclude general use among the majority of the people in the country. The rich seemed to be the primary population at risk.

By the mid-1980s, the supply of cocaine was sufficient to reduce the price significantly. Though still expensive, many middle-class consumers were able to occasionally purchase cocaine for recreational purposes through the very same distribution system used to sell marijuana and other popular, illicit substances. The essential meaning of the drug was positive for most users. It was something to spice up a social occasion, and the cost seemed to mitigate against habitual use. For abstainers, cocaine meant another threat to the established standards of behavior. As the use of cocaine became more widespread and popular, the legal, medical and political authorities convincingly and accurately associated the cocaine trade with the Columbian drug cartels, potential medical problems faced by habitual and occasional users, and the personal, financial difficulties of obtaining a drug that a middle-class individual really cannot afford. The public death of college basketball player Len Bias occurred as a crescendo of panic that swept the country.

Not coincidentally, the introduction of smokeable crack was occurring at about the same time. Previously, smoking cocaine had involved free-basing. Richard Pryor had almost burned himself to death, and Ricky Nelson and his band had died as a result of a plane crash in which a fire had apparently started while the passengers had been free-basing. Again, this had been a problem of the rich. But cocaine in crack form succeeded in two important respects. First, smoking crack delivers the drug much more quickly and efficiently to the brain. This results in a much more dramatic effect, increases the depressive kickback after the drug wears off, and heightens the individual's desire for another dose. Second, and probably most important, it made a form of cocaine available to consumers at a much lower cost. Distribution of the drug now could be extended to the working and the lower class neighborhoods, to the inner city and the ghettos. After the crack trade had been established in the African-American community, predictable problems became evident. The criminal enterprise controlling the crack trade through intimidation and violence, among other methods, became associated with crack houses, children distributing the product, murder, gangs, and heinous crimes. The economic reality of the trade in communities mired in poverty meant that there was a new product that could be sold to make money. The social reality of crack use was that the population had a drug available that was strongly associated with rich, sports and entertainment heroes. Obviously, it was embraced by many individuals as a very trendy, exciting, and profitable thing to do.

It would be a grave error to suggest that all or even most crack use is African-American, nor would it be accurate to suggest that all or even most African-Americans use crack. But to read the daily newspaper or watch the TV, one would assume that the crack "problem" is exclusively African-American. Reams of TV footage have been presented, showing raids and busts on crack houses, videos of gangs, and drug busts, which the authorities assure us will put a big dent in the criminal enterprise. These raids appear to target African-American communities almost exclusively (Shoemaker 1989). In 1995, there is not a great deal of concern about powdered cocaine, but "crack in the inner city" (euphemism for black neighborhoods) is constantly purported to be "the number one drug problem facing the country today." Even though crack is a significant problem, it is absolutely ludicrous to suggest that it is a greater threat to the health and welfare of the people in this country than even alcohol or tobacco consumption. But people believe it. Most white, middle-class people only associate crack with the African-American community. Law enforcement and political institutions feed the media information that generates and reinforces the association. Although it is not, by far, the worst drug problem Americans face, it is apparently comforting to believe that the worst problem is not one in which the predominant cultural group has any active culpability. This is the same racist propaganda that has accompanied almost every effort to prohibit drugs by law. In the meantime, the meaningful relationships between drugs, cultures, individuals, and American society remains obscured.

## CONCLUSIONS AND SUGGESTIONS

The "war on drugs" has been a miserable failure because it does not take into account the basic meaning of drugs to all users and abstainers. Nor do those who advocate such an approach understand that people use all drugs because they are meaningful. The ceremonial and ritual contexts of interaction within a drug culture do not just cause drug use, they generate beliefs and behaviors with respect to much more than just different drugs. Attempting to incarcerate just anyone who is a participating, cultural member of the wrong group is proving costly, ineffective, and counterproductive. Prison culture is also a reality, and those who spend time there generally learn and accept the predominant values. This fosters the continuing growth of an entire cultural group who most assuredly will become even more alienated from mainstream America and will not change any of their beliefs regarding drugs. As much as 40 percent of the prison population in this country are jailed because of drugs. Upon release, the problem is still there because the beliefs are still there (Wilcox 1994).

The prohibition of certain drug cultures also has had the unfortunate effect of supporting and maintaining a huge black market, criminal enterprise. The business is so lucrative that violent behavior is common in the United States and other countries. The worldwide production and distribution system is incredibly complex and efficient. Attempts to convince third-world countries to quit producing drugs never can be successful. Drug products have traditional meaning to poor, rural people, as well as the newer meaning of freedom from poverty, hunger, and disease. Sanctions to stop the distribution of illegal drugs in this country never will be any more successful than was Prohibition. The distribution system for illegal drugs is a grass roots operation. The demand and supply is there. Friends help each other acquire drugs. No neighborhood or community exists without connections.

The adoption of recreational marijuana use by a large majority of young people in the 1960s continued for at least a decade. During that time, the basic distribution system for nearly all illicit drugs was formidably developed by entrepreneurs who previously were restricted to very narrowly defined groups of customers. Marijuana use by such an overwhelming middle class population ensured that as new drugs were introduced, the economic system of distribution would be in place to sell them to a larger number and wider variety of people. It would be interesting to know what would have happened had the federal government legalized marijuana 25 years ago. Without the daily participation of middle class consumers in the distribution system, drugs such as speed, cocaine, crack, and heroin may have been much harder to acquire. Some of our fashionable drugs might not have caused as many problems as they have on such a broad scale in American society.

The conflict is not over the use of drugs as much as it is a conflict over the meaning of human life and the role of drugs in our lives. Fuzzy cultural beliefs must be replaced with facts. The meaning of drugs to the user and abstainer must be understood in a cultural context. The search for the culturally embedded meanings of drugs can lead researchers to examine reality rather than idealized illusions of the relationship between the individual, the culture, American society, and drugs. Based on such research we may be able to create rational domestic and foreign policies, and explain the desire, alienation, insecurity, cruelty, fear, and loathing that make so many of us believe we need chemically psychoactive assistance in our daily lives.

## REFERENCES

Douglas, M. 1987. *Constructive Drinking: Perspectives on Drink from Anthropology.* New York: Cambridge University Press.

Furst, P. 1972. *Flesh of the Gods: The Ritual Use of Hallucinogens.* New York: Praeger.

————1976. *Hallucinogens and Culture.* Novato, CA: Chandler & Sharpe Publishers.

Heath, D. B. 1981. *Alcohol Use and World Cultures: A Comprehensive Bibliography of Anthropological Sources.* Toronto: Addiction Research Foundation.

Heath, D. B. 1983. Sociocultural Perspectives on Addiction. In *Etiological Aspects of Alcohol and Drug Abuse*. E. Gottheil et al. (eds). Springfield, IL: Charles C. Thomas, pp. 223–237.

———1984. Cross Cultural Studies of Alcoholism. *Recent Developments in Alcoholism, Vol.* 2. M. Galanter (ed). New York: Plenum Press, pp. 405–416.

Inciardi, J. A. 1990. *Handbook of Drug Control in the United States*. Westport, CT: Greenwood Publishing.

———1991. *The Drug Legalization Debate*. New York: Sage Publications.

Levine, H. G. 1978. The Discovery of Addiction. *Journal of Studies on Alcohol* 39:143–174.

———1984. The Alcohol Problem in America: From Temperance to Alcoholism. *British Journal of Addiction* 79:109–119.

Leland, J. H. 1976. *Firewater Myths: North American Indian Drinking and Alcohol Addiction*. New Brunswick: Rutgers Center Alcohol Studies, Monograph 11.

Lyman, M. D. & Potter, G. W. 1991. *Drugs in Society: Causes, Concepts, and Control*. Cincinnati: Anderson Publishing Co.

MacAndrew, C. & Edgerton, R. B. 1969. *Drunken Comportment: A Social Explanation*. Chicago: Aldine Publishing.

Mandelbaum, D. G. 1965. Alcohol and Culture. *Current Anthropology* 6:281–293.

Marshall, M. 1979. *Beliefs, Behaviors, and Alcoholic Beverages: A Cross Cultural Survey*. Ann Arbor: University of Michigan Press.

Park, P. & Matveychuk, W. (eds). 1986. *Culture and Politics of Drugs*. Dubuque: Kendall / Hunt Publishing.

Radcliffe-Brown, A. R. 1952. *Structure and Function in Primitive Society*. New York: Free Press.

Shoemaker, P. (ed). 1989. *Communications Campaigns About Drugs: Government, Media and the Public*. Hillsdale, NJ: Lawrence Erlbaum & Associates.

Szasz, T. 1987. *Ceremonial Chemistry: The Ritual Persecution of Drugs, Addicts and Pushers*. Revised edition. Holmes Beach, FL: Learning Publications, Inc.

Wilcox, D. M. 1994. *Alcoholic Thinking: An Ethnographic Narrative of the Changing World View Among Recovering Urban Alcoholics in Alcoholics Anonymous*. Ann Arbor, MI: University Microfilms, Inc.

Zimring, F. & Hawkins, G. 1992. *The Search for Rational Drug Control*. New York: Cambridge University Press.

# 17

## New Religious Movements

### Gretchen Siegler

## INTRODUCTION

This chapter is concerned with diversity that comes from new religious groupings and, more precisely, with an example of the new religions as unique cultural groups in America. New religions throughout the world vary widely but also exhibit many similarities. Scholars have spent considerable time classifying these similarities and differences into typologies in order to increase our understanding of religious behavior. As may be seen throughout this volume, with all of the racial and ethnic categorizations, intellectual typologies if used improperly obscure more than they clarify. It must be understood that such categories are artificial since most groups fall somewhere in between on a continuum. Categorization is simply an attempt to increase our knowledge of them by allowing us to look at and understand their similarities and differences. With this limitation in mind, a few of these distinctions will be provided to help illustrate and help the reader understand. The main focus then will be to present a specific case study of one example of these new religions that make up one of the constituent cultural groups in the diversity of the U.S. culture.

### Denominations, Sects, and Cults

The most commonly heard distinctions when discussing religions are those among *denominations*, *sects*, and *cults*. *Denominations* are major religious groups that have established themselves as acceptable to a society and have become part of its "civil religion." A civil religion shapes the world view of the members of a society by embodying a belief system that incorporates that which comes out of the denominational faiths. It results in a totality of values, or ideals and beliefs based on those things which people feel strongly about. An adherence to these shared understandings about the proper ways of behaving sets American culture apart from other cultures, and provides an identity as a society. Compared to other societies, America exhibits a variety of denominations. This religious pluralism is primarily a result of the separation of church and state combined with ethnic diversity from immigration.

Splinter groups eventually tend to break away from denominations and form smaller groups called *sects*. Each sect's doctrines and behaviors depart in some ways from the denomination from which they came, but they continue to retain many of its characteristics. For example, a fundamentalist denomination consists of members who interpret the bible literally. A group within it might form who believe that the bible is made up of symbols that have alternative interpretations. Since these beliefs go against the fundamentalist doctrine of the larger denomination, this group will be forced to separate and form their own sect. The sect might become sufficiently organized with a well-established doctrine of its own to continue to attract a strong committed membership and become considered a new denomination. Or, it might not be able to establish an organization that can attract and retain members and eventually disperse. Its members also eventually could be reunited with the original denomination since sects, by definition, do not exhibit a significantly different cultural content from that of the established denomination.

This brings us to a third grouping called *cults*, a recent term when applied to American society, and previously known on a worldwide basis as "revitalization movements." Culture is not fixed, changeless, and universally accepted within any society. Cults play a prominent role as independent movements of culture change. They syncretize, or blend, elements drawn from a variety of sources, both internal and external to the society, religious and secular, and also often create new doctrine not previously known. Unlike the denominations or sects, cults are considered doctrinally precarious, with minimal organization, exhibiting loose relationships and little commitment from their members (Richardson 1979; Wallis 1975). Yet cults, like sects, also may or may not eventually become established denominations. The Church of Latter Day Saints, or Mormons, initially were considered a cult because their doctrine, while including major Christian beliefs, also contained new, dramatically different, precepts. It is now the fastest growing denomination in the world with an extremely well-organized, large, committed membership.

Cults have deep roots in American history, with a particularly strong increase in group numbers since the 1960s (Wuthrow 1985). They exhibit many of the same characteristics as revitalization movements throughout the world that have been described as "deliberate, organized, conscious efforts by members of a society to construct a more satisfying culture" (Wallace 1956:265). Sociologists attribute their recent upsurge in America to a variety of interrelated factors. Some believe that the public is experiencing impersonal relationships because of a loss of a sense of community. Cults bring back a sense of community and return meaning to people's lives. Others contend that there is an increase in secularization within the major denominations that results in a paradoxical increase in religious variation. Still others believe that a crisis of meaning in the country results in an attempt to order experience through the development of new symbols. These new symbols more appropriately reflect reality because they shift the world view of certain individuals

(Aidala 1984; Anthony & Robbins 1982; Bellah 1975). While explanations usually are based on assumptions of alienation or deviation, positive conditions that allow for the formation of these new innovative groups should not be overlooked. They introduce vitality into American culture, as the name revitalization implies.

## Intentional Communities

Cults whose participants form "intentional communities" become sufficiently different to warrant calling them separate constituent cultures. Members attempt to transform their physical, social, and psychological environment by consciously seeking an alternative life-style, exhibiting innovative values and beliefs. This cultural grouping becomes their key source of social-psychological attachment and begins to have more influence on the participants' behavior than does the larger society. Members develop ideas of in-group versus out-group, and tend to judge others by their standards and values. Depending on the degree to which they are able to separate themselves through such behaviors as a tendency to marry within the group, distinguishing traits such as distinctive dress and vocabulary may develop. It results in further increasing their identity as a cultural grouping.

Intentional religious communities in America vary from one another in beliefs. They may be looked at on a continuum with most falling somewhere in between. On one end, a group may adhere to traditional, authoritarian moral absolutism. In other words, it may sharply distinguish between good and evil, tend to be politically conservative, and have rigorous expectations regarding social conduct. On the other end, a group may envision an alternative social order, often drawing from Eastern religions and psychotherapy. It may evaluate morality relativistically, is concerned with the importance of individual consciousness, and hopes to recreate loving relationships as an extended family (Anthony & Robbins 1982).

Behaviors generally reflect where a group stands on this belief continuum. Most adhere to monogamy, although occasionally one may practice polygamy, group marriages, or open marriages. Some may maintain strict nuclear families, while others share the duties of child care with the community. While one group may organize itself in a strict hierarchy, another may allow all of its members to actively participate in decision-making. Furthermore, while some may be socially active and openly involved with the wider community, some close themselves off in insulated environments. In addition, such groups may rely on established businesses within communes to make their living, or members may work in various jobs apart from their fellow believers, then pooling or separating their resources.

## Cults as Deviant Groups

Cults usually are perceived negatively regardless of how much Americans voice acceptance of religious pluralism in their society. The public has developed preconceived notions, or stereotypes, of what a cult is that causes them to expect their members to behave deviantly. It generally will be described as authoritarian, consisting of passive believers who have been brainwashed by their power-hungry and manipulative leaders. Converts are expected to begin to act in uncustomary ways, quit their jobs, divorce their spouses, and are forced to give all of their money to the group. It is believed that this is initiated by the leaders through deprivation, thought reform, and false imprisonment when converts are systematically separated from loved ones. The public's prejudicial attitudes, or derogatory beliefs, toward what they think are cults often is expressed through discriminatory acts against them. The negative perception of cults is maintained and perpetuated by a number of sources. Of particular concern are the many anti-cult groups that have cropped up all over the country. The first was formed in 1972, to "liberate" followers of the Children of God, later known as The Family. This anti-cult group only began to organize with others after 900 members of the Peoples Temple committed suicide in Guyana in 1979. They allied under umbrella organizations called the Cult Awareness Network (CAN) and the American Family Foundation (AFF). The latter claims to conduct academic research to provide public education on cults, yet their research is often questionable. It usually consists of statements made by families of those who have joined new religions, and apostates, or ex-members, who have hard feelings for various reasons. Scholars who have dealt with members of CAN and AFF remark that they share an exaggerated fear of what they perceive as threats to the status quo (Kilbourne & Richardson 1986). They appear to be drawn together for the sole purpose of eradicating new religions, harassing them legally, through lawsuits in efforts to bankrupt them, and illegally, through the kidnaping of converts and attempts to deprogram, or deconvert, them. Their impact on such groups is even supported by the media which is known to reflect common assumptions. It often quotes these "experts," further labeling cults as deviant.

Others identified as being antagonistic to what are considered cults are selected members of the psychotherapeutic community and religious leaders from some major denominations. Psychotherapists sometimes view membership in cults as causing psychopathological behavior such as dissociative disorders. Yet there is an absence of empirical data to support this catchall phrase, which describes any temporary alteration in normal integrative functions. It has been suggested that these psychotherapists see new religions as competitors in the therapy market since many cults describe themselves as therapeutic communities and believe that their therapy is a way of life. Similarly, some religious leaders of established religions may feel threatened by new religions, possibly because they fear competition when they see their members join these groups (Kilbourne & Richardson 1984).

Public fears have forced both state and federal levels of government to consider anti-cult legislation at one time or another. Official studies of the "cult problem" have been sanctioned, which usually consist of efforts to deny them religious freedom. Solicitation of funds may be regulated, and decisions are made about tax freedom based on ideas about legitimate versus illegitimate religion. There have been hundreds of court cases concerning various aspects of these groups, and some of these cases have made it to the U.S. Supreme Court (Richardson 1991). Laws on the books often are manipulated in such a way that relatives are allowed to assume responsibility for members who are believed to be incapable of making decisions on their own, or attempts are made to define their religious activities as consumer products that need to be "quality controlled" by the government (Richardson 1986). Lately, child abuse laws also have been used as a mechanism to control new religions. Groups may be charged if their child-rearing practices conflict with more traditional family structures and practices, which they oftentimes do. For instance, they unconventionally may allow many adults, rather than simply the immediate family members, to interact with and discipline their children.

Members of cults most often feel targeted by the public and usually respond defensively. Criticisms often are interpreted as evidence that they have the truth and expect to be ostracized for it. It may cause them to isolate themselves further from the wider community, avoiding contacts with such major institutions as health care, choosing instead to treat illnesses within the group itself; education, preferring home schooling; and government, refusing to register births and deaths. Since this behavior only results in further misunderstandings, there is evidence that those new religions that manage to survive for a long period of time tend to move toward establishing behaviors considered more normal by their neighbors. The considerable negative attention paid to groups that have been labeled cults does not go unnoticed by scholars either. Most now avoid this label and refer to these groups as New Religious Movements (NRMs). Many share the assumption that it is not enough to know about NRMs from an "etic" perspective, or as an outsider perceives them. It is also important to try to know them as they see themselves, from their own "emic" perspective, based on their own perceptions and memories. This type of research is accomplished through ethnographic fieldwork, a method usually associated with anthropology but increasingly used in other disciplines. It consists of the researcher developing an intimate relationship with those being studied, by observing and participating in everything they do. It results in relieving many of the biases people tend to have of other people who are different from themselves. In fact, those who study NRMs by living with them have come to view them positively, or at least neutrally.

## A CASE STUDY OF A NEW RELIGIOUS MOVEMENT

### What They Believe

Fifteen years of periodic ethnographic research on an NRM and its neighbors illuminates characteristics similar to those found in other groups. A more complete description of this case study can be found in Siegler (1992). Members of In Search of Truth (ISOT) number approximately one hundred and fifty, live communally in a rural California town, and consider themselves to be Christians. They are led by a woman named Marie whose "prophetic" abilities to foretell events because of a direct connection with God are acknowledged by her followers. She has told them that they must transform themselves spiritually and become permanently *anointed*, or covered by God. It is believed that those who attain permanent anointment will be *chosen* by him to fulfill a *calling*. They will join a *Body* of people, rather than

Christ as is commonly believed by most Christians, to prepare the world for a prophesied time following the *millennium*, a 1,000-year period preceding the end of the world. The world is considered to be at the end of this 1,000-year period.

Members learn that they must partially separate themselves from the larger community through communal living which provides a necessary context for this self- transformation. At the heart of Marie's teachings is a *pattern* developed from her interpretation of the bible. Her followers learn that a knowledge of it provides a comprehensive world view, simplifying the bible's explanation of how God's plan is unfolding and therefore protecting them from a false interpretation of God's word. Its ethical guidance helps them to deny individualism and promote responsibility for others through an emphasis on self-discipline, self-reflection, and mutual respect. A very simplified description of the pattern shows that it consists of three circles which reflect the *Trinity*, or the three interrelated parts of God. He is made up of the physical realm consisting of the body, the mental realm composed of the word, and the spiritual realm signifying the spirit or emotions. Humans and the church community are believed to be made in God's image and therefore must balance the three circles. Humans in daily life move within these three circles. If they display behavior that is destructive to the body, it also will be destructive to the mind and to the emotions. The church community also must balance the circles that are exhibited in ritual, doctrine, and charismatic behavior. Movement within the pattern also is believed to be progressive, which is an important tool in understanding the community's belief of a developmental progression in the relationship with God. This movement is experienced during three periods of rebirth associated with each circle. *Life*, associated with the physical realm, is first brought to believers through "baptism of the water," known elsewhere as a "born again" experience. *Light*, as part of the mental realm, follows during "baptism of the word." Finally, *love*, in the spiritual realm, occurs when they experience "baptism of the spirit." Individuals, and the church community as a whole, strive eventually to fulfill their calling and move into a fourth circle. At that time they hope to be permanently anointed and acquire the nature of God.

### The Body

ISOT is affiliated with many other communities located primarily throughout North America, although there are also groups scattered throughout the world. These religious communities go by many different names, including Samaritan Farms, Blueberry, and Shepherds Inn, but they refer to themselves as a whole as the *Body*. Those affiliated with the Body loosely assemble around a traveling ministry who claim to be God's "apostles." They share some of the same general religious tenets as ISOT, such as the belief that God will call forward a Body of his chosen people at the end of the millennium. The communities differ from ISOT and from each other in how they go about preparing themselves for this post-millenniumistic role as moral reformers to the world. For instance, while ISOT members guide themselves with Marie's pattern, other groups have their own internal leaders who offer prophecies to their members. Important prophecies are presented to the apostles to be shared among the groups, but they may or may not be emphasized.

The groups comprising the Body benefit from the support that they offer each other. They come together during conventions and share newsletters and ministries. ISOT hosts a yearly convention on its property, and its members actively visit the other communities. Many send families who are experiencing difficulties raising their children to ISOT to temporarily live because ISOT has the reputation of being particularly knowledgeable about child-care issues. Some of these families stay, providing ISOT with a source of new members. The Body also offers ISOT children a pool of marriage partners that share similar beliefs. In addition, the ISOT community is not isolated when its members have the opportunity to share and evaluate their religious beliefs with others.

### Relations With Neighbors

ISOT was formed on the central California coast in the middle 1960s. Potential converts would visit the prophet's house and some stayed. A few were adults who were disillusioned with established churches and came to hear Marie's religious beliefs. Most were young and part of what is now known as the beginning of the "Jesus Movement." Initially, many were less attracted to specific religious beliefs than to her philosophy on life as taught through the patterns. They also enjoyed the social contact in a family-like environment. Because Marie took care of these youth, some of whom had been living on the streets, and offered an alternative to drugs, the group was considered valuable to those who lived in the wider community besieged by the influx of youth seeking a "hippie" life-style.

The ISOT's positive relationship with their neighbors changed when they moved closer to a rural town in the northeastern part of the state in the early 1970s. They numbered approximately the same as the number of residents in the town, known here as *locals*. Almost immediately, the group began to purchase a large proportion of the town's buildings, and was able to outbid the locals on construction and ranching jobs because they pooled their resources. They were highly visible because they moved throughout the town in large groups wearing distinctive dress. At that time women wore long dresses that reached the ground, while men had beards and often wore blue jeans and white shirts. Since this dress was associated with hippies, many locals assumed that the ISOTs took drugs. Most considered the group a cult that planned to take over their town. Consequently, they did not accord its members the privacy usually accorded to their neighbors. Acts of discrimination became common occurrences through such petty activities as letting the air out of the commune's vehicle's tires. Even more disruptive attempts of harassment included sabotaging their construction efforts by filing complaints to officials, writing derogatory letters to the newspaper about their supposed activities, and initiating unsubstantiated charges of child abuse against them. The members of ISOT reacted by strengthening their boundary maintaining behaviors. They hoped that by keeping largely to themselves and maintaining their identity as a separate group, it would reduce conflict with their neighbors. Furthermore, they believed that assimilation with the locals diminished the distinctive values and roles that they shared with each other. ISOT children were withdrawn from the public schools, and their parents refused to attend the wider community events.

## Financial Success

Yet the members of the commune could only partially separate themselves from their neighbors because of limited employment opportunities in the region. While they grew much of their own food and relied on meat from their ranch throughout the 1970s, they also were reliant on the locals to provide much of their income by supporting a variety of communally owned businesses, including a grocery store and a construction firm. They found it useful to become active in county govern-ment to ensure that public policy would be initiated to benefit, or at least not harm, their group. In the meantime, they concentrated on becoming independent by developing a business conducted within the commune in which all members could participate. By the 1980s, the ISOTs supported themselves solely by providing homes and counseling services for children who were listed as wards of the State of California. Eventually, they took into this "group home" as many as seventy children called "placements." They found that these efforts only served to expand their relationship with the wider community, particularly with state agencies that needed to be accommodated. In doing so, the members became more directly concerned with their image, finding it essential to normalize their behavior so that no one would think that something out of the ordinary was happening on their premises. Outsiders were hired to work in the group home, neighbors were invited to a yearly party in the ISOT park, and tours often were given of their property. Members also were educating themselves to legitimize their work with children who had multiple problems. Selected individuals who had been sent to colleges in the area eventually offered some college courses on their premises for the wider community. In addition, it became important to establish that the child-care business was separated from religious activities so that outsiders would not think that the state wards were being proselytized and made to convert. While this separation was very difficult for the ISOTs who believe that religion should be an everyday part of their lives, they were becoming financially secure for the first time in their short history.

## Charges of Child Abuse

In the early 1990s, charges of child abuse once again were brought against them, resulting in the loss of their child-care business. These accusations were much more serious then those previous because they were initiated by disgruntled ex-members and placements. The state also covertly planted an investigator in the commune. Rather than go to court, the ISOT community decided that it was in their best interest to work out a deal with the state to close the business if charges were dropped. The decision was made for the sake of privacy, not guilt, since some of the accusing ex-members were close relatives to leaders in the group. The ISOTs are now once again working in different parts of the wider community, this time in higher paying jobs because they are better educated. A major source of income comes from the reestablished construction business which this time relies on well paying federal contracts.

Close relatives often have presented innumerable problems for the ISOTs, but occasionally they also provide additional members for the group. In its early years, converts were young and so some families simply thought their children were going through a phase, or, similarly, anything was considered good that kept them away from the streets and drugs. But many reflected the general fear of cults and felt that their children were being manipulated by an unscrupulous leader. Certainly this image was reinforced when some of the members signed over their inheritances to the group, and loyalty to fellow believers was given priority over everyone else. Usually relatives reinitiate contact after their grandchildren are born. It is not seen to be in the best interest of the group to have their followers constantly leave the commune to visit with families because they are needed to work on the premises. At the same time, relatives of members are welcome to visit and some do. A few stay and become committed to the group, and others return periodically for lengthy visits, living in private trailers designated for that purpose. Recently an attempt has been made to create a communal household specifically for relatives who can no longer care for themselves, although so far it has attracted few. Anyone who stays in the group for any length of time must abide by the authority of its leaders, an uncomfortable long-term compromise for many outsiders.

### Who Has Authority?

The members of ISOT claim that everyone's authority is questioned because God leads the group. Since it also is agreed that Marie as a prophet has a direct connection with God's desires, she has a great deal of authority. Her husband, called Joseph, also has a strong voice and is considered the community's Executive Director. His status is not so much the result of his connection with Marie, but because of his personal attributes. He is considered to have a gift as an apostle, or leader. He has a Ph.D. in public administration, and is an astute businessman. A group of additional *Elders* help make most of the decisions for the community as a whole, as well as for families, since it is believed that individual problems affect the whole group. These Elders also have been chosen for their position based on personal talents. Since ISOT members share the belief in progressive spiritual development, perceptions of someone's spiritual level is a primary consideration. Spirituality is reflected in an individual's commitment to others in the group and the degree of conformity he or she exhibits on a daily basis to the religious precepts of the group. Subsequently, most of the Elders have been with the group for many years, and it is difficult for anyone else to obtain these limited positions. Recently a group of members have been chosen to take part in meetings as potential initiates to Eldership. Many of them are women, which has the potential to alleviate the present gender bias in higher levels of authority.

Other ISOTs may have limited authority in the six separate household clusters dispersed throughout the commune. Usually an Elder is selected to head a cluster, and different levels of decision-making are assigned to others living there. Clusters are composed of a central house where meals are served, along with surrounding buildings and trailers with bedrooms. Peripheral members and guests usually stay in separate quarters. Yet these living arrangements do not allow for autonomy from the wider community. A central meeting house provides an area where the whole community gathers for at least one daily meal, and for activities and special events. In addition, members are moved to new clusters periodically, sometimes as often as twice a year. In this way, they are not allowed to become too comfortable with one group of people, an act which it is feared will lessen their ties with others. They believe that it is important to their spiritual progress to be forced to "rub against one another."

### The Children

Children are valued in the group, and the birth of a child is celebrated. Families tend to limit themselves to no more than three, but women feel comfortable with early marriage and pregnancy because they have others to help them with their babies. Until recently, babies and children of preschool age lived in the same cluster as their parents but spent most of the day in a day care center so that their parents could work. Children in grade school moved away from their parent's cluster to a cluster specifically designated for them. Teenagers moved into Marie's and Joseph's household. Parents visited them on their days off, and they were allowed to visit their parents with permission from their *persons* (those assigned to care for them). Presently, children are more apt to live in the same cluster as their parents because placements no longer live in the commune. Those who want to live with the prophet or with other adults must request to do so. It is interesting to note that many who were raised in the group and now are having children of their own express an interest in reestablishing the designated children's house, agreeing that the life-style is beneficial to children.

### CONCLUSION

ISOT is a constituent cultural grouping within the larger American culture primarily because it is more than a religion for its members, it is their whole way of life. While they are similar to many other Americans in that they consider themselves Christian, that which they only share with each other is innovative and even differs from those in the Body with whom they are most closely affiliated. They have selectively developed a system of values, beliefs, and symbols that distinguish their cultural content from the dominant mainstream religions and that of the state. These differences are reflected in behaviors that provide them with in-group identity. A few of their unique distinctions include styles of dress, vocabulary that only has meaning to them, and adherence to a structure specifically designed to fulfill their needs.

ISOT has created a social experiment that is successful for a number of reasons. The cultural group presently consists of four generations. The parents of some of the original members live there, as well as children who were raised with the group and now are having children of their own. This community's ability to retain many of its original members and youth, and its survival for over twenty-five years, qualifies it to be considered a successful NRM (Kanter 1972). It continues to be meaningful for its participants because it provides a socially supportive environment in which they can experience their religious beliefs in everyday life. Members have organized themselves in a way that allows them to take care of the instrumental concerns of the group, and at the same time maintain the flexibility necessary to adapt to changing internal and external circumstances. Even while they are being described here, ISOT changes.

ISOT also is affected by the wider social climate and America's perceptions of NRMs. Occasionally a deviant religious group will refocus the public eye on any new religion that is considered different enough to warrant attention. Deviant groups often exist because a leader is allowed inordinate power or because he or she claims a right to power in the name of God. But these groups are rare and simply granted excessive media exposure. The attention that is generated rarely results in an attempt to understand new religions better, but instead, is most often negative. Consequently, intentional religious communities everywhere feel the backlash. For example, when it was discovered that the Branch Davidians were compiling large quantities of arms in Waco, Texas, the public assumed that others may be doing the same thing. The members of ISOT felt that it was important to assure me that they do not collect firearms and are patriotic. Their support of the government may have made them hesitant to express what must have frightened them the most, the disregard for religious freedom resulting in the government's rationalization for killing innocent members of the Davidian group.

We should question whether we actually live in a political environment that is open to cultural diversity and, in this case, religious diversity. Pluralism in the form of alternative life-styles revitalizes culture and helps it change by offering new approaches to life. Therefore, diversity is not only healthy in a society, but it may be necessary for the successful adaptation to changing circumstances. The American public voices an acceptance of pluralism, and may even behave itself regarding those who are different depending on the economic and political climate at the time. Unfortunately, those who are different often are blamed if the economy or the social circumstances take a turn for the worse, a time when new ideas should be shared. It seems that people often would rather hold on to old assumptions and maintain the status quo even if it is dissatisfactory and no longer works. Change is frightening. But there will always be innovators such as the members of ISOT who experiment with the unfamiliar, creatively designing, at least for themselves, a more satisfying way of life.

## REFERENCES

Aidala, A. A. 1984. Worldviews, ideologies and social experimentation: Clarification and replication of "the Consciousness Reformation." *Journal for the Scientific Study of Religion* 23(1):44–59.

Anthony, D. & Robbins, T. 1982. Spiritual innovation and the crisis of American civil religion. *Daedalus* 111(1):215–234.

Bellah, R. 1975. *The Broken Covenant*. New York: Seabury.

Kanter, R. M. 1972. *Commitment and Community: Communes and Utopias in Sociological Perspective*. Cambridge: Harvard University Press.

Kilbourne, B. K. & Richardson, J. T. 1984. Psychotherapy and new religions in a pluralistic society. *American Psychologist* 39:237–251.

———1986. Cultphobia. *Thought* 61(241):258–266.

Richardson, J. T. 1979. From cult to sect: Creative eclecticism in new religious movements. *Pacific Sociological Review* 22(2):139–166.

———1986. Consumer protection and deviant religion: A case study. *Review of Religious Research* 28(2):168–179.

———1991. Cult/brainwashing cases and freedom of religion. *Journal of Church and State* 33(1):55–74.

Siegler, G. 1992. The Structure of Anti-Structure: The Development and Organization of a Religious Community in a Small Western Town. Ph.D. dissertation, Department of Anthropology, University of Nevada at Reno.

Wallace, A.F.C. 1956. Acculturation: revitalization movements. *American Anthropologist* 58:264–281.

Wallis, R. (ed). 1975. *Sectarianism*. New York: Halstead.

Wuthnow, R. 1985. The growth of religious and reform movements. *Annals of Political and Social Sciences* 480:106–116.

# 18

# Deaf American Culture: Notes from the Periphery

## Kathee M. Christensen

Deaf people in America comprise a unique and powerful cultural unit. They are unique because of a world view that is, by necessity, visual in nature. They are powerful because of a vehement refusal to allow the discrimination, the *audism* as it has been called, of hearing persons to limit and proscribe Deaf cultural identity. The majority of my life has involved the social, political, and linguistic facets of the Deaf community even though I, myself, am not audiologically deaf. *Deaf America* will be the term used to designate the cultural group of this chapter.

In reality, I thought that the whole world knew sign language. I did not realize that most people are sign language-impaired until I was five years old. My first home was situated in close proximity to the primary school and dormitory which housed the youngest Deaf children in the school. My first playmates were the children from the primary unit. All of them signed, some of them talked, and all of the adults that supervised them could do both. Since my mother taught in the high school, she knew and hired the brightest and most capable Deaf girls as my babysitters. From them, and from my bilingual parents, I learned to sign and talk at more or less the same time. This was useful, since I rarely knew in advance whether or not the guest walking through our door on any given day would sign or talk to me. It really didn't matter! My parents used sign language as naturally as they spoke English and switched back and forth from one language to the other as the occasion required. As soon as I could toddle down the hill to the primary dorm playground, I found instant playmates and an abundance of toys to share. Communication was never an issue. As I look back on this time in my life, it seems that the majority of the people who came into and went out of our house on Miller Road at the edge of the MSD campus used American Sign Language (ASL). However, it was not called ASL at that time. It was just sign language, qualified occasionally as the "kind of sign language that the Deaf teachers use in the manual unit" or the "kind of sign language that the kids use on the playground." The official christening of ASL was yet to happen, although the actual language was being used consistently by most of the deaf people in my immediate environment.

I encountered the prejudice of hearing people against deafness and Deaf people when I entered kindergarten in the local public school. For the first time in my life, I was surrounded by children and adults who knew only one language, English. It was amazing, even more amazing were the words of my teacher, "We don't use that deaf and dumb talk here!" "Why not?" was my immediate reaction. After all, in my world even Santa Claus could sign!

In looking back on my early years, I realize that I was probably more fortunate than many of my Deaf friends when it comes to the issue of communication. Practically from birth I had the benefit of two rich languages, both of which were used consistently in my home and social environment. As my circle of Deaf friends grew over the years, and I listened to more and more stories about their early experiences, I was struck by the early social deprivation that many of them endured. Approximately 90 percent of Deaf children in America are born to parents who are not Deaf. The majority of these children do not encounter signed language until they enter a formal educational program; and if the school does not subscribe to a bilingual American Sign Language and English philosophy, the quality of signed language may vary from barely comprehensible to meaningless. Why does this condition exist? Perhaps it is because educators consider deafness to be a "low incidence disability" rather than a cultural and linguistic difference.

The number of Deaf children enrolled in public school programs in the United States is relatively small. More than 90 percent of the persons who teach these children are hearing, European American women who have a cursory knowledge of signed language. So, a Deaf child who enrolls in a public school in America rarely finds a cultural role model behind the teacher's desk. Role models can be found, however, and the most likely place to find them is at the state residential, or center, school.

Each state has at least one residential school for children who are Deaf. These schools are organized into campuses with complete residential, medical, social, and educational facilities. A typical residential school will employ more deaf staff, in various occupations, than will a general education program, or day school. Over the years, the state residential schools have been regarded as the "hub" of the Deaf culture. These schools provide access to signed communication through recreational and social programs as well as in the academic setting. In recent years, some positive changes have been occurring in many residential school programs. Educators who are themselves Deaf are more visible in positions of leadership, and a movement toward bilingual education has been one result of this informed leadership. Another positive trend is the examination of the sign language skills of professional educators who work with Deaf children. This long overdue concern for early, salient communication access was fomented by a position paper which asserted that "current approaches to deaf education continue to pursue English-only and speech-dominant approaches...which expect the children to learn curricular material through communication in a form which they can understand only imperfectly at best" (Johnson et al. 1989:11). Classroom teachers who employed signed language frequently were perceived to use sign language inefficiently and elliptically, thus providing a fractured visual model of a partial language. The educational problems created by this lack of access to a complete, salient receptive language were apparent particularly in the reading and writing performance of Deaf learners. Moving the focus away from the child's performance and toward the inadequate language input in most classrooms is critical to the reform of modern educational practice. Many educators, aware of the growing body of ASL linguistic research, are beginning to understand that, as William Stokoe so aptly stated, "language is not mouth stuff—it's brain stuff" (Wolkomir 1992). Deaf leaders are beginning to encourage a paradigm shift away from a medical disability perspective and toward a cultural and linguistic view of deafness as manifested in Deaf Culture. Language is the real key to unlocking cultural understanding, and, in particular, American Sign Language is the key to Deaf American culture.

In my opinion, the American Sign Language (ASL) is quite possibly the most misunderstood language in present-day society. This is true despite the fact that ASL is the fourth most commonly used language in contemporary America and ASL is included as one of the recognized languages of the American Council on the Teaching of Foreign Language (ACTFL). In fact, ASL has existed formally in a variety of educational and social programs in America since the mid-nineteenth century, 1830 to be exact (Scouten 1984). Why the misunderstanding? There are several possible explanations.

First of all, ASL is used primarily by a group of people who, for the most part, look and act like native English users and may, in fact, qualify for that category. For the most part, members of the Deaf American Culture do not come from a different country. And, with the possible exception of Martha's Vineyard in the 1800s where, due to the overwhelming presence of hereditary deafness, almost everyone was bilingual in English and ASL (Groce 1985), culturally Deaf people do not lay claim to any particular expanse of land.

ASL users are Deaf and hearing persons, most of whom are bilingual and many of whom have acquired English as a second language. People unfamiliar with Deaf culture typically observe ASL from the familiar vantage point of spoken standard English with its concomitant body of written literature. The non-ASL user may have a medical perspective of deafness as a disability rather than a language difference, and may not perceive signed languages as equal to spoken languages. Non-ASL users may be introduced to signed communication in a situation such as a theatrical performance or lecture where an ASL interpreter voices English in order to translate ASL to the entire audience. Or it could be that a non-ASL user has witnessed a hearing person who speaks English and simultaneously produces signed equivalents so that both hearing and Deaf persons can receive the same input. In simultaneous communication, signs are borrowed from ASL and placed within a spoken English format as a way of accommodating communication between English speakers and ASL signers. ASL users have learned to adapt to English, however, ASL is *not* a form of English. ASL is a visual-spatial language with its own syntax, semantics, and pragmatics and a unique literary tradition (Klima & Bellugi 1979).

Unless one has lived or grown up in the Deaf community, it may be difficult to understand the visual-spatial dimensions of this culture. Baker & Cokley (1980) proposed a model of Deaf culture that involves four essential factors:

1. audiological—one must have a hearing loss of some degree;
2. social—one must associate with Deaf people socially, e.g., go to Deaf clubs, attend a residential school for the deaf, marry a Deaf person;
3. political—serve as an officer of a Deaf organization such as the National Association of the Deaf (NAD) or one of its affiliates, or wield power in the Deaf community;
4. linguistic—ASL fluency—this is the most important factor.

According to Baker & Cokley, overarching these factors is ATTITUDE. A person with a positive attitude and involvement with at least three of the four factors listed above can be considered as a member of the Deaf culture. Therefore, hearing persons, for example hearing children of Deaf parents, may identify with Deaf culture more comfortably than the so-called "hearing" culture, or they may perceive themselves bicultural. Cultural identity is a personal choice and not an imposition.

Padden and Humphries (1988) offer another definition of Deaf culture. They assert that "people who are Deaf can have a range of hearing abilities from 'hard of hearing' to 'profoundly deaf,' and, conversely, there are people with severe or profound hearing impairment who do not participate in the community of Deaf people." They have suggested that "we use lowercase *deaf* when referring to the audiological condition of not hearing, and the uppercase *Deaf* when referring to a particular group of deaf people who share a language—American Sign Language— and a culture" (1988:2).

Padden and Humphries further point out that ASL users have the opportunity to perceive communication from a unique cultural center. ASL users construct their worlds and choose their words from a center that takes complete advantage of the communicative resources of movement, form, facial expressions, and a unique application of sound. ASL user s broaden their understanding of communication through the use of a variety of dynamic components. This open-mindedness to multiple facets of communication may be an advantage that allows culturally Deaf persons to deal more effectively with the diversity in our increasingly multicultural contemporary society. Since Deaf people, as a rule, are accustomed to encountering language barriers as a natural part of everyday life, they become proficient at negotiating communication, through various means including writing, miming, gesturing, speech reading, and other creative options, with persons who are able to use only spoken language. For Deaf people, easy, accessible communication on a daily basis is not taken for granted.

It is difficult for many hearing individuals to consider the possibility of someone communicating solely through a spatial medium. Those who have acquired ASL as a first language and those who have achieved fluency through study and use of the language have a different perspective. If asked to describe the differences between the two languages, the ASL-second language user might identify the task of translating an English idiom into a visual-spatial equivalent, or vice versa. The concept may "suffer in the translation," as is often the case with translation from one spoken language to another. The process of ASL acquisition and use is a fairly recent topic of academic research. Pioneers in the field include William Stokoe at Gallaudet University and Ursula Bellugi at the Salk Institute. Their work has brought signed language into the forefront of innovative linguistic research and has helped to solidify, popularize, and provide academic credibility to the term ASL.

It is interesting to trace the evolution of the terminology used for Deaf language. For example, "sign language" became "Ameslan" (Fant 1972 ) and "Ameslan," ultimately, became "American Sign Language" or "ASL" (Klima & Bellugi 1979). At the turn of the century, persons who could not hear were referred to as "deaf." In the 1970's the terms "deaf and hard-of-hearing" were replaced by a generic term "hearing-impaired." In the late 1980s, the distinction was made between culturally "Deaf" individuals and medically "deaf and hard-of-hearing" persons. Gates (1994) has made the observation that the "linguistic trend toward condensation is strong," that is, we tend to economize our language, over time. Telephone becomes phone, television becomes TV, bicycle becomes bike and so forth. In his book entitled *Colored People*, Gates even predicts that the African American community will eventually give up terms such as "people of color" and will once again revert to the term of choice of the 1950s, colored people." If the rule of condensation can be applied to all cultures, one might predict the eventual and exclusive use of the single word "Deaf" to describe, in general, persons in the Deaf American community.

The extent to which the brain uses signed language to enhance communication and cognitive development is the subject of some innovative current research. The work of Bellugi and other linguists at the Salk Institute in San Diego has provided insights into the acquisition and use of visual-spatial languages as they are passed from one generation to the next. Their research has shed some new light on the determinants of hemispheric specialization for language, suggesting that "the left hemisphere in humans may have an innate predisposition for language, regardless of the modality" (Belllugi 1991:32). Interesting new research at the University of California—Davis is considering the potential of signed language as a means of enhancing the cognitive development of babies who have intact hearing ability. Quite possibly this work will parallel the research of Pettito (1994), which studies the equipotentiality of signed and spoken languages in infants and toddlers, both Deaf and hearing. There is  much to be learned from these and other studies, and from members of the Deaf community who inform these research projects.

Inherent in Deaf culture, and an enhancement to the study of ASL and ASL literature, are the visual arts. The metaphor that guides one gifted ASL storyteller is his ability to "paint poetry in the air" (Bragg 1994). Those fortunate enough to see such a performance, and to understand it without translation, experience a vibrant combination of literature, art, and theater in a truly  unique dimension. Hearing ASL users often describe such an experience, say a production of the National Theater of the Deaf, as less dynamic with the presence of a voice interpreter who laboriously gives spoken words to a visual act that communicates eloquently through hands, face, and body to the eyes and minds of the audience in a language designed to be seen and not heard. In some cases, hearing ASL users learn to "turn off their hearing" in order to appreciate more fully the signed experience. Deaf West Theater in Los Angeles provides a wonderful service to hearing theater-goers who can listen to voice interpreters through earphones, thus allowing a visual theatrical experience for those who prefer to watch undisturbed by vocal translations.

Society, in general, is becoming more aware of Deaf culture through a number of opportunities that are available now. Linda Bove, a Deaf actress, is a resident on Sesame Street; Marlee Matlin, an award-winning Deaf actress, appears quite regularly on television and in film, Miss America 1994–1995 was the Deaf dancer, Heather Whitestone; and more and more televised commercials include persons who use signed language. Schools and universities around the United States have begun to offer American Sign Language as an alternative for "foreign" language requirements. Hearing authors such as Harlan Lane (1992) and Oliver Sacks (1989) have described Deaf culture and the Deaf community in popular books. In *Seeing Voices,* for example, Sacks uses the Deaf community as a springboard to ponder such issues as formation of communities, worlds, and cultures and the interface of language, biology, and culture. As exposure of Deaf American culture grows across the nation, Deaf people are becoming more visible and recognized for their talents.

As I reflect on my personal experience as a marginal member of the Deaf culture, I realize that I can never know what it is like to be physically Deaf. I can view Deaf culture only from the periphery, with profound respect for the persons who must encounter discrimination in practically every aspect of life. In this regard, Deaf American culture can be compared to other American cultural groups who also have endured discrimination and suppression by an insensitive majority. Langston Hughes, the acclaimed African-American poet of the Harlem Renaissance, speaks eloquently to this point. In "Note on Commercial Theater" he laments that "You've taken my blues and gone." Replace the word *blues* with the word *signs* and you have the situation of an attempt to destroy ASL through the creation of artificial sign systems. In the poem "Note," he alludes to the spirit of survival—"Tomorrow belongs to me"—which was so evident in the Deaf President Now revolt at Gallaudet University in 1988. In both cases, the oppression of a dominant culture is evident through an attempt of the majority culture to limit opportunities and suppress self-expression. Deaf people are the experts in defining and constructing their own cultural experience—in identifying themselves and describing their journey. For years, for generations, the control of the Deaf community has been in the inept hands of hearing educators and members of the medical community. For years, for generations, Deaf people have been limited by obstacles that hearing people create. Rather than noticing the connections between their cultures, Deaf and hearing persons often shut themselves off from one another, avoiding the effort, or risk, of honest two-way communication. In fact, the ability to share one's culture with another is a precious, personal gift. We are beginning gradually to see the benefits of more cross-cultural communication among Deaf and hearing people, particularly in settings where very young Deaf and hearing children are learning to communicate with each other through visual-spatial means. The notion that these children will grow up with a positive attitude toward cultural and linguistic diversity, a healthy respect for more visual-spatial communication, and greater opportunities for cross-cultural understanding is, at this point, a dream. And, as

Langston Hughes wrote, "This dream today embattled, With its back against the wall—To save the dream for one—It must be saved for all."

## REFERENCES

Baker, C. & Cokley, D. 1980. *American Sign Language: A Teacher's Resource Text on Grammar and Culture.* Silver Spring, MD: T. J. Publishers.

Bellugi, U. 1991. The link between the hand and brain: Implications from a visual language. In *Advances in Cognition, Education, and Deafness.* D. Martin (ed). Washington, DC: Gallaudet University Press.

Berry, F. (ed). 1992. *Good Morning Revolution: Uncollected Writings of Social Protest by Langston Hughes.* New York: Citadel Press.

Bragg, B. 1994. *Meeting Halfway in American Sign Language: A Common Ground for Effective Communication Among Deaf and Hearing People.* Rochester, NY: Deaf Life Press.

Fant, L. 1972. *Ameslan: An Introduction to American Sign Language.* Northridge, CA: Joyce Motion Picture Co.

Gates, H. 1994. *Colored People: A Memoir.* New York: Knopf.

Groce, N. 1985. *Everyone Here Spoke Sign Language: Hereditary Deafness on Martha's Vineyard.* Cambridge: Harvard University Press.

Johnson, R., Liddell, S., & Erting, C. 1989. *Unlocking the Curriculum: Principles for Achieving Access in Deaf Education.* Washington, DC: Gallaudet Research Institute.

Klima, E. & Bellugi, U. 1979. *The Signs of Language.* Cambridge: Harvard University Press.

Lane, H. 1992. *The Mask of Benevolence: Disabling the Deaf Community.* New York: Knopf.

Padden, C. & Humphries, T. 1988. *Deaf in America: Voices from a Culture.* Cambridge: Harvard University Press.

Pettito, L. 1994. On the equipotentiality of signed and spoken language in early language ontogeny. In. *Post Milan: ASL & English literacy.* B. Snider (ed). Washington, DC: Gallaudet University Press.

Sacks, O. 1989. *Seeing Voices: A Journey Into the World of the Deaf.* Berkeley: University of California Press.

Scouten, E. 1984. *Turning Points in the Education of Deaf People.* Danville, IL: Interstate Printers & Publishers.

Wolkomir, R. 1992. The quiet revolution in 'hand talk.' *Smithsonian* 23:30–42.

# 19

# Business and Organizational Culture

## Ann T. Jordan

Business and occupational culture represent special interest cultural groupings. Business culture usually is called "organizational culture" or "corporate culture." Organizational culture is the study of an organization as if it were a culture in order to understand better the behavior in the organization. In anthropology the approach to organizational culture is focused on the use of the construct "culture" and ethnographic methods to analyze human behavior in complex organizations. Here the anthropologist studies both for-profit organizations such as General Motors as well as non-profit organizations such as the Red Cross. It also includes government organizations at the local, state and federal levels. It includes organizations of any size, from large corporations like Toyota to small family-owned businesses like your local veterinary clinic. In short, any business can be studied as a special interest cultural grouping.

Occupational culture is a related field of study. It refers to the study of single occupations as cultures. For example, one might study the culture of physicians, the culture of engineers, or the culture of college students. Typically there are several occupational cultural groupings represented in the organizational culture of any business, and thus the anthropologist attempting to study the organizational culture must understand the relevant occupational cultures as well. Specific examples of occupational cultures are described somewhat in the chapters on professional culture groupings (e.g., social services and medical professions) located elsewhere in this volume.

## THE DEFINING CHARACTERISTIC OF BUSINESS CULTURE: DIVERSITY

Organizational cultures represent very complex special interest groups. The first reason for this is that the work force is very diverse. In the United States, business organizations that employ only U.S. residents exemplify a great deal of work-force diversity, and if the organization is multinational and has any non-U.S. branches, its diversity is greatly magnified. The cultural makeup of the U. S. work force is a reflection of the cultural makeup of the United States.

In the 1980s the U.S. Department of Labor commissioned the Hudson Institute to study of the work force of the twenty-first century (1987). In its report, the Institute made some predictions about the demographic composition of the U.S. population and work force until the year 2000. It predicted that of the 25 million people who will enter the workplace between 1985 and 2000, 85 percent will be minorities and women. This means that of this predicted net new work force through the year 2000, only 15 percent will be native white men;  42 percent of the net new work force will be native white women, 13 percent will be native nonwhite women, 7 percent native nonwhite men, 9 percent will be immigrant women, and 13 percent immigrant men (Morrison 1992:14). By the year 2000, the Hispanic and Asian populations each will grow by 48 percent, the black population will grow by 28 percent, and the white population will grow by only 5.6 percent. The Institute further predicted that sometime in the next century, non-Hispanic whites no longer will retain their majority status in the United States (Kogad 1994:28). By the year 2050, one-half of the country's population will be African American, Hispanic American, Native American, and Asian American. In addition, 500,000 immigrants arrive in the United States legally every year. The United States, which has only 5 percent of the world's population, takes in almost 50 percent of the world's migrants, excluding refugees (Fernandez 1991:5).

So if one wished to describe the special interest grouping of business culture, one would have to describe the culture of the entire U.S. population. Diversity is the most prominent characteristic of business culture. Most important within that diversity is gender and ethnic diversity as described above. However, as a reflection of the diversity of the U. S. culture, work-force diversity includes almost all other cultural groupings found in the United States. It includes sexual life-style grouping political groupings, and religious groupings, for example. Another significant aspect of diversity in the workplace is region. Workers from different geographical regions of the United States represent cultural groupings. For example, workers from the southern states may have different behavior patterns than ones from the Northeast or from the West. A manager from New York who is moved by his corporation to a manager position in Georgia may have difficulty with co-workers due to the difference in regional cultural beliefs and behaviors.

One set of workplace groupings that is not reflective of the general population are the age groupings. Child labor laws prevent individuals younger than 16 from working, and many individuals retire from the work force at age 65. Consequently, while age differences are significant in studying business culture, the age range is narrower than in the population as a whole.

Furthermore, if the business organization one is studying has multinational branches, the diversity becomes all that much greater. Some of the largest U.S. companies derive more than 35 percent of their revenues from their overseas operations. Eighty percent of industry of the United States faces international competition, according to the National Foreign Trade Council. In the United States there are more than 25,000 companies with overseas branche and affiliates, 3,500 multinational corporations, 30,000 exporting manufacturers, and over 40,000 firms operating abroad on an ad-hoc basis. The Commerce Department reports that foreign investors spent more than $10 billion to gain entry or control in U.S. firms (Harris & Moran 1987:14, 25). Consequently, a characteristic of the special interest cultural grouping of business culture is that its diversity includes diverse cultures all over the world. U.S. businesses are part of a global marketplace. U. S. residents are likely to work for companies that have offices in Hong Kong, Munich, and Cairo. In such situations, the company must adjust its business practices to the culture of the foreign location, and the U.S. residents who are employees also must adjust. In addition, many U. S. citizens working in the United States work for foreign-owned companies in their American branch or subsidiary. For those workers, while they work on home soil, they must adjust to a set of culturally different business practices. A leading industrial statesman in Japan remarked that the approaches and operations of U.S. and Japanese companies are 95 percent alike but that it is the 5 percent difference that really matters (Harris & Moran 1987:x). To understand business culture, one must understand the relevant national cultures.

In addition to this extreme degree of diversity, there is a second reason why business organizations undertake such complex units of study. They typically are structurally further divided into many subunits. For example, if one looks at the organization chart of a company that sells computer equipment and has 200 employees and two stores, one finds many different organizational subunits. One finds managers, sales personnel, cashiers, stockroom employees, and so on. Each of these groups represents a different subcultural grouping that is part of the culture of the organization in addition to the gender, ethnic, and regional cultural groupings mentioned above.

## UNDERSTANDING CULTURE IN BUSINESS ORGANIZATIONS

How does an anthropologist understand a business organization as a culture? How does the anthropologist deal with all of this diversity? The anthropologist's understanding is based on the traditional anthropological construct of culture described earlier in Chapter 1. Organizational culture is an integrated system of shared ideas (thoughts, ideals, attitudes), behaviors (actions), and material artifacts (objects) that are characteristic of an organization. Using ABC Computer as an example, a shared idea that is part of the organizational culture might be the stated goal of one million dollars in sales for the next fiscal year, or it might be the sentiment on the poster in the stockroom that reads "The customer is always right." Examples of shared behaviors might be the dress code that requires all employees wear the company shirt or the rule that employees are expected to arrive 30 minutes prior to the stated time of their floor shift. Shared material artifacts would include the two store buildings and all objects in them. Frequently when one considers all of the beliefs, behaviors, and artifacts, one finds some contradictions that lead to employee confusion. For example, company owners at ABC Computer may state that they put their employees first (a belief), but never actually meet the employees (behavior) and provide no employee break room (material artifact). The employees experience a contradictory situation and are likely to suspect that the owners who never meet them and do not consider their needs for a break room do not really put employees first. One of the tasks of the anthropologist is to sort out all of the conflicting cultural messages.

So, the organization is seen *as* a culture, and all of the components of the organization, its organization structure, reward system, rules of behavior, and goals, are components of the culture. An organization is a web of interacting cultures. Not only does the organization as a whole have a culture, but each department may as well. There are also likely to be cultures that cross-cut the organization, like a sales culture or a secretarial culture. In addition, individuals are members of national, ethnic, regional, gender, and perhaps even professional cultures outside of the organization, which contributes to the greater cultural picture. Consequently, from the anthropological perspective, the organization is a web of interacting cultural groupings. Using the computer company mentioned above as an example, we can describe some of the cultural groupings that it might included. The company, ABC Computer, has an organizational culture of its own. It is also a subculture within the business and U.S. cultures. Within ABC Computer there are nested subcultures such as computer sales representatives. Further, there is even a cross-cutting of African-American culture and European American cultures.

It is important to understand how the individual fits into this web of overlapping and interconnected cultural groupings. The actual individual is a member of several different cultural groupings. Sam Hanover, a computer sales manager at ABC Computer, for example, might be part of the ethnic grouping of African-Americans and the gender grouping of males, as well as two occupational groupings, managers and salesmen, respectively, and the organizational grouping of ABC Computer. His cultural behavior at ABC is determined by all of those groupings. He might at one point behave in a manner consistent with the norms of the computer salesman cultural grouping and at another point in a manner consistent with the norms of the African-American cultural grouping.

While all individuals are part of cultural groupings and behave to some extent in accordance with the norms of their cultural group, their individual behavior is still important. It is a characteristic of human beings that they exhibit free will, and no human is "programmed" by their culture. From an anthropological perspective, however, *the individual is actually understood in terms of his/her group behavior.* Individual behavior either conforms to or deviates from the accepted norms, and much individual behavior can be understood as the simple acting out of cultural norms or, in some cases, as the acting out of the ambiguity of cultural norms. The anthropological focus is on patterned group behavior rather than individual behavior. Individual behavior that is not understandable in terms of the group pattern is considered *idiosyncratic* and outside the scope of culture. Consequently, much of the study of individual behavior would not be subsumed under "culture " but instead represents the study of idiosyncratic behavior. An example of work that

Table 19.1
Universal Components of Culture and Organizational Culture

| Culture | Organizational Culture |
|---|---|
| Patterns of subsistence | Type of technology <br> Division of labor |
| Religion and magic | Values, goals, ceremonies, myths, assumptions |
| Economic system | Reward system |
| Political system | Organizational structure <br> Leadership behavior <br> Power and politics <br> Conflict management |
| Language and communication | Communication |
| Social Structure | Group formation other than formal organizational structure |
| Art | Organizational artifacts: Dress, building type, logos |

*Source*: Jordan 1995:133

represents the study of idiosyncratic behavior is that which explains what motivates individuals or describes personality types in the workplace. This work usually is conducted by psychologists. This is not to say that understanding culture does not contribute to understanding motivation and personality. Motivation factors often reflect cultural assumptions and cannot be understood outside of those. Personality traits (or the construction of these traits by psychologists) commonly are influenced by cultural norms and cannot be understood outside of those norms. To the extent that motivation factors are common to a cultural grouping, they are cultural. Cultural norms often include assumptions about motivation. For instance, in a social service agency, the opportunity to help others is a culturally accepted motivation for performing work, while in a for-profit corporation the opportunity to earn large sums of money is traditionally a more culturally accepted motivation for performing work.

The "holism" of the culture from the anthropological perspective is quite important in studying business organizational culture. Anthropologically, every group pattern is part of culture. This can be demonstrated by comparing cultural universals with a list of important characteristics of an organization. A long-held view in anthropology is that every human culture includes a set of universal components: subsistence patterns, religion, an economic system, a political system, a language, social structure, and art. These universal components of culture are listed in Table 19.1. On the right side is a list of important aspects of a business organization. Anthropologically, each one of these organizational topics is part of the cultural whole. The reward systems, for example, cannot be separated from organizational culture. Such systems are in fact but one set of ideas and behaviors that contribute to and are integrated with all of the other aspects of the culture. Anthropologists would study them as part of the culture's economic system. The organization chart would provide information about the political system as the organizational structure would describe the political structure of the organization, which again is part of the whole culture. All of these cultural universals represent components that are related and continually interact. Much of this interaction is well documented in organization studies. For example, a political structure (organization structure) of hierarchical bureaucracy needs to fit the subsistence pattern (type of technology) of a slowly changing marketplace. The strength of the anthropological concept of culture is that it views all of these components as parts of the cultural whole and therefore interrelated.

Referring to Table 19.1 again, most of the perceptions and behaviors typically associated with "culture" in the corporate cultural perspective found in the popular press can be equated with a universal component of magic and religion. That is the component which includes values and beliefs and their accompanying ceremonies and myths. For the anthropologist, this is just one component of culture, not culture in its entirety. The anthropologist sees the "culture" as including *all* of these ideas, behaviors, and artifacts. Thus the subsistence function of an organization such as automobile assembly or software development, support systems such as accounting and marketing, the organization structure, and even the management process are all components of any organizational culture. One looks for "culture" in every group within the organization as a whole. This is the holistic and integrated characteristic of culture.

## THE VALUE OF VIEWING ORGANIZATIONS AS CULTURES

One might wonder whether organizational culture as described here is an appropriate use of the anthropological concept "culture." After all, the accustomed patterns of behavior and beliefs shared by workers in one company do not constitute "a culture" in the same way that the people of the Trobriand Islands had "a culture." To use the construct "culture" for studying groupings in a business may be inaccurate and dilute its value. Such a view is in one sense correct. In the traditional anthropological sense, these patterns may not constitute a culture because they do not result from primary enculturation. There is clearly a difference, for example, between the "culture" of the Trobrianders and the "culture" of General Motors. In an organization, the patterns of behavior and beliefs result from a secondary enculturation process, one that begins at the time of an individual's employment. Formal training programs, asides from more seasoned employees, observations regarding rewarded and punished behavior, and a host of other elements contribute to the enculturation that makes an individual a member of the organization's culture. In addition, the new employees are already members of more traditionally defined cultures resulting from enculturation from birth. If one assumes that an organization has a culture, then it follows that any voluntary association, gender grouping, and a host of other structures have culture. It is difficult to see how one could actually understand cultural behavior if a single individual can belong to so many cultural groups and if culture is so easy to acquire. On the other hand, the construct "culture" is a powerful tool to use in understanding human behavior in organizations. It does indeed fill in some gaps and provide some understanding of behavior that other ways of looking at organizations might miss. For the way in which most anthropologists study culture in organizational settings, the comments of John Bennett are appropriate. As an anthropologist, one is "an expert on the patterned aspects of group behavior" (1954:171). One is doing what James Clifford suggests that "fieldworkers have always done, building up social wholes ('culture' in the American tradition) through a concentration on significant elements" (Clifford 1989:63).

## UNDERSTANDING DIVERSITY IN ORGANIZATIONS

When it comes to understanding diversity in organizations, the anthropological perspective can help organizational members understand and appreciate the complexity of organizational diversity (Jordan 1994). As already was explained, each circle nested within the larger organization oval potentially represents a subculture within the organization, defined by department or role (manager, staff, etc.), while the cross-cutting ovals represent cultures identified by ethnicity, nationality, gender, and so on. The anthropologist uses the culture concept and ethnographic methods to learn to understand each culture well enough to broker between diverse cultures and subcultures, pointing out areas of misunderstanding and areas in which the members of the culture are confusing cultural behavior with natural behaviors. These areas for misunderstanding can as easily include the subcultures' embedded ideas about reward systems or division of labor as the more commonly ascribed values and beliefs.

So, this concept of culture is the basis for the anthropological approach to understanding diversity. To understand workplace diversity one must translate between cultures. One barrier is that humans characteristically mistake their own cultural behavior for natural, panhuman behavior. For example, feelings of affection are typical of all humans; they are panhuman. The manner in which affection is expressed, however, is cultural. The kiss is not universally accepted as a symbol of affection; some societies consider it suggestive of cannibalism. To give another example, in the United States eating three meals a day with no snacks is considered to be the correct, healthy way to give the body nourishment. Few non-western societies adhere to such an eating schedule. Many adhere to no schedules of any kind since clock time is cultural time and is not applicable in their culture. The U.S. eating schedule is a cultural definition of healthy eating, not a natural one.

Thus each society views its own culturally sanctioned behaviors as "natural." Our culturally diverse society and multinational corporations afford American managers many opportunities to view their own behavior as natural rather than cultural, and to misunderstand other cultural groups in the workplace. American corporations with interests overseas recognize the importance of undestanding foreign cultures but insist on doing things the American way even when on foreign soil. In the United States, problems with race relations in the workplace are seen anthropologically as a problem in understanding diversity, where each cultural group views their own behavior as natural and therefore correct. One of the tasks of the anthropologist is to act as a culture broker and explain how each set of views is "cultural."

Crucial to an anthropological understanding of managing cultural diversity is the process of culture borrowing. The integrated nature of cultures creates an interesting situation when two cultures interact and borrow from each other. Frequently, when one culture borrows from another, it extracts a trait from a cultural pattern to borrow, but it does not borrow the entire pattern. The reason for this is that the entire pattern does not fit into the recipient culture's patterns. For example, when Europeans first arrived on the North American continent, they were amazed by the ways of the aboriginal tribes they encountered. While most of what they witnessed was not understandable to them and of little use in their own lives, they did borrow some of the culture traits they observed. Tobacco is a well-known example. Sir Walter Raleigh recognized the usefulness of tobacco, transported it back to England, and the tobacco industry as we now know it was born. The Europeans borrowed a single cultural artifact, tobacco, from American Indians, but they did not borrow the complex of culture traits that accompanied the use of tobacco. For American Indians tobacco was sacred and used in religious contexts. Since this religious pattern did not fit into the European cultural patterns, it was not borrowed. Cultures form a complex whole of interrelated traits and a borrowed trait must be adapted to fit into the existing integrated pattern of the borrower. Any behavior characteristics surrounding this trait that do not fit the new cultural pattern will be left behind. The culture borrowing process is useful in translating between cultures and subcultures in an organization and learning to understand diversity in the workplace. Consider the following two examples.

Lee Baker (1995) has studied forms of address in the workplace. The traditional African-American form of address used within structured settings such as church, office, or school is anthropologically identified as *title + name reciprocity*. This means that an individual would greet another by title and last name, and the other individual would respond in the same manner.

Staff 1: Hello, May I please speak with Mr. Foley?
Staff 1: It's Ms. Johnson.
Staff 1: Mr. Foley, it's Ms. Johnson in Admissions. I would like to know...(Baker 1995:191).

The general impetus for this particular form of address is respect and deference, not demarcating social hierarchies, which is the pattern associated with the European American use of the title and name form of address. On the other hand, European Americans frequently use *first name reciprocity* as the preferred form of address in organizations. One reason for this is to give the impression of equality, even if it is not a conversation between organizational equals.

Manager: Billy, how's the monthly plan coming?  We need it tomorrow.
Assistant Manager: Rick, you know I'll have it (Baker 1995:190).

In each case the speakers consider their form of address to be the most "natural." They do not consider that in each case the difference is "cultural," representing a cultural difference between European Americans and African-Americans. This allows for misinterpretation when an individual uses his own cultural form of address with members of the other cultural groupings. It is the avowed role of the anthropologist as culture broker to explain this difference and, by doing so, to prevent misunderstanding.

Tomoko Hamada (1995) has studied the cultural misunderstandings involved in a sexual harassment charge brought by a female European American worker against her Japanese manager in a Japanese-owned factory located in the United States. One of the acts of sexual harassment the female European American worker cited was gift-giving. Her manager had given her several gifts such as bottles of liquor. The Japanese manager explained, however, that it is a Japanese custom to give gifts to good employees, and that he gave gifts to several employees as recognition for their good work.  Just as in the case of African-American and European American forms of address, individuals take a course of action based on certain cultural assumptions. Others of a different cultural background act according to a different set of cultural assumptions. In the sexual harassment example, actions were misinterpreted as a result.The Japanese manager gave gifts (an action) with the Japanese cultural assumption that this action would be understood as a sign that he recognized good work. The European American female worker was unaware of this Japanese cultural meaning and instead assumed a female European American one, namely, that the manager was interested in sexual favors. The anthropologist, again, can act as culture broker and sort out the misunderstandings that occur across cultural groupings.

## CONCLUSIONS

Business and occupational cultures represent special interest culture groups that contribute to the cultural diversity of the United States. Business culture usually is called "organizational culture" or "corporate culture." Organizational culture is the study of an organization as if it were a culture in order to understand better behavior in the organization. Organizational cultures represent very complex special interest groups. The first reason for this is that the work force is very diverse. The cultural makeup of the work force in the United States is a reflection of the cultural makeup of the United States as a whole. In addition, the United States is part of a global marketplace and many business organizations are multinational. The second reason why organizational cultures represent very complex special interest groups is that organizations are structurally divided into many subunits.

Organizational culture has been defined as an integrated system of shared ideas (thoughts, ideals, attitudes), behaviors (actions), and material artifacts (objects) that are characteristic of an organization. Not only does the organization as a whole have a culture, but it also consists of an intricate web of interacting cultural groupings representing many ethnic, regional, gender, occupational, and other special interest groups. The task of the anthropologist in understanding organizational culture is to act as culture broker and assist the diverse cultural groupings in the organization in understanding what behavior is cultural for each grouping and what behavior is natural to all humans.

## REFERENCES

Baker, L. D. 1995.  Racism in Professional Settings: Forms of Address as Clues to Power Relations. *Journal of Applied Behavioral Science* 31(2):186–201.

Bennett, J. 1954. Interdisciplinary Research and the Concept of Culture. *American Anthropologist* 56:169–179.

Clifford, J. 1988. *The Predicament of Culture: Twentieth Century Ethnography and Art.* Cambridge: Harvard University Press.

Fernandez, J. 1991. *Managing a Diverse Work Force.* Lexington, MA: Lexington Books.

Hamada, T. 1995. Inventing cultural others in organizations: A case of anthropological reflexivity in a multinational firm. *Journal of Applied Behavioral Science* 31(2):162–185.

Harris, P. & Moran, R. T. 1987. *Managing Cultural Difference.* Houston: Gulf Publishing Company.

Hudson Institute. 1987. *Workforce 2000: Work and Workers for the Twenty-First Century.* Indianapolis: Hudson Institute.

Jordan, A. T. 1994. *Practicing Anthropology in Corporate America: Consulting on Organizational Culture.* NAPA Bulletin 14. Washington, DC: American Anthropological Association.

————1995. Managing diversity: Translating anthropological insight for organizational studies. *Applied Behavior Science* 31–140.

Kogod, K. 1994. The bridges process: Enhancing organizational cultures to support diversity. In *Practicing Anthropology in Corporate America: Consulting on Organizational Culture.* A. T. Jordan (ed). NAPA Bulletin 14. Washington, DC: American Anthropological Association.

Morrison, A. M. 1992. *The New Leaders.* San Francisco: Jossey-Bass.

# PART V

## Dealing with Cultural Diversity

No volume on diversity would be complete without offering up some considerations and practical suggestions for those people who will live, work, or play in contexts of diversity. Although none of the authors would suggest that they have all of the answers to all of the particular problems or difficulties generated by diversity in any context, they do attempt to convey some of the lessons and insights born of their experiences. The few presented here are hardly indicative of all of the contexts one might find themselves in, but the considerations, issues, and aspects are going to be similar. Again, as with other sections, some selection has been made based on the significance of particular contexts to social debates currently going on and where diversity presents some particular and glaring problems (e.g., in health care and aging, in areas of social services, and in education).

Throughout the first four sections of this volume, the reader was periodically exposed to at least some basic things to consider when interacting with people representing different racial, ethnic, and special interests groups as the authors directed their primary attention to conveying some of the problems of generalization and some basic knowledge concerning specific cultural groupings. Chapter authors of this last section are specifically concerned with some practical suggestions and considerations which operationalize that knowledge as people go about working or simply living in contexts of diversity. In Chapter 20, Deborah Reed-Danahay delves into cultural diversity and the health-care system, focusing her discussion around the nursing home and the aging population of America. She points out that the care giver is frequently from a very different cultural background than that of the patients with whom they work. To eliminate or minimize some of the misunderstandings, miscommunications, and mistrust that can characterize such interactions in health care, people need to be aware of this possibility and the implications of this to the quality of health care that can be provided. In Chapter 21, Richard Enos looks at social work practices with ethnic and minority persons, and strongly proposes that understanding some of the cultural specific values of the diverse groups in America is indispensable for the professional social worker who wants to deliver more ethnically and culturally sensitive serv ices. The author also provides us with some suggested techniques for enhancing the effectiveness of social workers in managing cultural values that so often lie at the heart of a successful or an unsuccessful interaction between people representing different cultures. Stanton W. Green and Stephen M. Perlman look at diversity in the context of American education in Chapter 22. In nearly every discussion of how to address the problems of cultural diversity, education has been proposed as part of the solution. The authors of this chapter discuss the problem of balancing a diversity of behavior with a solidified American culture—the stated goal of the educational system. They conclude that a better understanding of the diversity of America will help us come to grips with the role of education in American society, and that moving beyond mere token appreciation of American diversity is the way to deal with diversity in a dynamic, multifaceted, and changing American culture.

In Chapter 23, Gloria Contreras sums up the practical considerations for living and working in contexts of diversity. Contreras brings to the attention of the reader the various controversies surrounding diversity that are being hotly debated in the America today. The author rejects the ideas of "color blindness" and the rejection of differences that came from the 1970s that remain widely popular in the country today. She argues that such ideas go directly counter to what diversity means and how one must deal with the problems generated by it. The author suggests a strategy of tolerance and the acquistion of better interactional skills. The main ingredient of successful interaction (skill) is not going to come from an individual perspective but when individuals see things from the point of view of others. Although the author concludes that there is an increasing move to recognize cultural differences, and because in the future there will be even more such differences, the goal for us must be to capture it and define it better than we have up to this point.

# 20

# Cultural Diversity and Health Care: The Nursing Home

## Deborah Reed-Danahay

Cultural diversity in the health-care system touches the lives of many Americans in one way or another. No matter what our own cultural background is, when we go to receive medical care, we may encounter a care giver who comes from a different cultural background than ours.This can lead to cultural misunderstanding, mistrust, and miscommunication. The problems of "cultural discontinuity" long have been recognized as important in the ethnographic study of schooling (Ogbu 1982; Macias 1987; Reed-Danahay & Anderson-Levitt 1991), but only recently have begun to be noticed in the ethnography of long-term, institutionalized care of the elderly in nursing homes. In the field of anthropology and education, it has been documented that when teachers and students fail to share the same culture, there can be problems in learning, and that when teachers become sensitive to the cultural backgrounds of students, many communication obstacles can be overcome (Heath 1983). In this chapter, I will apply that insight to the study of nursing homes and focus on issues of cultural diversity that arise in such settings. I will explore the factors of ethnic and racial diversity among patients and staff, and pose questions about the role that cultural discontinuity or homogeneity plays in the quality of care that the elderly receive in nursing homes. After presenting some cases drawn from the ethnographic literature on nursing homes, I will discuss the particular case of Rosewood, where I conducted research on nursing assistant work culture in a unit devoted to the care of Alzheimer's patients under a grant from the National Institute on Aging for NIA Collaborative Studies (Special Care Units for Alzheimer's Disease) and two other grants from the NIA.

Old people in American society are viewed as "different" and "deviant" from younger adults, and often are isolated from mainstream society. Care givers in nursing homes are, in the vast majority of cases, much younger than their elderly patients. The younger person caring for an aged person therefore already perceives a "we-they" gap between herself, as either a young or middle-aged person, and the elderly patient as an "old" person. When the elderly person is physically frail and/or suffering from some form of dementia, the gap between the care giver and care recipient is wider. If one adds to this situation such factors as ethnic, racial, and/or cultural difference between the aged nursing home patient and the younger care giver, "we-they" distinctions are intensified to an even greater degree. If an elderly person is cared for by non-family care givers who do not share the same cultural backgrounds, the social distance between care giver and patient can be extreme and can foster situations of indifference. However, this social distance related to cultural discontinuity must be viewed within the wider institutional context in which care giving occurs. What has been called "elder abuse" has been documented in family settings, when care giver and care recipient share emotional as well as cultural bonds, as well as in nursing homes. Good-quality care giving is, it appears, related to recognition of a common human bond between the elderly person and his/her care givers, despite any diversity in age, social class, or ethnic/ cultural background. Whether it is the elderly person who views the care giver as "different," or the care giver who views the older person as "different", care will be affected by such "we–they" divisions.

The cultural and ethnic factors in aging are increasingly being investigated by anthropologists in order to focus on an issue that was long neglected (Sokolovsky 1990). Interest in cultural diversity among the aged in the United States is part of a wider trend to look at these issues in a wide range of health-care contexts. Most attention thus far has been directed to the study of those recipients of care who differ from the mainstream American medical culture in their cultural ideas and traditions about health and illness. The problem has been how to reach out to these groups in terms that they understand in order to provide good medical care to them (Spector 1985). The assumption generally has been that the health-care practitioners who care for minority-culture patients are predominantly white, Anglo Americans who are not sufficiently sensitive to the cultural values of ethnic Americans or recent immigrants. This is based on the fact that most doctors and registered nurses are European American and are frequently insensitive to the cultural differences between their own medical traditions and those of their patients.

The issues are different, however, among those health-care workers who provide the most direct care to patients in hospitals and nursing homes. The majority of health-care workers are themselves, increasingly, members of minority cultures. According to the U.S. Bureau of Labor Statistics, almost 40 percent of all nursing aides, attendants, and orderlies are either black Americans or Hispanic Americans. Therefore, cultural diversity is as important an issue for understanding the providers of health care as it is for understanding the recipients of that care. Cultural diversity becomes particularly relevant when there is a major difference between the cultural background of the provider and the recipient of health care. In nursing homes, where most patients are white and most care givers are nonwhite, ethnic and cultural diversity has become a crucial issue.

## NURSING HOMES AND THE NURSING ASSISTANT

Although there are some important exceptions, many nursing homes, particularly in urban settings, display a striking case of cultural and racial difference between the providers and recipients of care. Whereas 96 percent of all patients in nursing homes are white, the person who provides the most direct care to an elderly person in a nursing home is often a member of a minority U.S. culture, or is foreign-born. The main provider of daily care to nursing home patients is usually called a nursing assistant or a nursing aide. Almost 25 percent of all nursing assistants are black, and over 90 percent in this occupational category are female; no other occupational category do black females constitute such a large proportion. Considering that blacks comprise only 10 percent of the total civilian workforce, this shows that they are more than two times overrepresented in this field. For Hispanics, in contrast, the proportion of nursing aides is closer to their distribution in the total civilian workforce, which is almost 8 percent. The administrative and registered nursing staff in nursing homes is more exclusively white (over 95% in each case). It is important to bear in mind that nursing homes are primarily staffed with nursing aides or assistants. In the typical nursing home, there will be over six times more nursing aides than registered nurses and almost five times as many nurses aides as licensed practical nurses. Most employees will be female, given the high concentration of women in the nursing field.

The nursing assistant is, therefore, often a black female (either African-American or Caribbean American) with little education beyond high school. Nationwide, among both black and white nursing assistants, one-third of such workers lack a high school diploma. A nursing assistant's male peers, the orderlies and janitorial help at the nursing home, are also likely to be black or representative of another minority subculture. Since a nursing assistant's superiors as well as her patients will be white,more often than not, these circumstances ensure that issues of cultural diversity and of race will become daily issues for workers in many nursing homes. They also are going to be significant factors in the interactions that patients or the family members of resident patients will have with workers in such institutions. The most important issues facing nursing homes, whose numbers are increasing rapidly, are providing quality care for patients and ensuring good working conditions for the staff. Both of these issues depend upon an understanding of the role that culture and cultural diversity play in the nursing home.

### Nursing Homes and Diversity

Early ethnographic studies of nursing homes did not address issues of diversity, and focused attention on the institutional culture of nursing homes. Jaber Gubrium (1975), for example, tells a great deal about how a nursing home operates, but gives no detailed information about the cultural backgrounds of patients or staff members. In the case of a midwestern nursing home that he profiled, there may have been little diversity, but he does not tell us about that. Increasingly, more recent studies provide information about the ethnic, religious, gender, and racial characteristics of staff and patients, even if diversity is not the major concern of the researcher. A wide variety of additional cases of cultural diversity in nursing homes now have been documented. However, researchers do not agree about the role of cultural diversity in the quality of nursing home care.

Barbara Meyerhoff's classic work (1978) makes the Jewish religious and ethnic identity of the elderly she studied at a senior citizen's center central to her analysis. In this homogeneous ethnic setting, a close community of elders was formed based upon shared histories and religious traditions. Meyerhoff's study demonstrates the positive role that a shared cultural/religious background can have in promoting social solidarity among elderly individuals. Similarly, Jennie-Keith Ross (1977), in her study of a French retirement community, analyzes the positive advantages of associating with age mates who share social, cultural, and political backgrounds and interests. "Stated as a proposition," Ross suggests, "the greater the homogeneity of the individuals involved, the more likely they are to share we-feelings, and the more likely they are to develop common institutions" (1977:8). Both studies point to the advantages accruing to older people when they are able to form homogeneous communities in new institutional settings. However, both are based upon situations in which able-bodied and mentally alert older people voluntarily come together; but such is rarely the case in a nursing home.

Two comparative studies of nursing homes with varying degrees of cultural and ethnic diversity suggest that cultural discontinuity between staff and patients may be significant in patient care. In the first case, Jeanie Kayser-Jones (1981) compared a nursing home in Scotland, which she calls Scottsdale, with one in a metropolitan area of the United States, which she calls Pacific Grove. In the second, Wilbur Watson and Robert Maxwell (1977) compare a nursing home for the Jewish elderly with one for the black elderly—both of which are in the United States. I will turn first to Kayser-Jone's findings.

Scottsdale is located in what Kayser-Jones has referred to as the "homogeneous country" of Scotland. The patients are 100 percent white, 97 percent of whom are Presbyterian and 3 percent of whom are Roman Catholic. Although she does not give detailed statistics on the staff at Scottsdale, Kayser-Jones indicates that they share a cultural background with the patients. Scottsdale is described as a human, caring institution, in which the staff take a personal interest in their patients. In contrast to Scottsdale, Pacific Grove is marked by indifference to patients, and by what Kayser-Jones describes as frequently inhumane treatment. Like Scottsdale, Pacific Grove has an overwhelmingly white patient population (close to 96%), with some Asian but no black patients. The religious makeup of the Pacific Grove patient population is much more heterogeneous than at Scottsdale, including a mixture of Protestants, Catholics, and Jewish. However, the nonprofessional nursing staff is totally nonwhite. Kayser-Jones writes that "the homogeneity of staff and patients at Scottsdale may contribute to a higher level of care, whereas the heterogeneity of staff and patients at Pacific Grove may account for a lower level of care" (1981:58). However, she prefers not to conclude from her findings that neither ethnic or racial factors play a deterministic role in actual care giving. Rather, she suggests that, with proper administration, quality care can be given in any nursing home.

A different sort of conclusion is reached by Watson and Maxwell. In the Jewish nursing home they studied, an all-white patient population was being cared for by a "racially mixed" staff. In the case of the black nursing home, 98 percent of the patients were black, and the staff was also predominantly black. On the basis of observations of staff-patient interactions, the authors found that, in the latter case, there was more interaction. Introducing the concept of "status parity" to explain this, Watson and Maxwell suggest that shared racial identity was the main reason for the increased interaction. They write that "black nursing staff, especially lower status staff such as aides and orderlies, and black lower class elderly may sense a strong bond through their common plight in a society that punishes people for being black and lower class" (1977:109). "If this reasoning holds," they add, "interactions between white nursing staff and white elderly residents who share a common socioeconomic status should also reveal more approach than avoidance behavior" (1977:109). Watson and Maxwell conclude that the tendency to neglect or avoid the elderly, and especially the sick elderly, may be replaced by "deference and face-to-face interaction" in some situations where "the caretakers share with the elderly a common class and/or ethnic background" (1977:115).

Three other, more recent, studies, add more data on cultural diversity issues in nursing homes, but do not resolve the dilemma of the degree to which cultural discontinuity between staff and patients affects the quality of care. Renée Rose Shield (1988) describes a case in which Jewish patients are cared for by a non-Jewish, but ethnically diverse, staff. The Franklin Nursing Home, located in the northeast, is a nonprofit Jewish nursing home. Like the case in Meyerhoff's study, the residents share a religious and ethnic background. Shield reports (1988:10) that many knew each other before coming to the home. Located in an ethnically diverse city, Franklin has a staff marked by cultural diversity. Although mostly white, the staff included American and African black, Caribbean, Portuguese, and Indochinese workers. None of the nursing aides, who cared most closely for the patients, were Jewish. Although Shield describes Franklin as a good nursing home, it sometimes is marked by impersonal treatment of patients by staff. In her recommendations for improving the situation at Franklin (1988:218), Shield cites the need to enhance the independence of the residents and to create more community rituals for them. She also, however, advocates educating the staff in Jewish history, beliefs, and customs. Here, she suggests that cultural discontinuities and misunderstandings between staff and patients could be improved through education.

Joel Savishinsky (1991) describes a more homogeneous population of staff and patients in a village setting. Savishinsky writes that Elmwood Grove Nursing Home "served—and employed—a predominantly white and Christian population" (1991: 251). Like the case of Scottsdale described by Kayser-Jones, this led to a case in which both patient abuse and ethnic or racial tensions were virtually absent. Of almost 100 residents, only four to six were black, and Savishinsky notes that there was a "comparable number of minorities" on the staff of 120 people. Issues of racial difference between white patients and nonwhite staff did not gain much importance in the day-to-day life of the institution. "Black aides sometimes bridled at the racism of a handful of residents, but more often chose to ignore it as another symptom of 'people's crotchetyness'" (1991:192).

The last nursing home ethnography to be considered here before I turn to my own study is that of Nancy Foner, in a case that contrasts dramatically from that of Savishinsky. Foner (1994) is the most explicit of all the studies discussed so far in her treatment of the issues of race and ethnicity in nursing home care, describing a case of extreme cultural diversity in the nursing home. This particular study was carried out in New York City, in a good-quality nursing home located in a gentrified neighborhood. The Crescent Nursing Home serves a predominantly white (86%) population that is 50 percent Catholic and 35 percent Jewish. The nursing aides are all black women (except for two black males), and mostly from the Caribbean. However, the staff was highly diverse in ethnic background, including women from Haiti, Jamaica, Ecuador, Puerto Rico, Guyana, and the United States. Foner states clearly that "racial and ethnic cleavages create...barriers and misunderstandings between aides and residents" (1994:38). She cites incidents of both what she calls "worker abuse", in which patients physically attacked aides and used racial slurs with them, and of "elder abuse," in which aides physically neglected, but more often, verbally taunted patients—especially those suffering from dementia. Despite this situation in which racial tensions were often very high, Foner concludes, in agreement with Kayser-Jones, that cultural discontinuity does not have a direct influence on patient care. She writes:

Although the racial gulf between aides and patients heightens the aides' sense that patients, as a group, are in the opposite group, as far as I could tell, race had little, if any, effect on actual patient care in individual cases...From my observations, racial and ethnic similarity between patients and aides did not lead to better relations with patients or more sympathetic care. Interestingly, hardly any of the black or Hispanic patients were the aides' special favorites (1994:45).

Although Foner is hesitant to make a clear connection between racial tension and the problems of nursing care at Crescent Nursing Home, she does suggest that racial differences intensify social divisions (1994:148), and calls for further research on the actual role of race in patient care. As with other forms of cultural or ethnic discontinuity, racial difference can help to promote a "we-they" division between the staff and patients. Even though, as Foner points out, the nursing aides were ethnically divided themselves, they shared a bond of common race as well as bonds of gender, immigrant status, class, and occupation (1994:123). This promoted social solidarity among the nurse's aides, accentuating boundaries between staff and patients. Based on the cases presented thus far, the role of cultural discontinuity or homogeneity in patient care will vary according to the precise characteristics and sociocultural setting of the nursing home.

## THE CASE OF ROSEWOOD

The case of Rosewood presents a situation in which African-American and Afro-Caribbean nursing assistants care for upper-middle-class white patients. Rosewood is a special facility especially designed for Alzheimer's patients in a nursing home located in a large southern city. It is devoted to the care of elderly men and women with Alzheimer's disease who are not yet bed-ridden, but are able to get dressed and remain "up and about" during the day. It is considered a high-quality institution for the care of Alzheimer's patients, and has a good reputation in the community. In my study of nursing assistants at Rosewood, I used ethnographic methods that included informal interviews, observation of casual social interaction as well as of formal meetings, and working along with nursing assistants in their daily activities. The nursing assistants at Rosewood are called CNAs (certified nursing assistants), because they are required to have specialized training that leads to "certification" in this occupation. In keeping with that convention, therefore, I will refer to nursing assistants at Rosewood as CNAs. Because the staff at Rosewood referred to the Alzheimer's patients in the home as "residents," in order to lend more dignity to their status, that terminology will be adopted here.

There were approximately 85 residents at Rosewood during 1993, who lived in either private or semi-private rooms. All but two of the resident patients were white and upper middle class. These two residents were African-American (one male and one female). All but one of the more than 30 CNAs who cared for these residents were either ethnically African-American or Caribbean American (a category also called Afro-Caribbean). Rosewood is staffed, like most other residential facilities, according to shifts. There are three shifts during the day—one from 7 a.m. to 3 p.m., one from 3 p.m. to 11 p.m., and one from 11 p.m. to 7 a.m. On any given shift, there were usually seven CNAs on duty. The CNAs, LPNs (licensed practical nurses), housekeeping aides, and dietary aides all work according to shifts, and shift workers are almost all black. The professional staff work hours that approximate a 9-to-5 schedule. This category of workers includes two activities directors, a social worker, a program director, and a registered nurse (RN) who supervises the entire nursing staff. All but one of these professional staff members were white, and the entire staff working at Rosewood was female. Male staff included chaplains and other supervisory staff who occasionally visited Rosewood, but their visits were sporadic. Doctors rarely came to Rosewood, and patients generally had to leave the premises to visit doctors elsewhere.

## Work culture

The CNAs at Rosewood have a shared work culture that informs their daily interactions. Karen Sacks has defined work culture as "the understandings and values about work and workplace social relations that co-workers share and reinforce among themselves" (1988:70). This is a concept that has been used in many studies of female workers, particularly in factory settings. Cultural diversity and race play a significant role in the work culture of the CNAs at Rosewood, and both are an integral part of "understandings and values about...workplace social relations." Ideas of race, nationality, and regional origins are all part of the "work culture" of the CNAs. Race and culture are not, however, synonymous. The work culture at Rosewood produces contexts for social divisions among the CNAs as well as contexts for solidarity. Shared racial background leads to social cohesion and cooperation among the African-Americans at Rosewood, particularly those from the South, but cultural differences between African-American and Caribbean American workers contribute to occasional cultural conflicts within the total group of CNAs. Regional origins and ethnic background also provide divisions among the workers, as do generational differences between older and younger women. However, an overall shared racial identity as "black" did serve to reinforce distance between workers and patients, and workers and supervisors. Both African-American and Afro-Caribbean CNAs referred to themselves as "black" in comparison to what they termed "whites" (referring to all Anglo-Americans). They did not use such terms as "African-American," "Afro-Caribbean," or "Caribbean American" for themselves in everyday speech settings.

Despite the overall binary distinction that the CNAs made between themselves and the "whites" at Rosewood, the nursing assistants made very fine distinctions among themselves based on regional or national origin. The majority of CNAs at Rosewood were American black women from the South, and this group dominated the work culture of the CNAs. Those women from other cultural backgrounds were distinguished from this group, and accorded less status within the work culture of the CNAs. The CNAs from the Caribbean were labeled according to their country of origin, primarily as "Jamaican." They distinguished themselves from American blacks, and were perceived as culturally very different by most of the American-born nursing assistants. One Jamaican CNA told me that she preferred "white" people to American blacks, expressing her discomfort, I believe, with being an outsider among the group of southern CNAs. CNAs who were American-born also made distinctions among themselves based on regional origins. Among those who had worked together for several months, each knew the state in which the others had been born and raised. Even regional differences within the state in which Rosewood was located were highlighted by the CNAs. One nursing assistant from the more rural coastal region of the state was perceived as "different" from those who grew up around the urban area of Rosewood. A CNA from the northeastern part of the United States spoke to me of her disdain for some of her southern coworkers, who she felt were not sufficiently militant in their racial views. Although they may not all share the same culture of origin, the nursing assistants do share understandings about how to understand cultural identity that is part of their work culture. That is, they all agree on the distinctions that are made among them. The work culture of the CNAs at Rosewood is, in part, based upon a shared racial identity, despite the many cultural differences among this group of workers. It is also based upon a shared structural position in the hierarchy of the institution, as I outline below.

### The Nursing Hierarchy at Rosewood

In order to understand the work culture of the CNAs at Rosewood, it is necessary to place this within the overall context of the social hierarchy at Rosewood. The hierarchy of jobs at Rosewood is not based exclusively on either race or gender, since the staff is mostly female and there are black women in jobs with both more and less prestige than the CNAs. Most LPNs are black, and when I did my research, two professional nonnursing staff members were black. The women with the most power and authority in the system are, however, white. The residents are also, as I have mentioned previously, almost all white. Housekeeping staff, lower in the hierarchy than the CNAs and not part of the nursing staff, were like most of the CNAs, American-born black women. Because of their employment in the health-care field, and because nursing care is a highly respected occupation in the black community, CNAs enjoy some status among adults in their home communities. At Rosewood, however, they occupy the lowest position in the nursing hierarchy. The RN is highest in the nursing hierarchy and supervises all of the nursing care at Rosewood. RNs have little direct physical contact with residents. Next in line are the LPNs who are responsible for supervising the shift during which they work, and administering medication to the residents. CNAs work directly with residents. It is the CNAs who bathe and clean incontinent residents, help residents get dressed and washed and fed, etc.—what Gubrium (1975) has referred to as "bed and body work." CNAs are also responsible for more general and less easily defined tasks in resident care having to do with ensuring the safety of residents, taking them on walks if possible, and minimizing verbal or physical disruptions on the floors. CNAs at Rosewood are expected to maintain as "normal" as possible a life-style for the residents. This means that the CNAs must encourage residents to get up in the morning, get dressed and washed, come to the dining room for breakfast, and stay awake for most of the day before changing into bedclothes and getting into bed at night. Such a routine is not easy to accomplish with Alzheimer's patients, whose short-term memories are fading, who have little sense of time or even of social propriety, and who may be depressed and sad about their institutionalized status. The CNAs must employ many social skills in dealing with the residents in order to accomplish the physical tasks. Despite this, and despite their qualification as "certified," however, the stigma of dealing with the bodily functions of patients is central to the position of the CNAs within the hierarchy of the nursing staff at Rosewood. An indication of the CNAs low status in the nursing profession is revealed in an expression used by CNAs at Rosewood to describe what others think of them—that they are "ass-wipers." This unfortunate term symbolizes the feelings of being stigmatized that CNAs sense while at work, but it also serves to promote solidarity among them vis-a-vis their superiors. Their low position in the nursing hierarchy fuels CNA feelings of resentment, feelings that they are not sufficiently paid, appreciated, or recognized for the work that they do. This alone would tend to detract from their devotion to their work and to patients, without adding the factor of ethnic, race, class, and cultural diversity.

### CNA–Resident Interaction

Other features of diversity, besides that of race, affect relationships between CNAs and the residents for whom they provide daily care at Rosewood. Residents are not only white, but also predominantly upper middle class. In addition, they are from an older generation, who were youths in a very different time. Finally, these residents have Alzheimer's disease, a form of senile dementia that interferes with their ability to remember people, events, places, and time. For a variety of reasons, therefore, the CNAs tend to view the residents at Rosewood as "different." The strong solidarity of the work culture of the CNAs reinforces "we-they" divisions. Despite their Alzheimer's disease, many of the residents also are able to define the CNAs as "different" from their co-residents. This is mainly based upon obvious racial differences and, as at other nursing homes like those studied by Foner and Savishinsky noted above, racial slurs and comments often are made by residents toward their caretakers.

Despite these common conditions under which all of the CNAs work, there is a great deal of individual variation in interactions between CNAs and residents. The CNAs do not depersonalize and neglect all residents, and this is not simply because such behavior would cost them their jobs. There are many other factors that foster personal and often caring relationships between CNAs and residents. These include: 1) a shared regional culture between most CNAs and residents, who are natives of the American South; 2) the fact that residents are in the early stages of Alzheimer's and able to converse with CNAs (even if their conversations do not always make sense!); and 3) the tendency of the CNAs to create life stories about the residents that promote a recognition of their human side. Each of these factors will be taken in turn.

Even though the CNAs are black and all but two of the residents are white, many of them share a common regional background. Although racism permeated the experience of blacks historically in this region, similar experiences of strong religious values and of place between the blacks and whites create understandings between CNAs and residents. Protestantism dominates the institutional culture of Rosewood, as it does in the urban community in which it is located, CNAs often cited their own Christian religious values to me as sources of strength in confronting the racial slurs of many residents. Their confrontation with racism in Rosewood, therefore, was not a new experience, but one that generations in their families have had to face. Most of the CNAs are of southern origins, while wounded by racial comments, take them in stride. Because they perceive the residents to come from an earlier generation of southerners, one less enlightened than their contemporaries, they are inclined to forgive many of the comments. Such behavior among younger white people is not, however, excused.

A second factor in care is related to the active nature of the residents' behavior. Because many of the residents at Rosewood get dressed each day, eat in the communal dining room, and spend much of their day in the common room watching TV or moving about in the halls, they resist neglectful behaviors on the part of their care givers, and often seek out attention. Many of the CNAs at Rosewood are highly respectful of the elderly as a general category, and told me that they have received good advice on personal issues from those residents who are more mentally alert than others. Some told me that they felt sorry for these old people who had been "rejected" by their families, and harbored much more ill-will for the obviously well-to-do family members who come to visit patients than for the residents themselves.

Obviously, the situation at Rosewood differs here from those nursing homes that cater to the very physically frail elderly who are bed-ridden.

The third factor that worked toward quality care at Rosewood was that the CNAs had a tendency to create life narratives about the residents and to swap stories about their former lives. In this, they personalized the residents. As was their interest in soap opera stories strong, so was their interest in any dramatic narrative that they could learn about a resident. Those particular residents whose lives had been either very traumatic or marked by glamorous professional employment were particularly noticed at Rosewood. CNAs were fascinated by the story of two lovers at Rosewood who had been separated as youths and had found each other again at the nursing home. There was the story of the resident who had many misfortunes in her younger years, and another about a resident who had been a highly successful businessman. A sense of common humanity, of common experiences of human tragedy and love, were fostered by these stories. Hence, the "we-they" divisions were undermined in many cases. Sometimes, however, when lives were viewed as less glamorous, or if they represented experiences about which the CNAs were ambivalent, their negative attitudes toward residents were fostered through such stories. This was particularly true in the case of women who had been housewives, perceived by CNAs as "easy" and uninteresting lives. The CNAs, working women who had working mothers, found it less easy to be kind to white women who did not have to work than to professionals. Such women, labeled as "housewives," could be the butt of cruel jokes, but I never saw cases of outright physical abuse of them.

The CNAs, as the examples above illustrate, sought out ways to find common human threads linking them to the residents, and these often worked against the social divisions that cultural diversity and cultural discontinuity can foster. What about the two black residents at Rosewood? These cases illustrate the ways in which other factors mediate the factor of race. One resident, a black male, was a particular "favorite" of the CNAs. He was from a modest social class background, and had become a resident of Rosewood through former employment circumstances, rather than family means. As a favorite of the CNAs, he was given many privileges, and treated with a great deal of respect. In this case, a feeling of common racial, class, and regional cultural background aroused sympathy among the CNAs for this resident. In addition, he was an easy-going, likeable person. The case illustrates the positive role that shared identity can play in nursing home care, as suggested by Watson and Maxwell in the study cited earlier.

In contrast, the female black resident at Rosewood, while not physically abused in any way, received little attention that actually could be attributed to shared cultural background. She was perceived as "different" from the CNAs because of her high educational level and professional status. Class differences between this resident and the CNAs, despite shared racial identity, undercut any advantages to her over the white residents. That she was a shy, reclusive person, who didn't seek much attention, also kept her interactions with CNAs to a minimal level. Many white residents received much more attention and affection than did this resident, supporting Foner's findings at Crescent nursing home (cited above) that black CNAs do not always favor black residents.

## SUMMARY AND CONCLUSIONS

The case of Rosewood suggests that not only must cultural diversity be examined in the context of nursing homes, but that the wider regional culture in which nursing home care takes place also must be taken into account. It appears likely, for instance, that cultural diversity between white residents and black nurses' aides in New York City may have different meanings than it does in a southern city. The degree of diversity among staff members as well as the degree of cultural distance between staff and residents also will be important variables in care. In service institutions, whether they are schools or nursing homes, when cultural differences are perceived between staff and clients, there are bound to be implications for the interactions between them. Further research on these diversity issues of the nursing homes and in health care generally, will help to further specify the role that cultural diversity plays (which should not always be assumed to be negative) and the ways in which a common ground can be reached between all parties in order to ensure good quality care.

## REFERENCES

Foner, N. 1994. *The Caregiving Dilemma: Work in an American Nursing Home.* Berkeley: University of California Press.

Gubrium, J. F. 1975. *Living and Dying at Murray Manor.* New York: St. Martin's Press.

Heath, S. B. 1983. *Ways With Words: Language, Life and Work in Communities and Classrooms.* Cambridge: Cambridge University Press.

Kayser-Jones, J. S. 1981. *Old, Alone, and Neglected: Care of the Aged in Scotland and the United States.* Berkeley: University of California Press.

Macias, J. 1987. The hidden curriculum of Papago teachers: American Indian strategies for mitigating cultural discontinuity in early schooling. In *Interpretive Ethnography of Education: At Home and Abroad.* G. Spindler & L. Spindler (eds). Hillsdale, NJ: Lawrence Erlbaum Associates, pp. 363–384.

Meyerhoff, B. 1978. *Number Our Days.* New York: E. P. Dutton

Ogbu, J. 1982. Cultural discontinuities and schooling. *Anthropology and Education Quarterly* 13(4): 290–307.

Reed-Danahay, D. & Anderson-Levitt, K. M. 1991. Backward countryside, troubled city: French teachers' images of rural and working-class families. *American Ethnologist* 18(3):546–564.

Ross, J. K. 1977. *Old People, New Lives: Community Creation in a Retirement Residence.* Chicago: University of Chicago Press.

Sacks, K. B. 1988. *Caring by the Hour: Women, Work, and Organizing at Duke Medical Center.* Chicago: University of Illinois Press.

Savishinsky, J. S. 1991. *The Ends of Time: Life and Work in a Nursing Home.* New York: Bergin & Garvey.

Shield, R.R. 1988. *Uneasy Ending: Daily Life in an American Nursing Home.* Ithaca: Cornell University Press.

Sokolovsky, J. (ed). 1990. *The Cultural Context of Aging: Worldwide Perspectives.* New York: Bergin & Garvey.

Spector, R. E. 1985. *Cultural Diversity in Health and Illness*, 2nd edition. Norwalk, CT: Appleton-Century-Crofts.

Vesperi, M. D. & Henderson, J. N. 1995. Introduction. In *The Culture of Long Term Care: Nursing Home Ethnography*. J. N. Henderson & M.D. Vesperi (eds). Westport, CT: Bergin & Garvey, pp. 1–6.

Watson, W. H. & Maxwell, R. J. (eds). 1977. *Human Aging and Dying: A Study in Sociocultural Gerontology*. New York: St. Martin's Press.

# 21

# Social Work Practice with Ethnic Minority Persons

### Richard Enos

A better understanding ethnic minority groups within the American cultural mosaic enhances the potential of professional social workers to become more successful practitioners because cross-cultural awareness can result in more culturally focused and informed practice with the ethnic minority clients. Traditional models of social work practice, for the most part, have been based upon psychological and social psychological theories with respect to understanding the dynamics of human growth and behavior. We know that there are some limitations to these approaches with respect to working with ethnic minority clients. Erickson (1963), for example, has noted the importance of understanding psychiatric symptoms from the standpoint of the cultural and community context in which these symptoms occurred.

In this chapter, the writer will describe some of the important family, religious, and spiritual values among several major ethnic minority groups that social workers are likely to encounter in their work. This will be followed by a presentation of some techniques for more ethnic-sensitive social work practice with ethnic minority persons.

## FAMILY, RELIGIOUS, AND SPIRITUAL VALUES
## AMONG ETHNIC MINORITY GROUPS

The social work and related social science research literature contain a relatively robust amount of empirical data with respect to the family, religious, and spiritual values among ethnic minority persons. The writer believes that knowledge about family, and the religious and spiritual values of ethnic minority persons and groups, is a key element in developing a better understanding of minority groups and in working effectively with ethnic minority persons across various types of social service settings. Before proceeding however, it should be emphasized that although the discussion will focus upon some central cultural attributes that members of various ethnic minority groups appear to hold in unison, the writer is not suggesting that all or that even some of these characteristics are held by all the members of these groups. Other than the errors that are always inherent in generalizations and reductionism, ascribing characteristics can become problematic for a number of other reasons. Chief among such reasons is the issue of how close or distant the minority group is to the "mother" culture. Obviously, recent Hispanic immigrants who live near the border between the United States and Mexico and who may be less influenced in the direction of acculturation as compared to the self-described "Spanish" of northern New Mexico, who can trace their roots to the pre-colonial America-Spanish empire. Thus, geographic location, immigration status, and date of immigration can influence the degree of assimilation. In addition, ethnic groups are inherently very diverse. Consider, for example, the term, "Asian Americans." This term actually encompasses Indochinese, Chinese, Filipino, Japanese, Koreans, Asian Indians, and even vaious Pacific Islanders, such as the Hawaiians, Samoans, and Chamorros. Finally, not only are ethnic minority groups quite diverse, but even within major groupings one finds different cultural values, beliefs, and practices. Perhaps surprisingly to some, many Hispanics are evangelical Christians rather than Roman Catholics. Also, there are many Hispanics who are fluent in Spanish, or they speak a "patois", or an idiomatic version of it, or do not speak Spanish at all.

The difficulty of attempting to characterize ethnic minority groups and persons has been further compounded by federal directives that attempt to classify ethnic minority persons and groups by region or by country of origin. For example, the federal government  defines an "Hispanic" as an individual whose origin is from Mexico, Cuba, Puerto Rico, Central or South America, or from another Spanish culture, regardless of race (Office of Management and Budget 1978). This sort of definition assumes that all of these people have in common a primary Spanish culture. Castex points out the problems (and, perhaps, the rationale) of this kind of governmental behavior. She describes it as an attempt to create "an ethnic group in a dialectic with the state..." and, for Hispanics, as a process that "was bidirectional, involving state institutions and those so ascribed, to identify, control, and provide needed services to members of the new group" (1994:289). Thus, definitions of ethnic minority groups may have direct political significance. Castex also points out that this same process has occurred with African Americans and Native Americans.

### The Family

The social science literature concerning the dynamics of ethnic minority families is quite extensive. In focusing on some of the more current literature, one notes that Mindel et al. (1988) found that ethnic minority families function to socialize their children into their ethnic culture through family life-styles and through various community activities. Martin Luther King Day, now a national holiday, has been used by African-Americans  to celebrate pride in their ethnic heritage. In Texas, Hispanics celebrate "Cinco de Mayo," which is a public celebration honoring the defeat of the Napoleonic regime in Mexico in 1867.

Concerning African-American families, Jenkins (1981) noted  that many of these families can be characterized as having a vertical hierarchy with respect to parental authority. Invariably, the father is the primary parental authority and is an object of obedience. In discussing Asian American families, Lum (l986) indicated that these families traditionally emphasized the importance of the family structure. He also noted that with Chinese-Americans, the family is a source of personal identity and serves as a reference group. This provides for emotional security. He further states that: "It (the Chinese-American family) exerts control over interpersonal conduct, social relations, and occupational and marital selection" (1986:64).

Japanese-Americans also highly value and place much importance on the family structure. Culturally, Japanese-American families strongly emphasize a spirit of family cohesion and cooperation, respect for the elders, and obedience to the male head of the family or patriarch (filial piety). In the Filipino culture, great importance is placed upon the obligation of the young to take care of their elders ("utang na loob"). There are a number of other family values inherent in Japanese culture that may apply to other Asian American groups or they may not. Browne and Broderick (1994) have attempted to identify some of these traits from the ethnographic literature. Among the traits they identified are the obedience to family rules and roles, "enryo," or self-effacement, a sense of fatalism, "hiya," or the avoidance of shame, and respect for authority. Lum (l986) adds the use of modesty and indirect communication .

Generally speaking, the Hispanic family, like the African American and Asian American families, has many characteristics in common with respect to family structure and function. Patterns of authority, in the form of a vertical hierarchy with the father at the apex of authority, appear to be a common dimension. The term "respeto," or respect, can be used to define this type of structure in that respect is a means for enforcing the authority of the father in relation to the behavior of the children and the mother. The ideal child respects his or her father and mother. The ideal wife is submissive. In terms of child rearing, respeto is the norm of child development and socialization.

An understanding of the concept of "machismo" helps to clarify Hispanic family relationships. There are numerous definitions of this term. However, in the literal sense, machismo refers to manliness and also to sexual vitality and power.It also refers to the male role of protecting and defending the honor of women. In a cultural sense it means that the male is the defender of the family and is its chief provider. The related term, "mariansimo," refers to an idealized personality construct for women. More exactly, it defines the ideal wife and mother. Marianismo may be better understood by way of an analogy to the Virgin Mary or Madonna of Roman Catholicism: the wife/mother is expected to be pure and spiritually better than men; but at the same time, like the Virgin, she will be long-suffering and will place the needs of her husband and children before her own wishes and needs. Oftentimes, the grandmother, or "madre," occupies a central role in the family hierarchy as well. She often looks after the children when the parents are working; she can be a major force in child rearing.

Hispanic families, in the main, like other ethnic minority families, also appear to be mutually self-supportive, cohesive, and have extended family and kinship systems that can provide natural support networks. Extended family and kinship systems sometimes are referred to as the "compadrazo." This is the network that usually is established between the godparents and the godchildren ("padrinos" and "ahijados") at the baptism of the child. This creates a system of mutual aid between the godparents and the godchild, and between the godparents and the parents, who thus become co-parents, ("compadres") for children. In general, Hispanic families can be characterized as being "familial" in that family loyalty, interdependence, cooperation, and noncompetition among members are valued. It appears that the presence of extended family and kinship support systems has helped many ethnic minority families adjust to and deal with individual and group problems and dysfunctions, thus abrogating the need for social service or mental health treatment programs.

Native Americans, because they are perhaps the most diverse group among all American ethnic minority groups and seem to contain the most numerous subgroups (tribes), are the most difficult to characterize with respect to family values. Most of the current research seems to suggest that Native Americans also feel strong family obligations and responsibilities. They are also characterized by the extended family and strong kinship relationships. Non-interference in the affairs of others seems to be an additional trait of most of these families.

### Religious And Spiritual Belief Systems

Frazier (1963), concluded from his seminal study of African-American families, that the African-American church historically provided a place African-Americans could find refuge from the hostile white world. This would seem to be a continuing function of many African-American churches even today. More precisely, Frazier identified the importance of the African-American church as a place where families and individuals could find "a structured social life in which the Negro could give expression to his deepest feelings and at the same time achieve status and find a meaningful existence..." (1963:44). Staples (1976) reiterates the theme of the refuge from a hostile white world, but makes the point that these churches also have helped African-Americans deal with the detrimental forces of racism, while providing a means for reducing stress and tension. For Staples, the African-American church has, very importantly "given credibility to cultural heritage, validated the worth of Black people, and provided for the future" (1976:32). For African-Americans, the church has remained, along with the family, as a continuous and fundamental social and cultural institution. In addition, the African-American church historically has been a source of power with respect to attaining civil rights and social justice.

The Roman Catholic church has been the central social and cultural institution for Hispanics in general, although Protestantism has made major inroads among some groups of them. In the main, however, Catholicism has remained as the central religious value and ideology of Hispanics. The neighborhood church, in particular, is often the center of many religious and cultural activities in the barrio. The local priest is a central figure in Hispanic neighborhoods since he provides for religious services, and often for social services as well. Catholic Social Services agencies provide an extensive array of social programs to help meet the needs of Hispanic populations.

It is interesting to note that, in many Hispanic communities, some theological aspects of Roman Catholicism have been combined with various "folk cultural" ideas. These folk cultural ideas have been influenced by Native American and African-American belief systems. An analysis of Puerto Rican folk culture can provide insight about this phenomena. As Borrello and Mathias (1977) described it, a melding has occurred, centered in the Caribbean area, among Catholic, Native-American, and African belief systems. This has resulted in a spiritual system called "santeria." They note that "botanicas," or stores that sell herbal medicines along with religious images, are neighborhood centers that provide physical as well as spiritual services to the people in the community. These are also centers wherein one can become informed about the practices and nuances of santeria. Botanicas are readily encountered in areas of heavy Hispanic population, for example, in Santa Fe, New Mexico.

There are other folk cultural rituals and spiritual beliefs and practices that are important in the lives of many Hispanics as well. The most important is probably the notion of "curanderismo," a very difficult idea to describe. With respect to spiritual beliefs, it suggests that a person's soul can, by a magical process or ritual, be lost or stolen. This can occur by means of "susto," which is a kind of magically induced fright, or by an evil eye or hex ("mal puesto"). Often, hexes occur because of romantic jealousy or envy ("envida") by a former lover. The writer can recall numerous incidents of hex anxiety while working as a consultant to an early childhood development program in a rural area of Colorado. Frequently, Hispanic women from migrant labor families would cover up the faces of their infants when they entered the center because of the fear that a hex would be placed upon their child by the evil-eye gaze or "ojo" of "Anglo" staff members. It is important to consult with a "curandera," or faith healer, when working with Hispanic families who hold these kinds of folk culture beliefs.

Native Americans, in general, see life as a partnership with the forces of nature. Nature permeates all aspects of Native American life and influences their behavior and belief systems. In type of religion, Native American beliefs are characterized as animistic. Animism maintains that spirits are present and operating in the world both in the form of people, and in the form of inanimate objects, such as the mountains and rivers, and/or in the form of physical forces, such as the wind and the rain. Based upon his work among the Mescalero Apaches of New Mexico, the psychoanalyst Boyer (1964), has given us some important insights into Apache religious values that may have implications for other Native American groups. He discovered that these Apaches viewed religion as a kind obscure and dispersed spiritual force that occasionally permeated the environment and gave inanimate objects, such as rocks and trees, the power to become animate objects. The spiritual force worked through inanimate objects as these objects were used by the Apaches in everyday life. At some point, the spiritual power appears to a person, often via a hallucination, or while in a trance, or in a dream, as a personified semblance, and gives or helps this person obtain supernatural powers. As the author noted, a person who has received supernatural powers could use these powers for either good or evil purposes. The shaman uses it for tribal good, while the witch might use it for evil purposes. In a theological sense, it is important to note that: "This power has no intrinsic attribute of good or evil; its virtue is its potency" (1964:523). As Boyer viewed it, in a religious sense, the shaman had the power to deal with supernatural powers, witches, and the ghosts of the dead. He could, through various spiritual ceremonies and rituals, counterbalance the supernatural powers or forces that may have been insulted by members of the tribe. This writer has observed that some Native American groups utilize community religious ceremonies as a kind of group endeavor to obtain spiritual healing by putting members of the tribe, and other persons as well, in contact with natural forces and spirits. This often is done though various kinds of ceremonial events, such as dream and vision sessions, dancing, rhythmic drumming, and chanting, or by contact with medicine men.

As with other ethnic minority categories or specific cultural groups, the Asian Americans hold in importance the role of the family, and religious and spiritual values. As was mentioned earlier, Asian Americans comprise a very diverse and heterogeneous group. It is not possible to comment about all of the religious and spiritual values within this group. It is possible to focus upon the primary belief systems and spiritual values of the three major religions that impact upon Asian Americans: Hinduism, Buddhism, and Confucianism.

An understanding of Hinduism is important for social workers in terms of working with many Asian Indians. Hinduism differs from Christian theologies on one primary dimension. In Christianity, mankind was created by God in his image. Man, in the Christian religious belief system, is imperfect. Through faith, words, and deeds, he can be made perfect and, therefore, achieve salvation. In Hinduism, there was no "fall from grace" or "original sin." Individuals are not estranged from God because of some personal or human imperfection, such as sin. In Hinduism, all humans are god-like in that they all manifest and contain divine power. To achieve perfection, we need to express that divine nature. Campbell explains it this way: (Man only needs to bring) "the spontaneous activity of his mind stuff to a state of stillness and he will experience that divine principle within him which is the very essence of his existence" (1959:57). The divine power within each of us is our sense of "self." It is very similar to the construct of the ego in psychoanalytic theory. Self refers to our sense of independence, intellect, rationality, and self-worth. The path to perfection, while living in this world, is to actualize that divine self within each of us. However, we must not place our self in opposition to other people in the world. We must harmonize our self with the selves of other persons (Campbell 1959). The goal is to achieve a perfected or harmonious world. In other words, imperfection, or, in a sense, aberrant behavior, can be explained as an attempt to place ones self needs before the needs of others, thus creating problems in society.

There are four central spiritual beliefs in Buddhism that are important for social workers to understand in order to enhance their effectiveness in working with Asian American clients. By way of an overview, Buddhism is not a religion that has a "god," nor does it define a human as possessing a "soul." Nor does it acknowledge a supernatural power or any other force that could help mankind surmount human existence. The core of Buddhism has been described as consisting of four "noble truths." "The first of the four is that existence is unhappiness; second, unhappiness is caused by selfish craving; third, selfish craving can be destroyed; fourth, it can be destroyed by following the eightfold path" (Burtt 1959:81–82).

The notion that existence is unhappiness means that all of us are born into a world that it basically evil. This is the case because mankind consists of a blending of both good and evil; God and non-God. The antidote to evil is the avoidance of ignorance. The second "truth" of Buddhism locates the source of unhappiness in our preoccupation with selfish cravings or desires (Ringgren & Strom 1967). In this belief system, the deviant person may be seen as being preoccupied with selfish needs. With respect to the "third truth," these kinds of selfish cravings can be destroyed by patterning one's life in such a way as to acknowledge and assume the responsibility for one's behavior. Furthermore, we must actively strive to change our behavior. This point resonates well with the various social work practices derived from cognitive-behavioral theories. The fourth and last "truth" consists of a number of specific steps, which, if followed, will remove our cravings and ignorance and lead us toward salvation. These steps help the individual recognize that he or she is part of a larger whole, and that liberation from ignorance and from self-desire is the appropriate path to personal salvation or godliness. The process of the fourth "truth" path has much in common with the "twelve-step" Alcoholics Anonymous support group approach to the treatment of alcoholism.

Understanding Confucianism is a prerequisite for social workers who work with Asian Americans, especially Chinese-Americans, as well as with many Southeast Asian refugees. Confucianism is not so much a religion as it is a way of practicing a righteous life-style. Its chief differentiation from Christianity is contained in the term "hsiao" or piety. This means that those who are now living are linked with their ancestors as well as with the institutions of society (Ringgren & Strom 1967). The living have been given life, and they now are challenged to live a good and virtuous life. Many spiritual beliefs of Confucianism are expressed in parables and morality tales in much the same manner as Jesus Christ expressed his religious beliefs as described in the *New Testament*.

It can be argued that deBary (1959) gets at the core of Confucianism when he interprets the story of Confucius' response to the ruler who asked him to explain the meanings of virtue and humanity. From this particular story about Confucius' response, deBary is able to extract some of the core beliefs and spiritual values of Confucianism:

1. The ability to achieve self-understanding by being willing to look inward or become introspective.
2. The ability to appreciate the feelings, needs and desires of other persons.
3. The ability to acknowledge our limitations, while still demanding the most of ourselves.
4. The understanding that changing the world requires a collective action; one cannot do it by oneself (1959:105–106).

What Confucianism seems to say, especially with its core belief about the ladder among ancestors, living people, and society, is that we all can learn from other persons and from other experiences. This is a key therapeutic point that can be used in a meaningful way when working with ethnic minority persons. The learning is, of course, a two-way process: client to social worker, and social worker to client. This is analgous to the symmetry of transference and counter-transference in current psychoanalytic theory.

## Techniques for More Ethnic-Sensitive Social Work Practice with Ethnic Minority Clients

Some general postulates are in order before discussing some of the techniques for working with ethnic minority clients. Based on the research that has been done, we know several things about ethnic minority groups that may correlate quite well with successful social work practice:

1. The importance of sociocultural history, traditions, and ceremonies in personal and group identity formation.
2. The importance of the socialization and  acculturation roles of the family and the kinship network.
3. The significance of various religious and spiritual beliefs and practices.
4. The role of the historical experiences of ethnic groups since these experiences are often used as a means to filter or "reality test" the activities, motives, or behaviors of members of other groups.
5. The notion of the "dual perspective" (Norton, 1978). This means that ethnic minority persons derive strength, identity, stability, and a sense of group solidarity from their ethnicity; and, conversely,  these factors also create personal stress and strain as they attempt to accommodate their ethnic identity values with the majority culture values without becoming culturally marginized or perceived as "Uncle Toms".

Beyond these general assumptions, there are some specific techniques for effective social work practice with ethnic minority persons.

### The Significance of Time and Present Orientation

When working with ethnic minority persons, it is important to focus on the here and now: the present time. The reality of the needs and problems to be addressed in the current context is most important. A full-blown diagnostic picture is generally not feasible or useful. Unfortunately, there are very few culturally relevant clinical assessment and diagnostic tools. The problems that most ethnic minority persons face are most often the result of socioeconomic and environmental forces, such as poverty, unemployment, lack of education, cultural and religious differences, and language barriers. In most cases, ethnic minority clients are experiencing stress from the immediate impact of these kinds of problems. The ethnic minority client  needs a practice approach that is time-limited, highly focused, and crisis-oriented. The intent should be to impact and influence their social and physical environments. The focus should be upon obtaining "concrete" or tangible services, such as public welfare assistance, job training, education, housing, medical, or other direct social services.

## The Relevance of Psychotherapeutic Approaches

It is in no small measure true that ethnic minority persons, per se, cannot use and benefit from psychotherapeutic approaches. However, many ethnic minority group members have not had a history of or an acquaintance with psychotherapeutic approaches to problem-solving. Psychotherapies are idiosyncratically Western-culture–specific in nature. In addition, these approaches work best with clients who have adequate education levels, well-developed cognitive processes, and verbal skills and language abilities. It is also very problematic as to whether or not other counseling approaches, such as social learning, reality therapies, and cognitive therapies, are effective as well. Nonracial/ethnic minority persons seem to relate more easily to approaches that involve an exploration of the traumatic incidents in one's developmental history, reflection upon that history, and development of insight derived from that exploratory and reflective process. Because of these factors, the use of these kinds of helping approaches with ethnic minority persons may be highly problematic and therapeutically nonproductive.

However, there are some relevant folk cultural approaches that are somewhat analogous to psychotherapies. Gomez and Cook (1977), for example, describe the widespread practice of "platicando" among Hispanics. Platicando is a type of counseling approach that is highly personalized. It is highly personalized in the sense that it contains strong elements of acceptance of the person, or empathy, by the social worker. It is also highly personalized because in this form of encounter the social worker becomes a personal helper for the client. In a sense, the client operates via the ego of the social worker, a phenomena Hispanics refer to as "personalismo." Personalismo is manifested, particularly among Hispanic clients, by a strong preference for a particular social worker, combined with the inclination to establish a therapeutic relationship with only one particular professional person. Platicando is used as a means to address situational problems that arise from social and environmental stress. Platicando involves advice-giving and the conveying of information. But, as Gomez and Cook view it, it can go beyond mere advice-giving. It can become a supportive therapy. This occurs when the method is used to help individuals develop skills for coping with problems. At this level the emphasis can center upon the client's feelings about the problem, his or her reactions to the problem, and upon effective and ineffective ways used in the past to cope with problems. In other words, it can become a kind of relationship therapy.

What ultimately may be most helpful, in the therapeutic sense, with ethnic minority clients, is a kind of "ethnotherapy." This refers to practices that focus, when necessary for problem solving, upon race, culture, and ethnicity. Feelings can be explored when the client is asked questions that require personal reflection and consideration, for example: "How does it feel to be an African-American?"; or "What was it like growing up in the barrio?", or "Do you believe that I, a white person, can understand you and your problems?"

It is especially important to engage the client when the social worker perceives or feels that issues about race and culture which affect the relationship or impact on the client's ability to engage in problem-solving have not been dealt with. Solomon (1976) is very insightful about the genesis of this problem. She feels that it is very threatening for many nonethnic minority social workers to deal with racial issues, especially if the issues may lead to confrontation. Instead, they often prefer to withdraw or avoid racial and cultural issues. The caveat for the social worker is that the issues of race and ethnicity must be engaged actively if the client has distorted or misinterpreted the behavior of the social worker with respect to such issues.

Historically, clinical research concerning therapeutic outcomes comparing the same or different clients and therapists with respect to the variables of race and ethnicity generally has been inconclusive. The writer believes, however, that two key dimensions are at the core of successful practice with ethnic minority persons. First, the social worker (regardless of his or her race, gender, or ethnic minority status) has to be perceived as being believable. The ethnic minority client has to feel that the social worker can make a difference in their life. This is the issue of the credibility of the practitioner. The second point is more obvious: The ethnic minority client must believe that the social worker is knowledgeable about and sensitive to their ethnic minority background.

The issue of the dual perspective is at the core of "doing" any effective sort of psychotherapy or counseling with any ethnic minority individuals. From the dual perspective notion, one might hypothesize that the best way to "reach" ethnic minority clients through social work practice lies in dealing with their sense of personal fragmentation and identity loss and crisis that they may be experiencing as their cultural anchors increasingly become marginalized through interactions with the dominant societal values and culture (beliefs and behaviors). To reach an accommodation or change in behavior, or rehabilitation of deviant patterns of behavior, the practitioner would use "ethnocultural identification...(to help) the patient manage cultural values, negotiate transitional experiences, and cope with identity readjustment in an alien cultural environment" (Comas-Diaz 1988:340).

### Folk Cultural Beliefs

Several folk cultural beliefs, which generally can be classified as representing "mental health" notions, are important for social workers to understand and refer to when working with some ethnic minority persons. Many of these kinds of beliefs are pervasive among various Hispanic groups. Some of these beliefs are inseparable from religious belief systems and spiritual values that were discussed previously. "Espiritismo" is one of these folk cultural beliefs. It is especially important for the social worker to understand espiritismo when working with Puerto Rican clients. The espirita is a spiritualist, medium, or fortune-teller. She usually gives advice about such things as life, love, and fortune. However, much of her "trade" centers upon psychosomatic problems and illnesses. She can be a key person to consult in the attempt to understand the relationship between the physical and psychological difficulties that the client may be experiencing. In a way, she is a folk or "street" psychiatrist.

"Simpatico" is another Hispanic folk culture belief of some importance. This is the belief that one ought to always remain personable and pleasant in interactions with other people. It emphasizes avoiding disagreements, confrontation, and any kind of dissension. It values the notion of seeking consensus rather than conflict in intergroup relationships. Simpatico sometimes can be inferred by the behavior of individuals who appear to be passive, dependent, and lack affect or demonstrable feelings. As clients, these persons often are prone to suppress feelings, especially feelings of anger, hostility, and frustration.

There is a delicate balance in working with ethnic minority clients who subscribe to these kinds of beliefs. Many times, a warm, supporting , and highly personalized relationship can be effective in working with such clients. However, the exigencies of the social welfare system require that the social worker confront them with respect to their behavior. Clients who exhibit these kinds of behaviors are very trying and frustrating to work with. Usually, very little therapeutic progress is made. A proper decision about how to deal with them only can be made after completing an extensive assessment and diagnostic process. This is particularly important since their behavior may be masking serious problems in social functioning or a life-threatening depression.

## SUMMARY AND CONCLUSIONS

This chapter has presented some information about the characteristics of major ethnic minority groups in the United States in order to help professional social workers deliver more ethnically and culturally sensitive services. Obviously, a great deal more could be said about this topic. Indeed, there are many resources in the social work literature that directly address many of these issues. The need for the professional social worker to understand that certain cultural values and experiences have important meaning for ethnic minority individuals and groups was pointed out. It also was pointed out that this seems to be the case especially among ethnic minority groups with respect to certain ethnocultural values and patterns, such as the role of the family, and religious and spiritual values.

There are some techniques that can be used to enhance the effectiveness of social work practice when working with ethnic minority clients. These techniques were thought to be most effective when the social worker uses them in order to enhance their ability to manage their cultural values, and use these values in dealing with changing passages and transitions in their lives. It was suggested that many folk cultural beliefs could be utilized, often in conjunction with more traditional counseling methods, to help ethnic minority persons understand and cope with the problems of daily life, with what they may perceive as a hostile and alien world.

## REFERENCES

Borrello, M. A. & Mathias, E. (1977). Botanicas: Puerto Rican folk pharmacies. *Natural History* 86:64–73.

Boyer, L. B. 1964. Psychoanalytic insights in working with ethnic minorities. *Social Casework* 45:519–526.

Browne, C. & Broderick, A. 1994. Asian and Pacific island elders: Issues for social work practice and education. *Social Work* 39:252–259.

Burtt, E. A. 1959. Buddhism. In *Basic Beliefs*. J. E. Fairchild (ed). New York: Sheridan House, pp. 73–90.

Campbell, J. 1959. Hinduism. In *Basic Beliefs*. J. E. Fairchild (ed). New York: Sheridan House, pp. 54–72.

Castex, G. M. 1994. Providing services to Hispanic/Latino populations: Profiles in diversity. *Social Work* 39:288-296.

Comas-Diaz, L. 1988. Cross-cultural mental health treatment. In *Clinical Guidelines in Cross-Cultural Mental Health*. L. Comas-Diaz & E. H. Griffith (eds). New York: John Wiley & Sons, pp. 337–361.

deBary, W. T. 1959. Confucianism. In *Basic Beliefs*. J. E. Fairchild (ed). New York: Sheridan House, pp. 92–113.

Erickson, E. 1963. *Childhood and Society*. New York: W. W. Norton.

Frazier, E. F. 1963. *The Negro Church in America*. New York: Schochen Books.

Gomez, E. & Cook, K. 1977. *Chicano Culture and Mental Health: Trees in Search of a Forest*. Monograph No. 1, Centro Del Barrio. San Antonio: Worden School of Social Service, Our Lady of the Lake University.

Jenkins, S. 1981. *The Ethnic Dilemma in Social Services*. New York: Free Press.

Lum, D. 1986. *Social Work Practice and People of Color: A Process-Stage Approach*. Monterey, CA: Brooks / Cole.

Mindel, C. H., Habenstein, R. W., & Wright, Jr., R. W. 1988. Family lifestyles of America's ethnic minorities: An introduction. In *Ethnic Families in America*, 3rd edition. C. H. Mindel, R. W. Habenstein, & R. W. Wright, Jr. (eds). New York: Elsevier, pp. 1–14.

Norton, D. G. 1978. *The Ddual Perspective: Inclusion of Ethnic Minority Content in the Social Work Curriculum*. New York: Council on Social Work Education.

Office of Management and Budget. (1978, May 4). Directive 15: Race and ethnic standards for federal statistics and administrative reporting. *Federal Register* 43: 19269.

Ringgren, H. & Strom, A. V. 1967. *Religions of Mankind*. Philadelphia: Fortress Press.

Solomon, B. B. 1976. *Black Empowerment: Social Work in Oppressed Communities*. New York: Columbia University Press.

Staples, R. 1976. *Introduction to Black Sociology*. New York: McGraw-Hill.

# 22

## Education, Diversity, and American Culture

Stanton W. Green & Stephen M. Perlman

### INTRODUCTION

Americans long have viewed the democratization of public education with some ambivalence. On the one hand, education is seen as a means of providing people the opportunity to better themselves by pulling themselves up the socioeconomic ladder through increased literacy and college attendance. On the other hand, as education has expanded, public discontent with decreasing standards and student performance often has been blamed on the cultural and especially linguistic diversity of students. In a sense, this ambivalence indicates how American education serves as a mirror of American society as it grapples with its history as an immigrant-based nation. The questions for education are the same as they are for the nation: Does student diversity strengthen or weaken the system? Does the multicultural student body threaten the existing cultural coherence of our public schools? Does diversity affect outcomes? In practical terms: How do we teach students with diverse backgrounds. What do we teach them? Should everything be taught in standard English? Is there, indeed, "a body of information that each American should know to take part in our shared culture?" (Hirsch 1987).

This chapter approaches the anwers to these questions from the perspective of the anthropologist. We examine education as a part of culture. Formal education is one of several processes that transmits culture between generations. Education assumes many cultural forms ranging from socialization within the family through formalized learning and training within the school (Gardner 1993). Teaching and learning, the basic components of education, are played out within specific cultural settings. As Gardner (1993) has poignantly illustrated, the education of a person really involves the interaction of three domains: the intellectual proclivities of an individual (what he terms intelligences), the opportunities and constraints of one's culture, and the social setting that judges an individual's performance. His work as an educational psychologist focuses on the variety of intelligences we all possess (e.g., spatial, mathematical, linguistic, musical, and kinesthetic intelligence). But he does not stop at the individual. He argues that culture must not be seen merely as a backdrop to our individual abilities, but as an active ingredient in making us what we are. An individual's culture(s) and intelligence interact dynamically. This chapter examines culture as that vital aspect of learning and teaching wherein education and culture are presented as processes that produce social patterns. These patterns include the ways in which different culture groups interrelate and how these change over time. If we examine the processes that determine these patterns, we can begin to sort out the problems concerning cultural diversity and the American education system.

## EDUCATION AND CULTURAL DIVERSITY

Culturally diverse societies such as that of the United States face the problem of balancing the diversity of behaviors, ideas, and attitudes of its citizens with the solidarity of the idealized American culture. Adding to the ever continuing saga of immigration to America, we are confronted with the daunting task of passing on a continually changing and diversifying culture to succeeding generations. Where do the traditions of the older generations fit in? How about languages? How can we balance American's highly valued respect for individualism with the need to define what it is to be an American?

The relationship of educational and cultural settings is fundamental to both anthropological (Mead 1951) and educational literature (Gardner 1993), where teaching and learning have been shown to be particularly sensitive to cultural diversity. The dilemma in American education is a mirror of society at large and can come down to one's interpretation of *e pluribus unum*. The melting pot or the salad bowl? As educators, do we describe American culture as one of homogenized ingredients or of many separate but related parts? Much of this argument relates to how one treats the process of assimilation. Do we expect immigrants to become part of an Anglo-American culture—or to retain parts of their identity that they then contribute to a diverse American culture (Kazal 1995)?

The way we answer these questions determines the way we view the goals of educating immigrants. At the same time, immigrants come with their own varying beliefs, attitudes and expectations. Voluntary immigrants are inclined to reject their traditional culture and language for one or two generations, after which they often try to reclaim it. As involuntary immigrants of color, African-Americans have developed different coping strategies for dealing with long-term discrimination and oppression (Ogbu 1991). What is common to all immigrants is the centrality of education in their assimilation (or lack of assimilation). This being the case, they often find themselves embroiled in the educational debate of the time. Diversity and immigration continue to be tied intricately to America's continuing discontent with its educational system.

Rose (1989) shows a continuing discontent with reports of student performance (specifically writing) over the past 120 years. In the 1870s, Professor Sherman

Adams offered the following assessment of Harvard students: "Every year Harvard graduates a certain number of men some of them high scholars whose manuscripts would disgrace a boy of twelve" (Rose 1989:xx). In 1896, The magazine *Nation* produced an article entitled "The growing illiteracy of American boys," and in 1898 the University of California's subject A exam produced a failure rate of 30–40 percent in English, a rate that continues today (Rose 1989:6). In contrast to a perceived lack of change in performance and competence, the scope and standards of the educational system have been revolutionized. Some statistics based on Rose (1989:67) reveal this.

Table 22.1
Trends in American Education: 1890 and 1970s

|  | 1890 | 1970s |
|---|---|---|
| High School Attendance | 6.7% | 94.1% (1976) |
| High School Graduates | 3.5% | 75.6% (Americans, 1970) |
|  |  | 45–50% (Swedes, 1970) |
|  |  | 15% (Germans, 1970) |
| College Attendance | 4% | 50% (of 18 to 19 year olds) |

Not only has secondary and post-secondary education been expanded to include an increasingly diversified student body, but this expansion has been paralleled by increased expectations. Functional literacy, once defined as having three or more years of schooling, increased to five or more in 1947, to the sixth grade in 1952, the eighth grade in 1960, and by the late 1970s it had been increased to high school graduation (Rose 1989:6).

Given all of this, the perceived decline of education would seem more fiction than fact. A greater number and diversity of students is being educated to higher levels and standards than ever before. Education would appear to be an adaptive part of the American immigrant-based society where increasing diversity has been an historical pattern. At the same time, discontent continues and the immigrants of the particular time, the Irish of the late nineteenth century or the Mexicans of the late twentieth century, often take on the brunt of the criticism for the so-called "failure of American education." Our cultural values highlight education as a right and as an entrance to American social mobility. Our standards for education broaden and increase as we include immigrant and previously marginalized groups (such as women) and move into a more technological and future-oriented society. Yet, our discontent continues to be laid at diversity's doorstep. What can be made of this? Is there a logical process that can explain these seemingly contradictory viewpoints? A beginning to the answer to these questions is a consideration of how education functions as a part of culture.

## Culture

Culture is learned; it is shared by groups of people, and it concerns ideas, values, attitudes, and behaviors. That culture is learned distinguishes it from the innate or instinctual aspects of human behavior, but this does not, or course, imply that all learning is culture. Individual learning is done thorough simple trial and error as well as imitation. What makes learning cultural is the ability to use symbols to communicate (Fried 1967). The cultural world is created by groups of people. Symbols are sounds, pictures, inscriptions, and images that are given meaning through human language. Although symbolic learning has been attributed to other species such as chimpanzees, gorillas, whales, and dolphins, the human species has elaborated symbolic communication qualitatively beyond these fellow creatures.

Cultural groups share a viewpoint on the ways in which the world works and ought to work. It is very important to understand that sharing does not denote homogeneity. Rather, we would describe cultural sharing as a network of created understandings. Similarities in thinking, knowing, and behaving are greater within cultures and cultural groupings than between them. Two simple examples of cultural constructs are colors and foods. People from all cultures are sensitive to same range of the light spectrum (except for individuals with particular defects such as color blindness). When one compares the ways in which different cultures describe color, we see a wide range of categories. Similarly, as classic primate omnivores, human beings are capable of eating and enjoying a wide range of plant and animal foods. The definition of what is edible and what is not, of course, ranges widely between cultures. We could continue with the more complex examples of how we define relatives (the study of kinship), the related matter of who we are allowed to (or prescribed to) marry, and how work is divided between men and women and boys and girls (the sexual division of labor). All of these sets of cultural categories make sense of a world of almost infinite possibilities created by and implemented through symbolic language. Language, then, is important to discuss as the primary connector between culture and behavior.

## Language and Literacy

Language is the essence of human interaction. People relate to each other through mutually understandable ways of speaking, writing, and behaving, which, taken together, is what we call a discourse (Gee 1991). We learn to interact in a variety of social settings, each of which requires its own way of interacting. We can understand this if we think about the different ways in which we speak and interact with others in the classroom, in the workplace, and in our family. We speak and interact differently with a teacher, a supervisor, and a parent. Moreover, in the former two, we might find a person whose first language is different from ours.

Although we often think of literacy as the ability to read and write, we can define it more broadly to include the ability to interact using a particular discourse. We have to become literate in a variety of discourses to meet the variety of social settings we encounter through our lives. Beyond one's primary literacy, for example standard American English, Native-born Americans seek to acquire a variety of secondary discourses such as a foreign language (all too infrequently) and the ability to communicate using computers (sometimes called computer literacy). Immigrants and other cultural groups have their own set of discourses in most cases including a primary language other than standard American English.

## Education and the Process of Becoming Literate

The process of becoming literate is different in different educational settings. Gee (1991) draws a fundamental distinction between the social and formal contexts of learning. Social settings, such as the family, provide subconscious avenues for learning. Classroom settings are avenues for formal learning. Gardner (1993:339) describes educational settings as having three parts: the general context (family, classroom), the agent (parents, teachers), the location (kitchen table, classroom), and the media (conversation, book, computer).

Socialization provides the widest constellation of language and communication skills including nonverbal skills, and concepts of time and space. Formal learning may involve some of this, but the emphasis is on formal language and discourse, not on the broader aspects of communication, attitudes, and behaviors. To be literate in American English, therefore, is not simply mastering the oral and written form of the language. Only in the most limited versions of learning, such as learning specific vocabulary of a particular discipline, can literacy be thought of as just learning a language (and even in this case, certain intellectual attitudes and values are tied into particular intellectual traditions). Literacy is always broad and cultural.

## The Politics of Education

We now can begin to understand some of the politics underlying education and cultural diversity. There are, of course, pedagogical choices to be made in order to educate a culturally diverse student body. Whether non-English speaking students should be taught in English or in their native language is a legitimate pedagogical question. But the way we deal with diversity in the classroom goes well beyond this. The language of use and the goal of language training is a part of the larger question of the dominant cultures expectations of the assimilating student.

"Literacy," as Collins notes, " is never purely technical but always a profoundly political matter" (1991:231). The language of the dominant culture sets the general standards for publicly perceived literacy and the literacy in public places. In the United States, we see this battle in debates on the teaching of English as a second language. In Canada, the Quebecois movement argues for French dominance in public places. But it is important to understand that this problem is limited neither to the late twentieth century nor to the North American continent. As Said (1993) notes, we find these very same issues in the words of Stephen Daedelus in Joyce's "Portrait of an Artist as a Young Man" as he thinks of the use of the British-English language by an English Catholic priest.

The language we are speaking is his before mine. How different are the words, Christ, ale, master, on his lips and on mine! I cannot speak or write these words without unrest of spirit. His language, so familiar and so foreign, will always be for me acquired speech. I have not made or accepted its words. My voice holds them at bay. My soul frets in the shadow of his language. (Said 1993:223–224).

It is important to remember that the priest's language and Stephen's language are both forms of English. It is the cultural context and the difference between British and Irish dialects that makes them foreign tongues. The tension between American English and the great variety of languages brought to our schools by immigrants represents the same political struggle that Stephen describes, a struggle that results from our ambivalence about our society's cultural diversity.

### Education and Culture as Dynamic Processes

Education transmits culture from generation to generation. If it is anything, culture is ever-changing. Sometimes fast, sometimes slow, but always changing. Cultures and their associated discourses and literacies change as a result of their own internal dynamics and in relation to other cultures. Cultural change is an inevitable, unavoidable historical progression. Cultures change as shared ideas, values, attitudes, and behaviors are altered as a consequence of interaction among members of a culture and between members of different cultures. The question then becomes: How can the educators grab hold of this malleable and ever-changing phenomenon of culture so that they can pass it on to the next generation?

For this, we can turn to Margaret Mead's examination of American education and its relationship to culture change during the middle of the twentieth century (1951, 1970). She assesses the American discontent with the educational system by challenging one of education's primary assumptions: that the communication and education gap between the generations is the result of the younger generation simply not gaining the wisdom of the former generation (either because of their inability to learn it or the elder's inability to teach it). Provocatively, she looks for an explanation of the perceived communication problems between generations (inside and outside of the classroom) in the way culture changes. She does not accept the seemingly time-old explanation that kids today just are not learning. Rather, she looks toward cultural and historical processes as an explanation for the gap between the generations and for the discontent of the older generation about educational outcomes. It is not sufficient, Mead argues, to observe that times change and generations differ. It is necessary to understand that culture changes in different ways and at different rates. Educational problems may well be solved by looking at the way and speed in which any culture changes (Green and Perlman 1993). The argument on educational problems of Margaret Mead goes as follows.

In traditional societies, change is relatively slow (but not nonexistent). Culture is passed on from the elders to the younger through multiple-generation households. Wendell Berry (1970) describes this as basically a coherent oral tradition. This pattern changes in twentieth-century America as immigration breaks the continuity of experience in American society and culture change quickens. Peer learning becomes more important as a wider variety of viewpoints become available through immigration and global communication. In today's culture, change is so quick that the future can be essentially independent from the past and the present. Change is accelerated, time is fragmented, and knowledge is global and instantaneous. News is as fast as the speed of light. The history of the Persian Gulf War was viewed as it happened. Millions of people around the world watched the skies of Baghdad explode with missiles, bombs, and antiaircraft fire. How does one teach the Gulf War as history to students who viewed parts of it? The delay of watching news digests or reading next-day newspaper accounts are quite literally secondary to many current students. Indeed, the whole visual-image (or what some might term digital) orientation of today's student changes the very way information is passed on, where it is, and by whom it is passed on. The context, agent, locus, and media of learning (Gardner 1993) are revolutionized. Mead's summary is particularly poignant.

Today, nowhere in the world are there elders who know what the children know, no matter how remote and simple the societies are in which the children live. In the past, there were always some leaders who knew more than any children in terms of their experience of having grown up within a cultural system. Today there are none. It is not only that parents are no longer guides, but that there are no guides whether one seeks them in one country or abroad. There are no elders who know what those who have been reared within the last twenty years know about the world into which they were born (1970:75).

The older generation can never say they were once young, because they were never young in the world of the current generation (Mead 1970).

How do we educate students in such a time of culture change? What, indeed, do we teach them? Mead's lesson is that we cannot succeed in passing on our core cultural values to succeeding generations unless we confront the fact that culture change is different in today's world than it was in the past and it will differ in the future. If our educational system is not attuned to the nature of the cultural dynamic, then the generations will not be able to communicate and the next generation will not be reached. Although we cannot abandon the teachings of previous generations, we also cannot proceed with the traditional model that sees learning as occurring essentially, if not solely, down the ladder of generations through the teaching of elders.

### Balancing Tradition and Change and Coping with Diversity

But what of past traditions and culture history? Are they not necessary to pass on such truths and morals such as fairness, honesty, and sympathy that transcend generations and cultures (Wilson 1994)? Of course they are. Traditions pass on to children the values of our culture. But the swift culture change of today produces generations that are living in a world that in some ways is disconnected from the generations of our parents and grandparents. Each generation consists of, in Mead's words, "immigrants in time" (1979:71). How can we balance tradition and change in order to guide future generations?

At least part of the answer lies in how we as a society view American cultural diversity and how we cope with it. Some would argue for a reliance on the teaching of the traditions of an idealized Anglo-American culture (Schlesinger 1993). In this view, American culture is a coherent, well-bounded, and largely unchanging whole. Different cultural groups are essentially different and can be likened to a set of ingredients waiting to be mixed into a batter and baked into a cake. Assimilation is seen as the process of mixing and baking. Immigrants are expected to become Americans (if not Anglo-Americans); those who do not are marginalized.

Our argument leads us to a contrasting view. We view culture as a dynamic, historic process and culture diversity as a natural outcome of culture change. If this is true, diversity will not disappear through assimilation, it will only change. Diversity defines American culture. The society remains diverse and culture ever-changing. But how do we cope with the diverse viewpoints of cultural groupings within American society? Doesn't a viewpoint that recognizes cultural diversity promote cultural division in the form of multiple languages and even cultural ghettos?

If we accept culture as a process, then the pattern of tension and division that we see in contemporary America can be explained as the result of attempts to suppress diversity and resist cultural change. Emergent cultural groupings, or subcultures as some prefer to term them (Schlesinger 1993), are actually the natural outcomes of American cultural history. To return to our metaphor, they are ingredients that resist the baking process. The political tension would seem to be a consequence of our ambivalence toward our history as an immigrant nation. If we accept diversity, we take the first step toward coping with it. American education then is faced with the daunting tasks of creating productive American citizens and providing the bases for cultural literacy (and its subsidiary specialized literacies) within a diverse and ever-changing culture. However, the attitude we bring to the classroom is quite different if we accept diversity rather than attempt to eliminate it. The key is to understand education as a part of an ever-changing society and culture. Then we can attend to culture as a dynamic force in the classroom (Green & Perlman 1995).

## Strategies for Coping with Cultural Diversity

There have been a variety of rationales given for an educational system that recognizes and addresses cultural diversity. These include supporting the identity formation of students, recognizing the diversity of American ethnic groups and giving them equal support in the curriculum, and teaching an accurate culture history of America (Takaki 1993). We certainly agree with these goals. What is provocative to us is how we as educators really can achieve these goals within an understanding of contemporary cultural change. If we view generational differences as cultural differences, then any teacher–student interaction becomes intercultural. The increasingly diverse and global dimension of today's world adds additional intercultural relationships in the classroom. One key to communication in such a classroom culture can come from actively involving students in developing topics of discussion and the language in which these topics are discussed. This approach often is called active learning.

In effect, active learning allows for student cultures to meet and interact with other student cultures as well as teacher cultures. Controversies surrounding active learning and multicultural education derive from the difficulties of balancing the teaching of traditional information and values, and engaging the contemporary culture of students. Although active learning does not imply that students set the agenda, it does recognize that student and teacher discourse must be made mutually intelligible. Although multiculturalism does not imply that anything goes in the classroom (what some might call moral relativism), it does assert that all cultures need to be recognized (cultural relativism, Herskovitz 1972 ). Active, multicultural educational approaches recognize and appreciate the actual diversity of cultural backgrounds of students so that teaching and learning can bridge the cultural gap between teaching and student generations and their associated cultures. This is balanced with the teacher's cultural background so that both traditional and current cultures are represented in the classroom. In conclusion, let us try for the moment, to pull away from our general arguments and the politics of multiculturalism, and offer an example of how the awareness of cultural diversity can be heightened through an active learning experiment about culture in the classroom.

## AN EXPERIMENT IN CULTURAL AWARENESS

We will conclude this chapter with a little experiment designed to simulate what it is like to be a part of another way of knowing things, that is, what it is like to be a member of another culture. To do this we turn back to our example of food as a cultural construct. Food is, after all, something we all need and all relate to, despite the fact that cultures vary a great deal in the way they define it. In addition, food is often a dividing boundary between cultures and a significant way in which people perceive other cultures.

The lesson of this role-playing experiment is to get students to begin seeing food and diet as a cultural construct. Although cultural traditions play a role in the diet, the key is for students to see diet not as inherently different, but as a different view of food and eating. Students generally believe that their behavior is a matter of personal choice. The notion that much of our behavior is the result of circumstance contradicts one of our central values that we create our destinies. The key to this experiment, then, is to show how circumstance defines one's viewpoint. The goal is to help students understand the cultural foundation for many parts of their lives, so that it becomes more difficult for them to reject the life-styles of others out of hand and, most importantly, to provide them with a means for becoming more accepting of other cultural viewpoints. Hence we offer this little food and culture experiment.

A class of eighth graders were divided into groups and told to select a diet from a list of foods. They were allowed to choose as they wished as long as their menu was sufficient to feed a family of four. The only other constraint was the amount of money each group was given to accomplish the task. Group allocations ranged from just a few dollars a day to an unlimited amount. The results proved revealing in several ways.

When the groups compared their diets they could see that those with few dollars to spend selected essentially the same diets. Groups with larger allocations selected a wider diversity of foods. Through discussion, students learned that family menus are not just the result of personal or cultural choice, but they are also related to the social and economic circumstances of each family. They also learned that they all used similar decision-making criteria. Differences in diet that they had observed and experienced in the past were no longer seen as only the result of cultural preference. They could better appreciate the basis for these choices and therefore were less likely to be as judgmental and ethnocentric about other group's choices. People became, to a degree, themselves under different circumstances.

Despite the simplicity of this experiment, it shows the power of active learning about culture. It allows students to build bridges across cultural differences through an understanding of culture as a complex and ever-changing process. An active understanding of culture aids the students in understanding the basis for cultural differences so that they then can examine and appreciate the particulars that make different cultures different. These cultural particulars, then, do not immediately turn into cultural barriers and the basis for immediate cultural judgments.

## CONCLUSION

The dilemma of American education as it deals with the diversity of our country reflects our society's schizophrenia about its multicultural basis and the role of our educational system in the process of creating an American culture. We are, on the one hand, proud of our immigrant history and the success and strength its diversity brings to our society. At the same time, the ever-broadening problems brought on by cultural and technological changes often are laid at the feet of the multicultural nature of our society. Education is caught in this dilemma as it increases access, services, and standards.

Education is aimed at a cultural target that is moving on several axes. The first axis might represent standards, the second diversity, and the third culture change. Accepted standards and cultural diversity continuously change and usually broaden the objectives of education. These shifting educational objectives must pass through a constantly changing culture that redefines the relationships between generations and the way they interact on a regular basis.

A better understanding of cultural diversity and change can lead us to a better understanding of the role of education in our society. We need to move beyond the token recognition and appreciation of cultural diversity. Such a token understanding represents cultures as essentially different and mutually unintelligible. At best, this leads to the celebration of separate cultures, at worst, tokenism leads to disrespect, mutual distrust, and prejudice. We must understand the significance of a cultural group's history and tradition as a part of a dynamic and multifaceted American culture. Although families are the primary purveyors of culture, educators are next in line. As such, we must develop curricula and pedagogies that incorporate an understanding of cultural process and cultural continuity and change within the framework of American cultural diversity.

## REFERENCES

Berry, W. 1970. In Defense of Literacy. In *A Continuous Harmony: Essays Cultural and Agricultural.* New York: Harcourt Brace Javanovich, pp. 169–173.

Carroll, T. 1990. Who owns culture? In *Cultural Diversity and American Education: Visions of the Future.* T. G. Carroll & Schensul, J. J. (eds). *Education and Urban Society* 22 (4):346–355.

Collins, J. 1991. Hegemonic Practice: Literacy and standard language in public education. In *Rewriting Literacy: Culture and the Discourse of the Other.* C. Mitchell & K. Weiler (eds). New York: Bergin & Garvey, pp 229–254.

Fried, M. 1967. *The Evolution of Political Society: An Essay in Political Anthropology.* New York: Random House.

Gardner, H. 1993. *Frames of Mind: A Theory of MultipleIintelligences.* New York: Basic Books.

Gee, J. P. 1991. What is literacy. In *Rewriting Literacy: Culture and the Discourse of the Other.* C. Mitchell & K. Weiler (eds). New York: Bergin & Garvey, pp. 3–12.

Green, S. & Perlman, S. 1993. Putting culture into multicultural education: Toward a critical model of cultural literacy. In *Interdisciplinary Curricula, General Education and Liberal Learning.* R. Kelder (ed). New Paltz, NY: The Institute for the Study of Post Secondary Pedagogy, pp. 18–29.

————1995. Multicultural education and culture change: An anthropological perspective. *Multicultural Education* (Summer).

Herskowitz, M. 1972. *Cultural Relativism: Perspective on Cultural Pluralism.* New York: Vintage Books.

Hirsch, E. D. 1987. *Cultural Literacy.* New York: Vintage Books (Random House).

Kazal, R. 1995. Revisiting assimilation: The rise, fall and reappraisal of a concept in American ethnic history. *The American Historical Review* 100 (2):437–471.

Mead, M. 1951. *The School in American Culture.* Cambridge: Harvard University Press.

————1970. *Culture and Commitment.* New York: Columbia University Press.

Ogbu, J. 1991. Minority status and literacy in comparative perspective. In *Literacy: An Overview by 14 experts.* S.R. Graubard (ed). New York: Noonday Press.

Rose, M. 1989. *Lives on the Boundary.* New York: Free Press.

Said, E. 1993. *Culture and Imperialism.* New York: Knopf.

Schlesinger, A. 1993. *The Disuniting of America.* New York: W. W. Norton.

Takaki, R. T. 1993. *A Different Mirror: A History of Multicultural America*. Boston: Little, Brown & Co.

Wilson, J. 1994. *The Moral Sense*. New York: Free Press.

# 23

# Practical Considerations for Living and Working in Contexts of Diversity

## Gloria Contreras

Where does one acquire a set of practical considerations or skills for interacting effectively in contexts of diversity? Recently, one college student of mine wrote about his upbringing in the following manner: "All through my life I have been taught by my parents to be tolerant of other cultures and encouraged to ask questions of those who are different than myself and, more importantly, listen and learn." Tolerance is perhaps the skill most often identified by educators as the most important multicultural competency for today's diverse society.

Of course, not all students credit their upbringing and home environment for their multicultural perspective on life. For some people, however, one should not underestimate the power of the schools and teachers to effectively convey an anti-bias curriculum, particularly in the earlier childhood years (Derman-Sparks 1989). An anti-bias curriculum in this particular case refers to an active approach to challenging prejudice, stereotyping, and bias, for at a very young age children can be harmed either because they themselves struggle against a bias or because they learn that they are superior as a result of being white, able-bodied, male, etc. Still other students acquire anti-bias attitudes upon beginning their college careers as they enter settings that are far more diverse than they have ever before experienced. For these particular individuals the "hidden curriculum" offers a rich opportunity to acquire an important multicultural knowledge base.

Before plunging into a set of practical considerations for living and working in contexts of diversity, it is important to address the context of controversy that currently threatens the principles of multiculturalism, pluralism, and/or diversity, both on the inside and on the outside of most university campus communities. One recent issue that generated some very heated debates in the living rooms of America, came with the release of the National History Standards to the media, primarily through talk show hosts. These National History Standards are really about students becoming better historical thinkers have been highly criticized as political correctness and multicultural excesses (Nash 1995). To some of the

American public the world history standards have been linked to left-wing revisionism, while others are now just plain confused over the issue of how to provide students with a more comprehensive and challenging education for the twenty-first century. As the recent Gallup Poll "Of the Public's Attitude Toward the Public Schools" reveals, people are almost evenly divided on whether history teaching is more or less accurate than in the past (33% more accurately and 37% less accurately), with a sizable number saying that they do not know (22%). To the charge that the standards do not sufficiently emphasize Western civilization, Nash (1995) reminds us that the nation's new immigrants are reason enough for all Americans to learn about the entire human community. What, then, are the implications of this kind of multicultural controversy for the contexts of diversity in which people live, work, and play? Notwithstanding the continuing debates surrounding the issues of diversity, pluralism, or multiculturalism, whatever the label, ethnic, language, religious, racial, and international diversity is increasing at every level of society—in communities, in the schools, and in the workplace. Other issues related to exceptionality, sexual orientation, and gender bias will only grow, too.

## PRACTICAL CONSIDERATIONS

Most individuals are quite capable of forming opinions without adequate prior knowledge, thus forming a prejudgment either for or against a group, idea, or person. For example, after learning about the bombing of the federal building in Oklahoma, how many people immediately thought the explosion had been the work Arab terrorists? Of course, it is a human response to make sense out of confusion and to explain things that surround us. However, individuals also have the capacity for developing a defense mechanism against developing prejudice (Pate 1995). Learning to understand our own personal cultural conditioning and the assumptions we draw from experiences form the basis of this chapter. The following six considerations for interacting effectively in diverse contexts are drawn from a life-long commitment to multiculturalism, personal observations, and experiences living in a bilingual/bicultural community, exposure to a large body of literature on multicultural education, and some 20 years of teaching and administrative experience related to multicultural education issues: tolerance, positive self-image, listening skills, critical thinking skills, admitting discomfort, and experiencing differences.

### Tolerance

Tolerance is frequently the response given to the following question, "What is a major practical consideration for living and working in contexts of diversity?" Tolerance, however, is rarely defined operationally by those who deem it an essential element. Certainly, an imperative of the label is an open mind along with effective listening and critical thinking skills (discussed separately). The ability to question assumptions, the competence to withhold judgment, and the capacity to admit a misperception is a high-level form of self-scrutiny, indeed. Thus, authentic tolerance is at its best when we examine our own background and experience in order to dig out and eliminate stereotypes.

A valuable exercise for developing tolerance is called "first thoughts." This skill is acquired from years of leading sensitivity/prejudice reduction training sessions through the National Coalition Building Institute in Washington, DC. This self-scrutiny exercise serves to uncover the stereotypes we have learned about groups other than our own. It is thought that what we have heard or been told about other groups is internalized in the form of a "recording" that we carry with us throughout our lives. Although our own experiences and thinking may actually refute these "records" or stereotypes, they still remain inside of us. The idea behind "first thoughts" is to begin to confront these records and to break or replace them with more accurate ones. One simply repeats the select term (such as blacks, gays, men, women, Asians, Christians, etc.) to him/herself and permits one's uncensored recordings to come out. This mental exercise allows one to recognize and analyze bias in a personal and honest way.

The application of this exercise can be appreciated in the following anecdote involving a trip to Southeast Asia. Two years ago I traveled to Vietnam with a delegation of social studies educators from the United States to study Vietnam's history, culture, educational system, the legacy of the war, and to learn about the impact of the U.S. economic embargo on that country. Now as a college student of the 1960s, the notion of Vietnam conjured up painful memories of the war and the images of classmates who died in the war. My brother also had served in Vietnam and had worked toward the release of POWs. As an educator, social studies teacher, and textbook author, I was compelled to take on this emotional sojourn. Of course, a personal reason was connected to the healing process that many of my generation have been undergoing in the recent past.

A major objective of the trip, then, was to to acquire a new framework for teaching Vietnamese culture and history in the social studies curriculum, for the time had come to teach beyond the Vietnam war and the deep emotional scars that both sides endured from the war. At this point I began to prepare mentally by practicing pre-trip "first thoughts" of Vietnam. Not surprisingly, my very first uncensored thoughts about Vietnam came out in the form of stereotyped images I had learned of the Vietnamese peasants and Viet Cong fighters. Racial epithets flowed out as well, with the names of Manuel Hernandez, Robert Burciega, and Eddie Ayala, classmates who had lost their lives in the Vietnam conflict while I attended college.

Because I practice this exercise privately, I did not freeze or censor and block my first thoughts on Vietnam. This type of self-scrutiny enables one to recognize and analyze their own biases. Admittedly, my first thoughts only reflected my own accumulated experiences and not a universal truth about a whole group of people. Recognizing that there is much more that we do not know about a group of people is critical to the notion of tolerance. I should note that, today post–Vietnam first thoughts evoke an entirely different array of images and notions that portray the Vietnamese as a friendly people, one of laughing children, water puppets, musical performances, delicious foods, and business development as well as the war images.

It also should be noted that in the process of recognizing and analyzing one's biases, one should not feel guilty. Many biases are simply old "records" playing out their songs and not what an individual actually believes, thinks, or acts upon. Assuredly, my own experience with a Vietnamese bilingual education program served to counter the stereotyped images that the war had ingrained in my mind. And certainly I acknowledged that discrimination against Vietnamese refugees was even more abhorrent given the fact that it was the U.S. foreign policy in Southeast Asia that resulted in a flow of war refugees to the United States. The next major consideration for living and working effectively in diverse contexts, that of maintaining a positive self-image, enables an individual to better practice authentic tolerance.

## Positive Self-Image

To be tolerant and accepting of others requires that we like ourselves and take pride in our own identity. The research on self-esteem reveals that a person with low self-esteem will easily become defensive and frustrated (Candfield & Wells 1994). Therefore, an important consideration for individuals living and working in diverse settings is to maintain a sense of complete pride in their personal identity. Recently, a bright and thoroughly delightful student of mine from an upper-class background revealed to me that her rich upbringing was actually an embarrassment to her. She told of how she had tried to conceal this background information about herself from the other students in class. It is apparent in this situation that this young woman is mistaking pride in oneself and a positive self-image for arrogance, conceit, or pomposity. Real pride in a diverse setting means that one is not ashamed of the groups or categories to which one belongs (i.e., religion, class, gender, race, ethnicity, sexual preference). In this young woman's case, shame of being a rich white Anglo is not especially helpful in ending prejudice. It is important that people feel good about themselves so that they then can be optimistic and accepting of others.

## Critical Thinking

Inextricably linked to an authentic tolerance is real critical thinking, another imperative for living and working effectively in contexts of diversity. Critical thinking involves logical and analytical thought that prevents one from jumping to conclusions and overgeneralizing. Critical thinking has widespread use in a multicultural society, for diversity issues crop up continuously and stereotypes are abundant. One can examine critical thinking, for example, as it might relate to something like the "tomahawk chop" issue. The "tomahawk chop," invented by the Atlanta Braves baseball fans, and the antics that accompany such symbols prevent millions of people from understanding the authentic Native American, both historically and today. Imagine that a discussion ensues from the following remark, "So what's all the hoopla with the tomahawk chop? In this case, an open mind is imperative in order to understand the issue from any Native American perspective. A critical thinker in this situation might begin by asking why this issue is of major concern to tens of thousands of American Indians? Why are certain symbols offensive? Are tribal communities split on this issue? And who is the Native American?

In the process of genuinely considering the problem, one might learn that the 1990 Census recorded 1,959, 234 American Indians and Alaskan Natives living in the United States, and that there are 510 federally recognized tribes, 278 reservations, and 187 different languages. Assuming no great knowledge base on the subject, over time one could nevertheless acquire sufficient information on the subject to understand the issue from more than one perspective in order to form a more educated opinion about the controversial subject.

To extend this example, one might inquire even further into this culturally sensitive issue to learn how schools with various American Indian mascots and nicknames have resolved the issue. In this instance, Cornel Pewewardy, principal of the Mounds Park All-Nations Magnet School in the St. Paul, Minnesota, Public Schools and 1991 National Indian Educator of the Year, sheds some light on the matter (1993). Some guidelines actually have been formulated to guide educators in responding appropriately to the issue of Native American mascots and nicknames in schools. Some sample questions follow.

1. Do mascot sponsors choreograph skits to please the audience regardless of the "cute" nuances that may be psychologically harmful to representative tribal groups? Are the skits written from a Native-American world view?
2. Is the culture of the contemporary Indian mascot portrayed as a modern-day people contributing to society, rather than as a static noncontributing image that is a burden upon society?
3. Do Indian mascots adequately and accurately represent the lives of contemporary Native Americans within the context of the tribe being portrayed?

As this case demonstrates, to the tolerant critical thinker there is more than meets the eye in the "Why all the hoopla?" remark.


## Listening Skills

Multicultural competency for effective living in a diverse society involves the ability to acknowledge differences and take an interest in the unsimilar. When one keeps an open mind and is genuinely interested in others, good listening skills generally follow. Consider that the contexts of diversity where we live and work are filled with people who are unique individuals. To be attentive to others is to be genuinely interested in their ideas, their homes, their families, and their work. However humble the people one encounters might be, one can always regard the individual as a person of importance by employing good listening skills.

It is more challenging to be a good listener in a diverse context, however, when exploding pluralism turns from interesting to divisive (Haynes 1992). A case in point is the increasing religious diversity that can at times deeply divide people. According to Haynes (1992:23–24), "The language of pluralism may no longer be confined to the 'Protestant, Catholic, Jewish' discussion prevalent in the 1950s. Religious pluralism today includes believers from virtually all of the world's faiths and increasing numbers of people who indicate that they have no religious preference at all (up from 2 percent of population in the 1960s to nearly 12 percent in the 1990s). Islam, to mention just one highly significant example, will soon be, if it is not already, the second largest faith in the United States after Christianity generally." Presumably, the risk of not learning about one another in an age of increasing pluralism is much greater than the risk of confronting any differences. Listening with respect and civility to others who are different from oneself is imperative to making diversity contexts places of authentic tolerance.

Additionally, when differences are conflictive, it is important to remember that listening should not be mistaken for agreement. Listening carefully, even to a bigot, in certain contexts may be one of the most important communication skills for the twenty-first century. Recently, President Clinton asked rhetorically when the last time was that we had *really* listened to somebody express an opinion different that was from ours! That notion is the idea behind effective listening skills in a diverse society.

### Admitting Discomfort

The ability to recognize and analyze one's biases is closely related to one's capacity to admit discomfort about a given subject. To admit discomfort is a straightforward and honest policy to live by. Discomfort, however, might also cause us to launch into something of which one knows little about, that is, the very topic that makes us feel uncomfortable. Caution should be exercised against this type of nervous response. To illustrate the notion of dealing with discomfort, the subject of sexual differences provides good background. For example, the literature in teacher education is just now beginning to address sexual diversity in the classroom (Sears 1994). According to that literature, the gay or lesbian student is sitting in every school and classroom across America (Vigliotti 1994). Admittedly, heterosexual teachers who are homophobic will be hard pressed to support their lesbian and gay students. Indeed, many of those who would never consider uttering a racial or religious epithet still carelessly toss around such labels as "faggot" or "sissy."

In this situation, before people can act against homophobia, they will need to examine their attitudes toward sexual orientation and admit the discomfort that the subject causes. At this point, good listening skills kick into the picture so that one can listen to learn about a subject. Although the situation may cause some discomfort, how does it feel to be gay or lesbian in a school context? What is the personal impact of homophobic prejudice? Learning about the context in which one lives and works is usually interesting and fun to do; however, learning about the special characteristics of groups to whom one does not belong can sometimes cause temporary discomfort. Grin and bear it if you really should know!

### Experience Differences

Variety is the spice the life! So goes the old adage that translates into another practical consideration for living and working in contexts of diversity. If one cannot experience diverse contexts first hand, reading about the lives of people whose cultural backgrounds are different is one way to acquire an appreciation for those who are different. Effective teachers who are committed to tolerance, for example, often use novels and short stories to help students explore people's differences (Bauman 1995). Of course the younger one is, the more likely one can be drawn to stories that show the world through another person's eyes.

Of course, experiencing different contexts, rather than just reading about them, that is, the hands-on approach to learning, is the best teacher. This is better understood through the words of a student who remembered an early travel experience. "When I was eleven years old, I visited Holland for a month and learned that the world was much bigger than I could have possibly understood otherwise. What a great learning experience. I was encouraged by my sixth grade teachers to take the trip and told by them that I would retain knowledge from that trip far more than I would by staying in the classroom. They were absolutely right." Curiosity and an interest in places, things, and people who are different can provide one with life experiences on an international scale. Not everyone, however, would agree that a global experience is desirable.

James Banks (1994), a leading researcher in multicultural education, suggests that there is a typology of stages of ethnicity that can help individuals explore and clarify their personal ethnic identities. A brief description of Banks' typology that attempts to outline the basic stages of the development of ethnicity among individual members of ethnic groups follows. According to Banks, at Stage 1, Ethnic Psychological Captivity, the individual absorbs the negative ideologies and beliefs about his or her group that are institutionalized with the society. Stage 2 is characterized by ethnic exclusiveness, including voluntary separatism. At Stage 3, Ethnic Identity Clarification, the individual is able to clarify personal attitudes and their ethnic identity, to reduce intrapsychic conflict, and to develop clarified positive attitudes toward his or her ethnic group. With self-acceptance comes the ability to accept and respond positively to outside ethnic groups. Bi-ethnicity, Stage 4, gives an individual a healthy sense of ethnic identity and the skills needed to participate in the contexts of other ethnic cultures, too. In Stage 5, Multi-ethnicity and Reflective Nationalism, individuals are self-actualized and function, beyond superficial levels, within several ethnic cultures equally well. Finally, in Stage 6, Globalism and Global Competency, individuals come to possess all of the knowledge, skills, and attitudes needed to function effectively within ethnic cultures in the society as well as on an international scene.

If Bank's typology basically holds true, appreciating differences is a behavior that can be learned. Contexts of diversity can contribute toward self-actualization and the ability to function comfortably within various social and ethnic groups.

## CONCLUSION

Granting that all the terms multiculturalism, diversity, and pluralism are quite ambiguous, any interpretation of them as they pertain to the social structure will continue to stir intense emotions and debates among many of us (Schlesinger 1992; Takaki 1993). Still others will continue to invoke the "color blind" test, refusing to acknowledge differences and claiming to see only individuals. Regretably, it is almost impossible to live in this society without internalizing "records" of stereotyped ethnic, racial, cultural, religious, socioeconomic, or other social groupings. Better to recognize and analyze these "records" than to suppress differences! For the individual in the fast lane toward rich multicultural experiences and understandings, a wealth of resources exist, or are increasingly being marketed to reinforce the practical considerations for living, working and playing in the diversity contexts that have been presented here. Multicultural sensitivity training, diversity training, prejudice-reduction workshops, and other related activities are growing in number across campuses and the workplace. A World of Difference, a prejudice-reduction training program to address this issue has been designed by the Anti-Defamation League. It is being implemented in elementary and high schools all across the country. Other interactive video training programs, speaker bureaus for multicultural experts, diversity training institutes, multicultural education conferences, and an over-abundance of other audio-visual and teaching materials are flooding the marketplace. Multicultural resource centers on many university campuses also can direct the reader to a multitude of training opportunities and information.

On yet another front, the Educational Testing Service from Princeton, New Jersey, this year formulated a test for the purpose of assessing "Cultural Diversity in Education in the United States." The material in the test is generally taught in baccalaureate-level courses. Presumably, the examination is designed to encourage people who have a basic knowledge of the subject to seek college credit for that knowledge. The National Council for the Social Studies recently revised the "Curriculum Guidelines for Multicultural Education" (1992). And although these guidelines have come under attack for not providing a more clear and concise plan to ameliorate intergroup relations, these guidelines continue to be dis-seminated and used by educators throughout the country (Kleg 1993). All of these efforts are an indication that practices pertaining to American pluralism and multiculturalism, although controversial in many respects, will continue to evolve.

# REFERENCES

Banks, J. 1994. *Multiethnic Education: Theory and Practice*. Boston: Allyn & Bacon.
Bauman, S. 1995. Literature as a tool for tolerance. *Teaching Tolerance* 12:16–19.
Canfield, J. & Wells, H. C. 1994. *100 Ways to Enhance Self-Concept in the Classroom*. Boston: Allyn & Bacon.
Derman-Sparks, L. 1989. *Anti-Bias Curriculum: Tools for Empowering Young Children*. Washington, DC: National Association for the Education of Young Children.
Haynes, C. C. 1992. Living with our deepest differences: Religious diversity in the classroom. In *Common Bonds Anti-Bias Teaching in a Diverse Society*. D. A. Byrnes, & G. Kiger (eds). Wheaton, MD: Association for Childhood Education International.
Kleg, M. 1993. On the NCSS curriculum guidelines for multicultural education. *Social Education* 57:58–59.
Nash, G. B. & Dunn, R. E. 1995. History standards and culture wars. *Social Education* 59:5–7.
NCSS Task Force on Ethnic Studies Curriculum Guidelines. 1992. Curriculum guidelines for multicultural education. *Social Education* 56:274–294.
Pate, G. S. 1995. Bias defense. *Teaching Tolerance* 4(2):6.
Pewewardy, C. D. 1993. The tomahawk chop: The continuous struggle of unlearning 'Indian' stereotypes. *Multicultural Education* 1(2):14–15.

Rincon, E. 1995. Espanol: Judge needs to hear case for bilingualism. *Dallas Morning News* (September 10), p. 6J.
Schlesinger, A. M. 1992. *The Disuniting of America: Reflections on a Multicultural Society*. New York: W. W. Norton.
Sears, J. T. (ed). 1994. *Bound by Diversity*. Columbia, SC: Sebastian Press.
Takaki, R. T. 1993. *A Different Mirror: A History of Multicultural America*. Boston: Little, Brown & Co.
Vigliotti, J. 1994. What every teacher should know. In *Bound by Diversity*. J. T. Sears (ed). Columbia, SC: Sebastian Press, pp. 127–131.

# Postscript

Through the various chapters of this volume, you have been taken through only a small part of the actual diversity that can be found in American (U.S.) culture. By now you must recognize that this collection hardly represents all of American diversity. Altogether, the collection represents little more than a beginning. But, that has been the goal of this volume, to serve as an introduction and to help people begin the lifelong process of developing increased awareness, understanding, and appreciation of the diversity of America. For most people, attaining the goals of awareness, greater understanding, and appreciation of other cultures will not come from books—this one or any other. Sensitivity and tolerance, appreciation, and understanding will not be taught in America's classrooms or universities, nor will it come through legislation. It only will come with an increased awareness of the issues related to diversity (e.g., immigration, affirmative action, etc.). It only will come as individuals gain a better understand of the historical context of ethnicity and learn of the contributions of all ethnic groups to the United States. It only will come with people accepting the legitimacy of all cultural groupings, and in the recognition of who has power and who does not. It only will come as people of various cultural groups interact with people representing other groups, as they learn to listen and try to perceive things from the point of view of others. It will only come as people come to understand that everyone is in a sense like themselves, even if they seem to believe and do things differently. Those "other people" are not necessarily wrong or bad because of it—they are just different, and there is surely a place for differences. It will come as people recognize their own ethnocentrism and where it comes from.

To attain the kind of appreciation and understanding that has been advocated throughout this reader, individuals need to understand that this process must be an ongoing one throughout their lives. This is the most fundamental point—the process is forever ongoing. Education can start the individual down this path, but it is the individual that must carry it through. It must become a pervasive element of an individual's life, seen in everything, in all settings, and as basic to everything. The individual must experience and interact more effectively with others, and this means chosing to interact and incorporating with others. It is the responsibility of the individual to broaden their own horizons.

Culture has blessed the human and been its curse at the same time. It has made them all the same. It has made groups of them different, and it has produced the conflicts that naturally must accompany cultures in contact. In a world that moves increasingly toward greater inter-, intra-, and co-dependence, increased interactions, economic globalization, and the spread of the "information highway," cultural differences will not disappear; rather, they will become more pronounced, as will the conflicts that accompany them. Culture is "truth." It is what humans "know," and once learned, it will be strongly believed, defended, and the measure of all other cultures. Americans always have been willing and able to fight and die for what they believe. Other cultural groups are just as willing and just as committed to their "truth."

All of the contributors to this collection have attempted, in an admittedly brief manner, to convey some basic information about diversity and specific groups of people represented in the total diversity that has come to characterize the American culture, indeed, that characterizes most nation-state cultures in the world about to enter the twenty-first century. Altogether, they have been able to impart only a fraction of the actual cultural diversity obscured in the tendency for Americans to focus on diversity categories. These diversity categories based on some trait, perhaps a single physical characteristic, a common language, or a particular belief or practice (real or imaginary) do not represent the actual diversity of America with which people must come to grips. The real diversity comes with specific cultural groupings of people who learn and share beliefs, practices, and the products of these. No one should expect to come to grips with the problems of diversity by relying on such categorizations.

Cultural diversity is based on cultural differences, differences between groups that learn things, that distinguish them from others. Although such differences have probably always been with us throughout the human experience, the importance and significance of them has probably never been greater, nor has it posed such a threat. The complexity of modern nations has left this legacy for us and generations to come. The question is not whether such diversity exists, but whether our inability to come to terms with diversity might somehow lead to our demise as a species, as Americans, as humans, or as individuals. For well over 4 million years humans have existed because they have been different, because of their creativity, and because of their ability to overcome the problems that threatened their existence. While culture has contributed significantly to this heritage we all now share, culture has resulted in the greatest threat to our existence yet, and this does not come from our technology, from our weapons, or from any other of our artifacts. It has come with our ethnocentrism and the belief that only we in our own groups possess the really truest beliefs and the most correct behaviors. It has come with our conviction that our truth should be the truth for everyone and our efforts to impose it on others if we can.

As the globalization of the planet continues, as modern nations grow more complex, our contacts with others increase, and the number of cultural groups simply increase, culture differences will become highlighted and so, too, will the conflicts that accompany them. But it is important to periodically stop and remind ourselves of the achievements of our distant ancestors and the richness of what has come to pass because of them. Culture difference does not have to mean conflict. At this point in time it does because culture groups who exercise their truth, beliefs, and practices keep trying to impose that truth and way on everybody else. Surely, we must realize that while humans are different on one level, on another they are all the same. Personally, I have never met a person who was any different from me. People everywhere laugh when they are happy, cry when they are sad or hurt, seek sufficient food and shelter for themselves and their families, seek the same security and warmth that comes from our association with other humans as I do. It is only in how they may satisfy such things, that we can appear to end up so different. Perhaps we should de-emphasize differences and re-emphasize similarities, for in the final analysis, people are just like me. But that remains the goal, and to get to that, we have to begin where people are, not where we think they should be. That represents only the first step, perhaps it is the key to resolving the problems of diversity. Recognizing that, despite someone's physical appearance, despite one's preferences in religion, in custom, particular beliefs, or interests, they are just like me. On an individual basis, one on one, perhaps we can learn that from each other.

# Bibliography

Acosta-Belen, E. 1988. The Hispanic Legacy. In *The Hispanic Experience in the United States*. E. Acosta-Belen & B. Sjostrom (eds). New York: Praeger.

Acuña, R. 1981. *Occupied America,* 2nd edition. New York: Harper & Row.

Adler, J. 1995. Sweet Land of Liberties: If everyone has his own niche, what do we have in common anymore? *Newsweek* (July 10), pp. 18–23.

Aguero, K. (ed). 1993. *Daily Fare: Essays From the Multicultural Experience*. Athens: The University of Georgia Press.

Aidala, A. A. 1984. Worldviews, ideologies and social experimentation: Clarification and replication of "the Consciousness Reformation." *Journal for the Scientific Study of Religion* 23(1):44–59.

Alba, R. D. 1985. *Italian Americans*. Englewood Cliffs, NJ: Prentice-Hall.

———1990. *Ethnic Identity: The Transformation of White America*. New Haven: Yale University Press.

Allsup, C. 1982. *The American G.I. Forum: Origins and Evolution*. Austin: Center for Mexican American Studies, University of Texas Press.

Alvarez, R. 1985. The psycho-historical and socioeconomic development of the Chicano community in the United States. In *The Mexican American Experience: An Interdisciplinary Anthology*. R. O. de la Garza, et al (eds). Austin: University of Texas Press, pp. 33–56.

Ameisen, E. R. 1990. Exclusively in an Ethnic Elite: Racial Prejudice as Boundary Maintenance. In *Encounters with American Ethnic Realities*. P. Kilbride, J. Goodale, & E. Ameisen (eds), in collaboration with C. G. Friedman. Tuscaloosa: University of Alabama Press, pp. 25–76.

Amory, C. 1947. *The Proper Bostonians*. New York: E. P. Dutton & Company, Inc.

Amott, T. & Matthaei, J. 1991. *Race, Gender and Work*. Boston: South End Press.

Andersen, M. L. & Collins, P. H. 1992. *Race, Class, and Gender*. Belmont, CA: Wadsworth.

Anderson, T. 1990. Black studies: Overview and theoretical perspectives. In *Black Studies*. T. Anderson (ed). Pullman, WA: State University Press, pp. 1–10.

Anthony, D. & Robbins, T. 1982. Spiritual Innovation and the Crisis of American Civil Religion. *Daedalus* 111(1):215–234.

Aptheker, H. 1973. *Afro-American History*. Secaucas, NJ: The Citadel Press.
———1969. *To Be Free: Studies In American Negro History*. New York: International Publishers Company Inc.
Arens, W. & Montague, S. P. (eds). 1976. *The American Dimension: Cultural Myths and Social Realities*. Port Washington, NY: Alfred Publishing.
Azores, T. 1986-87. Educational Attainment and Upward Mobility: Prospects for Filipino-Americans. *Amerasia Journal* 13(1):39–52.
Baker, C. & Cokley, D. 1980. *American Sign Language: A Teacher's Resource Text on Grammar and Culture*. Silver Spring, MD: T. J. Publishers, Inc.
Baker, L. D. 1995. Racism in Professional Settings: Forms of Address as Clues to Power Relations. *Journal of Applied Behavioral Science* 31(2):186–201.
Balderrama, F. 1982. *In Deffense of La Raza*. Tucson: University of Arizona Press.
Baltzell, E. D. 1964. *The Protestant Establishment: Aristocracy and Caste in America*. New Haven: Yale University Press.
———1979. *Puritan Boston and Quaker Philadelphia: Two Protestant Ethics and the Spirit of Class Authority and Leadership*. New York: Free Press.
Banks, J. 1994. *Multiethnic Education: Theory and Practice*. Boston: Allyn & Bacon.
Banton, M. 1986. Ethnic Bargaining. In *Ethnicity, Politics, and Development*. D. L. Thompson & D. Ronen (eds). Boulder: Lynne Reiner, pp. 11–24.
Barkan, E. 1992. *The Retreat of Scientific Racism*. Cambridge: Cambridge University Press.
Barrett, R. A. 1984. *Culture and Conduct*, 2nd edition. Belmont, CA: Wadsworth.
Barringer, H. R. & Liu, N. 1994. The Demographic, Social, and Economic Status of Native Hawaiians. Report prepared for Alu Like, Inc. March.
Barringer, H. R., Gardner, R. W. & Levin, M. J. 1993. *Asians and Pacific Islanders in the United States*. New York: Russell Sage Foundation.
Barringer, H. R., Takeuchi, D. T., & Xenos, P. 1990. Education, Occupational Prestige, and Income of Asian Americans. *Sociology of Education* 63(1):27–43.
Barth, F. (ed). 1969. *Ethnic Groups and Boundaries*. Boston: Little, Brown & Company.
Bass, C. 1960. *Forty Years: Memoirs From the Pages of a Newspaper*. Los Angeles, CA: Charlotta Bass.
Batteau, A. 1990. *The Invention of Applalachia*. Tucson: University of Arizona Press.
Bauman, S. 1995. Literature as a tool for tolerance. *Teaching Tolerance* 12:16–19.
Bayer, R. 1981. *Homosexuality and American Psychiatry*. New York: Basic Books.
Bayor, R. H. 1978. *Neighbors in Conflict: The Irish, German, Jews and Italians of New York City 1929–1941*. Baltimore: Johns Hopkins Press.
Bellah, R. 1975. *The Broken Covenant*. New York: Seabury.
Bellugi, U. 1991. The link between the hand and brain: Implications from a visual language. In *Advances in Cognition, Education, and Deafness*. D. Martin (ed). Washington, DC: Gallaudet University Press.
Bennett, J. 1954. Interdisciplinary Research and the Concept of Culture. *American Anthropologist* 56:169–179.
Berlin, I. 1974. *Slaves Without Masters: The Free Negro in the Antebellum South*. New York: Vintage.
Berry, F. (ed). 1992. *Good morning revolution: Uncollected writings of social protest by Langston Hughes*. New York: Citadel Press.
Berry, W. 1970. In Defense of Literacy. In *A Continuous Harmony: Essays Cultural and Agricultural*. New York: Harcourt Brace Javanovich, pp. 169–173.
Blackwood, E. 1986. *The Many Faces of Homosexuality*. New York: Harrington Press.
Blakely, M. K. 1994. *American Mom*. Chapel Hill, NC: Algonquin.

Block, N. J. & Dworkin, G. 1976. *The I. Q. Controversy: Critical Readings*. New York: Panteon Books.

Blumenfeld, W. & Raymond, D. 1993. *Looking at Gay and Lesbian Life*. Boston: Beacon Press.

Blumenthal, S. 1995. The political scene: Her own private Idaho. *The New Yorker*, (July 10), pp. 27–33.

Bolton, C. 1994. *Poor Whites of the Antebellum South: Tenants and Laborers in Central North Carolina and Northeast Missippi*. Durham: Duke University Press.

Borrello, M. A. & Mathias, E. 1977. Botanicas: Puerto Rican folk pharmacies. *Natural History* 86:64–73.

Boyer, L. B. 1964. Psychoanalytic insights in working with ethnic minorities. *Social Casework* 45:519–526.

Brack, G. 1976. Mexican opinion, American racism, and the War of 1846. In *Three Perspectives of Ethnicity*. C. E. Cortes, A. I. Ginsburg, A. W. F. Green, & J. A. Joseph (eds). New York: G. P. Putnam's Sons, pp. 94–103.

Bragg, B. 1994. *Meeting Halfway in American Sign Language: A Common Ground for Effective Communication Among Deaf and Hearing People*. Rochester, NY: Deaf Life Press.

Branscome, J. 1978. Annihilating the hillbilly: The Appalachians struggle with America's Institutions. In *Colonialism in Modern America*. H. Matthews, L. Johnson, & D. Askins (eds). Boone, NC: Appalachian Consortium Press.

Brislin, R. W., Cushner, K., Cherrie, C., & Yong, M. 1986. *Intercultural Interactions: A Practical Guide*, Beverly Hills: Sage Publications.

Brophy, W. & Aberle, S. (eds). 1966. *The Indian: America's Unfinished Business*. Norman: University of Oklahoma Press.

Browne, C. & Broderick, A. 1994. Asian and Pacific island elders: Issues for social work practice and education. *Social Work* 39:252–259.

Bulosan, C. 1973. *America is in the Heart*. Seattle: University of Washington Press. Original, 1943.

Burtt, E. A. 1959. Buddhism. In *Basic Beliefs*. J. E. Fairchild (ed). New York: Sheridan House, pp. 73–90.

Cabezas, A., Shinagawa, L. & Kawaguchi, G. 1986–87. New Inquiries into the socioeconomic status of Pilipino Americans in California. *Amerasia Journal* 13(1):1–21.

Campbell, J. 1959. Hinduism. In *Basic Beliefs*. J. E. Fairchild (ed). New York: Sheridan House, pp. 54–72.

Camper, C. 1994. *Miscegenation Blues: Voices of Mixed Race Women*. Toronto, Ontario: Sister Vision.

Canfield, J. & Wells, H. C. 1994. *100 Ways to Enhance Self-Concept in the Classroom*. Boston: Allyn & Bacon.

Cariaga, R. R. 1936. The Filipinos in Hawaii: A Survey of Their Economic and Social Conditions. Master's thesis, University of Hawaii.

Carino, B. V., Fawcett, J. T., Gardner, R. W., & Arnold, F. 1990. The New Filipino Immigrants to the United States: Increasing diversity and change. *Papers of the East-West Population Institute*, No. 115.

Carroll, T. 1990. Who Owns Culture? In *Cultural Diversity and American Education: Visions of the Future*. T. G. Carroll & Schensul, J. J. (eds). *Education and Urban Society* 22 (4):346–355.

Castex, G. M. (1994). Providing services to Hispanic/Latino populations: Profiles in diversity. *Social Work* 39:288-296.

Chambliss, W. J. 1994. Policing the ghetto underclass: The politics of law and law enforcement. *Social Problems* 24:177–194.

Christopher, R. C. 1989. *Crashing the Gates: The De-WASPing of America's Power Elite.* New York: Simon & Schuster.

Ciria-Cruz, R. P. 1994. How far have we come? *Filipinas* 3(10):40–44.

Clark, D. 1986. *Hibernia-America: The Irish and Regional Cultures.* Westport, CT: Greenwood Press.

Clay, J. W. 1990. What's a nation? *Mother Jones* 15(7):28.

Clifford, J. 1988. *The Predicament of Culture: Twentieth Century Ethnography and Art.* Cambridge: Harvard University Press.

Cockoroft, J. D. 1986. *Outlaws in the Promised Land.* New York: Grove Weidenfield.

Cohen, A. (ed). 1974. *Urban Ethnicity.* A.S.A. Monograph no. 12. London: Tavistock.

Cohen, R. 1978. Ethnicity: Problem and focus in anthropology. *Annual Review of Anthropology* 7:379–403.

————1995. Surprise? Fuhrman tape doesn't shock blacks. *Dallas Morning News* (August 18), p. 25A.

Collins, J. 1991. Hegemonic Practice: Literacy and standard language in public education. In *Rewriting Literacy: Culture and the Discourse of the Other.* C. Mitchell & K. Weiler (eds). New York: Bergin & Garvey, pp 229–254.

Collins, P. H. 1994. Black women and motherhood. In *Living With Contradictions.* A. Jaggar (ed). Boulder: Westview.

Comas-Diaz, L. 1988. Cross-cultural mental health treatment. In *Clinical Guidelines in Cross-Cultural Mental Health.* L. Comas-Diaz, & E. H. Griffith (eds). New York: John Wiley & Sons, pp. 337–361.

Conover, T. 1987. *Coyotes.* New York: Vintage Books.

Cooke, S. 1976. *From Tobacco Road to Route 66: The Southern Poor White in Fiction.* Chapel Hill: University of North Carolina Press.

Cooper, Z. 1977. *Black Settlers in Rural Wisconsin.* Madison, WI: The State Historical Society.

Cornellius, W. 1978. *Mexican Migration to the United States: Causes, Consequences, and U.S. Responses.* Cambridge: Center for International Studies, MIT.

Cortes, C. 1980. Mexicans. In *Harvard Encyclopedia of American Ethnic Groups.* S. Thernstrom, A. Orlov, & O. Handlin (eds). Cambridge: Belknap, pp. 697–719.

Cortes, C. et al. 1976. *Three Perspectives on Ethnicity.* New York: G. P. Putnam's Sons.

Cory, D. 1964. *The Lesbian in America.* New York: Citadel Press.

Crimp, D. 1991. *AIDS, Cultural Analysis, Cultural Activism..* Cambridge: MIT Press.

Crowder, M. 1964. *A Short History Of Nigeria.* New York: Frederick A. Praeger.

Cucchiari, S. 1988. Adapted for heaven: Conversion and culture in western Sicily. *American Ethnologist* 15:417–441.

————1990. Between shame and sanctification: Patriarchy and its transformation in Sicilian Pentacostalism. *American Ethnologist* 17:687–707.

Curry, L. 1981. *The Free Blacks in Urban America, 1800–1850: The Shadow of a Dream.* Chicago: University of Chicago Press.

Daniel, P. 1985. *Breaking the Land: The Transformation of Cotton, Tobacco, and Rice Cultures Since 1880.* Urbana: University of Illinois Press.

de la Garza, R. O. et al (eds). *The Mexican American Experience: An Interdisciplinary Anthology.* Austin: University of Texas Press, pp. 33–56.

De Beauvoir, S. 1953. *The Second Sex*. New York: Knopf.

deBary, W. T. l959. Confucianism. In *Basic Beliefs*. J. E. Fairchild (ed). New York: Sheridan House, pp. 92–113.

Derman-Sparks, L. 1989. *Anti-Bias Curriculum: Tools for Empowering Young Children*. Washington, DC: National Association for the Education of Young Children.

di Leonardo, M. 1984. *The Varieties of Ethnic Experience: Kinship, Class and Gender Among California Italian-Americans*. Ithaca: Cornell University Press.

Dillard, A. 1987. *An American Childhood*. New York: Harper & Row.

Disney Corporation. 1995. *Pocahontas*. Feature film. Hollywood: Disney Corporation.

Dolan, J. P. 1975. *The Immigrant Church: New York's Irish and German Catholics 1815–1865*. Baltimore: Johns Hopkins Press.

Douglas, M. 1987. *Constructive Drinking: Perspectives on Drink from Anthropology*. New York: Cambridge University Press.

Downs, J. F. 1975. *Cultures in Crisis*, 2nd edition. Beverly Hills: Glencoe Press.

Dubberman, M. 1991. *Stonewall*. New York: Plum.

Duff, J. B. 1971. *The Irish in the United States*. Belmont, CA: Wadsworth.

Duster, A. (ed). 1970. *Crusade for Justice: The Autobiography of Ida B. Wells*. Chicago: University of Chicago Press.

Duster, R. 1993. The diversity of California at Berkeley: An emerging reformulation of 'competetence' in an increasinging multicultural world. In *Beyond a Dream Defrerred: Multicultural Education and The Politics of Excellence*. B. W. Thompson & S. Tyagi (eds). Minneapolis: University of Minnesota Press, pp. 231–255.

———1995. The new crisis of legitimacy in control, prisons, and legal structures. *The American Sociologist* 26:20–28.

East-West Population Institute. 1990. Recent Filipino Immigration to the United States: A Profile. Population Institute, East-West Center.

Ehrenreich, B. 1990. *Fear of Falling: The Inner Life of the Middle Class*. New York: Harper Books.

Erchack, G. 1992. *The Anthropology of Self and Behavior*. New Brunswick: Rutgers University Press.

Erickson, E. l963. *Childhood and Society*. New York: W. W. Norton.

Etheridge, E. 1988. Pellagra: An unappreciated reminder of southern distinctiveness. In *Disease and Distinctiveness in the American South*. T. Savitt & J. Young (eds). Knoxville: University of Tennesse Press.

Fant, L. 1972. *Ameslan:An Introduction to American Sign Language*. Northridge, CA: Joyce Motion Picture Co.

Farley, J. 1995. *Majority-Minority Relations*. Englewood Cliffs: Prentice Hall.

Farnham, T. 1976. The indolent, mixed race of California. In *Three Perspectives on Ethnicity*. C. Cortes, A. I. Ginsburg, A.W.F. Green, & J. A. Joseph (eds). New York: G. P. Putnam's Sons, pp. 60–62.

Feagin, J. & Booher Feagin, C. 1993. *Racial and Ethnic Relations*. Englewood Cliffs: Prentice-Hall.

Feagin, J. R. & Feagin, C. B. 1993. *Racial and Ethnic Relations*, 4th edition. Englewood Cliffs: Prentice-Hall.

Feagin, J. R. & Vera, H. 1995. *White Racism*. New York: Routledge.

Fernandez, J. 1982. *Bwiti: An Ethnography of the Religious Imagination in Africa*. Princeton: Princeton University Press.

———1991. *Managing a Diverse Work Force*. Lexington, MA: Lexington Books

*Filipinas.* 1994. Signed, Sealed, Delivered. December, pp. 16–18.

Firth, R. 1954. Social Organization and Social Change. *Journal of the Royal Anthropological Institute* 84:1–20.

Flynt, W. 1989. *Poor But Proud: Alabama's Poor Whites.* Tuscaloosa: University of Alabama Press.

Foner, N. 1994. *The Caregiving Dilemma: Work in an American Nursing Home.* Berkeley: University of California Press.

Forman, S. M. 1991. Filipino Participation in civil rights policies and practices in Hawaii. In *The Filipino-American Experience in Hawaii.* J. Y. Okamura, A. R. Agbayani, & M. T. Kerkvliet (eds). *Social Process in Hawai* 33:1–11. Honolulu: University of Hawaii Press.

Frankenberg, R. 1993. *White Women, Race Matters: The Social Construction of Whiteness.* Minneapolis: University of Minnesota Press.

Frazier, E. F. l963. *The Negro Church in America.* New York: Schochen Books.

Frederickson, G. 1965. *The inner Civil War: Northern Intellectuals and the Crisis of the Union.* New York: Harper & Row.

Freilich, M. (ed). 1972. *The Meaning of Culture.* Lexington, MA: Xerox College.

Frey, W. & Tilove, J. 1995. Immigrants In, Natives Out. *The New York Times Magazine* (August 20).

Fried, M. 1967. *The Evolution of Political Society: An Essay in Political Anthropology.* New York: Random House.

Friedman, T.L. 1995. Me fellow immigrants. *The New York Times* (September 10), p. E17.

Furst, P. 1972. *Flesh of the Gods: The Ritual Use of Hallucinogens.* New York: Praeger.

———1976. *Hallucinogens and Culture.* Novato, CA: Chandler & Sharpe Publishers.

Gamst, F. C. & Norbeck, E. 1976. *Ideas of Culture: Sources and Uses.* New York: Holt, Rinehart & Winston.

Garcia, J. 1981. Yo Soy Mexicano...:Self-identity and sociodemographic correlates. *Social Science Quaterly* 62:88–89.

Gardner, H. 1993. *Frames of Mind: A Theory of MultipleIintelligences.* New York: Basic Books.

Gates, H. 1994. *Colored People: A Memoir.* New York: Knopf.

Gates, H. L., Jr. 1992. *Ethnic and Minority Studies: Introduction to Scholarship.* J. Gibaldi (ed). New York: Modern. Language Association of America, pp. 288–302.

Gee, J. P. 1991. What is literacy. In *Rewriting Literacy: Culture and the Discourse of the Other.* C. Mitchell & K. Weiler (eds). New York: Bergin & Garvey, pp. 3–12.

Geldner, L. 1994. A lesbian family. In *Living With Contradictions.* A. Jaggar (ed). Boulder: Westview.

Genovese, E. 1974. *Roll, Jordan, Roll: The World the Slaves Made.* New York: Pantheon Books.

Giddings, P. 1984. *When and Where I Enter: The Impact of Black Women on Race and Sex in America.* New York: William Morrow & Company, Inc.

Gilligan, C. 1982. *In a Different Voice: Psychological Theory and Women's Development.* Boston: Harvard University Press.

Gilmore, D. 1990. Men and women in southern Spain: "Domestic" power revisited. *American Anthropologist* 92: 953–970.

Gingrich, N. 1995. Renewing America: In his new book, Newt says stop whining. *Newsweek,* (July 10), pp. 26–27.

Glazer, N. & Moynihan, P. 1963. *Beyond the Melting Pot: The Negroes, Puerto Ricans, Jews, Italians, and Irish.* New York: Cambridge, MIT Press.

Goffman, E. 1959. *Presentation of Self in Everyday Life.* New York: Doubleday.

Gomez, E. & Cook, K. (1977). *Chicano Culture and Mental Health: Trees in Search of a Forest.* Monograph No. 1, Centro Del Barrio. San Antonio: Worden School of Social Service, Our Lady of the Lake University.

Gonzales Jr., J. L. 1993 [1990]. *Racial and Ethnic Groups in America*, 2nd edition. Dubuque: Kendall / Hunt Publishing Company.

Goodenough, W. H. 1961. Comment on Cultural Evolution. *Daedalus* 90:521–528.

Gordon, C. C. 1993. *Race, Ethnicity, and Applied Bioanthropology.* Arlington, VA: American Anthropological Association.

Gordon, M. M. 1964. *Assimilation in American Life: The Role of Race, Religion, and National Origins.* New York: Oxford University Press.

Gould, S. J. 1981. *The Mismeasure of Man.* New York: W. W. Norton.

Grahn, J. 1984. *Another Mother Tongue.* Boston: Beacon Press.

Grant, J. 1968. *Black Protest: History, Documents and Analyses, 1619 to the Present.* Greenwich, CT: Fawcett Publications Inc.

Greeley, A. M. 1969. *Why Can't They Be Like Us: Facts and Fallacies About Ethnic Group Differences and Group Conflicts in America.* New York: Institute of Human Relations Press.

———1981. *The Irish American: The Rise to Money and Power.* New York: Harper & Row.

Green, S. & Perlman, S. 1993. Putting culture into multicultural education: Toward a critical model of cultural literacy. In *Interdisciplinary Curricula, General Education and Liberal Learning.* R. Kelder (ed). New Paltz, NY: The Institute for the Study of Post Secondary Pedagogy, pp. 18–29.

———1995. Multicultural education and culture change: An anthropological perspective. *Multicultural Education* (Summer).

Greenstone, J. D. & Peterson, P. E. 1973. *Race and Authority in Urban Politics: Community Participation and the War on Poverty.* Chicago: University of Chicago Press.

Gregory, J. 1989. *American Exodous: The Dust Bowl Migration and Okie Culture in California.* New York: Oxford University Press.

Groce, N. 1985. *Everyone Here Spoke Sign Language: Hereditary Deafness on Martha's Vineyard.* Cambridge: Harvard University Press.

Gubrium, J. F. 1975. *Living and Dying at Murray Manor.* New York: St. Martin's Press.

Gunn, B. 1992. *Redrawing Boundaries.* New York: Modern Language Association.

Gutman, H. 1976. *The Black Family in Slavery and Freedom:1750–1925.* New York: Pantheon Books.

Gwaltney, J. 1980. *Drylongso: A Self-Portrait of Black America.* New York: Vintage Books.

Hamada, T. 1995. Inventing cultural others in organizations: A case of anthropological reflexivity in a multinational firm. *Journal of Applied Behavioral Science* 31(2):162–185.

Handler, R. & Segal, J. 1990. *Jane Austen and the Fiction of Culture.* Tucson: University of Arizona Press.

Harris, M. 1968. *The Rise of Anthropological Theory.* New York: Thomas Y. Crowell Company.

Harris, P. & Moran, R. T. 1987. *Managing Cultural Difference.* Houston: Gulf Publishing Company.

Harrison, R. J. & Bennett, C. E. 1995. Racial and ethnic diversity. In *State of the Union America in the 1990s. Volume Two: Social Trends*. R. Farley (ed). New York: Russell Sage, pp. 141–210.

Hartigan, J. 1996a. Name calling: objectifying "poor whites" and "white trash." In *White Trash: Race and Class in American Culture*. M. Wray & A. Newitz (eds). New York: Routledge.

———n.d. Unpopular culture: The case of "white trash." Cultural Studies, (forthcoming volume). New York: Routledge.

Haviland, W. A. 1994. *Anthropology*, 7th edition. Fort Worth: Harcourt Brace College Publishers.

Haynes, C. C. 1992. Living with our deepest differences: Religious diversity in the classroom. In *Common Bonds Anti-Bias Teaching in a Diverse Society*. D. A. Byrnes, & G. Kiger (eds). Wheaton, MD: Association for Childhood Education International.

Heath, D. B. 1981. *Alcohol Use and World Cultures: A Comprehensive Bibliography of Anthropological Sources*. Toronto: Addiction Research Foundation.

———1983. Sociocultural Perspectives on Addiction. In *Etiological Aspects of Alcohol and Drug Abuse*. E. Gottheil et al. (eds). Springfield: Charles C. Thomas, pp. 223–237.

———1984. Cross Cultural Studies of Alcoholism. *Recent Developments in Alcoholism, Vol.* 2. M. Galanter (ed). New York: Plenum Press, pp. 405–416.

Heath, S. B. 1983. *Ways With Words: Language, Life and Work in Communities and Classrooms*. Cambridge: Cambridge University Press.

Hechter, M, (ed). 1983. *The Microfoundations of Macrosociology*. Philadelphia: Temple University.

Height, D. 1989. Self-Help—A black tradition. *Nations Magazine* (July 24/31), pp. 136–138.

Henderson, L. 1994. African Americans in the urban milieu: Conditions, trends, and developing needs. In *The State of Black America*. B. Tidwell (ed). New York: The National Urban League, Inc., pp. 11–30.

Henry, W. 1990. Beyond the melting pot. *Time Magazine* (April 9), pp. 28–31.

Herrnstein, R. J. & Murray, C. 1994. *The Bell Curve*. New York: Free Press.

Herskowitz, M. 1972. *Cultural Relativism: Perspective on Cultural Pluralism*. New York: Vintage Books.

Higham, J. 1988. *Strangers in the Land: Patterns of American Nativism: 1860–1925*. New Brunswick: Rutgers University Press.

Hirsch, E. D. 1987. *Cultural Literacy*. New York: Vintage Books (Random House).

Hobswam, E. J. & Ranger, T. O. (eds). 1983. *The Invention of Tradition*. Cambridge: Cambridge University Press.

Hoetinik, H. 1967. *The Two Variants in Caribbean Race Relations: A Contribution to the Sociology of Segmented Societies*. New York: Oxford University Press.

Hogan-Garcia, M. 1985. Adaptation Strategies of the Los Angeles black community: 1883–1919. Ph.D. Dissertation. University of California, Irvine.

Hooks, B 1990. Homeplace (a site of resistance). In *Yearning: Race,Gender,and Culture Politics*. Boston: South End.

Hudson Institute. 1987 *Workforce 2000: Work and Workers for the Twenty-First Century*. Indianapolis: Hudson Institute.

Inciardi, J. A. 1990. *Handbook of Drug Control in the United States*. Westport, CT: Greenwood.

———1991. *The Drug Legalization Debate*. New York: Sage Publications.

Jackon, E. 1993. Whiting-out difference: Why U.S. nursing research fails black families. *Medical Anthropology Quarterly* 7(4).

Jenkins, S. (1981). *The Ethnic Dilemma in Social Services*. New York: Free Press.

Johnson, L. B. 1990. Perspective on black family empirical research—1978. In *Black Families*, 2nd edition. H. P. McAdoo (ed). Newbury Park, CA: Sage Publications, pp. 91–106.

Johnson, R., Liddell, S., & Erting, C. 1989. *Unlocking the Curriculum: Principles for Achieving Access in Deaf Education*. Washington, DC: Gallaudet Research Institute.

Jones, D. J. & Harrison, G. 1994. Fast facts: Comparative views of African American status and progress. In *The State of Black America*. B. Tidwell (ed). New York: The National Urban League, Inc., pp. 213–236.

Jones, J. 1992. *The Dispossessed: America's Underclass from the Civil War to the Present*. New York: Basic Books.

Jordan, A. T. 1994. *Practicing Anthropology in Corporate America: Consulting on Organizational Culture*. NAPA Bulletin 14. Washington, DC: American Anthropological Association.

———1995. Managing diversity: Translating anthropological insight for organizational studies. *Applied Behavior Science* 31–140.

Jordan, W. 1969. *White Over Black: American Attitudes Towards the Negro, 1550–1812*. Baltimore: Penguin Books.

Josephy, Jr., A. M. 1971. *Red Power*. New York: McGraw-Hill.

Kanter, R. M. 1972. *Commitment and Community: Communes and Utopias in Sociological Perspective*. Cambridge: Harvard University Press.

Kayser-Jones, J. S. 1981. *Old, Alone, and Neglected: Care of the Aged in Scotland and the United States*. Berkeley: University of California Press.

Kazal, R. 1995. Revisiting assimilation: The rise, fall and reappraisal of a concept in American ethnic history. *The American Historical Review* 100 (2):437–471.

Kelly, M. 1995. A reporter at large: The road to paranoia. *The New Yorker*, (June 19), pp. 60–75.

Kephart, W. M. 1982. *Extraordinary Groups: The Sociology of Unconventional Life-Styles*, 2nd edition. New York: St. Martin's Press.

Kilbourne, B. K. & Richardson, J. T. 1984. Psychotherapy and new religions in a pluralistic society. *American Psychologist* 39:237–251.

———1986. Cultphobia. *Thought* 61(241):258–266.

King, J. A. & Fitzgerald, M. F. 1990. *The Uncounted Irish in Canada and the United States*. Port Credit, Ontario: P.D. Meany.

Kinsey, A. 1948. *Sexual Behavior in the Human Female*. Philadelphia: Saunders.

Kleg, M. 1993. On the NCSS curriculum guidelines for multicultural education. *Social Education* 57:58–59.

Klima, E. & Bellugi, U. 1979. *The Signs of Language*. Cambridge: Harvard University Press.

Klopf, D. 1991. *Intercultural Encounters: The Fundamentals of Intercultural Communication*. Englewood, CO: Morton Publishing Co.

Klor de Alva, J. 1988. Telling Hispanics apart: Latin sociocultural diversity. In *The Hispanic Experience in the United States*. E. Acosta-Belen & B. Sjostrom (eds). New York: Praeger.

Kogod, K. 1994. The bridges process: Enhancing organizational cultures to support diversity. In *Practicing Anthropology in Corporate America: Consulting on*

*Organizational Culture.* A. T. Jordan (ed). NAPA Bulletin 14. Washington, DC: American Anthropological Association.

Kossoudji, S. & Ranney, S. 1985. The labor market experience of female migrants: The case of temporary Mexican migration to the U.S. *International Migration Review* 18(4): 1121–1143.

Kottak, C. P. (ed). 1982. *Researching American Culture.* Ann Arbor: The University of Michigan Press.

Kroeber, A. & Kluckhohn, C. 1952. *Culture: A Critical Review of Concepts and Definitions.* Papers of the Peabody Museum of American Archaeology and Ethnology, Vol. 1. Cambridge: Harvard University Press.

Lamphere, L., Stepick, A. & Grenier, G., (eds). 1994. *Newcomers in the Workplace: Immigrants and the Restructuring of the U.S. Economy.* Philadelphia: Temple University Press.

Lane, H. 1992. *The Mask of Benevolence: Disabling the Deaf Community.* New York: Knopf.

Larson, E. 1995. *Sex, Race, and Science: Eugenics in the Deep South.* Baltimore: Johns Hopkins University Press.

Lasman, L., Buluran, O. J., Nolan, J. & O'Neil, L. 1971. A Study of Attitudes of Filipino Immigrants about Hawaii. Master's thesis, University of Hawaii.

Lawson, E. & Thompson, A. 1995. Black men make sense of marital stress and divorce. *Family Relations* 44:211–218.

Leighton, A. H. & Leighton, D. C. 1944. *The Navaho Door.* New York: Russell & Russell.

———1946. *The Navaho.* Cambridge: Harvard University Press.

Leland, J. H. 1976. *Firewater Myths: North American Indian Drinking and Alcohol Addiction.* New Brunswick: Rutgers Center Alcohol Studies, Monograph 11.

Lemann, N. 1991. *The Promised Land: The Great Black Migration and How it Changed America.* New York: Vintage Books.

Levine, H. G. 1978. The Discovery of Addiction. *Journal of Studies on Alcohol* 39:143–174.

———1984. The Alcohol Problem in America: From Temperance to Alcoholism. *British Journal of Addiction* 79:109–119.

Lewis, O. 1966. *La Vida: A Puerto Rican Family in the Culture of Poverty.* New York: Vintage Books.

Lieberson, S. 1985. *Unhyphenated Whites in the United States.* In *Ethnicity and Race in the USA: Towards the Twenty-First Century.* R. Alba (ed). Boston: Routledge & Kegan Paul.

Liebow, E. 1967. *Talley's Corner: A Study of Negro Streetcorner Men.* Boston: Little, Brown & Co.

Lind, A. W. 1980. *Hawaii's People.* Honolulu: University of Hawaii Press.

Linnekin, J. & Poyer, L. 1990. *Cultural Identity and Ethnicity in Oceania.* Honolulu: University Press of Hawaii.

Litwack, L. 1961. *North of Slavery: The Negro in the Free State, 1790–1860.* Chicago: University of Chicago Press.

Liu, J. M., Ong, P. M., & Rosenstein, C. 1988. Dual chain migration: Post-1965 Filipino immigration to the United States. *International Migration Review* 25(3):487–513.

Loewenberg, B. & Bogin, R. (eds). 1976. *Black Women in Nineteenth-Century American Life: Their Words, Their Thoughts, Their Feelings.* University Park, PA: Pennsylvania State University Press.

*Los Angeles Times.* 1977. The garden Grace built. (January 18), Section B, P. 41.

Lowie, A. 1937. *The History of Ethnological Theory*. New York: Farrar & Rinehart.

Lum, D. (1986). *Social Work Practice and People of Color: A Process-Stage Approach*. Monterey, CA: Brooks / Cole.

Lyman, M. D. & Potter, G. W. 1991. *Drugs in Society: Causes, Concepts, and Control*. Cincinnati: Anderson Publishing Co.

MacAndrew, C. & Edgerton, R. B. 1969. *Drunken Comportment: A Social Explanation*. Chicago: Aldine Publishing.

MacCannell, D. 1992. *Empty Meeting Grounds: The Tourist Papers*. London: Routledge.

Macias, J. 1987. The hidden curriculum of Papago teachers: American Indian strategies for mitigating cultural discontinuity in early schooling. In *Interpretive Ethnography of Education: At Home and Abroad*. G. Spindler & L. Spindler (eds). Hillsdale, NJ: Lawrence Erlbaum Associates, pp. 363–384.

Mairs, N. 1986. On Being a Cripple. In *Plaintext*. Tucson: University of Arizona Press.

Malveaux, J. 1990. The economic statuses of black families. In *Black Families*, 2nd edition. H. P. McAdoo (ed). Newbury Park, CA: Sage Publications, pp. 133–147.

Mandelbaum, D. G. 1965. Alcohol and Culture. *Current Anthropology* 6:281–293.

Mangione, J. *1981. Mont' Allegro*. New York: Columbia University Press. Original, 1942.

Marable, M. 1995. Black studies, multiculturalism, and the future of American education. *Items* (June–September) 49:49–56. New York: Social Science Research Council

Marcus, A. 1988. The South's Native Foriegners: Hookworm as a Factor in Southern Distinctiveness. In *Disease and Distinctiveness in the American South*. T. Savitt & J. Young (eds). Knoxville: University of Tennesse Press.

Marshall, M. 1979. *Beliefs, Behaviors, and Alcoholic Beverages: A Cross Cultural Survey*. Ann Arbor: University of Michigan Press.

Massey, D. S. & Denton, N. A. 1993. *American Apartheid*. Cambridge: Harvard University Press.

McKee, J. B. 1993. *Sociology and the Race Problem: The Failure of a Perspective*. Urbana: University of Illinois Press.

McLemore, D. & Romo. R. 1985. The origins and development of the Mexican American people. In *The Mexican American Experience: An Interdisciplinary Anthology*. R. de la Garza et al. (eds). Austin: University of Texas Press, pp. 3–32.

McNeil, W. K. 1989. *Appalachian Images in Folk and Popular Culture*. Ann Arbor: UMI Research Press.

McNickle, D. 1973. *Native American Tribalism*. New York: Oxford University Press.

McWhiniey, G. 1988. *Cracker Culture: Celtic Ways in the the Old South*. Tuscaloosa: University of Alabama Press.

Mead, M. 1951. *The School in American Culture*. Cambridge: Harvard University Press.
———*1970. Culture and Commitment*. New York: Columbia University Press.

Meier, A. & Rudwick, E. 1976. *From Plantation to Ghetto*. New York: Hill & Wang.

Meier, M. & Ribera, F. 1993. *Mexican Americans, American Mexicans*, 4th edition. New York: Hill & Wary.

Melendy, H. B. 1977. *Asians in America: Filipinos, Koreans and East Indians*. Boston: Twayne Publishers.

Metress, S. P. 1981. *The Irish American Experience: A Guide to the Literature*. Lanham, MD: University Press of America.
———1990. Black on the Green: A Historical Perspective. *The Irish People* 14:6.
———1995. *The American Irish and Irish Nationalism*. Lanham, MD: Scarecrow Press.

Meyerhoff, B. 1978. *Number Our Days*. New York: E. P. Dutton.

Meyers, M. A. 1995. Cyber U: Whither the modern university in this age of technological quakes? *The Pennsylvania Gazette: Alumni Magazine of the University of Pennsylvania*, (May), pp. 30–35, 41.

Miller, K. 1985. *Emigrants and Exiles: Ireland and Irish Exodus to North America*. New York: Oxford University Press.

Miller, K. & Wagner, P. 1994. *Out of Ireland*. Washington, DC: Elliott & Clark.

Miller, N. 1995. *Out of the Past*. New York: Vintage Books.

Mills, C. W. 1956. *The Power Elite*. New York: Oxford University Press.

Mindel, C. H., Habenstein, R. W., & Wright, Jr., R. W. 1988. Family lifestyles of America's ethnic minorities: An introduction. In *Ethnic Families in America*, 3rd edition. C. H. Mindel, R. W. Habenstein, & R. W. Wright, Jr. (eds). New York: Elsevier, pp. 1–14.

Montague, S. P. 1976. How Nancy gets her man: An investigation of success models in American adolescent pulp literature. In *The American Dimension*. S. P. Montague & W. Arens (eds). Sherman Oaks, CA: Alfred Publishing., pp.99–116.

Montague, A. 1964. *The Concept of Race*. New York: Free Press.

—— 1965. *The Idea of Race*. Lincoln: The University of Nebraska Press.

Moore, J. 1976. *Mexican Americans*. Englewood Cliffs: Prentice-Hall.

Morgan, E. 1975. *American Slavery, American Freedom.*. New York: Hill & Wang.

Morrison, A. M. 1992. *The New Leaders*. San Francisco: Jossey-Bass.

Moynihan, D. 1965. *The Negro Family: The Case for National Action*. Washington, DC: The United States Labor Department.

Muller, T. 1984. *The Fourth Wave: California Newest Immigrants*. Washington DC: The Urban Institute.

Myrdal, G. 1944. *An American Dilemma*. New York: McGraw-Hill.

Nash, G. B. & Dunn, R. E. 1995. History standards and culture wars. *Social Education* 59:5–7.

Naylor, L. L. 1996. *Culture and Change: An Introduction*. Westport, CT: Bergin & Garvey.

NCSS Task Force on Ethnic Studies Curriculum Guidelines. 1992. Curriculum guidelines for multicultural education. *Social Education* 56:274–294.

Newport, J. 1989. Steps to help the urban black man. *Fortune Magazine* (December 18), pp. 164–166.

Norton, D. G. (1978). *The Dual Perspective: Inclusion of Ethnic Minority Content in the Social Work Curriculum*. New York: Council on Social Work Education.

Novak, M. 1973. *The Rise of the Unmeltable Ethnic: Politics and Culture in the 70s*. New York: Collier.

Oberg, K. 1979. Culture Shock and the Problems of Adjustment in New Cultural Environments. In *Toward Internationalism: Readings in Cross-Cultural Communication*. E. Smith & L. Luce (eds). Rowley, MA: Newbury House.

Office of Management and Budget. 1978. Directive 15: Race and ethnic standards for federal statistics and administrative reporting. *Federal Register* 43:19269.

Ogbu, J. 1982. Cultural discontinuities and schooling. *Anthropology and Education Quarterly* 13(4): 290–307.

——1991. Minority status and literacy in comparative perspective. In *Literacy: An Overview by 14 experts*. S. R. Graubard (ed). New York: Noonday Press.

Okamura, J. Y. 1983. Immigrant Filipino Ethnicity in Honolulu, Hawaii. Unpublished doctoral dissertation, University of London.

Okamura, J. Y. 1984. Kinship and community: Filipino immigrants in Honolulu. *Dialogue* 20(1):27-43.

———1990. Ethnicity and Stratification in Hawaii. *Operation Manong Resource Papers*, No.1. Operation Manong Program, University of Hawaii.

———1991. Filipino educational status and achievement at the University of Hawaii. In *The Filipino-American Experience in Hawaii*. J. Y. Okamura, A. R. Agbayani, M. T. Kerkvliet (eds). *Social Process in Hawaii* 33:107-129. Honolulu: University of Hawaii Press.

———1995. The Global Filipino Diaspora as an Imagined Community. Paper presented at conference on Contemporary Diasporas: Focus on Asian Pacifics. Los Angeles, California, February.

Padden, C. & Humphries, T. 1988. *Deaf in America: Voices from a Culture*. Cambridge: Harvard University Press.

Page, H. & Brooke, T. 1994. White public space and the construction of white privilege in U.S. health care. *Medical Anthropology Quarterly* 8 (1).

Paredes, A. 1958. *With His Pistol in His Hand*. Austin: University of Texas Press.

Parillo, V. 1994. *Strangers to These Shores*. New York: McMillan Publishing.

Park, P. & Matveychuk, W. (eds). 1986. *Culture and Politics of Drugs*. Dubuque: Kendall / Hunt Publishing.

Pate, G. S. 1995. Bias defense. *Teaching Tolerance* 4(2):6.

Peoples, J. & Bailey, G. 1991. *Humanity*. New York: West Publishing Company.

Pettito, L. 1994. On the equipotentiality of signed and spoken language in early language ontogeny. In *Post Milan: ASL & English literacy*. B. Snider (ed). Washington, DC: Gallaudet University Press.

Pewewardy, C. D. 1993. The tomahawk chop: The continuous struggle of unlearning 'Indian' stereotypes. *Multicultural Education* 1(2):14-15.

Philip, R. 1991. *The Surgical Solution: A History of Involuntary Sterilization in the United States*. Baltimore: Johns Hopkins University Press.

*Philippine News*. 1994. Prime Time TV Slurs RP, Filipinas. December 7–13, pp. A1, A15.

———1995a. Union Rep Will File Suit for Language Prejudice. March 1–7, pp. A1, A15.

———1995b. Hate Crimes Against Asian Americans Rising. August 6–12, pp. A1, A12.

Phillips, G. 1989. Personal interview, November 17.

Piven, F. F. & Cloward, R. 1979. *Poor People's Movements: Why They Succeed, How They Fail*. New York: Vintage Books.

Polenberg, R. 1980. *One Nation Divisible: Class, Race, and Ethnicity in the United States Since 1938*. New York: Penguin Books.

Raboteau, A. 1978. Slave religion: The "Invisible Institution." In *The Antebellum South*. New York: Oxford University Press.

Radcliffe-Brown, A. R. 1952. *Structure and Function in Primitive Society*. New York: Free Press.

Rafter, N. 1988. *White Trash: The Eugenic Family Field Studies, 1872–1922*. Boston: Northeastern University Press.

Rapp, R. 1987. Urban kinship in contemporary America: Families, classes, and ideology. In *Cities of the United States*. L. Mullings (ed). New York: Columbia University Press, pp. 219–242.

Rawick, G. 1972. *From Sundown to Sunup: The Making of the Black Community*. Westport, CT: Greenwood Publishing Company.

Reed-Danahay, D. & Anderson-Levitt, K. M. 1991. Backward countryside, troubled city: French teachers' images of rural and working-class families. *American Ethnologist* 18(3):546–564.

Rich, A. 1986. Compulsory Heterosexuality and Lesbian Existence. In *Blood, Bread, and Poetry:1979–1985*. New York: W. W. Norton.

Richardson, F. 1994. Mission to mandate: Self development through the black church. In *The State of Black America*. B. Tidwell (ed). New York: The National Urban League, Inc., pp. 113–126.

Richardson, J. T. 1979. From cult to sect: Creative eclecticism in new religious movements. *Pacific Sociological Review* 22(2):139–166.

———1986. Consumer protection and deviant religion: A case study. *Review of Religious Research* 28(2):168–179.

———1991. Cult/brainwashing cases and freedom of religion. *Journal of Church and State* 33(1):55–74.

Rincon, E. 1995. Espanol: Judge needs to hear case for bilingualism. *Dallas Morning News* (September 10), p. 6J.

Ringgren, H. & Strom, A. V. (1967). *Religions of Mankind*. Philadelphia: Fortress Press.

Rodriguez, N. & Nunez, R. T. 1986. An exploration of factors that contribute to differentiation between Chicanos and Indocumentados. In *Mexican Immigrants and Mexican Americans*. H. L. Browing & R. de la Garza (eds). Austin: Center for American Studies, University of Texas Press.

Roediger, D. 1991. *The Wages of Whiteness: Race and the Making of the American Working Class*. London: Verso.

———Roediger, D. 1993. *Towards the Abolition of Whiteness: Essays on Race, Politics, and Working Class History*. London: Verso.

Rollins, J. 1985. *Between Women*. Philadelphia: Temple University Press.

Rose, M. 1989. *Lives on the Boundary*. New York: Free Press.

Ross, J. K. 1977. *Old People, New Lives: Community Creation in a Retirement Residence*. Chicago: University of Chicago Press.

Sacks, K. 1989. Toward a unified theory of class, race, and gender. *American Anthropologist* 16:534–550.

Sacks, K. B. 1988. *Caring by the Hour: Women, Work, and Organizing at Duke Medical Center*. Chicago: University of Illinois Press.

Sacks, O. 1989. *Seeing Voices: A Journey Into the World of the Deaf*. Berkeley: University of California Press.

Said, E. 1993. *Culture and Imperialism*. New York: Knopf.

Salamone, F. A. 1975. Becoming Hausa—Ethnic identity change and its implications for the study of ethnic pluralism and stratification. *Africa* 45:401–420.

———1979. Hausa ethnicity in Ibadan. *Afrika and Ubersee* 56:115–125.

———1985. *Gods and Goods in Africa*. Salem: Sheffield Press.

San Juan, Jr., E. 1994. Configuring the Filipino Diaspora in the United States. *Diaspora* 3(2):117–133.

San Miguel, Jr., G. 1987. *"Let all of Them Take Heed": Mexican Aemricans and the Campaign for Educational Equality in Texas, 1910–1981*. Austin: University of Texas Press.

Savishinsky, J. S. 1991. *The Ends of Time: Life and Work in a Nursing Home*. New York: Bergin & Garvey.

Saxton, A. 1990. *The Rise and Fall of the White Republic: Class Politics and Mass Culture in Nineteenth-Century America*. London: Verso.

Saxton, M. & Howe, F. (eds). 1987. *With Wings: An Anthology of Literature By and About Women with Disabilities*. New York: Feminist Press / CUNY.

Schlesinger, A. M. 1992. *The Disuniting of America: Reflections on a Multicultural Society*. New York: W. W. Norton.

Scouten, E. 1984. *Turning Points in the Education of Deaf People*. Danville, IL: Interstate Printers & Publishers.

Sears, J. T. (ed). 1994. *Bound by Diversity*. Columbia, SC: Sebastian Press.

Shapiro, H. 1978. *Appalachia on Our Mind: The Southern Mountains and Mountaineers in the American Consciousness, 1870–1920*. Chapel Hill: University of North Carolina Press.

Shield, R. R. 1988. *Uneasy Ending: Daily Life in an American Nursing Home*. Ithaca: Cornell University Press.

Shipman, P. 1994. *The Evolution of Racism*. New York: Simon & Schuster.

Shoemaker, P. (ed). 1989. *Communications Campaigns About Drugs: Government, Media and the Public*. Hillsdale, NJ: Lawrence Erlbaum & Associates, Publishers.

Siegler, G. 1992. The Structure of Anti-Structure: The Development and Organization of a Religious Community in a Small Western Town. Ph.D. dissertation, Department of Anthropology, University of Nevada at Reno.

Simon, R. & DeLey, M. 1985. The work experience of undocumented Mexican women immigrants in Los Angeles. *International Migration Review* 18(4):1212–1229.

Sokolovsky, J. (ed). 1990. *The Cultural Context of Aging: Worldwide Perspectives*. New York: Bergin & Garvey.

Sollors, W. 1986. *Beyond Ethnicity: Consent and Descent in American Culture*. New York: Oxford University Press.

Solomon, B. B. 1976. *Black Empowerment: Social Work in Oppressed Communities*. New York: Columbia University Press.

Spector, R. E. 1985. *Cultural Diversity in Health and Illness*, 2nd edition. Norwalk, CT: Appleton-Century-Crofts.

Spicer, E. H. 1969. *A Short History of the Indians of the United States*. New York: Van Nostrand.

Spradley, J. P. & McCurdy, D. W. 1972. *The Cultural Experience*. Prospect Heights: Waveland Press.

———1989. *Anthropology: The Cultural Perspective*. Prospect Heights: Waveland Press.

Staples, R. (1976). *Introduction to Black Sociology*. New York: McGraw-Hill.

Steiner, S. 1968. *The New Indians*. New York: Harper & Row.

———1979. *The Mexican Americans*. London: Minority Rights Group.

Stuckey, S. 1987. *Slave Culture*. New York: Oxford University Press.

Szasz, T. 1987. *Ceremonial Chemistry: The Ritual Persecution of Drugs, Addicts and Pushers*. Revised edition. Holmes Beach, FL: Learning Publications, Inc.

Takaki, R. T. 1993. *A Different Mirror: A History of Multicultural America*. Boston: Little, Brown & Co.

Tan, A. 1989. *The Joy Luck Club*. New York: Ballantine.

Terkel, S. 1992. *Race: How Blacks and Whites Think and Feel About the American Obsession*. New York: New Press.

Thompson, D. L. & Ronen, D. (eds). 1986. *Ethnicity, Politics, and Development*. Boulder: Lynne Reiner.

Tidwell, B. (ed). 1994. *The State of Black America*. New York: The National Urban League, Inc.

U.S. Bureau of the Census. 1988. We, the Asian and Pacific Islander Americans. September.
———1989. Washington, DC: Government Printing Office.
———1993. We, the American...Asians. September.
Vesperi, M. D. & Henderson, J. N. 1995. Introduction. In *The Culture of Long Term Care: Nursing Home Ethnography.* J. N. Henderson & M. D. Vesperi (eds). Westport, CT: Bergin & Garvey, pp. 1–6.
Vigliotti, J. 1994. What every teacher should know. In *Bound by Diversity.* J. T. Sears (ed). Columbia, SC: Sebastian Press, pp. 127–131.
Vincent, J. 1974. The structuring of ethnicity. *Human Organization* 33:375–379.
———1982. *Teso in Transformation: The Political Economy of Peasants in East Africa.* Berkeley: University of California Press.
———1990. *Anthropology and Politics: Visions, Traditions, and Trends.* Tucson: University of Arizona Press.
Walker, A. 1974. *In Search of Our Mothers' Gardens: Womanist Prose.* New York: Harcourt Brace Jovanovich.
Wallace, A. F. C. 1956. Acculturation: revitalization movements. *American Anthropologist* 58:264–281.
Wallis, R. (ed). 1975. *Sectarianism.* New York: Halstead.
Washburn, W. E. 1964. *The Indian and the White Man.* Garden City, NY: Anchor Books.
Wasylyshyn, J. 1982. A neo-Freudian analysis of the *Hardy Boys Mystery Series.* In *Researching American Culture.* C. Kottak (ed). Ann Arbor: University of Michigan Press, pp.111–115.
Watson, W. H. & Maxwell, R. J. (eds). 1977. *Human Aging and Dying: A Study in Sociocultural Gerontology.* New York: St. Martin's Press.
Weber, D. 1982. *The Mexican Frontier, 1821–1846: The American Southwest Under Mexico.* Alburquerque: University of New Mexico Press.
Weber, M. 1961. Ethnic groups. In *Theories of Society.* T. Parsons, E. Shills, K. D. Naegele, & J. Pitts (eds). New York: Free Press, pp. 301–309.
Weintraub, S. & Ross, S. 1980. *The Illegal Alien from Mexico: Policy Choices for an Intractable Issue.* Austin: Mexico–United States Border Research Program, University of Texas Press.
White, L. 1959. *The Evolution of Culture.* New York: McGraw-Hill.
Whyte, W. F. 1955. *Street Corner Society: The Social Structure of an Italian Slum,* 2nd edition. Chicago: University of Chicago Press.
Wilcox, D. M. 1994. *Alcoholic Thinking: An Ethnographic Narrative of the Changing World View Among Recovering Urban Alcoholics in Alcoholics Anonymous.* Ann Arbor, MI: University Microfilms, Inc.
Williams, J. E. & Coleman, A. M. 1992. *Lest We Forget: The Japanese and American's Wartime Mistake.* East Rockaway, NY: Cummings & Hathaway.
Williams, M. 1966. *The Strange Career of Jim Crow.* New York: Oxford University Press.
Williams, N., Himmel K. F., Sjoberg, A. & Torrez, D. J. 1995. The assimilation model, family life, and race and ethnicity in the United States. *Journal of Family Issues* (May):380–405.
Williams, N. & Sjoberg, A. 1993. Ethnicity and gender: The view from above versus the view from below. In *A Critique of Contemporary American Sociology.* T. R. Vaughan, G. Sjoberg, & L. T. Reynolds (eds). Dix Hills, NY: General Hall, pp. 160–202.

Williamson, J. 1984. *The Crucible of Race: Black and White Relations in the American South Since Emancipation*. New York: Oxford University Press.

Wilson, J. 1994. *The Moral Sense*. New York: Free Press.

Wilson, W. J. 1978. *The Declining Significance of Race:Blacks and Changing American Institutions*. Chicago: University of Chicago Press.

————1987. *The Truly Disadvantaged: The Inner City, The Underclass, and Public Policy*. Chicago: University of Chicago Press.

Wolf, E. 1959. *Sons of the Shaking Earth*. Chicago: University of Chicago Press.

Wolkomir, R. 1992. The quiet revolution in 'hand talk.' *Smithsonian* 23:30–42.

Wollstonecraft, M. 1792. *A Vindication of the Rights of Woman*. (Reprint) New York: W. W. Norton, 1988.

Woolf, H. B. (ed). 1974. *The Merriam-Webster Dictionary*. New York: Pocket Books.

Wrone, D. R. & Nelson, Jr., R. S. 1973. *Who's the Savage?* Greenwich, CT: Fawcett Publications, Inc.

Wuthnow, R. 1985. The growth of religious and reform movements. *Annals of Political and Social Sciences* 480:106–116.

Zimring, F. & Hawkins, G. 1992. *The Search for Rational Drug Control*. New York: Cambridge University Press.

# Index

# About the Editor and Contributors

**Charles Cambridge** is an enrolled member of the Navaho Tribe and received his Ph.D. in anthropology from the University of Colorado at Boulder. Having taught at several universities during his career, he is presently continuing his interest in appropriate technology and traditional architectural designs in the Solar Hogan Project at the University of Colorado.

**Mikel Hogan-Garcia** is an associate professor in human services and anthropology at California State University, Fullerton. She received her Ph.D. in anthropology from the University of California at Irvine. As an applied anthropologist, she has done much research on the Los Angeles black community and in the area of work organization. She also has published widely in the area of teaching methods for multicultural students.

**Kathee Mangan Christensen** is a professor in communicative disorders, San Diego State University and is a nationally recognized authority on the bilingual/trilingual education of children who are deaf. She has developed an assessment instrument, Nonverbal and Verbal Communication Assessment (NaVCA), and published widely on deafness and deaf-blindness. Most recently, she co-edited *Multicultural Issues in Deafness*, Longman Publishers (1994). She is the immediate past president of the National Council on Education of the Deaf (CED).

**Gloria Contreras** is a professor of education at the University of North Texas and received her Ed.D. from the University of Georgia. Her major interests are in social science education and curriculum development. Her most recent publication is entitled *The World Around Us: A Social Studies Program for K-7* (1993). Formerly, Dr. Contreras served as the Assistant Vice President and Director of the Office of Multicultural Affairs, University of North Texas, and currently serves as the editor for *The Social Studies,* a journal for elementary and secondary school teachers.

**Deborah Reed-Danahay** is an assistant professor of anthropology at the University of Texas at Arlington. She received her Ph.D. from Brandeis University. Her major interests revolve around cultural identity, personal narrative, and political and social theory. She was the author of *Education and Identity in Rural France: The Politics of Schooling* (1995).

**Richard Enos** is a professor of criminal justice and social work at the University of North Texas. He holds a doctorate in social work, is a licensed Master Social Worker / Advanced Clinical Practitoner in Texas, and has practiced in a variety of settings. He has authored or co-authored three books in the areas of social work, criminal justice, and sociology.

**Tyson Gibbs** is an assistant professor of anthropology at the University of North Texas. He received his Ph.D. in anthropology (medical) from the University of Florida. During his career he has served as the Director of Programs, Geriatric Center, Emory University, and as Program Director of the Gerontology Program, West Georgia College.

**Stanton W. Green** is currently the Dean of Arts and Sciences at Clarion University of Pennsylvania. He received his Ph.D. in anthropology from the University of Massachusetts and taught at the University of South Carolina before moving to Clarion. His main interests lie in the social and ecological causes of agriculture, multiculturalism, and education. He has edited *The Archaeology of Frontiers and Boundaries* in cooperation with S. M. Perlman (1980), and *Interpreting Space: GIS and Archaeology* with K. Allen & E. Zubrow (1990).

**John Hartigan** is an associate professor of anthropology in the Department of sociology & anthropology, Knox College, Galesberg, Illinois. He received his Ph.D. in the History of Consciousness program, University of California at Santa Cruz. He formerly served as a Fellow with the National Museum of Natural History in the Smithsonian Institute in Washington, D.C. His primary interest has been on the subject of cultural construction of whiteness in distinct class communities of Detroit.

**Ann T. Jordan** is an assistant professor of anthropology at the University of North Texas. She received her Ph.D. in anthropology from the University of Oklahoma. She has edited *Practicing Anthropology in Corporate American, Cross-Cultural Management and Organizational Culture* (edited with T. Hamada), and *Managing Diversity: Anthropology's Contribution to Theory and Practice* (edited with C. Walck).

**Michael D. Lieber** is a professor of anthropology at the University of Illinois at Chicago. He received his Ph.D. from the University of Pittsburgh. His research has focused on folklore and leprosy among Polynesians, Micronesians, Afro-Americans, and the Shoshone, as well as university/community relationships in Chicago.

**Kimberly P. Martin** is an associate professor of behavioral science at the University of La Verne, California. She received her Ph.D. in anthropology from the University of California at Riverside. In addition to teaching, she conducts multicultural workshps for educators and social service organizations.

**Seamus P. Metress** is a professor of anthropology at the University of Toledo. His primary interest has been on the Irish-American community in the United States, and his most recent publication is *The American Irish and Irish Nationalism* (1995).

**Larry L. Naylor** is an associate professor of anthropology and Director of the Cultural Research and Training Center at the University of North Texas. He received his Ph.D. from Southern Illinois University. Prior to his current position, he was with the University of Alaska at Fairbanks and did impact studies on the Trans-Alaskan Oil, Proposed Gas Pipelines, as well as other topics, ans served as the Chair of anthropology at the University of North Texas. He has done culture change studies and applied anthropology projects in Alaska, New Guinea, and Latin America. He is the author of *Culture and Change: An Introduction*, Bergin & Garvey (1996), *Anthropology: Computerized Study Guide (1993),*and *Cultural Anthropology: Computerized Study Guide* (1993), *Interactive Study Guide for Anthropology*, and co-authored *Eskimos, Reindeer and Land* (1980).

**Jonathan Y. Okamura** is a researcher in the Student Equity, Excellence and Diversity Office, University of Hawai'i. As a social anthropologist by training, he has undertaken research primarily in the Philippines.

**Stephen M. Perlman** currently serves as the Director of Employee Training and Development for Dominion Realty Trust, Richmond, Virgina. He received his Ph.D. from the University of Massachusetts and a M.Ed. from Virginia Commonwealth University. Prior to his current position, he taught at the University of Southern Maine and Virginia Commonwealth University. His primary interests focus on evolutionary models and social systems, and he edited *The Archaeology of Frontiers and Boundaries* (1980) with Stanton W. Green.

**Alicia Re Cruz** is an assistant professor of anthropology at the University of North Texas. She received her Ph.D. from the State University of New York at Albany. Her major research interests have focused on the Maya and Spanish-speaking immigrants in north Texas. She is the author of *The Two Milpas of Chan Kom: Scenarios of a Maya Village Life* (1996).

**Tiffany D. Rogers** is currently a student of anthropology at the University of North Texas. Prior to returning to complete her college education, she formerly served with the U.S. Navy (Seabees).

**Frank A. Salamone** is a professor of anthropology at Iona College, New Rochelle, New York. He received his Ph.D. from the State University of New York at

Buffalo. He authored *Gods and Goods in Africa* (1983), edited, along with Bruce Grindal, *Bridges to Humanity* (1995), and *Who Speaks for the Yanomami*, which he published as part of the Studies in the Third World Society (1995).

**Gretchen Siegler** is an assistant professor of anthropology and sociology at Westminster College, Salt Lake City. She received her Ph.D. from the University of Nevada at Reno. She has done her most extensive work in the area of religion, Pentecostals, and charismatic movements in North America.

**Shari Neller Starrett** is an assistant professor of philosophy and teaches in the Women's Studies Program at California State University, Fullerton. She received her Ph.D. from the University of California, Riverside. Her research centers on the philosophical analysis of women and the relations between the sexes, and has published several articles about women, her latest as a chapter entitled "Critical Relations in Hegel: Women, Family, and the Devine," in *Feminist Interpretations of Hegel*, edited by Patricia J. Mills (1995).

**Laura Zimmer-Tamakoshi** is an associate professor of anthropology at Truman State University. She received her Ph.D. in anthropology from Bryn Mawr College. Prior to assuming her present position, she did resrearch in Papua New Guinea and taught at the University of Papua New Guinea. Her latest publication is *Modern Papua New Guinea Society* (1995).

**Norma Williams** is an associate professor of sociology and the Assistant Vice President for Multicultural Affairs and Director of the Center for Cultural Diversity at the University of North Texas. She received her Ph.D. from the University of Texas. Most of her work has focused on the Mexican- American community in the United States, and is the author of *The Mexican American Family: Tradition and Change* (1990).

**Danny Monroe Wilcox** is an adjunct professor of anthropology at the University of North Texas. He received his Ph.D. from Southern Methodist University. While his specific specialty is in linguistic anthropology, he has worked extensively with recovering alcoholics and others involved with drug use.

ISBN 0-89789-478-2

9 780897 894784

HARDCOVER BAR CODE